MARITIME POWER
&
THE STRUGGLE FOR FREEDOM

Other books by the same author

BIOGRAPHY
Dönitz: The Last Führer
Himmler: Reichsführer-SS
Hess: Flight for the Führer

NAVAL AND MARITIME HISTORY
Maritime Supremacy and the Opening of the Western Mind: Naval
Campaigns that Shaped the Modern World 1588–1782
(Available from Overlook)
The Sea is a Magic Carpet
The *Titanic* and the *Californian*
An Agony of Collisions
Aim Straight: A Biography of Admiral Sir Percy Scott
Broke and the *Shannon*: A Biography of Admiral Sir Philip Broke
The Battleship Era
Guns at Sea: A History of Naval Gunnery
The Great Naval Race: Anglo-German Naval Rivalry, 1900–1914
Nelson's War
Tide of Empires: Decisive Naval Campaigns in the Rise of the West
Volume I: 1481–1654
Volume II: 1654–1763
Rule Britannia: The Victorian and Edwardian Navy
Beneath the Houseflag of the P & O: A Social History
Armada: A Celebration of the 400th Anniversary of the Defeat of
the Spanish Armada
War Beneath the Sea: Submarine Conflict 1939–1945

NOVELS
The Lion's Claw
The Unquiet Gods
Gold Chains of Empire
Salt and Steel

MARITIME POWER
POWER
&
THE STRUGGLE
FOR
FREEDOM

Naval Campaigns that Shaped
the Modern World
1788-1851

PETER PADFIELD

THE OVERLOOK PRESS
Woodstock & New York

First published in the United States in 2005 by
The Overlook Press, Peter Mayer Publishers, Inc.
Woodstock & New York

WOODSTOCK:
One Overlook Drive
Woodstock, NY 12498

NEW YORK:
141 Wooster Street
New York, NY 10012

Manufactured in the United States of America

ISBN 1-58567-589-X

Contents

Illustrations

The author and publishers would like to thank the following for permission to reproduce illustrations: Plates 1, 12, 18, 19 and 20, Private Collection; 2, Cecil Higgins Art Gallery, Bedford/Bridgeman Art Library, London; 3, Gianni Dagli Orti/CORBIS; 4, 6 and 28, Bettmann/CORBIS; 5, Leonard de Selva/CORBIS; 7, Philip Mould, Historical Portraits Ltd/Bridgeman Art Library, London; 8, 10, 13 and 17, National Portrait Gallery, London; 9, The Stapleton Collection/ Bridgeman Art Library, London; 11 and 22, National Maritime Museum, London; 14, Photo RNM/Gérard Blot; 15, Giraudon/ Bridgeman Art Library, London; 16, Bonhams, London/Bridgeman Art Library, London; 21, The Crown Estate/Bridgeman Art Library, London; 23, Topham Picturepoint/Bridgeman Art Library, London; 24, Lauros/Giraudon/Bridgeman Art Library, London; 26, Private Collection/Bridgeman Art Library, London; 27, David Messum Gallery, London/Bridgeman Art Library, London; 29 and 31, Stapleton Collection/CORBIS; 30, I. N. Phelps Stokes Collection, Miriam and Ira D. Wallach Division of Art, Prints and Photographs, The New York Public Library, Astor, Lenox and Tilden Foundations.

Maps and Diagrams

Acknowledgements

First, I thank Jane, my wife, for researching aspects of this book, for translations of French material and for interpreting during our research trips to France, for communication and support services, and much else besides. Our son, Guy, assisted with French translation and interpretation, internet research, guidance and advice for my occasional forays into philosophy. Without Jane and Guy, this would have been less of a book, and for me a far less enjoyable, indeed less instructive, personal journey.

I should like to acknowledge my debt to Grant McIntyre of John Murray for his moral support over the long haul, even when it turned out that this volume was concluding considerably short of the time frame originally envisaged, and that another volume would be necessary. And I should like to thank Howard Davies for his creative suggestions and meticulous editing; remaining solecisms are due to my obstinate preference for the sound of a phrase over strict syntax. John Murray are to be applauded for continuing, against current trends, the tradition of excellence in copy-editing.

I was fortunate that Robin Jessup, who drew the maps and battle diagrams for my previous *Maritime Supremacy*, was able to produce the graphics for this volume with equal skill and clarity. And I am grateful to Lord de Saumarez for making available paintings from his collection, and for granting permission to reproduce them.

I am grateful to the following authors or editors and publishers for granting permission to quote from their books: Elizabeth Sparrow for

Secret Service: British Agents in France, 1792–1815, and Norman Scarfe, *Innocent Espionage: The La Rochefoucauld Brothers' Tour of England in 1785*, both from the Boydell Press, Woodbridge; J. M. Golby, editor of *Culture and Society in Britain, 1850–1890*, Roger Lonsdale, *The New Oxford Book of Eighteenth Century Verse*, and D. R. Headrick, *The Tools of Empire*, all from Oxford University Press; HarperCollins for *Pückler's Progress: The Adventures of Prince Pückler-Muskau in England, Wales and Ireland . . .*; the Navy Records Society for A. N. Ryan (ed.), *The Saumarez Papers*; H. G. Thursfield (ed.), *Five Naval Journals, 1789–1817*; and T. Sturges Jackson (ed.), *Logs of the Great Sea Fights*; and the editor of the *Mariner's Mirror*, the journal of the Society for Nautical Research, and Ole Feldbaek for permission to quote from his 'Humanity or Ruse de Guerre? Nelson's Letter to the Danes'.

If there is anyone I have omitted, I apologize for the oversight.

Introduction

In *Maritime Supremacy and the Opening of the Western Mind* I suggested that we, the liberal western nations, are the heirs of maritime supremacy: that is to say, our beliefs and the present dominance of those beliefs throughout much of the world are the result, not of any natural progression of the human mind towards the rational or the good, but rather a consequence of the global distribution of sea and land masses which has conferred strategic advantage on powers able to use and dominate the seas. The system of government and beliefs natural to such powers has, therefore, prevailed. In this sense the first maritime power in the modern era was the seventeenth-century Dutch republic; the British superseded the Dutch in the eighteenth century and were in turn superseded by the Americans in the twentieth century.

During their periods of dominance these three powers were fundamentally different from rivals whose power was based on territorial dominion. The difference was merchant government. The supreme maritime powers were run by and for merchants; their navies, their administrative and financial systems and their beliefs evolved from merchant necessities, and their policies were directed exclusively towards increasing national wealth through commerce. Their entanglements in great power politics were never from choice, but were rather a necessary strategy to preserve or enlarge their trade or colonies, or to protect the homeland itself from jealous territorial powers. In territorial courts inspired with a warrior ethic ministers of the maritime powers were disdained as mere tradesmen who put profit before glory. This was, indeed, their essence.

The merchant system was prefigured in the Mediterranean city states of the Renaissance. The grandest of these, Venice in the fifteenth century, exhibited all the distinguishing marks and most of the institutions of maritime supremacy. Her wealth and power were dependent on trade. Her navy dominated the Adriatic and eastern Mediterranean, directing the exchange of such essential commodities as salt and grain through her wholesale market, the Rialto; there her merchants as middlemen took the profits on buying and selling, and the government collected revenue from the taxes on transactions. But above all, Venice enjoyed a prime middleman position in the rich long-distance trades between Europe and the east. Her buyers were pre-eminent at Alexandria, Acre, Beirut, Tyre, Constantinople, and other Levantine terminals of luxury products and exotic seasonings from China, India and the spice islands. Regular twice-yearly convoys of Venetian merchant ships freighted the cargoes home through seas defended by war squadrons operating from occupied island or coastal bases along the routes. Shipping was her largest industry; the arsenal which built and maintained her war galleys was the largest industrial establishment in the world.

As was to be expected, her business methods and institutions were highly developed: voyages were financed by networks of partnerships and loans; risks were spread to specialist marine underwriters who insured ships and cargoes against natural hazards and the piracy endemic to the sea; property rights and contracts were enforced by law. Bankers facilitated payments between individuals by simple book transfers between accounts; for transactions abroad bills of exchange were honoured wherever Venetians traded; double-entry book-keeping in Arabic rather than Roman numerals was employed for accounts, debits in the left-hand column, credits in the right, entries cross-referenced between journal and ledgers. As for public finances, spending above the revenue from taxes and duties was spread over the long term in the form of consolidated state debt which rose to dangerous heights during wars, especially with her great trading rival, Genoa, and in 'peace' was reduced by means of a sinking fund; the 5 per cent bonds were traded as securities by Venetians and foreigners alike, such was confidence in the probity of the city's institutions.

In this exclusively mercantile republic the elite was formed of the leading merchant families. The system of government which had been evolved by and for themselves was a testament to one thing above all:

fear of concentrated hereditary power. There was no written constitution. Authority was diffused through councils whose membership was arrived at by an arcane combination of lotteries and elections; committees appointed by councils for specific functions were checked by other committees or councils. Significantly the council responsible for foreign affairs was also responsible for overseas shipping, the organization of convoys and commercial privileges. At the top of the pyramid of consultative bodies which formed the government was the Ducal Council of six members who held office for a year or less and could not be re-elected for two years after the end of their term. They acted as an initiating and coordinating body, yet had to abide by the majority decision of the councils to whom they delegated policy-making; similarly they had to ensure that the head of state, the Doge, who was elected for life from among the elite, acted in accordance with these decisions. The Doge, enjoying permanent office while his councillors constantly changed, could exert leadership, yet in the last resort was constrained by law; he was in effect a constitutional prince.

Constraint on executive power is, it seems, the defining characteristic of merchant power in government. The Dutch republic, the United Provinces, which was similarly ruled by an elite of wealthy merchants, styled Regents, was the first nation to achieve on a worldwide scale the kind of maritime and trading supremacy Venice attained in the eastern Mediterrarean. Like the Doge, the hereditary ruler from the House of Orange was constrained in all important areas of policy by the decision of the Regents' highest consultative body, the States General. And England, which succeeded the United Provinces as the supreme maritime power, only did so after her absolutist Stuart monarchy had been deposed by William III of Orange in the coup known as 'the Glorious Revolution'. When William and his wife, Mary, were crowned at Westminster in 1689 they accepted a 'Bill of Rights' subordinating the royal prerogative to Parliament. Thereafter there were no essential differences between the political systems of England and the United Provinces: both, as a Dutch political commentator expressed it, acknowledged an 'eminent head' who scrupulously observed the constitutional limits of his authority.[1]

In both cases fear that the ruler would be drawn into unnecessary adventures whose costs would ruin trade and financial probity led the merchant interest – in the English instance with considerable aristocratic support – to shackle the ruler. The theoretical underpinning of the system was provided, at about the time of England's sudden conversion to the 'Dutch' system in 1689, by the philosopher John Locke who made his appeal primarily to individual freedoms and property rights. His emphasis on these elements echoed writers of the Dutch 'Golden Age' who had laid stress on 'true liberty' and 'security of possessions' as essential foundations for their trading wealth.[2] Simply put, Locke's premise was that governments were instituted by free and rational men to make laws to preserve their liberties – 'For Liberty is to be free from restraint and violence from others which cannot be when there is no law'.[3] The prime liberty, it seems, was ownership of property: 'The great and chief end of men uniting into Commonwealths, and putting themselves under government, is the preservation of their property',[4] a sentiment so attuned to merchant necessities, Locke might have been spokesman for the moneyed interest.

Locke's other great contribution to political theory, again surely derived from the Dutch example, was his insistence that, to prevent the abuse of power, government itself should be subject to the rule of law. To ensure this it was necessary that the legislature, Parliament, should be separate from the executive, the king; whilst the governed, who elected the legislature, had the same right to depose it. Though Locke failed to make any mention of the judiciary in this doctrine, Parliament in 1700 in effect completed the separation of powers by removing the Crown's right to dismiss judges.

Locke's prescriptions, or more properly the example of the extraordinary liberties enjoyed by the English/British under the constitutional monarchy he advocated, were celebrated particularly in the great territorial rival, France, where all powers and property were legally at the king's disposal. In practice Bourbon authority was far from absolute: it was restricted by public opinion and custom; and class, church, provincial and corporate privileges rendered it weaker in many respects than that of English ministries, nowhere more than in the vital matter of raising revenue through taxation. Nonetheless, it stood at the opposite pole to the principles of English – or Dutch or Venetian – government. Beneath the forms of an ancient feudal order that had long lost substance, all power had been gathered to the king. The legislative, administrative and higher judicial functions of state were all joined in his council of ministers, the Conseil d'État du Roi, whose chosen representatives, styled *Intendants*, took the law to the provinces.

The *Intendants* were the governors of France, responsible for maintaining order in their region, administering justice, apportioning and over-seeing the collection of taxes, distributing famine relief, levying the con-scripts required by the Conseil for military or naval service and forced labour for the road or canal building or other public works ordered by the Conseil; they were also responsible for armies of petty functionaries whose job was to ensure compliance with the decrees and regulations handed down by the Conseil year by year directing practically every area of economic and social life. Local institutions, undermined by this web of rules from the centre, had lost their authority, individual French men and women their habits of political association and the desire to improve their lot by their own initiative. Beneath a hollow but still brilliant show of noble authority the dead hand of officialdom lay across France. There were, of course, exceptions, especially in the great port cities; but in general, French society and economic activity in France had been ren-dered uniform and static, in marked contrast to the mobility and dyna-mism evident in English society and commerce. Above all, for the intelligentsia, religious and political censorship stifled the free expression of ideas.

For those Frenchmen of the Enlightenment, worshipping reason, English intellectual freedoms provided the most conspicuous proofs of Locke's theories on government. They were brought to France chiefly through the works of Voltaire, who had been thrown arbitrarily into the Bastille for lampooning the Regent then acting for the infant Louis XV, and had subsequently fled into exile in England; and Montesquieu, another satirist of French government and society who spent time in England and, like Voltaire, had many friends in the English political and literary worlds.

Voltaire first contrasted English liberty with French tyranny in a play, *Brutus* (1730), but his defining study of the English way in politics, phil-osophy and economic and social behaviour came out in London three years later as *Letters Concerning the English Nation*. These fictitious letters extolled a society in which anyone was free to say or publish what they pleased, all religions were tolerated and there was no torture or arbitrary imprisonment. 'To be free', he observed, echoing Locke, 'is to be dependent on the laws'; and the English loved their laws 'because they are, or at least think themselves, the framers of them'.[5] The first French edition of this panegyric to English liberties, entitled *Lettres philosophiques*, came out the following year. It was immediately proscribed, torn up and burned by the Paris hangman, the offending bookseller was sent to the

Bastille and a warrant was taken out for Voltaire's arrest, obliging him to leave Paris. He lay low for a while in the country, later moved to Geneva, and finally established himself close to the French-Swiss border from whence he could escape rapidly from either country.

Montesquieu reported on England in the same vein as 'the freest country in the world . '. . And I call it free because the sovereign, whose person is controlled and limited, is unable to inflict any imaginable harm on anyone.'[6] Voltaire had specified Locke's principle of separating executive and legislative power as the means by which the English constrained their kings; Montesquieu added the judiciary to the independent divisions of government necessary to promote liberty. The doctrine, modelled on what he had observed in England, appeared in his major work, *De l'esprit des loix* (1748) – in English translation *The Spirit of the Laws* (1750). It became at once the cornerstone of political theory in intellectual circles in France and Europe generally.

The final supreme maritime power, the United States of America, which was to take over world dominion in the twentieth century, emerged in the last quarter of the eighteenth century from the British colonies along the eastern seaboard of north America, naturally inheriting from the colonists English systems of law and government, English liberties and the social mobility and self-improving energy they bred – sharpened by the pioneering life on the new continent.

The different ethos in those north American colonies originally settled by the French is instructive: it was observed in lower Canada by the French political analyst, Alexis de Tocqueville, during a tour of north America early in the nineteenth century. He was immediately struck by the contrast with what he had seen in New England: in place of elected magistrates and local self-government by democratically elected assemblies, involving the inhabitants closely in local concerns, he found among descendants of French settlers in lower Canada 'centralized administration, lack of confidence in local government and bureaucratic regimentation'; instead of vigour and prosperity, a society which had 'remained stationary, gaining neither strength nor riches'.[7] The contrast was so vivid it seemed to him to have the clarity of a scientific experiment, providing him with crucial insights into the deadly effects of administrative centralization which he was to deploy later in a seminal enquiry into the origins of the French Revolution.

Like Voltaire and Montesquieu, he was dazzled by Anglo-American expressions of individual liberty; he linked them rather more to the habits of civic association and local self-government he had witnessed – what he termed decentralization – than to the institutional framework of central government, jotting in his notebook during his American journey, 'The greatest merit of the government of the United States is that it is *powerless* and *passive*',[8] and writing to his father that in administration, the United States seemed to have taken precisely the opposite direction to France: 'With us [France] the government is involved in everything . . . [Here] there is no, or at least there doesn't appear to be any government at all.'[9]

His views on decentralization were reinforced by observations made in England on his return from America. His English notebook contains a record of a conversation with the economist, Sir John Bowring, who told him that England was the country of decentralization, continuing:

> We have got a government, but we have not got a central administration. Each county, each town, each parish looks after its own interests. Industry is left to itself . . . In your country industry is subject to endless interference; here it is infinitely more free.[10]

Centralization, Bowring told him, was a magnificent idea, but impossible to carry out since a central government could not, by the nature of things, watch over all the needs of a great nation; in France, he suggested, what prevented decentralization was the perceived need to apply the same rule at the same time to the whole of their vast territory.[11] 'However enlightened and however skilful a central power may be,' de Tocqueville wrote, 'it cannot of itself embrace all the details of the existence of a great nation. Such vigilance exceeds the powers of man.'[12]

Belief in the minimum government necessary to secure individual liberties and protection from foreign enemies was, of course, pure Locke. That these principles were practised in the eighteenth century and at least the first half of the nineteenth in both Great Britain and the United States – the reigning and the future supreme maritime and world powers – is evident from Voltaire, Montesquieu and de Tocqueville. At the same time France, the great territorial power of western Europe in this period, remained – like the other European territorial powers, Austria, Prussia, Russia – in the grip of administrative regimentation from the centre. This was not the result of chance, or of racial or religious disposition: the two Anglo-Saxon powers were following a pattern set by Venice in the eastern Mediterranean and the Dutch in their Golden Age, a distinctive pattern that set them apart.

The pattern, as noted, derived from merchant government – in England's case, crossed with the aristocratic and landowning interests involved in commercial enterprise. Placing the highest values on the sanctity of private property and of contract guaranteed by law, the merchant system could not tolerate any authority powerful enough to override or circumvent the law, or inclined to tax wealth for its own ends; hence the dispersal of government into separated organs and local administrations. In turn the individual freedoms based on property rights and the limited powers of government spread to all areas of life: freedom of expression was a particular hallmark of the merchant system; another was toleration of different religions, races and customs, for trade knew no boundaries and its only creed was profit. Freedom and the cash nexus also gave rise to a more fluid society, breaking barriers between classes, demolishing received ideas and releasing enterprise. As de Tocqueville noted during his American journey – and confirmed in England – 'Liberty . . . infuses throughout the body social an activity, a force and an energy which never exist without it, and which bring forth wonders.'[13] Montesquieu even credited the market exchanges of a commercial society with a civilizing effect on manners and morals, as did the pioneer of modern economic theory, Adam Smith. The opinion was expressed before either, by one Samuel Ricard in 1704:

> Through commerce, man learns to deliberate, to be honest, to acquire manners, to be prudent and reserved in both talk and action. Sensing the necessity to be wise and honest in order to succeed, he flees vice, or at least his demeanour exhibits decency and seriousness so as not to arouse any adverse judgement.[14]

This might be a description of the bourgeois. Like Dutch society in the seventeenth century, English society became increasingly urban and bourgeois during the eighteenth century; while Americans, according to the English radical economist John Stuart Mill, were '*all* middle class' by the early nineteenth century.[15]

It was different in the great powers of continental Europe. Here the rulers were concerned with extending or defending their land borders against rivals and containing the centrifugal tendencies of different provinces that had been absorbed through conquest, treaty or dynastic marriage. The army was crucial in both roles; the elites were thus imbued with martial values – including contempt for trade. Power was necessarily concentrated at the centre and administered through professional bureaucracies whose aims were to knit different regions of the state together under a system of uniform regulation. The institutions varied widely in the different nations or empires, but the effects were similar: static hierarchical societies intolerant of departures from the norm, including the state-imposed religion; repression, censorship and the suppression of local and individual initiative that de Tocqueville noted in France. Another effect of downwards command, seen in all autocratic societies, was a tendency to improve reports to superiors, resulting in a sort of institutional distortion of reality – heightened by a complete lack of transparency in government – all of which produced communities whose characteristics were at the opposite pole to those promoted by merchant government.

Nonetheless, trade and industry, despite the contempt in which they were held by the ruling elite, were recognized in all territorial powers as of the highest importance for the national treasury, and were supported and often directed by the government for the benefit of the state. This was one of many areas, however, where paradox rather than rationality held sway: while frequently very successful in desired directions, central control of trade and industry rendered the economy as a whole inefficient by comparison with those of maritime merchant states. Adam Smith explained one aspect:

> No regulation of commerce can increase the quantity of industry in any society beyond what its capital can maintain. It can only divert a part of it into a direction into which it might not otherwise have gone; and it is by no means certain that this artificial direction is likely to be more advantageous to the society than that into which it would have gone of its own accord.[16]

The paradox, apparent in the practice of all maritime powers, was that state interest was best served when merchants pursued their own self-interest; as Adam Smith put it, 'the study of [the individual's] own advantage naturally, or rather necessarily, leads him to prefer that employment [for his capital] which is most advantageous to the society.'[17] Or, what he famously described as the 'invisible hand' of competition in free markets rendered economies based on individual self-interest more effective than those directed for state interest.

There were more potent historical causes for the failure of territorial powers. These showed up particularly in war when the resources needed by central government to support an industry or monopoly company, and the warships protecting overseas trade, were redirected for more pressing needs on their borders.

More crucially, the sophisticated financial institutions developed under maritime power could not evolve in absolute regimes where there was no public scrutiny of revenue and expenditure, not even a ministerial audit, and no certainty that the consequent chaos in the public accounts would not impel an unfettered government to seize private funds or property or renege on payments on the accumulated debt; indeed, in crises caused by the extraordinary costs of war it was certain to do so. Thus, while maritime powers were able to borrow at low rates of interest on the security of a funded public or national debt in which the people had confidence, absolute continental monarchies had to borrow on the reputation of the king's government at rates which rose steeply as the financial situation deteriorated during the course of a war. Great wars were decided largely on margins of interest.

Since war was the inevitable and constant feature of international mercantile rivalry, comparative advantage tipped towards maritime power. The pattern scarcely varied. By the eighteenth century the ultimate aims of both chief territorial and maritime protagonists, France and Great Britain, were to defend and extend their overseas colonies, especially those in the West Indies and America, since transatlantic colonial produce underlay the fastest growing and most profitable trade of both nations. British strategy, like that of the United Provinces in the previous century, was to subsidize France's territorial rivals in order to engage and bleed her on land, while themselves gaining command at sea by outbuilding the French battle fleet, blockading it in its bases or crippling it in battle – in successful campaigns combining all methods. After this Britain was able to pick off French overseas colonies and cut her sea trade, so depressing French industries and the revenue reaching her treasury, and thus forcing financial crisis. In this situation French governments would reveal their territorial basis by reducing the funding for the battle fleet – or laying up the big ships altogether – in order to concentrate on the land struggle, so contributing further to the British maritime grip. France's only remedies against failure at sea were to attempt the invasion of England – invariably thwarted – or seize continental bargaining counters to exchange for her lost overseas colonies at the peace negotiations that would follow when both powers were sufficiently exhausted.

The exception to this pattern was the War of American Independence when Britain could not construct the usual continental alliance against France. With funding thus flowing freely to the navy, the French battle fleet, in alliance with the Bourbon Spanish fleet, was able to achieve strategic concentrations which cost Great Britain most of her north American colonies. It is significant, nonetheless, that although Britain lost the American end of the war, Admiral Sir George Rodney's victory at the Saints soon afterwards in 1782 re-established British naval ascendancy in the vital struggle against the Bourbons; even more significantly, although financially much exhausted, Britain ended the war in far better shape than France or Spain. The French minister chiefly responsible for Louis XV entering the American war in the first place was by the end imploring Spain to join them in concluding it:

> The English have to some degree regenerated their navy while ours has been used up . . . Join to that the diminution of our financial means . . . That inconvenience is common, no doubt, also to England, but her constitution gives her in that regard advantages which our monarchical forms do not give us.[18]

He was referring to parliamentary scrutiny of public accounts, so entirely lacking in France or Spain, and the equally transparent system of collecting the taxes on which British government loans were secured, which contrasted with the hidden and in many respects arbitrary tax system of the Bourbons.

These complementary advantages had allowed Britain to fund the war at peacetime rates of interest of about 3 per cent while France, largely because she lacked them, had been borrowing at between 8 and 10 per cent. Thus, although France achieved her primary war aim of ensuring the success of the American colonial rebellion, the burden of servicing the debt incurred wrecked her financial and political stability. She was soon to pay the final price in revolution. Great Britain by contrast, apparently the loser, had no real difficulty either in servicing her vastly increased national debt or in recapturing the markets in north America from which it had been France's main aim to remove her.

Such was the situation as this volume opens. The United States had just been founded. The colonists' original Declaration of Independence, written in the main by Thomas Jefferson, a disciple of John Locke, had laid down the premise that all men are created equal and endowed with 'certain unalienable Rights', among them 'Life, Liberty and the Pursuit of Happiness'. It continued:

That to secure these rights, Governments are instituted among Men, deriving their just powers from the consent of the governed – That whenever any form of Government becomes destructive of these ends it is the Right of the People to alter or abolish it, and to institute new Government.[19]

So the People, as opposed to any central power, had been established as sovereign. The constitution drawn up in 1787 after the successful war of liberation sought to ensure they remained so by separating the organs of government following the British example, as Locke, Montesquieu and their disciples had advocated. Legislative power was vested in Congress, comprising an upper and a lower chamber particularly responsible, like the British House of Commons, for financial control; executive power in a President elected for a fixed term of four years; and judicial power in a Supreme Court, whose judgement on constitutional or inter-state disputes would be final. This was assented to by popular vote and ratified in 1788, after which amendments were passed according United States citizens statutory rights which the English/British had acquired over the years under common law or by legislation: these included specific freedoms of religion, speech, the press and peaceful assembly, the right to 'a speedy and public trial, by an impartial jury of the State and district wherein the crime shall have been committed' and rights not to be oppressed by excessive bail, excessive fines or 'cruel and unusual punishments'.[20]

Besides deriving from the English model and the customs of the British colonies which had given birth to the new republic, the constitution of the United States was also the product of a merchant system driven by the mercantile elites of the seaport cities – Philadelphia, New York, Boston and Newport, Rhode Island – substantial sections of which had been foremost in the rebellion against British rule.[21] It was therefore in all respects a true reflection of a merchant society, and in the following century was to fulfil its mercantile destiny through overseas trade and internal commerce via rivers, canals and finally iron and steel railroads driven across the continent.

The manifestations of merchant power in government and society in the United States, as in Great Britain and the United Provinces before, could be attributed simply to free-market capitalism; but the description would not be complete. It would not hint at how or why capitalism triumphed when and where it did, nor why it failed in apparently similar conditions elsewhere, nor why it was frustrated in all major civilizations before the 'modern' era. These questions have been addressed by E. L. Jones in *Growth Recurring*, an analysis of economic change in past civilizations. He points to the largely unexamined but undoubted tendency towards economic growth in most societies throughout most of history; avoiding the term 'capitalism', which can mean different things to different economists, he investigates why general economic expansion has so seldom been converted into 'intensive growth', defined as a rise in average income per head of population. He refers to this failure in the great civilizations of the past as 'history's greatest frustration'.[22] It might be described as the frustration of successive peoples – as opposed to elites – whose material well-being did not greatly improve; but Professor Jones's term, 'history's frustration', will be used here.

The thesis of maritime supremacy suggests the conditions necessary to break through the constraints which have frustrated such civilizations. It implies wealth from trade, since most international trade has been and still is by sea, and naval dominance, since sea trade has always needed protection. In geo-historical terms it suggests that a city or state which acquires maritime supremacy enjoys both a prime middleman position on international trade routes and natural defences against attack by land, since these glittering centres of mercantile wealth on the periphery of land masses have always acted like magnets to warrior hordes from the hinterland. Here again is the essence of the opposition between territorial and maritime power, the contradiction between martial and merchant objectives. For once the maritime city or state is sacked or so weakened by constant warring as to become absorbed into its more populous territorial neighbour, its investment capital is dissipated in the preoccupations of the new suzerain, whether by further campaigns of plunder, defence against rivals, repression of internal rebellions, ostentatious display, funerary architecture or any number of non-market objectives espoused by the warrior or bureaucratic elite – even market investment when directed centrally by the state rather than by merchants for themselves. For, as noted earlier, the soldiers' and bureaucrats' requirement for central authority is incompatible with the financial institutions and individual freedoms necessary for merchants, and thus for capitalism.

This ultimately is the reason for 'history's greatest frustration': before the modern era and the development of the great-gunned sailing warship able to trade and achieve maritime supremacy around the globe, no maritime state could accumulate the wealth, and thus the strength, to do much more than coexist with neighbouring territorial empires. The first to gain dominance over them was the cluster of merchant cities in the Netherlands around which the United Provinces was founded. Achieving security by flooding low-lying border areas to form a defensive moat against the armies of Spain, then France, this small republic became the first merchant state with a global reach and the financial strength to manipulate the power balances of Europe; its commercial capital, Amsterdam, became the financial heart of the western world. In turn Great Britain, more secure behind the English Channel and with a larger area and population, took over as capitalism's standard-bearer; and London supplanted Amsterdam as the centre of the financial world. Finally the United States, far larger and eventually more populous than either, and separated by oceans, seized the trident; and London bowed to New York. As local war fleets in the Mediterranean had secured local capitalist economies at the time of the Renaissance, so global maritime supremacy, encircling and outflanking the Eurasian land mass, was the vehicle for global capitalism and the liberal values and institutions which grew from it and served it.

THE ARGUMENTS presented in *Maritime Supremacy and the Opening of the Western Mind* were challenged by some historians: most interestingly perhaps, it was asked why, if the merchants of trading states in the west so naturally captured and transformed their governments to their own purposes, a similar process did not take place in the east? China was technologically far ahead of Europe at the start of western oceanic expansion. As early as the eleventh century the Chinese had developed the use of coke for smelting iron in blast furnaces – one of the key innovations in the later British industrial revolution – and by the thirteenth century they were producing more iron per head of population than eighteenth-century Europe,[23] using it for weapons and tools for agriculture and manufacturing industry. Water-powered spinning machines were widespread; river navigation had been improved and north–south canals built – all recognizable components of the later Dutch and British industrial revolutions – and as a result transport costs had been cut, commodity markets widened, large cities supplied and consumer goods rendered plentiful, 'some of extremely high quality, but most designed for popular consumption'.[24]

Moreover, Chinese sea trade had spread across the Indian Ocean as far as the African coast taking iron weapons, silks, cottons, pepper, spices, porcelain – fragments of which have recently been found 'by the shovel-ful' along the entire east African coastline – and bringing back rhinoceros horn, pearls, aromatic substances, gums and the like. The spectacular cul-mination of Chinese ocean voyaging had come in the early fifteenth century when a series of grand treasure- or jewel-ship fleets headed by huge war junks of 1,500 tons or more armed with gunpowder weapons and packed with soldiers had sailed into the Indian Ocean as far as the Persian Gulf and the Zanzibar coast to overawe local rulers with the might of the Chinese emperor, 'the Son of Heaven', exact submission, encourage trade and, most importantly it seems, search for and bring back rarities and marvels, from precious stones, minerals, drugs and plants to ostriches, zebras and giraffes.[25]

The voyages reveal that the Chinese of the early fifteenth century were ahead in the art of building large deep-sea vessels, and at least the equal of the most advanced Europeans in oceanic navigation. Yet these grand expeditions, in contrast to the trading voyages which the Chinese had been making for centuries – and were still making – were not driven by merchant-mariners for profit but by the court for prestige, luxury and sheer curiosity, and were financed by the imperial treasury. When Confucian 'agriculturalists' at court gained the upper hand under a new emperor, and Mogul and Tartar invaders threatened the north-western provinces, the voyages were discontinued, never to be resumed. Sub-sequently the navy itself was allowed to disintegrate and anti-maritime policies were provoked by the inward-looking official culture. So great were the fears that merchants of the coastal provinces might make alli-ances with foreigners and spin out of control of the centre that by 1500 it was a capital offence in China to build a sea-going junk with more than two masts. This outcome was entirely predictable on the theory outlined in these pages: China was a huge territorial empire of diverse regions with vulnerable land borders, governed from the centre by a scholar-bureaucracy certain of its traditional values and superiority, abominat-ing and fearing foreign contamination.

But what of Japan? The Japanese islands were as strategically placed off the coast of east Asia as the British Isles off Europe; they possessed deep-water harbours and sheltered anchorages, a similarly temperate climate and an industrious population. While not on the route of such vital commodities as Baltic timber, naval stores and grain from which Dutch and British merchants and shipping profited, they were well placed for trade with China, Korea, the Philippines and the Indonesian spice islands, and exploited the position to the full. By the end of the fourteenth century their merchant trader-pirates dominated the commerce of the China Seas, and as the Chinese navy withered during the fifteenth century the Japanese ravaged the coastal shipping and cities of China as well. With sea trade, industries had been stimulated to such an extent that manufactured goods as well as raw materials were exported and a purely commercial-industrial city, Osaka, dominated by merchants outside the fief of territorial barons, had grown on the delta of the Yodo river where it met the Inland Sea at the southern end of the main island, Honshu. Agricultural productivity had also increased to support a population which had grown by the beginning of the fourteenth century to nearly ten million, some five times larger than the United Provinces or England.[26]

In all these respects Japan might be compared to the western maritime powers. Where it differed was in political structure. It retained a feudal system which by the fourteenth century had fragmented into a number of virtually independent domains under barons styled *daimyo*. These owed nominal allegiance to the emperor at Kyoto, some 30 miles inland from Osaka, but he was powerless against the leader, the *Shogun* – 'generalissimo' – of the strongest *daimyo* coalition, and the imperial court had degenerated into a refined but hollow pretence. In the final decades of the fifteenth century the ambitions of powerful *daimyo*, stimulated by the rapid increases in trade, industry and population, led to a series of civil wars during which all semblance of central authority was lost, and it was not until almost the end of the sixteenth century that the country was unified under the military dictatorship of Hideyoshi Toyotomi, a peasant's son who had risen in the service of a victorious *daimyo*. Even Hideyoshi lacked full control; no doubt at least partly for this reason he set about redirecting the martial dynamism generated by the internal wars into overseas aggression. It is testimony to the maritime, industrial and economic strength of the country by this date, and to the confidence engendered, that he aimed at the conquest of their huge but ailing territorial neighbour, China.

He ordered a great shipbuilding programme and in 1592 transported an army of some 200,000 men across the Strait of Tsushima to southern Korea, then advanced northward practically the length of the peninsula on the way to China. The Koreans, defeated on land, looked to their navy to extricate them by cutting Japanese sea lines of communication, constructing for this purpose so-called 'turtle ships'. These appear to have been a development of the Chinese war junk, built for speed, with a length–beam ratio of almost four to one – perhaps 110 feet by 28 feet[27] – a single tier of ten oarsmen each side and a single gun deck above pierced with 12 gun ports and 22 loopholes for musketeers and archers. This was completely covered with a sloping turtle-back deck studded with spikes and knives and, according to strong local tradition, sheathed with copper or iron plates, thus impervious to burning arrows and other Japanese incendiary devices. With two of these formidable craft, probably the first 'ironclad' warships, leading a fleet of conventional war junks, the Korean admiral Yi Sunsin routed Japanese supply squadrons and their escorts in a series of stand-off engagements in line-ahead formation – again to foil the Japanese penchant for boarding and entering men – and succeeded in cutting the Japanese army from its home base. Chinese forces then intervened on behalf of their satellite and the Japanese withdrew to their beachhead on the Strait of Tsushima. In 1597 Hideyoshi launched a second grand invasion across the Strait, but was again checked by a Chinese army entering Korea. The following year he died and the whole grandiose enterprise was abandoned.

The power struggle precipitated by his death was decided in 1600 at the battle of Sekigahara in favour of his chief lieutenant in eastern Japan, Tokugawa Ieyasu, whose castle seat was at the fishing village of Edo – future Tokyo – set in a deep inlet on the Pacific coast of Honshu. He was duly appointed *Shogun* by the impotent Kyoto court. From his earliest years Tokugawa had personal experience of the shifting coalitions, treachery and incessant warfare of the *daimyo*: when he was two his mother had been separated from his father's family because of a change of alliance and at seven he had been sent away to live with another powerful family as a hostage. Like Louis XIV of France, who in his early years saw his kingdom torn apart by the civil wars of the Fronde, he determined to build a power structure impervious to factional rebellion. Like Louis he succeeded remarkably: his dynasty, known as the Tokugawa, or Edo shogunate, was to provide Japan with unity and internal stability for the next two and a half centuries. The price was paid in repression, bureaucracy, uniformity, the stifling of social change and creative, scientific or religious deviation and to a large extent of economic progress – all the symptoms of territorial as opposed to maritime power writ large.

His methods were traditional; they included the rearrangement of domains to reward loyal *daimyo* and control others, restrictions on building or repairing castles, the requirement for *daimyo* to have their sons or wives living as hostages in his own castle at Edo which he extended with towering concentric walls, moats and high embankments into the largest castle complex in the world, over two miles in diameter – whose core now forms the grounds of the Imperial Palace in Tokyo – together with rigorous restrictions on carrying arms and a rigid freeze on class distinctions according to the 2,000-year-old Chinese Confucian formula: with warrior administrators – in Japan styled *Samurai* – at the top, followed by peasants, then artisans, and finally tradesmen – including merchants of high economic and social standing – at the very bottom. Confucianism held tradesmen unproductive. Tokugawa Ieyasu also took care to reduce the castle of his predecessor, Hideyoshi, at the merchant city of Osaka, and to eliminate the surviving family.

While none of these measures was original, indeed Hideyoshi had instituted most of them, including the forced separation of the four classes of society – *shi-nō-kō-shō* – Tokugawa created both an efficient central administration and a separate body of officials, *metsuke*, to police the bureaucrats and seek out groups throughout the land who might threaten the regime – said to be one of the first, if not the first extensive and efficient secret police system anywhere.[28]

Tokugawa Ieyasu died in 1616 having established the hereditary principle long before with a formal but bogus retirement in favour of his son, Hidetata, who in 1623 made a similar purely formal retirement to pass the title to his son Iemitsu. Under these two the Tokugawa system reached its logical conclusion. It was a hierarchical pyramid: at the apex the *Shogun* owned all the land in the country; he divided it among the *daimyo*, who in return owed him military and other services, including the duty of making a ceremonial visit to the Edo castle every year – a unique feature of Japanese feudalism – where they met wives and other family members living there as hostages. The *daimyo* were owed similar duties by their warrior retainers, but these instead of being granted divisions of land in the domain received stipends in rice.

At the base of the pyramid were the farmer-peasants who provided the economic foundation of the system and comprised 80 per cent of the population; they were organized at village and town level in matters of civic order and the payment of taxes – assessed in measures of rice by government officials on the basis of land surveys. They were prohibited from abandoning their land, changing their occupation or buying or selling land and were subject to restrictions on dress and mode of life, including a strict prohibition on carrying arms. They were serfs tied to the soil of their lord.

With hierarchy went a code of absolute obedience which was sanctified by the Confucian principles of *chu* and *ko* – loyalty and filial piety. This was applied equally within families where, as might be anticipated, women were placed at the bottom of the scale: the common concept of *danson-johi* translates as respect for the male, contempt for the female.

The first Tokugawa *Shogun*, Ieyasu, had recognized and encouraged foreign trade as an important source of wealth and strength for the regime. An English shipwright turned mariner named William Adams who had come to Japan as pilot of a Dutch ship in 1600 gained his confidence and became a trusted adviser on European customs and shipbuilding and trading practices; his influence led to the establishment of Dutch and English trade relations with Japan.[29] Adams also warned Ieyasu of the Jesuits in the Portuguese trading community. The Portuguese had been the first Europeans in Japan, arriving in the 1540s; they had combined commerce with a mission to propagate the true faith, and had been so successful in converting minor *daimyo* and Japanese of all classes that Hideyoshi had barred missionaries from the country. Ieyasu, keen to encourage the Portuguese to establish trading links with the Edo region, had annulled the ban. However, it was not long before he realized that the Jesuit campaign of conversion was subverting the social and political order and he banned Christianity altogether.

This proved the first step in rejecting all European contacts and ideas since his son and grandson took the policy to a ruthlessly logical conclusion: missionaries were executed, Japanese Christians forced to renounce the faith by trampling on the Cross, failing which they suffered death; Christian communities were slaughtered and all Japanese forced to register as members of a Buddhist temple; and foreigners were expelled from the country. To prevent further infiltration by their ideas, travel abroad was banned: Japanese living or trading abroad were prohibited from returning home and, as in China, the construction of ships large enough for overseas voyaging was forbidden, at a stroke confining Japan's vigorous mariners to coastal and inter-home island trading. Only one minute opening was permitted in the policy of national seclusion, or *sakoku*; this was at the port of Nagasaki at the western end of the western island, Kyushu – as far from the most productive and populous central plain of Honshu as it was possible to get; here Chinese were allowed to trade under strict supervision and a small island in the harbour was assigned for trade with the Dutch, the only Europeans permitted this privilege; unlike the Portuguese and Spanish they did not proselytize.

The Japanese retreat from the outside world coincided precisely with the rise to world trading supremacy of the Dutch republic of the United Provinces. The first long-haul company for trade with the east, the Compagnie van Verre, had been founded in Amsterdam four years after the unification of Japan under Hideoshi Toyotomi. By 1602, when Tokugawa Ieyasu had seized power, Dutch capital was invested in so many rival companies trading with the east that they were merged, in order to stabilize prices, into the United [Dutch] East India Company, Vereenigde Oost-Indische Compagnie, or VOC in short. In 1609 the VOC established a trading post on Hirado off north-western Kyushu; simultaneously at home the Bank of Amsterdam was founded: it was to prove the essential facilitator for Dutch capitalism, its bills of exchange the lubricant for world commerce. Over the following years the VOC pioneered a faster route to the Indonesian spice islands and established its main eastern base, Batavia, on Java to windward of the Portuguese main base at Malacca. With this advantage, more manoeuvrable and better gunned fighting galleons and overwhelmingly greater capital resources the VOC began to drive the Portuguese from the archipelago.

Meanwhile, in Japan the persecution of Christians began. The process was concluded in 1638 with the mass slaughter of the last resisting communities,[30] and by the following year, after the last foreigners had been expelled, the policy of isolation was complete. In the same year that Japan shut herself off, in the English Channel Maarten Tromp, Lieutenant Admiral of the United Provinces, routed a final armada sent north by Spain, effectively ending the great days of the Spanish empire and announcing the arrival of the Dutch republic as the leading naval, commercial, industrial and financial power of the western world. Dutch political and social freedoms, including far greater freedom for women than was found elsewhere, consultative government, an advanced market economy, mass consumption, leadership in intellectual enquiry, the sciences and technology placed them at the opposite pole to the inward-looking and repressive society of Tokugawa Japan. While the Japanese retreated to a systematically ordered and policed feudalism, the Dutch were – with hindsight – heralds of the modern liberal west.

The simple answer to the question of why both China and Japan – followed by Korea – ringed themselves with sea walls as western traders appeared in their waters is that more powerful long guns had been developed in the west and no eastern war junk could compete with the broadsides of western galleons. It is not clear why this should have been so, since gunpowder and guns were developed in China earlier than in Europe. However, what does seem clear is that it was the culture of the elite groups rather than simple impotence in naval warfare that forced the eastern nations into isolation. The merchants who undoubtedly thrived in the port cities had not been able to impose their incompatible values on the Confucian bureaucracy of China or the warring *daimyo* of Japan; both these groups retained an essentially territorial outlook founded on land and agricultural production, and the closer the city merchants came to the European traders with their very different values the more they threatened the ideological hold of the centre. Contact had to be sundered. As noted, this was entirely predictable in the case of China, a huge territorial empire. That it also happened in Japan despite her insularity and the success of her overseas trader-pirate mariners suggests that commerce had not yet permeated Japanese society to the extent that it had on the coastal fringes of western Europe, and Japan remained at bottom a territorial state dominated by landholders.

Commerce and industry continued to grow in the unified internal market achieved under the Tokugawa shogunate, but the absence of foreign competition and foreign models and the virtual inaccessibility of foreign markets left the country backward by comparison with its western rivals. As western commercial and industrial expansion gathered pace during the industrial revolution, Japan fell far behind, as did China. This was history's 'greatest frustration' in the east. It was paralleled in Mogul India, Ottoman Turkey and tsarist Russia.[31] It was the frustration of the merchant class.

WHAT MERCHANTS of the western maritime powers enjoyed was freedom to invest for maximum profit wherever they saw the opportunity; freedom to dispose of their property – which Locke defined in the broadest sense as composing 'their Persons as well as their Goods . . . [and] their life, liberties and estates'[32] protected by law from arbitrary restraint or violence, whether from kings, ministers, barons or commoners. Freedom was the bright thread running through successive maritime powers, for, as noted, the economic freedoms demanded by merchants, and achieved only in merchant-dominated governments, spread through and changed society.

It might be asked how deeply these freedoms penetrated. Evidently not down to slaves or labourers in overseas colonies who were held and worked like slaves; nor perhaps to sailors. It was contended in *Maritime Supremacy* that Dutch sailors 'were a particularly brutalized class . . . savage punishments, undermanning, short rations and death from disease were too often the realities beneath the civilized abstractions of the republic's liberal thinkers'.[33] And in the case of Great Britain:

> Seamen, on whom the whole edifice of freedom ultimately rested, were peculiarly exploited and liable to lose their own liberty. In war . . . they were seized from homecoming merchantmen or rounded up ashore by the impress service to complete the companies of men of war, and at the end of a cruise they were frequently 'turned over' to another of HM ships.[34]

An articulate British sailor was quoted excusing 'pressing as 'a hardship which nothing but absolute necessity can reconcile to our boasted freedom'.

The system compared unfavourably, in theory, with the rational manning policy of the archetypal territorial rival, Bourbon France; there, all seafaring men were compelled to register for naval service and were listed in 'classes' each of which was required to serve a year in the navy every three to five years. However, this neatly bureaucratic scheme invariably collapsed under the demands of war. There were too few sailors and naval service was generally loathed, with reason. It compared unfavourably with service in the British fleet in matters of shipboard cleanliness, victuals – hence disease – good order, pay and morale. Admiral de Grasse acknowledged as much when brought aboard Rodney's flagship after the battle of the Saints in 1782: admiring what he saw about him, he admitted that his own service was a hundred years behind. In consequence the most savage means were employed in the French service to enforce conscription, prevent desertion and subdue mutiny.[35]

So in practice the British sailor, while in wartime deprived of his freedom, probably suffered less than his French counterpart. And it is likely that in his life aboard he enjoyed more freedom to exercise initiative and rise as far as his abilities would take him less constrained by class or social barriers; for as N. A. M. Rodger has observed in *The Wooden World*, his classic revision of hitherto accepted ideas about naval life in the eighteenth century, 'the Navy resembled the society from which it was recruited in many more ways than it differed from it'.[36] And there is no doubt that eighteenth-century British society was far freer from legal or social restraints than that of France or any other European country except perhaps her maritime counterpart, the Dutch republic. This is clear from the observations of foreigners – already noted – who were amazed both at the freedom of political expression and the free and easy intercourse between classes in England; towards the end of the century a German visitor wrote:

> The sentiment of liberty and the ever-active protection of the laws are the causes why the common people testify but little consideration for persons of quality, and even for persons in office, except they have gained their affections by affable and popular manners.[37]

In France, by contrast, distinctions of rank remained rigid. Early the following century – after the French Revolution – de Tocqueville famously epitomized the social mobility of the English as against the rigidity of French class distinctions with one word drawn from each language:

> 'Gentleman' and 'gentilhomme' evidently have the same derivation, but 'gentleman' in England applies to every well-educated man whatever his birth, while in France 'gentilhomme' applies only to a noble by birth. The meaning of these two words of common origin has been so transformed by the different social climates of the two countries that today they simply cannot be translated . . . This grammatical observation is more illuminating than many long arguments.[38]

It has been mentioned that Samuel Ricard, Montesquieu, Adam Smith among others credited the market exchanges of English commercial society with a benign effect on manners and morals. The freer relationships between the classes was similarly ascribed to the mutualities of a commercial society, and also to parliamentary government; thus the moral philosopher, William Paley:

> Popular elections procure to the common people courtesy from their superiors. That contemptuous and overbearing insolence, with which the lower orders of the community are wont to be treated by the higher, is greatly mitigated where the people have something to give. The assiduity with which their favour is sought upon these occasions, serves to generate settled habits of condescension and respect.[39]

There was no such system of popular representation in France, consequently little pressure on the upper ranks to court their social inferiors.

The son of the inventor, James Watt, visiting Paris in 1784, was horrified at the way the nobles' coaches were driven with complete disregard for the safety of people in the street, and observed, 'One would think the common people here were looked upon as different creatures.'[40]

Thus while it is not possible to define precisely how far practical enjoyment of freedom extended through British society – or to what extent, if at all, 'pressed sailors benefited aboard ship from the customary freedoms of British life – freedom undoubtedly penetrated further and deeper in Britain than in France. It was a qualitative difference. The British were no less disorderly – it seems that execution rates in George III's London were far higher than in Louis XV's Paris – but whereas French society was in thrall to a web of regulations administered by state functionaries backed by civil police, the British, who refused to establish a professional police force, suffered few functionaries and insisted on parliamentary control of the comparatively small standing army, managed to preserve stability and order, certainly with savage punishments for even minor offences, but substantially through custom and a web of interdependent social relationships. The difference was an expression of the fundamental contrast between a still hierarchical order governed from the centre and a merchant order bound together by monetary exchanges and a representative system of government which mediated people's concerns and prevented serious oppression. William Paley expressed it in 1785: 'the representatives are so intermixed with the constituents and the constituents with the rest of the people, that they cannot, without a partiality too flagrant to be endured, impose any burden upon the subject, in which they do not share themselves.'[41]

Of course, both the commercial and parliamentary basis of British liberties had been evolving for centuries: as early as 1649 Sir John Fortescue defined the purpose of English government as the protection of persons and their belongings, for which reason kings could not impose taxes without their subjects' consent. In practice it was not always so: the English Civil War (1642–8) and the 'Glorious Revolution' (1688–9) resulted from Parliament – representing primarily landed and commercial interests – defending that principle against kings who sought to violate it. It was not until William of Orange seized the English Crown in the 'Glorious Revolution' and pledged not to suspend laws or levy taxes without the consent of Parliament that the monarchy was effectively constrained by law. This was the turning point. Without Parliament's absolute control of the nation's finances none of the vital financial institutions, particularly the Bank of England (1694) and long-term funded national as opposed to royal debt, could have been established. Without these, London could not have taken over from Amsterdam as the centre of world finance, and Great Britain could not have attained maritime supremacy in the sense defined here.

Viewed strictly in terms of history or prevailing ideology and political practice this outcome was an anomaly, a reversal of the trend elsewhere. In the years during which the English Parliament increased its influence and finally chained the Crown, its counterparts throughout Europe, especially in the great territorial empires, surrendered power and withered. By the eighteenth century the Estates General in France, the Cortes in Spain and virtually all other European national representative bodies had lost all influence. Various causes have been ascribed, not least chronic internal dissensions and religious conflicts which persuaded the representatives of the people to trade in their rights for a strong central authority that could ensure stability. For whatever reasons, by the eighteenth century representative central government was confined to two great powers, Great Britain and the United Provinces, and one lesser power, Sweden; towards the end of the century these were joined by the infant United States. Otherwise in western Europe absolute monarchy was the rule – apart from Poland where a Diet of nobles dominated and Switzerland which was comprised of thirteen independent cantonments ruled by urban oligarchies. In Russia and the great empires of Asia and the middle east autocratic or bureaucratic despotism prevailed.

The maritime powers were virtually unique. The reasons are not hard to find: they were governed by and for merchants or men of property, and were protected by the sea or low land which could be flooded from the onslaught of territorial autocrats coveting their wealth and jealous of their power. Japan, too, was protected by the sea and was the one eastern nation that might have been expected, according to the theory advanced here, to have developed in the same way as England. However, her merchants had not overcome the territorial centre; they remained closely regulated, and confined, at least in theory, to the lowest level of the class structure.

ANOTHER ARGUMENT against the thesis of *Maritime Supremacy* is that great wars have generally been decided by land campaigns. The deeper truth is that in such cases the victorious armies or coalitions were financed and supplied by the leading maritime power – in the seventeenth century the Dutch, in the eighteenth and early nineteenth centuries the British and in the twentieth century the Americans. But whether decided by land campaigns or, more frequently, by financial exhaustion, great wars have never in the modern era resulted in defeat for the coalition led by a supreme maritime power – despite these powers' failures in particular campaigns. Opposing great territorial powers, on the other hand, have often been humbled.

Other questions concern artistic advance, particularly the prominence accorded in *Maritime Supremacy* to the development of the novel in the free atmosphere of eighteenth-century England. It has been pointed out that at the same period the frontiers of musical form and expression were being extended in the distinctly territorial and absolutist regimes of the Habsburg empire and German principalities. There are fundamental differences: Bach, Haydn, Mozart were patronized by princes; Defoe, Richardson, Fielding relied on a public who bought their books. More importantly, while composers certainly expressed ideas of, for instance, political freedom, these came through in coded form, not in an accessible public language that could either be censored or used to promote policy. The point has been illustrated in modern times by Stalin's attempt to censor Shostakovich's 'petit bourgeois' music. It remains a question whether the Russian composer's mature works are hymns to Bolshevism or, more probably, cries of despair at the direction Communism had taken.

Novels, on the other hand, spoke unambiguously to their readers, as did satire, philosophical and economic treatises and handbills. Music might delight, excite, move, but writing, in addition, disseminated ideas which could directly or indirectly threaten the established order. It was the glory and uniqueness of the maritime powers that such writing was not usually censored. It might be argued that Jean-Jacques Rousseau, Denis Diderot and the *philosophes* who contributed to the famous *Encyclopédie* spread the most subversive ideas of the eighteenth century under the noses of the Bourbon monarchy. They were, of course, for the most part disseminating or expanding liberal ideas originally expressed in the freer air of the maritime powers. And most did suffer from official censorship: Rousseau was chased from France and his native Geneva, took refuge in England and finally returned to France incognito. Diderot was imprisoned for an early publication and work on his *Encyclopédie* was continually delayed by government and ecclesiastical censorship. So far as the latter was concerned, it is worth noting the views of his British contemporary, Edmund Burke, on the zeal with which the French literary establishment – of which he was a leading light – sought the destruction of Christianity. 'They were possessed with a spirit of proselytism in the most fanatical degree; and from thence, by an easy process, with the spirit of persecution . . . These Atheistical fathers have a bigotry of their own, and they have learnt to talk against monks with the spirit of a monk.'[42] This was to result during the Revolution in the oppression and pillage of the Church; it no doubt explains the ecclesiastical censorship.

As for the *Encyclopédie*, the publisher secretly removed some 300 pages of more compromising material before daring to print the first edition. Diderot's own commentary on the French explorer Bougainville's voyage to the Pacific in which he advocated a society based on tolerance and sexual liberty – or 'free love' – only circulated in manuscript before the Revolution. Nor were many other controversial contributions included until a new and enlarged edition appeared as the old regime was collapsing. By this time, it seems, the advocates of reason had accomplished their task and subverted the regime from within, as will appear; official censorship was frustrated by patrons in the highest ruling circles.[43] To put it another way, most influential sections of the French nobility and upper bourgeoisie had been so infected by 'Enlightenment' ideas through salon talk, circulated manuscripts, often banned books and scurrilous satires that, to cite Burke again, the persecution of the Encyclopedists and others in the dying years of the regime was 'desultory and faint', carried out 'more from compliance with form and decency than with serious resentment'.[44] The system had already been sapped from within – the result of ideas blown across from the shores of the maritime powers.

The English novel, which spread and was copied throughout continental Europe, was quite as subversive. Written by mainly middle-class authors for the fast-growing English middle class, it undermined aristocratic assumptions, replacing them with bourgeois values. In contrast to the high art that resulted from patronage, of which the great music of eighteenth-century Vienna was a surpassing example, the new art forms flourishing in the maritime powers were promoted by the people – those who bought them. The English novel was one; popular etching was another, which William Hogarth developed into a means of satirizing the pretensions and follies of society. What these and other forms had in common was a commercial and democratic quality; they were purchased by willing customers and served to promote their attitudes – in particular, for example, the concerns of women. The novel, with its wide readership, its ease of imitation and comparative immunity from censorship, was probably Britain's most seditious export to Europe: Rousseau's best-selling novel *Julie* escaped the censors who had condemned his *Social Contract* and other commentaries. In the process, the novel changed the way the world thought and promoted individuality more effectively than the *philosophes* or the English philosophical school which reached its eighteenth-century peak in David Hume's *A Treatise on Human Nature* (1739–40). In this sense Robinson Crusoe, Tom Jones and their successors had more impact than Bach, Mozart or Beethoven; more even than John Locke.

FINALLY, SHOULD any doubts remain about the distinctive expressions of maritime/merchant and territorial power, or the profound opposition between them, should there be any lingering claims that liberal values stem from the 'Enlightenment' rather than the necessities of trade and a monopoly of violence at sea, they should be stilled by the historic cataclysm with which this volume opens. If ever a transformation of society was predicated on the texts of the 'Enlightenment' – or indeed of eighteenth-century British ideals – it was the French Revolution of 1789. Yet within three years of the end of the 'old regime' the antithesis of the liberal state emerged: centralization was taken to new extremes and the institutions of twentieth-century dictatorship – secret police and family denunciations – were foreshadowed; and from the upheaval came the emperor Napoleon Bonaparte, the ultimate territorial warlord who aimed to give the law to Europe.

Counter-factual history is usually spurious, but it is worth considering in general terms whether, if Napoleon had triumphed over Great Britain, he would not have provided history's greatest frustration. It is for this reason that the events of the French Revolutionary and Napoleonic wars are covered in considerable detail in this volume.

I

The French Revolution, 1789

THE FRENCH REVOLUTION is represented as a grand turning point in western civilization when the ideas of the 'Enlightenment' assumed political form. It was the reverse. Judged by actions and results rather than words and the partisan gloss since applied, it was prototype and herald of the nationalist, totalitarian upheavals that disfigured the twentieth century.

It began in a golden glow of discourse. Those who took part remembered the years 1788–92 as a brilliant period when liberal aristocrats joined writers, philosophers, economists of enlightened views to fashion a fresh start for France and all humanity free from the artificial forms of the *ancien régime*. Germaine de Staël, daughter of one of the most brilliant salon hostesses in Paris, recalled it as a time when 'unlimited hope for unfettered happiness had taken hold of the nation, as it takes hold of men in their youth, with illusion and without caution'.[1]

There were many springs of the intellectual ferment. Among practical men of affairs, the British form of government with a limited monarchy, bicameral legislature and independent judiciary provided the model. A young noblewoman whose parents moved in the highest ministerial circles of the Bourbon regime afterwards recalled dinner parties at which she had to ask the meaning of the numerous English words totally unknown in France which peppered conversations – 'Club', 'motion', 'petition', 'majority', 'minority'.[2] Germaine de Staël's father, Jacques Necker, a Genevan-born banker, thrice Louis XVI's finance minister, was an influential champion of the 'English system'. During his first term of office, when seeking to raise funds for the heavily indebted French monarchy towards the end of the American War of Independence, he had tried to imitate the transparency at the heart of British financial management by publishing the first ever French government budget, the *Compte rendu au Roi* of 1781. However, he omitted the costs of war as 'exceptional expenditures', thereby producing an annual surplus of 10 million livres when there was an actual deficit nearer 50 millions (some £2.2 million). The artifice was a temporary success, but soon led to his dismissal; he had for the first time exposed to public scrutiny the extravagance of Louis' court. It made him a hero of the people, and added to accumulating dissatisfaction with the monarchy.

The British system was favoured by the hard-headed more for the evident benefits it conferred on Great Britain in terms of financial strength, naval and trading power and industrial dominance than for the theoretical merits promoted by Voltaire and Montesquieu. Everywhere British manufactures undersold their French counterparts; in Britain's new industrial heartlands French spies, official and unofficial, probed the practical secrets of the steam engines, power looms or coke-smelting blast furnaces which provided such significant cost advantages. But above all the French monarchy faced bankruptcy, and for financiers like Necker the chaotic and unaccountable methods of French revenue collection, ministerial expenditure and payment of debt had to be transformed; the British fiscal and budgeting procedures regulated openly in Parliament provided an enviably successful pattern.

Practical politicians and moneyed men like Necker were far outnumbered by theorists under the spell of that tremendous body of literature representing what came to be called the 'Enlightenment'. Central to this vision was belief in the efficiency of reason – as against the accretions of tradition, religious doctrine, political and social conventions by which men lived. Reason was, of course, a sound tool for mathematics, the sciences and philosophy; attempting to apply it to politics and society was, for the French at least, inappropriate. Whereas most British political thinkers and economists who laid the foundations for the 'Enlightenment' were either involved in practical politics or based their doctrines on strict observation of its workings, French *philosophes* inhabited planes of abstract thought divorced from the muddle of public affairs. This, according to de Tocqueville, was attributable to the way official functionaries answering to central government had taken over practically every aspect of French life, denying most of the population any meaningful political involvement or experience. So the French intelligentsia, in what de Tocqueville called their 'almost infinite detachment', produced what he described as a 'kind of abstract and literary politics'.[3]

Of the diverse forms this took, one of the more influential was the 'physiocratic' school which, rather in the manner of Confucian agriculturalists, regarded land and its produce as the only true source of wealth, and artisans and manufacturers as sterile classes adding nothing beyond their own labour. While in favour of free exchange in commerce and industry, physiocrats had no concept of political freedom and were as contemptuous of the British system of checks on power as of the apparently chaotic institutions of their own country. They wished to pull everything down and rebuild government and society on a *tabula rasa* according to reason and natural law, as they defined it. Recognizing that such a complete transformation could only be carried through by an absolute authority, they proposed strengthening the monarchy. Continuous public instruction in the essence of justice and the natural order would, they believed, prevent abuses of such concentrated power. De Tocqueville very reasonably described this as trifling gibberish.[4] But it was gibberish that was natural to a mainly agricultural country of diverse regions, as France was outside her few great commercial-industrial cities; it was no coincidence that the physiocrats looked to the great eastern territorial empire, China, for lessons in government.

Physiocrats believed in private property, but other schools of thought anticipated the most extreme forms of socialism – a word still to be coined – by calling for absolute equality, to be achieved through communal ownership of all land, property and goods; the necessary corollary was also an all-powerful state exercising a formative and regulatory tyranny, anticipating George Orwell's imagined regime of 1984, to rear, indoctrinate, employ and support every citizen.[5]

However, the single most important theorist for the Revolution was the Genevan-born Jean-Jacques Rousseau, who inaugurated a shift away from the primacy of reason towards the irrational, spontaneous, aesthetic, emotional and imaginative areas of the mind, heralding what came to be called the 'Romantic' movement. His earlier writings idealized the natural life of the *bon sauvage* and a conjectured era before man came together in society when all were free and equal; he contrasted this with the inequalities inherent in modern society with its unjust distribution of property, distinctions of rank and oppression of the poor by the wealthy. His first essay, which brought him to notice, even attacked the arts as purveyors of propaganda controlled by the rich to perpetuate social injustice.

His major work *Du contrat social* (*The Social Contract*) of 1762 might be described as inspiration, impractical handbook and testament to the Revolution; Maximilien Robespierre is said to have reread it every day. As suggested by its arresting opening, 'Man is born free, but he is everywhere in chains', it was essentially an exploration into how society might be so organized that all members preserved the freedom and equality Rousseau believed had been taken from them by unjust laws and artificial distinctions.

The answer he found was that peoples should form their own society. By joining together in a 'social contract' to choose their own form of government and laws, the people would be both sovereign and subjects – sovereign because they had created the constitution and could instal or remove its office-holders, subjects because they were bound to obey the laws and constitution so approved. By the act of association they would subsume their individual wills in what he famously termed the 'general will'. This term was hedged about by a theoretical distinction between the 'will of all' and the 'general will', but in practice seemed to mean the will of the majority; minorities would have to abide by majority decisions. He claimed on the one hand that the individual would be free since he shared sovereign authority in the constitution, which was bound therefore to uphold his rights, on the other hand that the individual was bound of his own free will to obey the 'general will', 'which is to say nothing else than that he [the individual] will be forced to be free'.[6]

If this was all highly paradoxical, or perhaps mere word play, it had to be since there is no categorical solution to the relationship between an individual and society. It has been suggested that Rousseau's ideas are better embodied in the modern United States of America, where his influence has been slight, than in most European nations. On the other hand Bertrand Russell saw the Nazi dictatorship as 'in part an outcome of Rousseau's teaching'[7] – an illustration of the difficulties of interpreting the message. In any case, the 'general will' was to prove an unfortunate concept for many thousands of French men and women when appropriated by the few and used to license tyranny.

Rousseau also wrote two influential novels, *Julie: ou, la nouvelle Héloïse* (1761), and *Émile: ou, de l'éducation* (1762) – which was more a tract on bringing up children uncorrupted by the fallacies and vices of adult society. Both books dealt with personal morality and individual fulfilment and virtue. Like the English novels they followed, they enjoyed a far wider readership, thus probably had more subversive effects on the established order than his or any other political treatises. Rousseau's personal life fell far short of the ideals exemplified by his fictional heroes and heroines; a modern scholar has suggested that by today's standards of mental health he would have been a candidate for psychiatric treatment:[8] Rousseau once confessed to the diarist, James Boswell, that he lived in a world of fantasies and could not tolerate the world as it was, adding like Jonathan Swift, 'mankind disgusts me'.[9] Nonetheless, the vision of moral progress he and his circle promulgated established a kind of collective hope for the transformation of society through individual virtue. This was, of course, at the opposite pole to the doctrine of the Church, which held that all were born to sin and could be saved only through the grace of God.

The American Revolution and the birth of the United States reinforced the idea of a revolution in moral values. The resonant phrases of the Declaration of Independence – 'all men are created equal . . . endowed by their Creator with certain unalienable Rights . . . Life, Liberty and the pursuit of Happiness . . . Governments . . . deriving their just powers from the consent of the governed' – and the framing of the US constitution which elevated 'the People' to sovereign authority appeared to embody Rousseau's concepts and to promise a new political dawn. Above all, the Americans, who were represented as a plain, homespun people living in freedom and harmony without distinctions of birth or rank, able to rise on merit alone – all of which was true by comparison with European society – provided a living model for the rebirth of civilization.

Besides these positive views tending to undermine the principles of Bourbon absolutism, the moral standing of the monarchy was weakened by negative images in the daily newspapers – a recent innovation in Paris – and a flood of satirical and pornographic pamphlets, particularly relating to Queen Marie Antoinette's supposed or alleged sexual perversions. As visions of reform had taken root in the liberal aristocracy, so these scurrilous tracts enjoyed the patronage of just those in the court and high nobility whose status they did most to threaten. Simon Schama has pointed out that stalls selling such erotica and salacious gossip sheets carried on business close by the royal palace at Versailles and in those towns to which the court moved in season.[10] For the elite, state censorship had virtually broken down. Subversive manuscripts circulated freely in the grand salons and chateaux, most notably Denis Diderot's essay on Bougainville's voyage to the Pacific, mentioned in the Introduction, which proposed a free and tolerant society modelled on the supposed virtues of Pacific islanders; and Beaumarchais' play, *The Marriage of Figaro*, banned because of its pyrotechnic attack on rank. Only the threat that this might be performed privately eventually persuaded Louis XVI to approve its public performance in Paris (1784). It might be said that the Revolution began in the hearts and minds of a substantial portion of the nobility it was destined to overthrow.

There was no pre-formed plan for revolution, merely a multitude of mostly utopian aspirations; the exception, as noted, was the wish of practical statesmen and financiers like Necker to harness Louis XVI as a 'constitutional' monarch in the British mode with an elected legislature on the Anglo-American model; the aim was to enhance France's power and enable her to compete more effectively with Great Britain in the world, particularly in the financial markets. Since the aim of the majority of the liberal nobility and government office-holders seems to have been the establishment of a reign of happiness, equality and freedom, there was a fundamental split in the ambitions of the elites from the start. And since the minds of all participating in government from ministers to petty functionaries had been formed in a milieu of regulation from the centre, there was a fundamental dichotomy between their desire to 'free' the people to participate in representative assemblies and their whole training in ordering the minutest details of community activity. They were indoctrinated exponents of Rousseau's paradox that people might be forced to be free.

Aggravating the differences in elite aims and means were the great regional diversities within the country, particularly the fundamental divide between Paris and a few thriving commercial port cities, where a wealthy merchant class held sway, and the rural interior where peasant landholdings had been fragmented by partition among families down the generations, where farming methods were backward by comparison with those of the Dutch and British, and communities adhered to a traditional way of life in which the Church was central – that Church which, to Parisian devotees of reason, had become a malignant relic of superstition and manipulation.

If there was one common perception linking the ordinary people of France, it was hunger. The exactions of the American revolutionary war, inefficient farming, regional barriers to a national market, a succession of poor harvests and rising bread prices, had combined to depress the economy, swell unemployment and reduce peasant and urban workers alike to destitution; in 1788 it was estimated that one-fifth of the population of Paris was dependent on charitable relief.[11]

In this setting, replete with high-minded optimism at the top, bitter grievances below and so many conflicting remedies, can it be wondered that the Revolution, instead of bringing a new, bright morning for mankind was to plunge Europe into the blackest night? It is no special reproach to the French; they simply illustrated the potential for human depravity beneath the most brilliant societies when the rules of law, custom and religion are dissolved. The odium should rather fall on those academics who have wilfully mistaken words for deeds and consequences and perpetuated a dangerous myth of revolutionary progress.

THE TRIGGER for the rolling revolutions that overtook France from 1787 was imminent bankruptcy: expenditure on wars and preparations for wars had outstripped the borrowing capacity of the Bourbon monarchy. The causes lay deep in the two great power systems in which France was enmeshed: the European territorial system and mercantilist competition for overseas trade and colonies. The costs finally overwhelmed the treasury and laid bare the limitations of the Bourbon form of government, unable either to exploit the full tax potential of the country or, as noted earlier, to command the confidence of international financiers to the same extent as the constitutional governments of the rival maritime powers, Great Britain and the United Provinces.[12]

This was well understood by Louis XVI's chief ministers. Yet they were locked into the systems. Attempted internal reforms over more than a century had been stalled by the privileged noble and ecclesiastical classes; and there was no escape from external wars both because they were integral to the mercantilist system and because colonial produce, its related industries and re-exports were the fastest growing elements of the national economy. The Comte de Vergennes, the chief minister who had engineered France's entry into the American revolutionary war for the expressed purpose of weakening Great Britain financially by cutting her trading links with her north American colonies, was preparing for the next war. It was this that plunged the government into crisis.

The underlying cause of the crisis was the British navy. France, even encumbered with the debts of the American war, had the resources to maintain her army at great power strength; what she could not afford was both a first-class army and a fleet to challenge the British fleet. Yet this is what Vergennes was attempting, backed enthusiastically by the ministers for the army and the navy, and driven apparently by remembrance of naval humiliations in the Seven Years War and consequent loss of French colonies in north America and India.[13] The navy minister was embarked on a construction programme designed to increase the battle fleet to eighty of the line headed by huge 118-gun first rates half as large again as the largest British flagships,[14] and a project to build an artificial harbour off Cherbourg to shelter French fleets in the English Channel and enable forces to be gathered there in safety for the invasion of England. Both schemes were fatally flawed, the former because experience in all previous wars against the maritime powers had shown France unable to man, let alone pay for smaller battle fleets than that now planned; the latter because of the unrealistic, indeed fantastical technology and equally huge cost. The Cherbourg scheme called for ninety hollow oak structures 142 feet in diameter at the base, narrowing to a flat top, which had to be towed into the roads, sunk and ballasted with rock to form an offshore barrier enclosing sheltered water.

Although French naval expansion was a response to the historic threat posed by the British navy, it was equally a positive drive to project French power and glory overseas and expand the empire. There are remarkable similarities with Germany's naval and world ambitions towards the end of the following century: in each case the monarch was obsessed by naval affairs; Louis XVI was as enthusiastic about ship design and construction, naval artillery, navigation, tactics and even the design of naval uniforms as Kaiser Wilhelm II, and as encyclopedically knowledgeable; like his ministers, Louis saw France's future riding on the oceans. In both cases a dominant British fleet blocked the way; in neither case was the policy thought through realistically and both attempts proved so ruinously expensive that they affected wider aspects of government policy – in the French case actually bringing the government down before the resulting world war. Finally, both navies failed dramatically. These parallels prompt questions as to whether the Bourbon policy was, like the Kaiser's later naval expansion, also an effort to rally disaffected classes and interest groups to the government under the banner of overseas success and national pride.[15]

It seems the only rational explanation. If so it rebounded disastrously. The quantities of timber and other raw materials demanded by the vast construction and attendant stock-piling programme exceeded domestic supply and imports were sucked in, exacerbating an economic and balance of trade crisis caused by British manufactured imports under-selling their French counterparts, while the need to emulate British naval advances, particularly the use of sheet copper to protect underwater timbers from boring worms and marine incrustations that slowed ships down, exposed the extent to which France had fallen behind Britain in industrial technology.[16] Above all, the money had to be borrowed.

The Cherbourg project was abandoned in 1788 – defeated by the elements as much as by finance – by which time it had consumed some 28 million livres (*c.* £1.2 million), a huge sum which had been literally cast upon the waters. The fleet-building programme never reached its target, although it did bequeath to successor revolutionary governments the largest navy France attained in the sailing era. This was still some 50 per cent smaller numerically than the British fleet, although the ships were larger on average, and it was little over 25 per cent inferior in aggregate tonnage.[17]

For this the Bourbon government had bankrupted itself. Viewed from a different perspective it was merely the project that finally exposed the financial ineptitude and inflexibility of the system. Accumulated borrowings from the American war and preparations for the next war had by 1786 pushed the total debt to something over four billion livres (nearly £200 million). Great Britain with a population scarcely half the size had a slightly larger debt of £215 million. Yet the contrast could not have been more marked. The French debt carried interest almost double that on the British, so cost twice as much to service. The reason and the fundamental difference between the two systems was, as noted earlier, that British revenue and expenditure were under constant scrutiny in Parliament and the British treasury was managing the debt by means of a sinking fund; French finances on the other hand were uncoordinated and secret. The Comptroller General of Finance, Charles-Alexandre de Calonne, had recently discovered that annual expenditure exceeded revenue by 80 million livres, revised upwards the following year to 110 million (*c.* £4.8 million),[18] which came as a considerable surprise and annoyance to the king and other ministers and to government creditors. Unless expenditure could be pruned, or revenue increased, the debt must continue to grow inexorably. Added to this a substantial parcel of short-term loans taken out in the American war was due for repayment. In practice French government credit was exhausted unless new taxes were raised as security for new loans to fill the gap left by repayments.

Yet existing taxes already caused serious disaffection – aggravated by the distressed state of the economy – and since Calonne had good reason to believe that the whole antique, inefficient and inequitable system of their imposition and collection was the real cause of his difficulties – not government overspending – he determined to combine the introduction of necessary new taxes with a fundamental restructuring of the system. His proposals were in line with physiocratic solutions, cast around a new tax on income from land to be paid by all irrespective of rank, so ensuring fairer contributions from the tax-exempt nobility; he also proposed liberating internal markets by removing regional tariffs, excise duties, provincial tax exemptions and other trade restrictions, and eliciting cooperation by setting up local consultative assemblies to be elected by all taxpayers whatever their rank.

Similar schemes of wholesale reform had caused the downfall of practically all his predecessors; Calonne was to prove no exception. This and the devious route he felt forced to take, convening an ancient forum called the 'Assembly of Notables' which had long fallen into disuse, and appointing its members himself, reveal the underlying problem of the Bourbon state: inability to adapt. The social order was so rigid – however much the nobility had in practice been diluted by the moneyed bourgeoisie it remained distinct in law – power was so centralized and consultative institutions so limited that peaceful constitutional change seems to have been impossible. Calonne's Notables agreed all his principal reforms, in some cases suggesting more radical solutions, but they rejected his scheme, and Louis dismissed him.

His successor retained his essential proposals and was also defeated, principally by the *Parlement* of Paris. *Parlements* were the nearest thing to institutional checks on government power in France; besides being supreme law courts and guardians of law enforcement and public morality within their regions, they shared some executive functions with *Intendants* and claimed the right to approve royal ordinances. However, their membership was by inheritance, not election or appointment or even purchase – unless from the owner of an inherited seat – and this self-perpetuating aristocracy, intermixed with and scarcely distinguishable from the ancient feudal nobility, whose income derived largely from the land and who enjoyed tax exempt status, naturally baulked at the proposed land tax and refused to register it.

The government reacted in May 1788 with ordinances reducing the power and status of *parlements*, in particular their authority to block legislation by refusing to register decrees. *Parlements* throughout France struck back by promoting themselves as champions of the people and provincial liberties against despotic central power, provoking riots in Paris and regional capitals; whereupon the government called out the military. On 7 June the first deaths occurred when the troops opened fire on demonstrators at Grenoble. This was the real start of the revolution; for during the popular unrest that summer all the dammed-up theories, hopes and aspirations of the years of salon discourse found public and extreme expression. A responsible consensus of the enlightened nobility, Church and commercial bourgeoisie wanted constitutional monarchy and an end to tax exemptions and, drawing on the American precedent for drafting a new constitution, demanded that Louis summon the Estates General, the ancient representative forum drawn from the three 'Orders' of the nobility, the Church and the commoners, or Third Estate, which had last met in 1614. In face of this nationwide pressure, popular lawlessness and now the acute financial crisis, Louis XVI drew back, restored the powers of the *parlements*, promised to convene the Estates General the following year and recalled Necker as Minister of Finance.

The course of events from the meeting of the Estates General in May 1789 to the imposition of state 'Terror' in 1793 is well known, but it poses a fundamental historical riddle: why, when practically all influential politicians, moneyed men, merchants and industrialists, including the new government Minister of Finance, Jacques Necker, were anticipating an outcome on the lines of the English settlement of 1689 and the more recent American constitution, did the French Revolution turn wildly back in the opposite direction towards extreme centralization and tyranny?

One obvious difference from the English model was the character of the king: whereas William III had been raised as a constitutional head of state before he seized the Crown of England, and was therefore prepared to accept the limitations imposed on him by the English Parliament, Louis XVI had been brought up to believe in his right to rule, by the Grace of God, as father of his people without any constraints whatever. And whereas William was a gifted leader with exceptional clarity and firmness of purpose, Louis proved in crisis fundamentally indecisive.

Important as these differences are, the contrast between two individuals, however highly placed, cannot of itself account for the diametrically opposed outcomes of the revolutions. This must surely have resulted from the differences between the two societies already outlined in the Introduction. By 1689 England was a commercial nation; the values associated with monetary exchange had permeated most classes, and merchants and financiers had been attempting to free themselves from royal interference for most of the century. William III, schooled in just such a merchant-dominated society, gave them their chance and they seized it.

France in 1789 remained, by contrast, a predominantly agricultural nation with commercial centres – the great port and industrial cities. It is true that the wealthy commercial bourgeoisie had infiltrated the land-holding nobility by purchase or merit to such an extent that some two-thirds of nobles were descended from commoners elevated during the seventeenth or eighteenth centuries;[19] however, far from imposing their own values on the nobility, they had imbibed the nobles' values, privileges and exclusivity. Thus France remained a rigidly hierarchical society governed by a central bureaucracy with scarcely any popular representative institutions. This was the essential difference. The French revolutionaries had neither the institutions nor the experience of practical consultative or representative politics on which to draw. Instead they had a riot of mostly impractical theories and driven ideologues to deploy them.

There was also great hunger due to the soaring cost of bread; an economic slump, unemployment and a widespread breakdown in civic order, which ranged in the countryside from defiance of the game laws by poaching on landed estates and attacks on grain transports and flour stores to rioting, looting and bloodshed in the cities. By spring 1789 the Marseilles–Toulon region had become virtually ungovernable and in Paris in late April, just before the Estates General was due to convene, troops opened fire on rioters, killing and wounding hundreds. Everywhere despair found expression in rage against the system and against those of wealth and rank seen as profiting from it at the expense of the common people. The April rioters in Paris shouted, 'Death to the rich! Death to aristocrats!'[20]

These were the crucial differences on the eve of revolution: England defined by commerce, France by bureaucracy; the English people with full stomachs, the French driven to violence by poverty and hunger. These differences were reflected in all that followed.

The majority of the delegates of the Third Estate who in June 1789 famously detached themselves from procedural arguments in the Estates General to convene in a nearby real tennis court and formally light the fuse of revolution by declaring themselves the 'National Assembly', vowing never to part until they had formed a new, just constitution, were lawyers; and the majority of these lawyers – 278 out of the 648 deputies (43 per cent of the total) – held government office. Only 85 deputies (13 per cent) were businessmen or merchants; 67 (10 per cent) were land- or property-owners, and some 5 per cent came from the professions.[21] From the beginning, then, the Revolution was largely in the hands of men raised within the centralized bureaucratic tradition of the country; and the proportion of such people never changed significantly in subsequent assemblies.

Moreover, they had to rely from the beginning on the people of Paris. They had no other defence against the regular troops which Louis XVI called up to disperse them. The people then took hold of the Revolution. Maddened by the price of bread and persisting rumours of an aristocratic conspiracy to starve them into submission, incensed by extremist orators and pamphleteers, they erupted in a discharge of elemental violence, wrecking customs posts in the city, looting foodstuffs, overrunning the fortress symbol of royal oppression, the Bastille, arbitrarily hacking off heads of leading 'conspirators' and parading them on pikes through the streets.

Similar rioting in provincial cities destroyed royal authority throughout France, while in the countryside lawlessness reached a pitch that obliged the National Assembly in Paris, in order to contain anarchy, to abolish all feudal, regional and city privileges and fiscal exemptions. This wholesale attempt to redress the grievances of the majority of the population, those who lived on the land, was led by a group of liberal nobles who had joined the Assembly. The privileges abolished included the game laws; the people were authorized to hunt and kill any animals for food or to protect crops – an enactment that survives, as do so many other aspects of the Revolution, in the annual decimation of small songbirds by French sportsmen.

It seems clear that it was the collapse of the economy, the gross inflation in food prices, the consequent acute distress of ordinary people, owners of small workshops, artisans, journeymen, peasants throughout the country that provided the dynamic of the Revolution. This had not happened in either the English revolution of 1688 or the more recent American revolution.

It was, nevertheless, the deputies of the National Assembly, renamed the 'Constituent' since they had authorized themselves to draw up a new constitution, who imposed the form. Their first production was a statement of principles entitled 'Declaration of the Rights of Man and of the Citizen', which was adopted on 26 August. It had obvious affinities with the American Declaration of Independence; indeed the French hero of the War of Independence, the Marquis de Lafayette, and the US Ambassador in Paris, Thomas Jefferson, were key contributors. The first article declared that 'Men are born free and equal in rights'; the second defined those rights as 'Liberty, Property, Safety and Resistance to Oppression'. It will be recalled that the American Declaration had adopted 'Life, Liberty and the pursuit of Happiness' as among the 'unalienable Rights' with which men were endowed.

'Liberty' was defined in Article 4 of the Declaration as the ability to do anything that did not harm others, and Article 5 stated that the law had the right to forbid only those actions injurious to society; Article 10 stated that no one might be disturbed on account of his opinions, even religious ones; and Article 11 ran: 'Any citizen may . . . speak, write and publish freely except what is tantamount to the abuse of this liberty in the cases determined by law.'

The right to property, placed second only to liberty in Article 2, was stressed in the final Article 17: 'Since the right to property is inviolable and sacred, no one may be deprived thereof, unless public necessity, legally ascertained, obviously requires it, and just and prior indemnity has been paid.'[22] Property was not defined. The article sounds like a response by the propertied delegates to the vandalism widespread through the country.

The Declaration marked the formal end of the old regime: the end of the three 'Orders' of society, since all were born equal in rights; the end of arbitrary imprisonment or sequestration of property; the end of censorship; and since Article 3 declared the source of all sovereignty to be 'the Nation', the end of the king's absolute right to rule. Who should rule and how was left for debate on the new constitution. There were signs, however, of the direction that would take. Most obvious was Article 6: 'The law is the expression of the general will. All citizens have the right to take part, personally or through their representatives, in its making. It must be the same for all.' The 'general will' was pure Rousseau.

Article 16 made reference to 'guaranteeing rights' and 'the separation of powers' and the Preamble referred to distinct 'legislative' and 'executive' powers. However, several articles appeared to look forward to an Athenian style of direct democracy by all citizens, and the Preamble concluded: 'the demands of the citizens, founded henceforth on simple and uncontestable principles, may always be directed toward the maintenance of the Constitution and the happiness of all.' Here is Rousseau's paradox of the free citizen bound by the communal will, as defined in this case by the Deputies themselves when they drew up the Constitution.[23]

The loose rhetoric is in marked contrast to the practical prescriptions of the English 'Bill of Rights' of 1689 and the United States Constitution of 1787–8, both of which were built on existing institutions and laws evolved through time and exigency. And since the freedoms supposedly guaranteed under the Declaration of the Rights of Man were substantially less than those long since won by the English in law and adopted by the Americans, it is hard to account for the hold the Declaration has since had on both the revolutionary and historiographical imagination.

In any event, the argument which is apparent in the Declaration between those wanting an English-style 'constitutional' monarchy with two consultative chambers and those adhering to Rousseau's concept of the 'general will' exercised through a single body representing the nation was won conclusively by the Rousseauists. One practical reason was that creating an upper and a lower debating chamber seemed rather like resurrecting the legal 'Orders' of society which had so recently been buried. The chief reason had to do with a patriotic, idealistic fervour for initiating a fresh chapter in human affairs without recourse to ancient forms, an Enlightenment faith in reason, an equally naive faith in Rousseau's nostrum of the 'general will' which by definition could not injure the interests of all those free wills of which it was composed and, perhaps most important of all, the unconscious habit of mind of all those lawyers who had served the Bourbon government machine, and others who wished to make France more efficient, and thus more powerful. All these could embrace direct lines of authority from a single body for the common good. Anglo-Saxon checks and balances could only introduce conflict, confusion, inefficiency and delay. This was the story of French bureaucracy. Like all organisms, it sought to reproduce itself. It might be said the country wished to reproduce itself in a more rational and effective way.

To a large extent the Constituent Assembly achieved such a transformation with the measures taken over the following months. The internal customs dues and levies which had distorted the internal market for centuries were abolished; provincial administrative distinctions were removed by dividing the country into eighty-three *départements* of almost equal size, each divided into nine *arrondissements*, in turn subdivided into nine *communes*, and powers were granted to elect local councils.

A start was made on standardizing a chaos of regional weights and measures by directing the Academy of Sciences to produce a uniform system. They set about the task in true Enlightenment style, fixing the basic unit of length which they named the *metre*, as one ten-millionth part of the meridian passing through Paris from the North Pole to the equator – found after a six-year survey to be some decimal points over 39.37 inches. They derived larger units from multiples of ten using Greek prefixes, *deca, hecto, kilo*, and smaller units by dividing by ten, using Roman prefixes, *deci, centi, milli*. Units of weight and capacity were similarly derived from the *metre*; thus a *gram* was a cubic *centimetre* of water, a *litre* was one thousandth of a cubic *metre*. When the new 'metric' system was declared the legal standard in 1799 the hope was expressed in true revolutionary style, that it would serve 'all people for all time'.

Similarly the accumulation of direct and indirect taxes and tax exemptions that had evolved over centuries was swept away and a unified system brought in owing much to the physiocrats, which taxed income from landed and other property and commercial profit. All these were precisely the sort of unifying reforms Bourbon finance ministers had been advocating or attempting for decades, if not centuries, without success. They were accompanied by measures to free up trade by suppressing craft guilds, corporations, chambers of commerce, the privileges of chartered companies, patents, trademarks and indeed all regulations tending to monopoly, even inspection and certification of products; although significantly the colonial trades, especially with the West Indies, were so vital to the economy that the mercantilist prohibitions on commerce between the colonies and any country other than France were retained.

The reforms changed France for ever, but in the short term they could not relieve the acute financial and food crises that had triggered the Revolution, nor resolve real regional differences and deep-seated class presumptions. Nobles of conservative mind who adhered to the warrior ethic of their caste, disdaining the bourgeoisie, followed Louis XVI's younger brothers, the Comtes de Provence and d'Artois, into foreign exile on the borders and plotted to restore Louis to his proper state. The people of Paris constituted a more immediate threat. Lafayette, who had been appointed Commandant of a volunteer militia labelled the National Guard, struggled heroically to preserve order and property in the city but could not prevent alarming acts of mob violence, pillage and bloody reprisal on suspected hoarders and profiteers. Women often inspired the riots; for freeing the markets had actually aggravated food shortages and increased price fluctuations.

In addition the new freedoms of expression and the press had released torrents of invective. Orators, intoxicated with sublime, often Rousseau-esque solutions to all problems of society and mankind harangued audiences at political clubs; pamphleteers and newspaper correspondents vilified scapegoats in the most extreme language. The feelings incited among politicized small tradesmen, artisans, journeymen and others who characterized themselves as *sans-culottes* – those who did not wear the knee breeches of nobility – were as anti-liberal as those of the conservative aristocracy; but they were anti-monarchical too and their solutions were egalitarian, communal and protectionist; abhorring the free market and capitalist employers, they called for price and wage controls and regulation of supplies of grain and other basics of existence. Their frustrations were channelled into fervent belief in the Revolution and the *Patrie* and hatred of enemies of either. These views were represented in local electoral district – or *section* – assemblies, political clubs and a central assembly of delegates from the different *sections* which met at the Hôtel de Ville as the Paris Commune, and more basically and bloodily in the streets.

Pressed between these threats of aristocratic counter-revolution, backed by the monarchies of Europe, and popular street democracy tending to anarchy, beset by impending bankruptcy and continuing grain shortages, the high-minded delegates of the Constituent Assembly revealed themselves as true successors to the old regime. First, one of the nobles who had thrown in his lot with the revolutionaries, Charles-Maurice de Talleyrand-Périgord, recently appointed Bishop of Autun – known to history as the notoriously amoral survivor Talleyrand – proposed transferring all church property to the state as security for a new loan. Initial astonishment that such a thing should be proposed by a bishop was accompanied by grave doubts about violating the rights of property, so recently declared 'inviolable and sacred'. Such scruples could not withstand the absolute need for funds or the personal needs of the holders of old government bonds to be redeemed by the new, since a great many of them sat as deputies; and on 2 November 1789 the deed was done – passed by 568 to 346 votes.[24] A decree transferred all church property to the nation, which took over responsibility for maintaining it, paying the clergy and administering ecclesiastical education and poor relief.

The following month it was resolved to sell up to 400 million livres' worth of church and crown lands to serve as security for a loan raised by issuing 5 per cent government bonds. The bonds, called *assignats*, were not redeemable in coin; they could only be used to purchase government land or property. And having been used in this way they were to be returned for destruction to a special treasury established for land sales, whereby it was hoped the entire government debt would gradually be eliminated. The issue saved the Assembly from immediate bankruptcy, but like similar Bourbon schemes not grounded on budget transparency and creditor confidence, it was to prove fundamentally destructive: *assignats* began to change hands as paper money and depreciate rapidly as more were printed.

There were more serious unintended consequences from taking the Church into state ownership. The next step for an Assembly claiming to represent the 'general will' of the people was to subordinate this powerful institution to its own will; any dual allegiance to Church and state was intolerable – especially since the Church owed its allegiance to Rome. Accordingly, in May 1790 the 'Civil Constitution of the Clergy' was adopted, placing the Church under democratic control, even to the popular election of bishops, in defiance of the Pope. Since this was intolerable to the majority of the clergy, the inevitable next stage for such an Assembly was to force all clergy to swear allegiance to the new constitution. This breathtaking series of acts which could never have been contemplated by the most desperate Bourbon administration – nor probably by any government not consumed with original virtue – further alienated the traditional God-fearing countryside from the enlightened Parisian intelligentsia, strengthening the forces of counter-revolution and transforming revolution into incipient civil war.

Meanwhile, in that summer of 1790 the Assembly established two executive committees designed to secure its control of events, the Comité des Rapports with powers to monitor and allow or disallow political appointments in the regions – significantly eroding the earlier move to local democracy – and the Comité des Recherches to head a state security service with powers of search, arrest and imprisonment without trial quite as arbitrary as those exercised under Bourbon governments, working through the same means of spies, informers and letter-openers.

Thus, scarcely a year after the 'Tennis Court Oath' the revolution had widened internal divisions and recreated the old absolutist organs of central control and repression; of course, these had their origins in the very same need to control separatist forces within the country. Crucially, the revolution had failed to preserve the rule of law or solve the financial problem; indeed this was exacerbated as the old taxes collected ruthlessly by tax farmers were abolished before the new tax system could come fully on stream. Moreover, the new constitution fashioned by the Assembly did little more than exchange for the fiction of absolute monarchy the fiction of the general will of the people.

Louis XVI was invested with a new title 'by the Grace of God and the Constitutional Law of the State, King of the French', and allowed to choose his own ministers, ambassadors and generals, but he was unable to take real decisions since his ministers and his council were in the final analysis answerable to the Legislative Assembly. He could delay legislation for up to six years but not veto it; nor could he dissolve the Assembly. Thus the Assembly was sovereign. Of course it was elected by the people, the repository of their 'general will'.

However, the vote was restricted to males over the age of twenty-five who paid tax equivalent to three days' labour; this disenfranchised practically all rural labourers, domestic servants, even some artisans – and of course all women – while a property qualification for election as a deputy limited the Assembly to the professional and intellectual elite.[25] For all their devotion to reason, the members of the Constituent Assembly were only men of their time. By setting up these hurdles they not only compromised the first article of their own Declaration that 'Men are born free and equal in Rights' – as the deputy for Arras, Maximilien de Robespierre, pointed out – they fatally diluted Rousseau's theory of the 'general will' under which they claimed legitimacy for the Assembly. In practice it was the will and oratory of the propertied and cultural establishment, the so-called 'Notables', ex-noble and non-noble alike, that would be served. And since the Locke–Montesquieu safeguard of a separation and balancing of powers between executive and legislative had also been fatally undermined, and the king reduced to a constitutional figurehead, the result was absolute power exercised by a single chamber – which might have been predicted from the composition of the Constituent Assembly and the physiocrats' emphasis on the need for uncurbed power to force through the necessary wholesale reforms against vested interests.

Louis XVI formally accepted the new constitution in September 1791. He had no choice; he had attempted escape from the country in June but had been caught and brought back to Paris. The new Legislative

Assembly convened in October. It faced huge challenges: from the émigré nobles on the border with links to Louis' court and royalists and refractory priests in the regions; from the two great monarchies, Austria and Prussia, alarmed by rhetoric suggesting that the revolutionaries aimed to 'liberate' peoples outside the borders of France; most immediately from militant women and sans-culottes roused by further food price rises due primarily to a depreciating *assignat*, and their spokesmen in the *section* assemblies, political clubs and the Paris Commune, which was assuming the status of a rival legislative chamber.

Inevitably the Assembly was pulled towards war. Denouncing émigrés and the states supporting them was the most effective way of diverting attention from the Revolution's failure to relieve the distress of ordinary French men and women, and win their backing. It was also a natural extension of the rhetoric of virtue; all who disagreed with the will of the people were branded traitors. Above all, perhaps, war against foreign 'tyrants' would set the seal on the revolution of 'liberty' by drawing the nation together under the new patriotic banner, the tricolour, formed from the red and blue of Paris and the white of the Bourbons; for the orators of the Legislative Assembly, war would be a veritable 'school of virtue'.[26] It would also expose those covert traitors within the court and clergy. For its part, the court also wanted war as the surest means of summoning foreign aid to defeat the Revolution and release Louis from his constitutional constraints. For, as Louis himself wrote to his agent at the Austrian court, 'The physical and moral condition of France is such as to make it impossible for her to resist even a partial campaign.'[27] His Austrian-born queen, Marie Antoinette, sent her relatives details of French military dispositions as discussed in the Royal Council.

War was declared against Austria and Prussia in April 1792. Although Assembly orators had elevated the offensive into a crusade to liberate the people of Europe and all mankind from monarchical and feudal despotism, the army was in no state even to secure the borders against the Austrians and Prussians in alliance. Slogans of equality and rights had subverted discipline; half the noble officers had emigrated; many of those who remained distrusted their men, who distrusted the generals. Unsurprisingly the opening months were marked by defeat and invasion. In Paris, heightened suspicions that the court and royalist spies had betrayed their armies generated a rising similar to that of 1789, this time marshalled by an 'Insurrectionary Committee' of delegates from the militant *sections*. Joined by several thousand National Guards from the provinces who had been sent to the capital for training before being posted to the front, the rebellious forces converged on the royal residence, the Tuileries, on 10 August and massacred the king's Swiss Guard in a fearful orgy of clubbing, hacking and mutilation; women stripped the bodies of clothes and possessions. The royal family who had taken refuge in the Assembly earlier in the day were later imprisoned in the Temple for their own safety.

If a main war aim had been to win support from the people, it had miscarried. Again the government had had no force capable of containing the street violence, and was now compelled to yield to popular demands for a new Assembly to be elected by universal male suffrage, a drive to hunt down royalist traitors and a Revolutionary Tribunal to try them. The Constituent Assembly had created the potential for continuing the traditional police state with the Comité des Recherches set up two years before; the provisional executive of the Legislative Assembly now laid the foundations for state terror. The machine invented by Dr Joseph-Ignace Guillotin in the first flush of revolutionary zeal to ensure that the noble privilege of beheading was extended to all, and that death would be as painless as possible, was set up in front of the Tuileries, while hundreds of suspects, mainly refractory priests, were thrown into mass confinement. The evil mood of the people at this time is conveyed by Madame de Staël in a description of her attempt to leave Paris in a six-horse carriage: 'a swarm of old ladies, emerging from hell, threw themselves on my horses, and cried that I should be arrested . . . common people with savage faces seized my postillions and ordered them to take me to the assembly of the neighbourhood where I lived.'[28]

Sans-culotte hostility towards traitors, food hoarders, wealthy speculators and 'aristocrats' – a general term for enemies of the people – was allied to a patriotic will to defend the country from foreign enemies. When the provisional government ordered a mass levy to reinforce the army there was no shortage of volunteers, but a great fear spread that, when the men departed, the capital would be at the mercy of the enemy within, and on 2 September news that the fortress of Verdun had fallen to the invaders provoked another outburst of primitive bloodletting. Prisons and other buildings where royalist suspects had been confined were stormed and over a thousand of the priests and others within, including common criminals, were bludgeoned, stabbed and hacked to death after a minimum of hostile interrogation. One of Marie Antoinette's retinue, the Princesse de Lamballe, who refused to swear that she hated the king and queen, was struck down, her head was hacked off and impaled on a pike and paraded before the windows of the Temple where the queen was held.

In such a savage environment, those leaders claiming to speak for the people, notably Jean-Paul Marat, Georges Danton and Maximilien Robespierre, all from the radical Jacobin Club, were able to seize the initiative and use the dynamic of the streets and political clubs to advance their power in a new Assembly known as the National Convention. It met for the first time on 20 September, elected by fewer than one million of five million eligible to vote – since royalists and moderates had been disqualified – and again 47 per cent were lawyers, a preponderance of whom had served in the Legislative Assembly, many in the original Constituent.[29] Its first acts were to abolish the monarchy, declare a republic and inaugurate a new calendar – from which some sense of the elevated mood of the deputies can be gauged: they named 20 September 1792 as the beginning of Year One of French Liberty. It was far from the beginning, but it did mark an acceleration of the drive to conscript all citizens for the war effort, control all ideas, eliminate all opposition and centralize all power.

By chance 20 September also marked the turning point of the invasion: the enemy was halted at Valmy and forced to retreat; the French armies followed, advancing through Belgium to Brussels. On 16 November the National Convention lifted the ban on navigation in the river Schelde with the intention of freeing Antwerp for trade, in defiance of international treaties to which France was a signatory. This threatened the prosperity of Amsterdam and alarmed London. On the 19th the Convention declared 'in the name of the French nation that it will extend fraternal feelings and aid to all people who wish to regain their liberty'.[30] What this meant became apparent in the conquered territories in December as revolutionary administrations were established and began a process of confiscating property belonging to the Church and enemies of the new regime to service *assignats*, abolishing feudal dues and imposing levies on the rich and extortionate war indemnities. Initial enthusiasm from the 'liberated' would soon turn to sullen mistrust. But for the liberators it was a breakthrough: they had found the key to paying their way. It had nothing to do with equality, fraternity or the Rights of Man, but was the law according to all predatory hordes from the dawn of history: to squeeze the conquered dry. It was not a long-term solution since it was inevitably self-defeating and must lead to the need for further conquest.

Nonetheless, it was to form a key pillar of French economic policy for the duration of the Revolution and subsequent military dictatorship.

The plan was for General Dumouriez, who had led his army to Brussels, to continue across the Maas into the United Provinces to bring Amsterdam and the Dutch cities with their financial and commercial strength into the French orbit. This had been a national aim since at least 1670 when Louis XIV and Charles II of England had agreed to fall simultaneously on the Dutch. Now the merchant republic appeared a riper plum for picking. It had been torn between rebellious 'Patriot' and conservative Orangist factions for a decade. The 'Patriots' were not so much revolutionaries in the Enlightenment sense of wanting a new beginning as reformers wishing to renew the ancient freedoms they believed diminished under the House of Orange, and seeking to recapture the administration for the people from an oligarchy of Regents by opening public office to talent.[31] Their movement had been suppressed in 1787 by the troops of Friedrich Wilhelm II of Prussia aided by British government money in support of William V of Orange, and many had fled to France. Patriot sentiment remained a strong and divisive force nonetheless, open for exploitation by numerous agents of subversion sent in to the republic by the National Convention, and there was no doubt that if Dumouriez were to march in he would be greeted as a liberator by substantial sections of the populace.

It became equally evident that the British government would not stand idly by while the Schelde and Dutch rivers and port cities fell to France. The independence of the republic was regarded as a vital British interest; indeed William V was virtually a British client, so much had the supreme merchant and naval power of the seventeenth century fallen under the shadow of her larger maritime rival across the water. The certainty of war with Great Britain gave the French government pause. Dumouriez was ordered to postpone further advance.

Meanwhile the National Convention, under pressure from *section* assemblies, political clubs, the Paris Commune and not least Robespierre and associates from the Jacobin Club, known collectively as 'the mountain' from the position they occupied high against the wall of the Convention chamber – although it could as well have derived from the lofty tone of their rhetoric – placed Louis XVI on trial. For 'the mountain' the death of the 'tyrant' was the logical and inevitable conclusion to the Revolution, which would otherwise never be stabilized. In a sense they were right. The Revolution had begun with the people demanding blood atonement for their wretchedness, and it had to be consummated with the blood symbol of the regime they had destroyed. The argument for stabilization was specious: taken to its logical conclusion it should have meant the execution of the seven-year-old dauphin named by royalists Louis XVII, who was lodged with the royal family in the Temple prison, and of Louis' younger brothers and other relatives organizing counter-revolution from exile.

The Convention found Louis XVI guilty of treason – he had of course colluded against the Revolutionary Constitution – and in January 1793 he was condemned to death by 387 votes to 334.[32] His last words to the crowd massed avidly around the guillotine were to pardon those who had brought about his end. After the blade had fallen and the executioner lifted the dripping head those spectators in a position to do so scrabbled their fingers in his blood.

By this time the Convention had steeled itself for war with Great Britain. It was believed that the British government was determined to harness the monarchies of Europe and the networks of royalist counter-revolutionaries within and outside France to destroy the Revolution. There were good grounds for this belief, as will appear. It was also believed that Britain herself was ripe for revolution. The secret agent accompanying an official French mission to London the previous October had gained entry to radical political clubs and reported their aim as the overthrow of the British constitution and its remodelling after the form of the new French regime; they had powerful support, he had noted.[33] It was anticipated that an invasion force landed on British soil would prove a catalyst for insurrection. The Minister of Marine ordered thirty of the line and twenty frigates prepared for sea.

To pay for the extension of the war to Great Britain and the Dutch republic, and to expand France to its 'natural frontiers' – defined by the Convention in December as the Pyrenees, Alps and Rhine, the Channel and the Mediterranean – the French government printed more *assignats*. The original 400 million livres' worth had already been increased to almost 2,400 millions, the last tranche of 400 millions since October 1792; now a further 800 millions' worth were added.[34] Inflation predictably followed. By February the notes were worth barely half their face value and were so distrusted that they were not readily exchangeable. Peasants had ceased to accept them for produce. Food shortages and escalating prices resulted, particularly in the cities, inspiring more riots, pillage and arbitrary 'revolutionary justice' towards suspected hoarders and profiteers and increasing the pressure from radical political clubs and *section* assemblies for control of prices and wages and the regulation of grain supplies.

The Revolution was now in the final coils of its vicious descending spiral and the ideologues of the National Convention, having exacerbated the chronic financial situation and worsened the living conditions of the people whose will they invoked as their warrant to rule, were obliged to harness the passions excited. In doing so they completed the transformation of the struggle for an Enlightenment ideal of liberty into a campaign against a world of enemies. It was both a spiritual and economic necessity. On 1 February 1793 the Convention declared war on Great Britain and the United Provinces, and the following month on Spain.

2

The Terror, 1793

AT THE BEGINNING of the Revolution British intellectuals and politicians of liberal mind had hailed the changes across the Channel in much the terms used by the revolutionaries themselves, as the dawn of a new era for mankind. A few poets, radicals and politicians in opposition managed, against all evidence, to maintain this interpretation. For most it had become a horror. The atrocities on the streets of Paris, the September massacres, the execution of the king, belligerent speeches in the National Convention and the government's contempt for international treaties had returned the bulk of the nation to a more realistic view of the traditional enemy with whom they had fought for primacy in Europe and overseas for a century. Jacobins had become objects of loathing and contempt.

The intellectual rebuttal of the Revolution had been led by Edmund Burke, a unique, if erratic genius born in Dublin, who joined deep reverence for the English constitution as consummated in the Glorious Revolution of 1688–9 with quicksilver imagination and poetic extravagance. As Member of Parliament for an English borough, he had introduced thoroughly un-English dimensions of eloquence to the House. Replete with abstract philosophical reasoning, passion, irony, invective, pathos and baroque decoration, his speeches were too much for the solid men of business and country squires on the Commons' benches, which tended to empty directly he rose – he was known as 'the dinner bell of the House'. His writings were nonetheless influential and his classic *Reflections on the Revolution in France* (1790) had captured the popular mood, selling 32,000 copies within a year.[1]

Reflections laid out the dangers inherent in the principles of the Revolution before the worst excesses occurred and while most of Burke's contemporaries were still spellbound by the rhetoric. Fundamentally he objected to men with necessarily limited perspectives attempting to over-turn society and impose wholesale schemes of change conceived in the abstract. He had a Darwinian view – long before Charles Darwin – of a nation's institutions as the tried and tested products of selection over centuries, the exquisitely balanced issue of men's actual conduct, not the conduct the reformers would have them exhibit. To abuse such institu-tions was to court disaster; and after the revolutionaries abolished the different Orders of society he had no hesitation in declaring the French 'the ablest architects of ruin who have hitherto existed in the world. In a short space of time they have pulled to the ground their army, their navy, their commerce, their arts, and their manufactures.'[2] In January 1790 this was a remarkably bold assertion; yet history has confirmed it in every respect – with the possible exception of the army which they later reinvigorated in a new form. Yet in the early years the Revolution was saved more by the disunity of its enemies than by its own troops.

Burke's attitude to 'natural rights' derived from the same vision of society as an organic creation mirroring the order of nature. He identified natural law with custom and usage hallowed by the historical process, thus in the legal sense of 'prescription' – custom which has existed so long it has become a right and passed into law – rather than with Rousseau's sup-posed past age of innocence or equally mythical 'social contract'. He believed individuals were served best within an ordered society where rights were defined by precedent and duty rather than imposed by consti-tutional instrument. Beside his arguments, which have resounded power-fully down the centuries, the certainties of the Enlightenment *philosophes* and revolutionary politicians and their British radical apologists seem friv-olously one-dimensional: where these saw only absolutes, Burke saw a miraculous fabric of social forces so interwoven that interference with any part or parts inevitably compromised others; where they imagined 'liberty' and 'equality', he recognized that achieving either must destroy the other. And in place of the abstract liberty they proposed, he celebrated practical British liberties 'as an entailed inheritance derived to us from our forefathers and to be transmitted to our posterity, as an estate specially belonging to the people of this kingdom, without reference to any other more general or prior right'.[3]

Burke drew from a long tradition of English pragmatism and was no opponent of change. He saw reforms addressed to specific practical problems as not only desirable but essential for a nation's health, thereby putting his finger on the underlying cause of the Revolution in France: 'A state without the means of some change is without the means of its conservation.' He also pinpointed the danger in the concept of the 'general will', foreseeing its outcome in what he termed 'despotic democracy',[4] the extreme version of which was to be realized under the Jacobins. Here he was expressing the fear of undiluted power that had shaped the British constitution, and the Dutch and Venetian before it, a tradition lacking in Paris or Versailles.

Above all, he was probably the first to interpret the Revolution as a new kind of political religion which transcended the frontiers of France. The view was to be endorsed by de Tocqueville, who likened the French revolutionary message to that of Islam, 'flooding the whole world with its soldiers, its apostles, its martyrs'.[5] Appalled by the prospect of such an evangelical secular faith spreading and subverting religion and all moral and political conventions, Burke called for a crusade by the monarchies of Europe to stamp it out at source.

His appeals had little effect on the British government. The Prime Minister was William Pitt 'the younger', son of the architect of Britain's most successful imperial war. Coming to power after the War of American Independence at the precocious age of twenty-four, he had set himself the task of reducing the huge national debt accumulated during that struggle against the combined powers of France and Spain. While the Comte de Vergennes and his army and navy ministers had been adding recklessly to French government debt with unaccountable expenditure in preparation for the next war, Pitt had increased British taxes, reduced customs and excise duties to discourage smuggling – gaining increased yields thereby – introduced more businesslike methods of financial administration and established a sinking fund on new principles to bring down the debt.

At the same time he had ensured sufficient warships were built to maintain superiority over the French fleet, and by continuing mercantilist policies in the carrying trades with the newly independent United States, barring their ships from bringing in to Britain anything but the products of their own country, and similarly regulating trade with the West Indies, he had presided over a spectacular increase in British merchant shipping from 615,000 tons in 1782 to 1,265,000 tons in 1788.[6]

For his financial policies to succeed, he needed peace above all. And misled by the financial chaos into which the revolutionary governments had plunged France, he had assumed she posed no serious danger. In the historic sense he was right: the need to restore financial equilibrium in the peace after great wars before engaging in the next round had been a constant feature of eighteenth-century Anglo-French rivalry. If prudence and precedent were guides France could not embark on another major war.

Internal subversion was another matter. Thomas Paine, a self-educated intellectual whose pamphlet *Common Sense*, published in Philadelphia in 1776, was credited with awakening the American colonists to hitherto unexpressed desires for independence, had returned to England and in March 1791 published an answer to Burke's *Reflections* entitled *Rights of Man*. It had struck a chord with the same politically marginalized classes as formed the core of the sans-culotte movement in Paris and quickly ran through at least eight editions. Burke replied, whereupon Paine struck back again in February 1792 with *Rights of Man, Part II*, a more inflammatory polemic equating the British monarchy with the despotic regimes of Europe, calling for a republic, universal manhood suffrage to elect annual, single-chamber parliaments and repudiation of the national debt, among other wholesale changes to the constitution and social reforms to improve the lot of the poor, the unemployed and the old. The popularity of these radical tracts, together with an increase in the membership of clubs for 'Constitutional Information' and 'Friends of the People' up and down the country, where Paine was read as gospel, alarmed Pitt's government more than events on the continent; for the political clubs were seen as copies of the Jacobins and other clubs in Paris with equivalent potential for inciting revolutionary violence. In May 1792 magistrates were instructed to take vigorous measures to suppress seditious publications and meetings and in June a Police Bill passed through Parliament.[7]

Up to this point Great Britain was the only country in Europe without professional police. It was one of the prized freedoms of the British not to be subject to a disciplined force answerable to the government. Below the level of riot, when the army was called in, the peace was kept by ordinary citizens raising a hue and cry when robbed or attacked, assisted perhaps by the parish constable, an unpaid official who undertook the duty in his spare time and served for one year. Local magistrates, also unpaid, were empowered to order arrests, examine prisoners and conduct trials. Like everything else in the country the system was penetrated by money: a constable could charge for his services; magistrates kept certain fees and fines and there were parliamentary rewards for bringing criminals to justice, graded on the severity of the offence.[8] However, the chief deterrent to crime – and indicator of the absence of serious means of prevention – was the severity of punishment. Petty offences such as stealing five shillings' worth of goods from a shop, stealing a sheep or stealing anything from a person were among 200 transgressions carrying the death penalty, although the disproportion often seems to have persuaded juries not to convict.[9]

This amateur yet commercialized system backed by savage retribution worked well enough in small communities where everyone knew everyone else, but it had patently failed in the growing conurbations; and London itself was the most lawless city in Europe, possibly the world.[10] It seems British conservatism was responsible for this situation quite as much as the boasted love of liberty. At all events, it was the dangerous political emanations from France that provided the spur for change.

An embryo police unit had been founded by a Westminster magistrate, the playwright and novelist Henry Fielding, on his own initiative and in his own house in 1749. The small force of thief catchers known as 'Bow Street Runners' had been expanded after Fielding's death, provided with a criminal record office and subsidized from the government's Secret Service fund. The 1792 Bill provided for seven further offices in the London area on the same lines, each with three salaried magistrates to sit in rotation so that one was always on duty, together with clerks and six detective constables or 'runners'; their specific remit was to prevent revolution. They were paid from Pitt's newly consolidated fund of Customs and Excise revenues and were answerable to the king and his ministers rather than Parliament.[11] The lawyer responsible for drafting the Police Bill and appointed first 'Receiver' or director of the new organization also established a loyalist society on behalf of the government and paid for initially from Police Office funds to counteract the radical clubs. Named the Association for Preserving Liberty and Property against Republicans and Levellers, it was usually referred to as the Constitutional Society or the Crown and Anchor Society, since its meetings were held at that tavern in the Strand.

Paine, meanwhile, avoided arrest on charges of treason by crossing to Calais where on the strength of his pro-revolutionary writings he was elected a deputy to the National Convention in Paris, though he spoke no French. He was tried *in absentia* in England, found guilty of seditious libel and declared an outlaw; and *Rights of Man* was suppressed. He had discovered the limits of Britain's famed freedoms of expression. Had the Parisian revolutionary leaders imposed similar curbs on the heady new rights to 'speak, write and publish freely' they might possibly have preserved those rights.

Pitt's Home Secretary followed the Police Bill with the Alien Act, another momentous departure from British precedent, passed on 8 January 1793. Framed on the advice of French émigrés in England and based on French practice, it required all foreigners to register personal details at a Police Office or with Customs officials at their port of entry to the country, and suspended habeas corpus for aliens, thereby permitting the arrest and imprisonment without trial of any foreigner on suspicion alone. The vast work entailed was coordinated at an Alien Office established at 20 Crown Street near the Foreign and Home Offices, formerly home to the Secret Office where incoming and outgoing correspondence of foreign embassies in London was opened, copied, deciphered and resealed for onward transmission by skilled engravers who fabricated stamps to match the original seals. This work was removed to the Lombard Street Post Office in the city of London.[12]

Besides examining foreigners, especially French émigrés, in order to uncover and deport republican spies and agents of subversion, the Alien Office acted as liaison with the de facto Bourbon government in exile, the Comité Française, through which it developed networks of secret agents within France. These were soon extended to royalist centres of resistance in France, among them a remarkable clerical organization, the Institut Philanthropique, ostensibly a charity for the relief of poverty, but concealing a secret inner core of priests hostile to the Revolution and working through chains of initiates throughout the country for the restoration of the monarchy. These and many other counter-revolutionary groups were supported by British government funds for the purpose of fanning the fires of revolt in the regions of France against the Paris Revolution.[13]

Pitt's overt preparations for war followed these internal and covert measures. He had held as long as he possibly could to the hope of preserving British neutrality. When the National Convention extinguished that hope towards the end of 1792 he had begun mobilizing the armed forces and cementing what is known as the 'first coalition' against France. Britain had existing alliances with Prussia and the Dutch republic; it remained to make treaties with Austria and Spain and negotiate for mercenary troops from minor European states to join the alliance armies – which served to confirm the French government in the belief that Pitt was resolved to destroy the Revolution.

This was not his aim. Had it been, he might perhaps have achieved it, for within weeks of the French declaration of war their army in Belgium was in full retreat before the allies, and their general, Dumouriez, disillusioned with the regicide government in Paris, had crossed the lines to the enemy. Lafayette had preceded him, as had increasing numbers of former nobles with or without their families since the September massacres. More serious for the government, whole regions of France were in open revolt against Paris.

In the west the peasants of a vast area stretching from the river Loire down through the Vendée and adjacent *départements* to the estuaries of the Gironde and inland as far as Poitiers had risen behind their nobles and priests against the republic. The region was an epitome of rural France, isolated by poor roads, backward in farming methods, unchanged in custom for centuries: wives took their meals standing while their menfolk ate seated on benches at table.[14] The Church and the priest, usually a clever local boy made good, were central to the life of the villages; yet many priests had refused the oath to the constitution and had been replaced by alien newcomers. After the disastrous start to the war against the coalition the National Convention passed a law to conscript 300,000 additional men for the army, and the arrival of recruiting officers in the region to claim young men in what was viewed as a 'blood tax' triggered revolt under the banner of the Church and the monarchy. It began with savage attacks on towns where republican authorities were established and where a new breed of merchants controlling a domestic weaving system reaching into the countryside were resented as intruders, particularly since depression in the textile industry and the depreciating *assignat* had caused widespread unemployment.

The rising in the Vendée was duplicated in other rural areas in Brittany, Normandy and the eastern border. The National Convention took drastic measures to save the republic: a central Revolutionary Tribunal was set up for the summary trial of counter-revolutionary suspects, its verdicts only acquittal or death with no appeal or review. Members of the Convention were sent out to the *départements* as *représentants en mission* with punitive powers to enforce compliance with the levies for the army and to root out traitors; commissioners with similarly unlimited powers were sent to the armies and the naval bases to investigate officers and men. *Comités de surveillance* were established in every *commune* throughout the country and in the *sections* of the large towns to hunt out foreigners and denounce traitors; and in early April a small inner cabinet was established, the notorious Committee of Public Safety of only nine members, later increased to twelve, to sit in closed session to coordinate the policy of all executive committees of government.

Most of these steps were carried through by the Jacobin 'mountain' with the support or at the instigation of the Paris sans-culottes against the protest of moderates loosely banded together under the title 'Girondins', who attempted to defend the liberalizing principles of the Revolution. To Girondin charges of 'dictatorship' Danton pointed to the disorder which their predecessors in the Legislative Assembly had failed to contain: 'Let us take terrible measures so that the people may not have to take them themselves.'[15] And Marat proclaimed, 'It is by means of violence that liberty must be established, and the moment has come for the temporary organization of the despotism of liberty in order to crush the despotism of kings.'[16] The paradox comes close to Rousseau's exposition of the 'general will' whereby the individual would be 'forced to be free'. Rousseau's most humourless disciple, Robespierre, wrote in his diary, 'What is needed is one single will . . . The dangers within France come from the middle classes, and to defeat them we must rally the people.'[17]

This was not difficult. The people's preoccupation was again acute hunger. Roused by demagogues dubbed *enragés* who blamed the old scapegoats – merchant aristocrats, hoarders, speculators and royalist plotters – they took to the streets and on 2 June surrounded the Convention in thousands demanding regulation of food prices, taxes on the rich to subsidize the poor and a trial of those deputies speaking for the merchant interest or in league with the renegade General Dumouriez. Twenty-nine Girondin deputies and the only two Girondin ministers were placed under house arrest; others, alarmed by the insurrection, had already left for the provinces. The Convention was now, more than ever, the creature of the 'mountain'. Robespierre's diary entry continued: 'The people must ally with the Convention and the Convention make use of the people.'[18]

Once again a combination of hunger-induced desperation and politicians avid to surf the swell of violence had shifted the Revolution decisively in a communal direction against counsels of moderation and the sophisticated needs of business. What followed pushed it to the extreme. The great cities, Lyons, Marseilles, Bordeaux, other important industrial and trading centres and the major naval bases, Brest and Toulon, also rose in rebellion against Paris. It was not a concerted royalist movement, but a series of revolts led by the merchant and cultural elites of the cities in defence of their own interests against the radical policies of the National Convention and local Jacobins. In a sense it was the extreme expression of existing centrifugal tendencies. With very different rebellions in the countryside in favour of priests and the old order and against a new class that had benefited from the sale of church lands, the Paris government found itself by the end of June openly opposed in some sixty of the eighty-three *départements*. Meanwhile the coalition armies were advancing on all the 'natural frontiers' of France, from the Channel coast, the Rhine and the Alps to the Pyrenees. Unsurprisingly the food crisis intensified, the *assignat* continued its descent until worth less than 30 per cent of face value and there was a flight of capital from the country.

In such desperate circumstances, under the necessity of survival, the territorial imperative – as against the maritime-commercial imperative – was finally realized in the Revolution. As in the previous century after bitter civil wars Louis XIV had united France under his own will, exercising authority through a central body of officials, so the National Convention, assuming the will of the people, discharged absolute power through the Committee of Public Safety. It was not what the fathers of the Revolution had intended. The sweeping reforms carried through by the Constituent Assembly show that they had wanted above all a modern, relatively decentralized free-trading economy like that of Great Britain, in which capital would flourish. Now the opposite was achieved. A command economy was established in which industries vital for the war effort were in effect nationalized; maximum grain prices were set, bread rationed and the price of essential foods controlled, crops and cattle requisitioned, the storage and movement of supplies regulated. Capital transmissions abroad and the export of French goods and produce were prohibited; French shipping was protected by a Navigation Law and no products from Great Britain or her empire were allowed in; by September 1793 the country was virtually cut off from world trade.

At the same time the people were mobilized for what would become known in the twentieth century as 'total war'. A *levée en masse* conscripted some 300,000 young men without children for the fighting fronts; fathers were directed to manufacture arms and ammunition in scores of small workshops and large-scale ironworks where they laboured under tight discipline for fourteen hours a day with one day off in ten; women made uniforms under similarly harsh regimes; old men were enjoined in the Convention decree 'to excite the courage of warriors, to preach hatred of kings and the unity of the Republic'.[19]

The attempt at total control was not due entirely to the zealotry of members of the Committee of Public Safety, which Robespierre joined in July. The rhetoric was anti-capital and virulently hostile to what was seen as Britain's ambition to engross the trade of the whole world, but the take-over and regulation of the economy was necessitated equally by the scale of dislocation of French industry and agriculture after the financial incompetence of successive revolutionary governments[20] and the inroads made in the French economy by British manufactured goods and British merchant shipping. French agriculture, industry, shipping and commerce had been so crippled by the Revolution – foreign trade had shrunk to a fifth of its 1780s volume – that the Committee of Public Safety had no option but to regulate, direct and fund national subsistence and the war effort. However, this was entirely consistent with the ideology driving the Committee: community as against individuals, crafts and trades as against big business employers, national self-sufficiency as against world trade; Republican France the expression of these virtues as against Great Britain, embodiment of all the abuses the Republic was fighting. In this sense and in the degree of prying and denunciation achieved, the control ultimately exercised by the Committee went far beyond the requirements of a directed war economy.[21]

It is interesting that Talleyrand, who had been condemned by the Convention for an incriminating document found among the king's papers and was now living as an émigré in London, had developed a totally opposite viewpoint. In a paper written the previous November, he had suggested that France should conclude industrial and commercial agreements with Great Britain for free trade between both countries and their respective colonies, and should make common cause in the liberation of the Spanish south American possessions by throwing open 'to free trade that vast part of the western world which lies in the Pacific Ocean and in the South Seas'.[22]

Of equal interest, in the same memorandum Talleyrand insisted that the new France created by the Revolution must adopt policies consistent with the philosophy of her new constitution. These included abandoning the old ambition to be the greatest power in Europe and the old drive for more territory, instead learning that 'for states as for individuals, real wealth consists not in acquiring or invading the domains of others, but in developing one's own' and that the real effect of 'all extensions of territory, all usurpations by force or fraud . . . is to increase the difficulty of administration and to diminish the happiness and security of the governed for the passing interest or vanity of those who govern'.[23]

The Committee of Public Safety was embarked on an opposite course. It legitimized the age-old customs of conquest by instructing the generals when in enemy territory to take hostages, levy taxes, requisition food, forage, cattle and draft animals, minerals, clothing, silver from churches, indeed any money or portable property, sending home to France the surplus above army requirements. This process had, of course, started in the conquered territories the previous year and was to form one of the core principles of French economic policy for the duration of the war against Great Britain.

Internally the Committee imposed control through terror. A 'Law of Suspects' widened the definitions of persons who could be arrested on suspicion of being enemies of the Revolution to include even those who could not justify their means of existence and performance of their civic duties, or members of former noble families who had not 'constantly manifested their loyalty to the Revolution'; the local *comités de surveillance* were charged with the task of drawing up lists of such suspects and issuing warrants against them and an *armée révolutionnaire* recruited from zealous Parisian sans-culottes provided *représentants en mission* to the provinces with a loyal guard to arrest the suspects, impose the controls decreed from Paris, ensure the provisioning of towns – usually by ransacking the countryside – striking fear into hoarders, the rich and counter-revolutionaries. As for those regions in open revolt, army units were deployed and a war of annihilation declared, extending to women, children and the entire society supporting the rebellion.

State control imposed by terror – 'the despotism of liberty' – was accompanied by the promotion through all media, arts and public symbolism of Republican virtue and reason; this extended to a violent campaign against the Church as the hypocritical purveyor of superstition which had enslaved the people and 'perpetuated the tyranny of the great'[24] – an offensive which justified stripping churches of gold and jewellery to pay members of the *armée révolutionnaire* and relieve the distress of the poor.

Robespierre, although a principal publicist and instructor in Republican virtue, denounced the atheistic content of the de-Christianizing campaign. Believing in a creator-God who had granted each human an immortal soul, he attempted to found a purer Republican religion shorn of the 'myths' of Christianity; he was to inaugurate it the following summer with a grand 'Festival of the Supreme Being and of Nature' staged in collaboration with the Revolution's premier artist, Jacques-Louis David. Robespierre himself presided holding a bouquet of flowers and a sheaf of corn, declaring 'Nature itself' the true priest of the Supreme Being.

Robespierre remains an enigma. He was described by Germaine de Staël as having ignoble features and a pale skin with veins of a greenish hue. She asserted that he soon lost whatever virtue he possessed because his character was fundamentally 'envious and spiteful' – a judgement that may be inferred from his deeds; her further claims that he 'supported the most absurd theses with a sangfroid that had an air of conviction', and that the source of his power was fanaticism are unquestionably true.[25] Some historians regard him as 'far-sighted and courageous', the 'only man in French history to merit the description "incorruptible"',[26] others as a tragic figure attempting to blend Rousseau's philosophy with practical political leadership.[27] To judge from his speeches he regarded the Republic, in Simon Schama's words, as 'an immense enterprise in moral instruction'.[28]

Certainly he regarded economics as a branch of ethics. Whether he had read Adam Smith on the self-interest of individuals advancing the interests of society through the 'invisible hand' of competition in a free market, he showed no sign of having grasped the concept. From the premise that all citizens had the right to subsistence, he proceeded to the proposition that only those funds over and above the total subsistence needs of the community might be employed for commerce. This aligned him with the sans-culottes whose simple economic credo was 'tax the rich', and served to justify the levies which, like all Bourbon governments before it, the Convention exacted on wealth – a further surrender of the property rights guaranteed as sacred in the Declaration of the Rights of Man. The aim, he declared in rhetorical terms, must be to make commerce 'a source of public wealth, not only of the monstrous affluence of a few families'.[29] Such unawareness of the forces driving trade and industry had an ancestry in French ministerial thought stretching back at least to Louis XIV's great administrator, Jean-Baptiste Colbert, who had despised merchants as egotistical profit-seekers with no concern for the general welfare of the state. 'But', Colbert wrote, 'we should raise ourselves above our private interests to seek the general good.'[30]

Robespierre had no better idea of what drove his fellow men. He viewed the terror, of which he was a principal architect, as a temporary but necessary prelude to the Republic of Virtue – the means justified by the ends. An ultimate product of the Enlightenment vision of moral progress, he appeared to believe that democracy and civic education would of themselves transform human beings and usher in a good society 'where all base and cruel feelings are suppressed, and where the law encourages beneficent and generous feelings'.[31] Meanwhile, those who disagreed with his solutions, including those Girondin deputies under arrest, must do penance on the guillotine. One is reminded of Rousseau's confession to Boswell that he lived in a world of fantasies and could not tolerate the world as it was: 'mankind disgusts me'.[32]

The terror signalled the end of any hopes that women had placed in the Revolution. From the beginning women had been among the most active agitators in the streets, extending their traditional role of demonstrating against food prices and shortages. Louis XVI and his family had been brought back to Paris from Versailles by a massed column of women escorted by National Guards. Women had founded their own political clubs and there had been a general expectation that they would share in the rights being claimed for men. An actress, Olympe de Gouges, had even presented a Declaration of the Rights of Women and Citizenesses to the Constituent Assembly – to no effect. Now, as the Revolution proceeded grimly against its internal and external enemies, summoning up the warrior virtues, women were officially denied a public voice or political rights: their clubs were shut down, their attendance at political assemblies forbidden, female gatherings banned.[33] Whilst evidently rooted deep in the warrior psyche, since something very similar was to occur in the Nazi Revolution in Germany,[34] the ideological demand for women to return to domesticity was also linked to a cult of maternal breast-feeding – as opposed to employing wet-nurses. Rousseau had claimed that the practice would lead to a general reform of society.[35]

Most women who left a record were by now sickened by the Revolution. They were indeed high among its victims. Deprived of their menfolk or mourning their death, or simply deserted, despairing the loss of their way of life, thousands forced into prostitution, they saw beneath the lofty abstractions of the politicians only violence and bloodshed.[36]

Of those known to history none did more for the honour of her country or her sex than Charlotte Corday. Twenty-five years old, she was

living in Caen in Normandy which had become a centre of revolt against
the Convention after the arrest of the Girondin deputies. Inspired by
loathing of the Jacobins for having brought the Republic so low, she travelled to Paris to assassinate Marat, a particular target of the Girondins for
his radicalism and the malign influence of his newspaper, *L'Ami du Peuple*.
She hoped to achieve maximum effect by doing the deed in the
Convention chamber in the presence of the deputies, but Marat was
suffering from a skin infection and staying at home. Obtaining entry to his
room on the pretext of supplying the names of counter-revolutionaries in
Normandy, and finding him in a medicinal bath, she took a knife from
beneath her clothes and stabbed him to the heart. In explanation, she said
simply that she believed he had been the principal figure inciting dissen-
sion in France and had wished to sacrifice her life for her country. She
went to the guillotine with the same composure and courage. For his part,
Marat became a martyr of the Revolution; his body was embalmed for
public display, his unheroic end in the bath immortalized by David.

In the event the ruthless determination and fanatic energy displayed
by the members of the Committee of Public Safety and their representatives in the regions, and increases in arms production and numbers of
troops achieved by the *levée en masse* saved the Republic, although the
coalition allies made major contributions to this outcome. The land
powers, Austria, Prussia and Spain, behaved in character by diverting
resources to the seizure of territory in respectively Alsace, Lorraine and
Roussillon, while in eastern Europe Austria and Prussia, in concert with
the other great land power, Russia, were already dividing Poland
between them. Great Britain, the anchor of the coalition, behaved in her
maritime character. Instead of concentrating means to support royalist
rebellions, especially in the west of France, her major efforts went into a
great expedition to seize France's West Indian colonies and to cut off her
overseas trade, the strategy that had served Pitt's father so well in the
Seven Years War. So the French Republic was allowed time to extinguish
her internal fires.

3

The Glorious First of June, 1794

NOWHERE IN BRITAIN was there more enthusiasm for the war against Republican France than amongst naval officers. For hundreds ashore on half pay, war meant employment again; for all it held the prospects of accelerated promotion and riches from prize money. Prize was the lure. Despite the unusual privations and dangers of naval life, the long separations from home in often debilitating conditions, able and bold spirits were attracted to the service by the possibilities of becoming rich from the capture of enemy ships and cargoes.

Prize was a direct inducement codified in the Convoys and Cruizers Act (1708), whereby the Crown had given up its rights in captured ships and cargoes to the captors specifically 'for the better and more effectual encouragement of the Sea Service'.[1] Thus proceeds from the sale of captures after they had been adjudged lawful prize by an Admiralty Court were distributed among the company of the capturing ship according to a scale of eighths: three-eighths went to the captain, unless acting under the direction of a flag officer, when one of the eighths went to the flag officer; one-eighth was shared amongst the ship's lieutenants, another eighth amongst warrant officers such as boatswain, gunner, carpenter, another amongst petty officers and midshipmen and the remaining two-eighths amongst the sailors, boys and others. For captured warships taken into naval service a bounty was awarded calculated on her complement at the start of the action, which was shared out in the same proportions.[2]

The Act was an illustration of the power the merchant/financial interest had acquired in Parliament by the early eighteenth century, for it was principally concerned with the protection of British maritime trade. A well-motivated naval officer corps was a prerequisite. The motivation served the complementary merchant and naval aim of crippling the enemy's trade and reducing his capacity to wage war. The younger Pitt's government pursued this strategy as rigorously as all previous British governments. In November 1793 instructions went out to HM ships and privateers to 'stop and detain all ships loaden with goods, the produce of any colony belonging to France . . . and bring the same, with their cargoes, to legal adjudication in our Court of Admiralty'.[3]

Traditionally the English/British had rejected the proposition associated particularly with the Dutch as universal carriers that the goods of a belligerent aboard a neutral ship enjoyed the protection of the neutral flag. In its latest manifestation, known as 'the Rule of the War of 1756' – the elder Pitt's war – the justification ran: 'a neutral cannot legally engage, in wartime, in the trade of a belligerent not open to that neutral in peacetime'.[4] Since French Navigation Laws banned foreign ships from her colonial trades in peacetime, any neutral found carrying French colonial produce in war was subject to this rule. The aim was to throttle French overseas trade and the wealth derived from colonies, which would then fall easy prey to British expeditionary forces.

For naval officers who carried out the policy, the chances of prize were better on some stations than others, better at the start of a war than later and better in frigates and smaller warships, where there were in any case fewer hands to share the booty, than in ships of the line in the battle fleets. It was a lottery. That small proportion who survived disease, the violence of the elements and the enemy[5] and had the right mixture of ability, patronage and good fortune to be promoted to command a small warship – particularly the comparatively few of these who achieved the final step up to 'post captain', entitled to command a frigate or a ship of the line, thence to rise strictly by seniority through the captains' list and on up the flag officers' lists – were the winners who could anticipate fortunes from prize. For this reason, and because the training at sea and a commission as a naval officer cost nothing, it was predominantly the younger sons of the aristocracy and gentry and youngsters from service, professional and merchant families without patronage or significant private means who were prepared to endure the harsh, austere and monotonous discipline of the sea service. In a society where money could buy social advantage, they had the chance of raising themselves spectacularly by their own efforts without significant financial outlay.[6] And in every war many of them did so. Jane Austen, two of whose brothers rose to flag rank at this time, portrays in her novel *Persuasion* a self-satisfied baronet of ancient lineage expressing strong objections to the naval service:

> First, as being the means of bringing persons of obscure birth into undue distinction, and raising men to honours which their fathers and grandfathers never dreamt of; and secondly, as it cuts up a man's youth and vigour most horribly; a sailor grows old sooner than any other man.[7]

The hero of *Persuasion*, a naval officer, Captain Wentworth, started without fortune:

> But he was confident that he should soon be rich; – full of life and ardour, he knew that he should soon have a ship, and soon be on a station that would lead to everything he wanted.[8]

So it proved: 'Ah!' he exclaims later:

> those were pleasant days when I had the *Laconia*! How fast I made money in her . . . after taking privateers enough to be very entertaining, I had the good luck, in my passage home the next autumn, to fall in with the very French frigate I wanted. – I brought her into Plymouth . . .[9]

where he was rewarded with the handsome bounty earned by such an important prize.

Many were the real-life models from whom Captain Wentworth was drawn. The officers of the Royal Navy, the striking arm of a predominantly commercial nation, were inspired by the same financial inducements as their freebooting predecessors in Elizabeth I's reign. So to an extent were the men they led, who could never amass the immense fortunes and titles harvested by admirals commanding on lucrative stations but might make a year's wages from a single fortunate encounter, or even gain enough to set up in business ashore.

This is not to suggest that narrow financial motives drove the naval service. Undoubtedly the quest for honour, glory, adventure, the call of patriotism, even the romance of exotic cruising and the deep satisfaction of mastering skills demanding art and judgement were factors, as was the close companionship born of shared hardship and danger. The complexity of aspiration is well illustrated in the figure who came to dominate this era of naval warfare, Horatio Nelson. The son of a Norfolk rector of modest means and without prospects, he had an uncle in the navy, his mother's brother, Captain Maurice Suckling, and at the age of twelve had asked his father to write to Uncle Maurice to say he would like to go to sea with him. This was by no means young for officer entry, and his uncle had agreed to take him, while expressing some surprise: 'What has poor Horace [as Horatio was known] done, who is so weak, that he above all the rest [of the Nelson siblings] should be sent to rough it out at sea?'[10] To a lad brought up frugally in a remote country parsonage, Captain Suckling must have appeared a romantic figure, and this might be sufficient to account for Nelson's choice of career. Who knows what his uncle might have told him about life at sea? On the other hand one of Nelson's first biographers stated: 'it was the wish of providing for himself by which Horatio was chiefly activated'; that is to say, he would make his own way, relieving his father of the necessity of laying out money for his career.[11]

Nelson's apprenticeship to the service was somewhat unusual, since it included a voyage in a merchant ship to the West Indies and an expedition of scientific discovery to the North Pole. It also included two years in a small warship in the East Indies where he caught one of the diseases so often fatal to Europeans and had to be shipped home in wasted condition and for a time unable to move his limbs. He was never to recover robust health again, if indeed his constitution had ever been strong, which seems doubtful. Nevertheless, in all ships he served in he had won the confidence of his commanders by the zeal, quick-thinking competence and eagerness for personal distinction which were to distinguish his later career.

Meanwhile his uncle had been appointed to the influential post of Comptroller of the Navy and was able to place him after his recovery as acting lieutenant aboard a ship of the line escorting a convoy to the Mediterranean. This was a mark of confidence beyond mere patronage for Nelson was barely eighteen, two years younger than the minimum age for lieutenants. On his return he passed the examination for lieutenant, still eighteen months short of the regulation age and short of the mandatory six years' sea time, despite which his uncle secured him a commission in that rank in the frigate *Lowestoffe* under orders for the Jamaica station. This was to be a formative period. The great war with France and Spain over American independence had just broken out, ensuring frequent action, and the frigate's captain, William Locker, with whom he formed a lasting friendship, proved an inspiring mentor. Years later Nelson wrote to him, 'It is you who taught me to board a Frenchman . . . it is you who always told me, "Lay a Frenchman close and you will always beat him." '[12] Another inspiration during this period was the captain of the *Lion*, William Cornwallis, who taught him, 'You can always beat a Frenchman if you fight him long enough', and 'When in doubt, to fight is always to err on the right side.'[13]

Recommended by Locker to the commander-in-chief on the station, Sir Peter Parker, Nelson was transferred to the flagship as Third Lieutenant. He quickly won over Sir Peter, as he had his previous commanders, by his activity and a personal charm and directness; by his twentieth birthday he had risen to First Lieutenant. Shortly afterwards Sir Peter appointed him commander of a gun brig and six months later gave him the vital step up to post captain of a captured enemy merchantman taken into the service and armed as a frigate. His uncle Maurice had died the previous year, but Nelson had in effect created his own patronage. This was how the system worked. It worked because the 'interest' or patronage by which officers advanced in the service was actually based on commanders' reports and judgement of an officer's merit, and all the way up the chain of command it was in everyone's interest that only the able earned promotion. Admiral Sir Peter Parker required live wires like young Nelson to command the vessels that would earn him his prize eighths.

Nelson was three months short of his twenty-first birthday when he was made 'post' and started on the seniority list that would take him up to flag rank in his prime: rear admiral of the blue at thirty-nine, vice admiral by forty-three. He was by no means exceptional in gaining his first post command in his early twenties; in consequence the Admiralty usually had a pool of youngish admirals to choose from for important commands. However suspect to modern eyes, there can be no question that this system of promotion by personal influence worked and brought good men to the top; as N. A. M. Rodger has argued, there is no other explanation for the Royal Navy's triumphant record in the eighteenth century.[14] It worked because of the ceaseless wars. It is hard to imagine it producing fighting sailors during a long period of peace, but nor has any other peacetime system of promotion.

When the great American war ended Nelson was, as he expressed it, 'without a fortune: but there is not a speck on my character. True honour, I hope, predominates in my mind far above riches.'[15] Whether he was attempting to console himself for disappointment, his actions in his first peace command, the frigate *Boreas*, prove the basic truth of the sentiment. He found himself senior captain, second only to the commander-in-chief, on the Leeward Islands station in the West Indies, where, he soon discovered, a regular trade was carried on with American ships contrary to the Navigation Laws – since the American states had become independent. Taking a fellow captain and lifelong friend, Cuthbert Collingwood, with him, Nelson confronted the commander-in-chief with the illegality of the American commerce, and afterwards took his complaint to the Governor of the islands. The latter, a military man, told him that old generals were not in the habit of taking advice from young gentlemen. Nelson was then twenty-six and appeared younger; he was slight, scarcely 5 feet 4½ inches tall, with lank, fair hair, seemingly 'the meerest boy of a captain'.[16]

'Sir,' he replied, 'I have the honour of being as old as the Prime Minister of England, and think myself as capable of commanding one of His Majesty's ships as that Minister is of governing the state.'[17]

Finding neither man willing to take action against the illegal trade in which the whole islands community – merchants, planters and Customs officials – was complicit, Nelson took it upon himself to stop it, again with Collingwood's support. After giving notice, he seized an American-owned and manned schooner attempting to evade the law with a British registration obtained on the island of St Christopher, and in the subsequent lawsuit argued the case that he had the right to seize such vessels which infringed the Navigation Laws; after which he took four more American ships. The Leeward Islands community erupted: writs for damages were issued against him and to avoid arrest he was obliged to remain aboard his ship, virtually a prisoner. He had no support from his commander-in-chief; as he put it to his former captain, Locker, 'I had the governor, the Customs, all the planters upon me . . . and the admiral stood neuter, although his flag was then in the roads.'[18]

With the British government's support, Nelson eventually prevailed and American ships were driven from the islands, replaced on the protectionist principles of the Navigation Laws by British-owned and manned vessels. The chief interest of the episode, perhaps, is as an illustration long before Nelson came to public attention of his outstanding moral courage, self-confidence, resolution and ability to master a brief and carry his case; it also indicates that the remarkable impression he made on his superiors owed nothing to sycophancy. His driving motive remained personal distinction; soon afterwards he wrote to a friend, perhaps in hope, 'a uniform conduct of honour and integrity seldom fails of bringing a man to the goal of fame at last.'[19]

During this uneasy period in the islands he fell for the niece of the President of the Council in Nevis, Frances Nisbet. She was a few months older than him, the widow of a Dr Josiah Nisbet, by whom she had one son, also Josiah. After intermittent courtship between cruises, Nelson married her on Nevis in March 1787, and three months later set sail for England. There, after the *Boreas* paid off at the end of the year, he languished, frustrated on every front: the Admiralty found no ship for him despite his repeated requests for employment, his new wife did not bear him a child, nor it seems ever become pregnant, and the two had very meagre allowances from their respective uncles to supplement his half pay of eight shillings a day. They settled with his father at the parsonage at Burnham Thorpe, where he attempted to occupy himself in the garden. He had little liking or aptitude for country sports; he was such a poor shot he was a danger to his companions.

The outbreak of war with Revolutionary France came as release. The Admiralty gave him a command in February 1793, the 64-gun line of battle ship *Agamemnon*, with orders to join the fleet under Lord Hood preparing for the Mediterranean. He took a number of midshipmen with him, including Josiah, now thirteen years old, whom he called his son-in-law. One of these midshipmen recalled his guidance: 'First, you must implicitly obey orders, without attempting to form any opinion of your own respecting their propriety; secondly you must consider every man as your enemy who speaks ill of your king; and thirdly you must hate a Frenchman as you do the devil!'[20] The last two precepts he followed himself with all his heart, not always the first.

Hood's fleet of fourteen of the line arrived off the French Mediterranean naval base, Toulon, in July at a critical time in that city's revolt against the Republic. The nearby commercial city of Marseilles was also in revolt, and both were prepared to declare for Louis XVII, son of the executed French king, and form an alliance with Britain to support them against Paris. The provincial urban revolts arose, as noted, from local conditions, particularly the defence by local elites of their property and interests against the communal aspirations and violence of local Jacobins inspired by the Paris government. They were supported by the majority of the people, who had been ground down by years of hunger and sickened by violence. Earlier the arsenal workers in Toulon had petitioned the National Convention in Paris for 'peace in our towns and bread for our families. A declining paper money and your terrible political squabbles suggest we will not obtain either.'[21] These were not so much royalist uprisings as desperate anti-Jacobin revolts on behalf of moderation and normality.

On the night of 23 August, at the prompting of a delegation from Marseilles, then about to fall to central government forces, Hood sent a declaration to the authorities in Toulon offering military aid to defend the city, crush the (Jacobin) factions and restore monarchical government; he guaranteed private property and promised that the port, its forts and the warships within would be held in trust and returned to France once peace was restored. The offer was put to a meeting of the Toulon *sections* the following night and naturally aroused deep divisions. It seems that stories of atrocities by government troops reported by streams of refugees from Marseilles finally induced doubters to accept Hood's offer in the hope of averting similar reprisals in Toulon.[22] However, when instructions were sent to the acting fleet commander to disarm his ships and allow the British in, he refused. For a time a battle between ships and shore seemed likely, with the city authorities threatening to use red-hot shot from the forts under their control. Instead the petty officers and sailors, who had been subject to intense political propaganda since the start of the Revolution four years before and were divided on ideological and regional lines, not least on where their ultimate loyalties lay, took the decision out of the hands of the fleet command by deserting, led by Toulon crews who had no desire to bombard their homes and families. By the morning of 28 August a number of ships were completely abandoned. The city authorities signalled to Hood to enter, and as the leading British sailed in and parties were rowed ashore to occupy the forts and batteries guarding the entrance, remaining resistance collapsed.

Nelson was not with the fleet as it took possession of the French Mediterranean squadron. Hood had ordered him to Naples the previous day with despatches requesting troops to garrison Toulon from the King of the Two Sicilies who ruled southern Italy. Since the queen was a sister of Marie Antoinette, the prime minister was an Englishman, Sir John Acton, and the French Revolutionary government was much feared, Nelson found himself fêted and Hood's request was easily granted. It was during his stay at Naples that Nelson first met Emma, the delectable young wife of the British Envoy and Minister Plenipotentiary to the Neapolitan Court, Sir William Hamilton. Nelson was always susceptible to feminine charm and it can hardly be doubted that in that warm southern clime Emma's vivid looks and spontaneity and her care for young Josiah whom he brought with him made an impression. To his wife he wrote, 'She is a young woman of amiable manners, and who does honour to the station to which she is raised.'[23] Sir William, for his part, recognized Nelson as 'no common being'.[24]

On 13 September, the day after Nelson dropped anchor in Naples Bay, the French Atlantic fleet mutinied. Neither this nor the disaffection among the Toulon crews two weeks earlier were freak events. The French navy, like the army, had been plagued with indiscipline since the start of the Revolution. In part this was due to dissonances between the revolutionaries' rhetoric of equality and the fact that the navy, a microcosm of the country, reserved rank and privilege almost exclusively to nobles. There were non-noble and temporary officers commissioned from the merchant service or from naval petty officers to fill expanded wartime fleets, but neither could expect important commands or flag rank; and despite efforts just before the Revolution to introduce promotion by merit, strains and antagonisms between the different classes of officers remained to supplement those between officers and sailors subject to Revolutionary propaganda in their home base.

The crucial difficulty, however, was the loss of authority of royal and central government to which the navy owed allegiance. In the fleet bases local Revolutionary committees had interfered in the management of the arsenals; in Toulon the commandant and other officers had been arrested. The Constituent Assembly in Paris, instead of supporting the naval authority and upholding a national chain of command, had appointed a committee to reorganize the service on Revolutionary principles. Meanwhile, local interference and outright hostility to the officer corps had continued, and sailors, exposed to Jacobin theory portraying nobles as enemies of the Revolution, had begun petitioning for rights and justifying insubordination as political protest. When in August 1790 the Paris Assembly had adopted a new naval penal code proposed by the committee, which included savage traditional punishments like keelhauling, flogging and leg irons, crews in Brest had mutinied and appealed to the Commune against such barbaric residues from the past. Again the Paris Assembly failed to uphold naval against local authority, or officers against defiant or violent sailors, with the inevitable result that indiscipline and mutiny became endemic throughout the service, and officers, unable to exercise control and often in danger of their lives, deserted in increasing numbers, many to join the émigré forces abroad.[25] At the root of the problem was the dichotomy between executive authority and the theory of the 'general will', and confusion among Revolutionary leaders as to where this popular will was located. By 1792 a majority of professional officers had left the service.

After the Vendée revolt in spring 1793 the Brest squadron was ordered to sea to prevent enemy forces supplying the rebels or attempting a landing to support them. The British government could have attempted either had they not been so intent on readying the great expedition for the West Indies. At all events, the Brest ships were in poor condition, their provisions inadequate, and the crews who were not allowed to land because rebels controlled the countryside, were by the summer going down with scurvy in great numbers. News of the treachery at Toulon came as the final aggravation and the dispirited men mutinied, demanding immediate return to prevent Brest likewise opening its gates to the British. The officers could do nothing against the militant mood and on 20 September the squadron weighed from its anchorage in Quiberon Bay and sailed for home.

The formalization of terror and the reclamation of all power from the regions to the Committee of Public Safety in Paris was well under way before the shocks of the loss of Toulon and the Mediterranean squadron and the mutiny in the Atlantic fleet; these bombshells merely accelerated both processes, further stimulating those inclined by temperament to passionate defence of the Republic against what they perceived as a vast web of treachery. It is interesting that the *représentant* of the Committee of Public Safety sent to Brest to sort out the naval problem, Jeanbon Saint-André, conjured up the same kind of enemies as were to be invoked one and a half centuries later in Nazi Germany: 'the speculators of London, the oppressors of Bengal, the disturbers of public peace in Europe'.[26]

Backed by radical Parisians formed into *armée révolutionnaire* companies, Jeanbon subordinated the Brest authorities to the national government and investigated and purged the fleet, dismissing three flag officers, punishing other officers and sending six captains to Paris to be tried for treason, three of whom were adjudged guilty and guillotined. Many officers were dismissed the service simply because they were nobles; other noble officers were evidently able to demonstrate politically sound views and remained.

He was equally uncompromising with the men, making it clear that they had no rights to question orders or petition captains. Failure to respond promptly to orders was to carry a punishment of four days in irons, assaulting an officer or inciting mutiny, death; and he made an example of four of the September mutineers by having a guillotine set up on a pontoon in Brest Roads and ordering the sides of the ships manned to witness their execution.

While he was reimposing a national chain of command and military discipline on the Atlantic fleet, the main centres of rebellion around the country capitulated to government forces. Marseilles had already been overcome in late August, its name changed to Ville-Sans-Nom and its merchant elite purged. On 9 October the citizens of Lyons, starving after months of siege, capitulated. Next day the National Convention passed a law focusing all executive, ministerial and military power in the Committee of Public Safety.[27] The Committee promptly appointed commissioners to punish the rebels of Lyons, with instructions both to destroy all quarters inhabited by the rich, leaving only the dwellings of patriots, industrial buildings and those devoted to humanity and education, and to erase the name of the city itself. The commission under Joseph Fouché and Collot d'Herbois exercised such zeal in the campaign that the city's name was permanently inscribed in the annals of atrocity.

Citizens denounced by a 'Republican Vigilance Commission' and judged guilty by members of a Revolutionary Tribunal who processed on average one man every two minutes, and sometimes ended the day drunk, were taken to the Plaine des Brotteaux, a meadow bordered by willows and poplars on the bank of the Rhône, where they were tied or chained together in a line and made the targets of several cannon charged with grapeshot; those not killed outright were despatched at close range with rifles or sabres. Others sentenced to death were executed by a guillotine set up before the Hôtel de Ville to impress those citizens unwilling or unable to make their way to Les Brotteaux. The surrounding earth became sodden and reeked, so the machine was moved to another square where a ditch was dug to channel away the blood. It failed to solve the problem. Daily successions of decapitated bodies spattered the inside of the structure with gore which putrefied giving off a hideous stench, and radical cleansing measures had to be adopted after each execution.[28] By the time the slaughter ceased the bodies of some 1,900 victims, a cross-section of Lyons society from nobles and merchants to artisans, servants and workers, had been tipped promiscuously into mass graves heaped with quicklime. At the same time the fortifications and wealthy quarters of the city – renamed Ville Affranchie or 'liberated town' – were demolished in accordance with the Committee's instructions by armies of labourers paid by levies from the rich and loot from the churches. The former silk manufacturing capital of France, indeed of Europe, had virtually ceased to exist.

According to Fouché, the object was not retribution but example. Toulon fell to government forces in mid-December during this orgy of violence, and Fouché wrote to Collot claiming that their work had contributed to its capture 'by spreading terror among the cowards who took shelter there, by offering to their view the thousands of corpses of their accomplices'.[29] The more obvious cause was the failure of Pitt's government to reinforce the small Spanish and Italian contingents and the few British marines supporting the royalists of the city. When the defence broke under cannon fire from batteries on the surrounding heights and Republican gunners occupied the forts commanding the harbour Hood evacuated the base, instructing one of the most enterprising of his captains, Sir Sidney Smith, to destroy the French ships. Smith failed to deal with all, but took out or burnt thirteen of the line.

The commander of the Republican artillery was a twenty-four-year-old Major Napoleon Buonaparte, or Bonaparte. Although born in Corsica shortly after that island had been ceded to France by Genoa, he had been sent to school at Autun in France at the age of nine. The following year, three months before his tenth birthday, he had been entered in the Military Academy at Brienne in the Champagne region. A part of one wing of the Academy has been preserved. Here, where he spent his most impressionable years, a museum has been devoted to his life and military campaigns. His entry form can be viewed, with his father's proofs of nobility; the subjects he studied and the books detailed in the syllabus are on display; the military traditions of France radiate from their pages. As a youth he was strikingly good-looking, but physically small in comparison with his fellows, as he was to remain in adult life, and as a Corsican who could barely speak French at the start, he felt an outsider and was driven in on himself. He read eagerly and indulged dreams of military glory: 'with my sword by my side and Homer in my pocket, I hope to carve my way through the world',[30] he wrote.

After five and a half years at Brienne he spent a year at the Military Academy in Paris, a finishing school for the sons of the nobility, with whom he felt nothing in common and whom he had grown to dislike.

He remained a solitary youth with a fierce sense of his own worth, proud, egotistical and ambitious. After graduating in the lowest quartile of his class he went home and made an unsuccessful foray into Corsican politics before returning to France and in June 1788 entering a training regiment for artillery officers as a Second Lieutenant. He had obtained his eminent position at the siege of Toulon through the influence of a family friend after the artillery commander was wounded. In recognition of the decisive part played by his batteries, he was promoted brigadier general three days after the city was retaken; and the government *représentant* to the army, Augustine de Robespierre, wrote to his brother Maximilien in Paris praising the young Republican's 'transcendent merit'. He had seized his chance. Two months later he would be appointed commander of the artillery in the French army of Italy.

Meanwhile the Vendéans were defeated. Their Royal and Catholic Army was routed at Angers in the Loire a few days after the fall of Toulon. The Republican commander reported to Paris that, complying with orders, he had 'crushed children under the feet of horses, massacred women . . . I have no prisoners with which to reproach myself.'[31] There followed a campaign of extermination of the inhabitants of the whole rebellious region more horrible than that at Lyons, embracing unspeakable atrocity, mutilation and sexual depravity. The process of dismantling the communities which had bred defiance of the Republic unleashed primal passions. Fields and woods were burned, livestock slaughtered, villages razed, their remaining inhabitants put to the sword and bayonet. In one episode foreshadowing an ideological extermination one and a half centuries later, some 200 old people, women and children were forced to dig their own mass grave, than shot at the edge so their bodies tumbled in. In another anticipation of a later genocide one of the senior military commanders suggested deporting the 'brigands' and recolonizing the area with 'pure' French.[32] The most notorious mass killings took place at Nantes where the *représentant en mission*, Jean-Baptiste Carrier, ordered bound prisoners placed in barges whose sides had been deliberately holed; these were then pushed out into the Loire to fill and sink with their human freight. Over 2,000 were despatched in this way; bodies washed up in the shallows for weeks.[33]

Republican armies boosted by the *levée en masse* were as successful in beating back the allied forces on the borders as in suppressing internal rebellions; indeed it was only after securing the northern frontier in Belgium that sufficient troops were released for the subjugation of the

Vendée. Now confident that the imminent peril for the Republic had been averted, the Committee of Public Safety turned to offensive planning and like countless Bourbon ministries before settled on invasion of Great Britain, the heart of the enemy alliance. To make up for the loss of ships at Toulon and mobilize the powerful battle fleet necessary, the Committee in January 1794 decreed a naval construction effort in parallel to the *levée en masse*. The task was slowed by shortages of timber, iron and naval stores which had to run the British naval blockade and was set back in early summer by losses in a major battle in the Atlantic.

Battle was not sought. It was forced by the need to cover a convoy of 127 French and chartered American merchantmen loaded with grain, flour and other foodstuffs purchased with 5 million livres' worth of gold in the United States. In view of the chronic food shortages in France and disruption caused by the rebellions in large areas of the countryside its safe arrival was vital if famine were to be avoided. Five of the line under Rear Admiral Joseph-Marie Nielly sailed from Brest in April to meet and reinforce the escort, but when a large British fleet was reported off Ushant in early May Jeanbon ordered the Brest fleet out. Earlier he had announced that he would accompany the fleet to sea and any captains not complying with signals from the flagship or failing to repeat them would face the guillotine; and he had initiated new signals to direct the instant dismissal or replacement of a vessel's commanding officer. Now he installed himself aboard the 120-gun *Le Montagne* flying the flag of Vice Admiral Louis-Thomas Villaret-Joyeuse, the officer he had picked as commander-in-chief.

Villaret, a noble by birth, was in his forty-sixth year. He had distinguished himself during the American war in Indian waters and in 1792, when France was still nominally a monarchy, had been promoted *capitaine de vaisseau*, roughly the equivalent of post captain. During the mutiny in the Brest fleet the following autumn he had maintained order and cleanliness aboard his ship, and it was his qualities as a disciplinarian who retained his men's loyalty and respect that had brought him to Jeanbon's attention. He was also exceptionally able as a tactician and fleet handler, as he was soon to show. For the captains of the twenty-five ships of the line under him were a mixed band, rather over half former *lieutenants* or *sous-lieutenants* in Louis XVI's navy, nine former merchant service captains or mates, one former boatswain and a former seaman,[34] and their station-keeping skills were equally mixed. Once a favourable wind on 16 May had allowed the fleet to sail from the roads, Jeanbon,

while discerning much enthusiasm in the ships, reported: 'several captains are well trained; but there are three or four whose ignorance is
beyond anything one could say.'[35]

VILLARET'S OPPONENT in command of the British Channel Fleet, Admiral
Lord Howe – 'Black Dick' to the men on account of his dark and sombre
countenance – was by common consent the finest fleet handler and tactician of the day – and possibly of all time. The only blemish on his vir-
tuosity was an awkwardness amounting at times to inability in expressing
his tactical intentions. By nature intensely reserved, he spoke or wrote
instructions in elliptical, often baffling dependent clauses, and such was
his aura that only the boldest dared question him.

As a captain he had earned a reputation for holding fire until almost
aboard the enemy, a traditional British aspiration that demanded exceptional courage and seamanship. At Lord Hawke's spectacular chasing
victory in Quiberon Bay in 1759 Howe had led the line in the *Magnanime*,
closing within pistol shot of the rear French flagship before delivering his
first broadside so that despite high seas scarcely a shot had missed the
enemy hull; the French who survived described the result as a 'massacre
rather than an engagement'.[36] Similarly leading the line against a fort near
Rochefort, he had stood on in *Magnanime* through all the shore gunners
could hurl at him until within 40 yards he had dropped anchor and opened
a terrific cannonade that reduced the walls to rubble in an hour. Hawke
said of him, 'He never asked me how to execute any service entrusted to
his charge, but always went straight forward and performed it.'[37]

As an admiral in the American war, and afterwards as First Lord of
the Admiralty, he had been at the forefront of attempts to develop new
tactics and reform the signalling system to make it more responsive to
tactical needs. The battle of Chesapeake Bay, or Virginia Capes, in 1781
when Rear Admiral Thomas Graves' signals had been misunderstood
by his flag officers and captains and his deliberate evolutions had allowed
the French fleet to regroup and prevent the relief of the British army
besieged at Yorktown – with the consequent loss to Britain of the
American colonies – had demonstrated the need for reform. Most other
fleet engagements of the American war had revealed the same short-
comings. Rodney had been frustrated on more than one occasion by the
failure of his captains to understand his intentions in action, and all
British officers knew that both French and Spanish fleets were adept at

avoiding decisive action by retiring downwind. This was not due to lack of courage, but to their traditional doctrine as generally the weaker navy of carrying out their mission rather than giving battle. The British aim was always to destroy the enemy main fleet and so win the freedom to carry out any mission anywhere on the high seas.

Yet it was evident to all thinking officers that the battle tactics handed down in the Admiralty 'Sailing and Fighting Instructions', little changed from the end of the seventeenth century, were deficient. They were designed, if forces were more or less equal, to bring about a battle in a single mutually supporting line extending the length of the enemy line and parallel to it on the same tack. In practice differences between ships in sailing and handling characteristics, exacerbated by early mast and rigging damage from enemy long-range high-angle fire, rendered the parallel line extraordinarily difficult to achieve. Further, if the French held the windward position they seldom used their advantage to close to decisive range, and when to leeward they were able to lask away to prevent the British closing. In consequence virtually all line battles between roughly equal fleets ended indecisively.

This had been inevitable in the seventeenth and early eighteenth centuries when there was little to choose between the different navies in fighting efficiency, but from the mid-eighteenth century the British had begun to achieve an ascendancy in gun discipline and accuracy and rate of fire which convinced them, as the aphorisms of Nelson's mentors have indicated, that if they could only hold a French ship to close action they would prevail. The result of the last great battle of the American war off the Saints in the West Indies when wind changes had thrown the formal lines into confusion and allowed parts of the British line in amongst the French in close mêlées had confirmed it: Rodney had achieved decisive victory. As noted earlier, the defeated French admiral, the Comte de Grasse, when brought aboard the British flagship, confessed that the French service was a hundred years behind. Hence the search for a new system of tactics that would allow British fleets to capitalize on their evident fighting superiority.

The answer seemed to lie in fighting from close to leeward, so preventing the enemy from retiring downwind. It carried the additional advantage that ships to leeward could, because of their angle of heel, use the lower tiers of the heaviest guns on the engaged side in sea conditions that would make it dangerous to open the lower gun ports of ships in the windward position. This was clear to thinking British officers before the

Saints; Rodney had a signal in his personal instructions which directed each ship when chasing to 'engage from the lee side and not to quit her opponent until she has struck'.[38] After flying this signal and achieving decisive victory over a Spanish fleet in 1780, he had written to the First Lord: 'as I told your Lordship, when the British fleet take the lee gage, the enemy cannot escape.'[39] A theoretician, John Clerk, Laird of Eldin, near Edinburgh, who had an obsessive interest in naval tactics and discussed manoeuvres with naval officers whenever he had opportunity, usually with the aid of small model ships he carried in his pockets, also promoted the advantages of giving battle from the lee berth in *An Essay on Naval Tactics*, first published for his friends in 1782 and issued for the public in 1790. This was the first original work on naval tactics published in English. Hitherto the French had monopolized theory.

The problem with the lee gage was the near impossibility of forcing an enemy to action. The fleet with the weather gage had all the advantages of giving or refusing battle and controlling the range at which it was fought. Attention, therefore, turned to the tactics employed in the mid-seventeenth-century Anglo-Dutch wars of breaking through the enemy line. This is what Rodney had done inadvertently as a result of the wind shifts at the Saints. Before that the unfortunate Thomas Graves, sailing with reinforcements for a second, ultimately vain attempt to relieve the British army at Yorktown and determined not to repeat the failure off Chesapeake Bay, had issued additional signals, three of which instructed his van, centre or rear to 'force through the enemy'.[40] And in the year before that in the Channel Fleet, from whence Graves had come to the north American station, Howe's chief collaborator in reform, Rear Admiral Richard Kempenfelt, had devised a book of signals, one of which signified: 'When fetching up with the enemy to leeward and on the contrary tack – to break through their line and endeavour to cut off part of their van or rear.'[41] The Saints served to confirm the merit of breaking through the enemy line.

Kempenfelt's Channel Fleet signal book of 1780 had marked a huge advance in signalling method. Hitherto flag hoists had referred to articles in the printed Admiralty 'Sailing and Fighting Instructions', and the often convoluted wording found there had to be interpreted in the light of the present situation of the fleet and the enemy. To complicate matters, hoists had different meanings according to the position from which they were flown, and as a further source of confusion, each commander-in-chief issued his own 'Additional' signals and instructions.

Kempenfelt's compilation was for the first time a true signal book since the meanings and instructions were contained in its pages alongside the representations of the flag hoists.

Kempenfelt lost his life in 1782 when his flagship sank while being heeled for repairs in Spithead, but Howe, appointed to command the Channel Fleet in 1790, took the signalling reforms to their logical conclusion by introducing a numerical code. Such a system had been invented by a French East India Company officer[42] over thirty years earlier, but it had not been adopted in the French service. During the American war Howe and Kempenfelt had played with the idea. Now Howe adopted it fully. He designed flags to indicate numerals nought to nine, assigned a number to each meaning or instruction he wished to communicate and signalled it with numeral flags hoisted singly or in pairs or threes. This represented a revolution in ease, speed and clarity of signalling – since flags could now be hoisted in the most visible position – and opened the way to an almost infinite extension of what could be conveyed. The system became standard through the British service. Hood issued an almost identical book to his fleet before sailing for the Mediterranean in 1793.[43]

There had been less incentive for change in the French navy. Despite defeat at the Saints, its performance in the American war was justly regarded with satisfaction. And although two experienced officers published treatises in the 1780s critical of the formal line of battle and advocating divisional formations to concentrate attack on a part of the enemy line, the official doctrine set out in *Tactique et Signaux* (1787) remained wedded to the single line and the orderly evolutions required to form it and match the enemy's every move. Breaking through the enemy line was described as a 'very difficult and daring' manoeuvre which could only be undertaken by a master of evolutions commanding a very well exercised and nimble fleet.[44]

The signalling system too was left unchanged. Meanings and instructions in the printed *Tactique et Signaux* were briefly summarized in a numerical table each of whose lines and columns was represented by a different flag. Thus a two-flag hoist, the upper denoting the column, the lower the line, designated a numbered instruction. It was clumsier than the new British method and less adaptable. The Republican navy inherited both this partial numerical system and the extremely formal tactical doctrine. For once, it appears, the British service was ahead in theory as well as practice.

On the outbreak of war in 1793 Howe, reappointed to command the

Channel Fleet, had issued a slightly amended version of his 1790 signal book, added an appendix of 'Additional Instructions' and constantly drilled his ships, focusing all the while on the problem of bringing and holding the French to close action. Strategically he aimed to entice the Brest fleet to sea by exercising an 'open' or distant blockade of the Brittany coast; tactically he had two novel plans: one, which had actually been used by the great Dutch admiral, de Ruyter, in 1672, was to form a fast advanced squadron to take station to windward and intercept and harass a part of the enemy in order to disrupt his formation and bring on a general action; the other, entirely new, was for each ship individually to steer through the enemy line and engage her opponent from the other side, thus breaking his line everywhere. This was not made absolutely clear in the instruction (number 34), which ran: 'when, having the weather gage of the enemy, the Admiral means to pass between the ships of the line for engaging them to leeward, or being to leeward, to pass between them for gaining the weather gage'. And, no doubt because of the extreme difficulty of the evolution against a disciplined opponent, he added a rider which further confused the object: 'NB – The different Captains and Commanders not being able to effect the specified intention in either case are at liberty to act as circumstances require.'[45]

He had sailed on his present cruise on 2 May, arriving off Ushant on the 5th, where his frigates reported about twenty-three of the line in the Goulet, the enclosed roads off Brest harbour, and ready to sail. So he steered out into the Atlantic, both to leave the door open for them and to seek the American grain convoy reported by agents in France and America. Failing to gain any intelligence of the convoy, he returned eastward, passing close by Villaret shortly after he emerged from the roads but denied a sight of him by thick weather. Off Ushant again on 19 May, he learnt from his frigates that the French fleet had sailed three days before. He steered west after them.

FOLLOWING INTELLIGENCE from merchantmen, he came up with the French fleet in the morning of 28 May some 350 miles west of Ushant. From his flagship, the 110-gun *Queen Charlotte*, they could be seen hull down over the southern horizon some 15 miles distant; the wind was in the south-south-west, giving them the weather gage. He set t'gallants and pressed into the wind on the starboard tack, stationing his advanced squadron of four fast 74s under Rear Admiral Sir Thomas Pasley in the *Bellerophon* to windward.

Villaret in *Le Montagne*, with Jeanbon at his elbow, also formed on the starboard tack, heading easterly, intent on holding the windward station and drawing the British away from the grain convoy somewhere in the west. The wind increased in squalls and backed southerly during the day, throwing up a heavy sea and forcing both fleets to shorten sail, despite which Howe tacked towards the French line so skilfully that by evening Pasley's advanced squadron had gained the wind of their rear and engaged. The captain of the last in the French line, the 110-gun *Révolutionnaire*, judging valour the better part, attempted to hold them off on his own and was crippled by successive opponents and forced to strike his colours; however, his final adversary, the *Audacious*, was too damaged to take possession during the night, and next morning the *Révolutionnaire* was saved by the appearance of Rear Admiral Nielly's squadron and taken under tow for home. The *Audacious* also parted from the fleet, eventually making Plymouth under jury rig.

The southerly wind held that day, the 29th, and Villaret, still to windward, maintained his easterly course close-hauled on the starboard tack. Howe formed in the same direction, instructing his ships to take station in line as most convenient without regard to their established positions, then tacked in succession, aiming to cut off the French rear and force a general action. Villaret countered by wearing in succession to a westerly course and succeeded in covering the threatened ships, whereupon, shortly after midday, Howe tacked again and made number 34 to signal his intention of breaking through the enemy line. However, his leading ships remained to leeward engaging each enemy as it went past on the opposite tack, and it was left to the *Queen Charlotte*, about tenth in the irregular formation, to press through a gap near the rear, followed by her next astern, Pasley's flagship *Bellerophon* and one other. All three then came round on the larboard tack – an indication that they had not suffered severely in masts and rigging as they broke through – to sail in the same direction as their opponents, engaging them from to windward. The leading British ships, meanwhile, sailing past the last of the French rear, also tacked and running back towards the enemy brought on just the confused mêlée Howe intended. When Villaret discerned through the drifting gunsmoke three of his embattled rear crippled and separating downwind, he wore round to their rescue, interposing between them and their opponents. In so doing he surrendered the weather gage. The seas were running high before a fresh wind and Howe, seeing several of his own ships damaged in masts and rigging, lay to to make repairs and regroup for the decisive action he intended to force next day.

Thus far Howe had dictated the action in masterly fashion from downwind against steep head seas, finally gaining the windward position of advantage. Villaret's performance with his far less practised fleet had been as good. He had lost one powerful three-decker in the night, and that day the 74-gun *Le Montagnard* failed to obey his last signal to wear, instead continuing westward and abandoning him. He had rescued another from the rear mêlée; another had been so shattered she had to be towed from the fleet by a frigate, but he had held his ships together and prevented Howe from pursuing the vital grain convoy.

Next day, 30 May, Rear Admiral Nielly joined him with three of his squadron – one had joined earlier – bringing the French fleet up to twenty-six of the line against twenty-five with Howe. Materially Villaret now had the advantage since his vessels were larger, class for class, better proportioned, carried more men and threw a greater weight of shot than their British counterparts. He could also expect his men's Republican fervour to count. But he had observed from the previous day's fighting that in seamanship and gun discipline his ships were at a severe disadvantage. It was not put to the test that day as fog closed down visibility, and the fog persisted long enough the following day, the 31st, to dissuade Howe from attacking.

Sunday 1 June – 13 *Prairial* in the Republican calendar – dawned fine and clear with a fresh breeze from the south. The opposing fleets lay within easy sight of each other, no more than five miles separating them, the French downwind, sunlight brightening their topsails. Howe, observing them form line on the larboard tack, heading westerly, gathered his fleet and bore down towards them on a north-westerly course, the best point of sailing with the wind on his quarter, sure at last he would gain the reward for his aggression and patience over the past days. By 7 that morning he was inside three miles, just beyond long gunshot, and he hauled round to a westerly course to parallel the enemy formation and dress his line. At 7.25, satisfied that all his ships were in station and aligned ahead and astern of the *Queen Charlotte*, he signalled the mode of attack, number 34: 'having the weather gage of the enemy, the Admiral means to pass between the ships of the line for engaging them to leeward', and he had a gun fired to draw it to attention as the hoist was broken out.[46] Yet the performance of several of his captains in the action of the 29th left him unsure how many would understand his purpose or have the resolution to carry it out, and he made a prediction to his first captain and chief adviser, Sir Roger Curtis, that they would take one French ship for every British ship that broke through the line.

In the meantime he had the signal flown for all hands to breakfast. Galley fires had been extinguished long since, and benches and mess tables together with cabin partitions and officers' furniture stowed in the holds. It was a cold meal of gruel and hard biscuit taken on deck between the timber carriages of the great guns whose muzzles had been run out through the open ports. The men were as confident of victory as Howe and his officers. After a century of warfare against the French and victorious propaganda spread especially in popular songs and ditties they were sure of their triumphant character as British seamen, considering themselves in the words of one observer 'at sea as rulers by birthright'.[47] Not all were British – a few were of other nationalities; most were very young; not all were fit – many suffered strains and ruptures caused by strenuous lifting and heaving combined with an unbalanced diet and vitamin deficiency; others had venereal diseases, others chronic catarrh or chest complaints caused by constant damp, wet hammocks and careless habits.

Some of those in ships which had sustained most casualties in the earlier engagements were no doubt apprehensive, but suppressed their fears. The general mood was elevated. Battle provided focus and relief from the monotony of cruising and constant drill. Kept in tight subordination, they could anticipate releasing the tensions of discipline and close confinement in the frenzy of action.[48] A proportion of those destined to survive the shot and showers of splinters about to bring death and mutilation between decks would have their minds permanently deranged by the horror and spend the rest of their days in asylums, yet in the heady mood of the morning this was unimaginable. Inured to hazard from an early age, careless of consequences in everything they did and with a fierce pride in the British seaman's reputation for courage, they showed, in the words of a fleet surgeon who knew them intimately, 'a degree of contempt for danger and death that is to be met nowhere else'.[49] These were the men on whom Great Britain and her seaborne trade and empire and her financial and political systems and bourgeois comforts and liberal values and culture ultimately depended. In the end all the constitutional theories and freedoms reduced to battle at sea and the unflinching spirit and internalized training of these young men and the resolution of their officers.

After breakfast drums beat to quarters. The guns' crews, bare-chested above loose-bottomed white duck or canvas trousers, and with gaily coloured or black silk scarves to bind around their ears as some protection from the stunning concussion of the great pieces they served, unhooked handspikes, rammers and sponges and worms from overhead beams and laid them to hand on decks being doused with sea water to prevent fire and spread with sand to soak up blood. Captains of guns checked the setting of flints in the firing locks, priming powder in the vent, and uncoiled their firing lanyards. The pieces were each loaded with two round shot or one round, one double-headed shot, the carronades on the upper deck with round and grape or canister shot filled with jagged metal pieces to spread and cut through rigging and exposed flesh at the close ranges anticipated. Midshipmen and lieutenants checked their sections as if at drill; presently ships' captains, resplendent in cocked hats, stooping somewhat to negotiate the low beams of the gun decks, hands on sword hilts, long blue cutaway coats trimmed with gold, white waistcoats, breeches and stockings, buckled shoes – in some cases more individualistic attire – accompanied by their first lieutenants with speaking trumpets and retinues of midshipmen aides, made their rounds, radiating purpose and confidence, throwing out encouraging phrases, reinforcing the air of vivid expectation.

Just before 8.30 Howe ordered the preparatory signal 36 for each ship independently to steer for and engage the ship opposed to her in the enemy line. Taken together with his previous number 34, this should have made his intention clear: each captain was to put his helm up, steer for his opposite number in the French line, and instead of rounding up and engaging from to windward in the conventional manner, continue on under his opponent's stern, then luff up to engage her from her lee side. Indeed in the 1799 Signal Book the wording of number 34 was to become: 'to break through the enemy's line in all parts where practicable.'[50] However, if the enemy maintained a close line and if their captains, realizing what was intended, made sail to close the gaps, the evolution was fraught with the danger of close-range raking fire, even collision or boarding. Several captains understood number 34 as permissive only; certainly the release clause at the end gave them liberty 'to act as circumstances require' if they could not fulfil the intention.[51] A few evidently did not understand the meaning or thought the signal superseded number 36, which they took as an order to close and engage from to windward in the time-honoured fashion. Several understood Howe's intention perfectly and resolved to hazard the attempt.

At 8.38 Howe had the preparatory flag above number 36 hauled down and a gun fired. In the quiet after the shot brief orders to bear up, slack the mizzen bowlines and lee braces and haul on the mizzen weather braces carried across the 300 yards or so between neighbouring ships. Quick seamen threw turns off the quarterdeck pins by reflex while teams of quartermasters heaved the great double steering wheels round; ropes creaked through tiller blocks below. High above topmen prepared to loose the t'gallants. As the mizzen canvas shivered, releasing the pressure aft, the straining head sails assisted the rudder in swinging ships' heads off the wind, and fleet line ahead was transformed into line of bearing, each vessel steering for a point some distance ahead of her opponent to allow for the way the close-hauled French line was making through the water. Captains, their first lieutenants and sailing masters leant against the heel of the quarterdeck or stepped up on gun carriages, the better to see over the hammock nettings the position of their consorts, eyes lifting to the stretched sails or the flagship's halyards, constantly checking the bearing of the enemy they were closing, but part of their mind filling with the scale and grandeur of the scene. 'I do not think there could have been a more noble sight', one lieutenant later recalled, 'than seeing twenty-five British line of battle ships intending to pass through the French line of twenty-six.'[52]

Bearing down in close formation at some five knots, bluff bows lifting to a heavy swell from the west, pushing out surges of lathered salt as they fell, bright sunlit and shadowed canvas straining in arcs above, it was a sight to stir the least reflective. 'Down we went under a crowd of sail,' Cuthbert Collingwood, flag captain of the 98-gun *Barfleur*, was to write afterwards, 'and in a manner that would have animated the coldest heart, and struck terror into the most intrepid enemy.'[53]

Howe, on the high poop of the *Queen Charlotte*, attended by Sir Roger Curtis, the junior captain, the sailing master, James Bowen, lieutenants and aides, told Sir Roger to have the signal for closer action prepared, adding, 'I only want that to be made in case of captains not doing their duty.' Then, turning to the others, he closed the small signal book he carried at all times in action.

'And now, gentlemen, no more book, no more signals! I look to you to do the duty of the *Queen Charlotte* in engaging the French admiral. I do

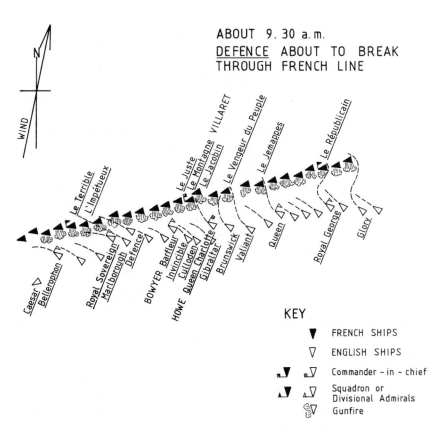

Battle diagram 1   The Glorious First of June, 1794

not wish the ships to be bilge and bilge, but if you can lock the yardarms together the action will be the sooner decided.'[54]

Inevitably the line grew irregular as the ships which sailed better than their consorts or carried more sail advanced more rapidly, while other captains, attempting to dress by their flagship, backed one or other topsail. The van, including the fast 74s of the advanced squadron, was foremost in closing, led by Pasley's *Bellerophon*, second in the line but soon far nearer the enemy than the leading ship, the new and equally fleet *Caesar*, whose captain had incurred Howe's displeasure during the engagement of the 29th by holding back, and now aroused universal criticism for backing his topsails and lieing to outside gun range while the rest of the van closed. He was later to be dismissed his ship after a court martial. Fifth in the line was the flagship of the van squadron, the 100-gun *Royal Sovereign*, flying the flag of Vice Admiral Thomas Graves, Howe's second in command, and determined to brighten a reputation overshadowed by the indecisive result off Chesapeake Bay. After her came two more fast 74s, the second of which, *Defence*, commanded by James Gambier – 'Preaching Jemmy' to his men on account of his austere religious sentiments – was the only ship with both fore and main t'gallants set and was far in advance of all her consorts except the *Bellerophon*.

'Look at the *Defence*!' Howe exclaimed, studying the scene through a telescope, 'See how nobly she goes into action!' Soon afterwards, as the *Queen Charlotte* herself advanced beyond her close seconds at the centre of the centre squadron, he called for the pennants of these ships to be made together with number 67 – 'Make more sail'.[55] The 74-gun *Culloden*, two ahead of the flagship in the line, responded by setting both her fore course and fore topmast staysail and was soon pulling so much ahead of station she came up with her second ahead, Collingwood's *Barfleur*, flying the flag of Rear Admiral Bowyer, interposing between her and the enemy line. Her captain was hailed by Bowyer and told he was obstructing his line of fire, at which he had the fore course and main topsails backed.

It was about this time, 9.24 according to a signal log kept aboard the *Queen Charlotte*, that the leading French ships opened the action at something over half a mile with high-angle shots. The British did not respond immediately. It was Howe's custom during the approach to have his men lie down on the disengaged side of the deck to minimize casualties before reaching effective range. The balls flew overhead with sounds like tearing canvas, occasionally holing a sail or parting rigging or thudding on masts or spars, gouging splintered bites from the timber. Fire soon spread along the French line to the rear, smoke issuing from gun ports, shrouding the deep red of the hull paint and hiding the lower masts and rigging before shredding away downwind.

As the British line closed the more advanced ships began to reply, partly to obscure themselves with gunsmoke blowing down the range, while French captains, perceiving that the British intended to go through between their ships, eased off the wind and made sail to close gaps in the line. Howe, conning the *Queen Charlotte* himself, made more sail in response, setting the fore course and fore and main t'gallants, and had number 5 hoisted with a red pennant over it – the prepared signal to engage more closely – and shortly afterwards number 67 to all ships to make more sail. The flagship was by this time under fire from the second vessel astern of Villaret's *Montagne*. Her own guns remained silent, their crews lying on the larboard, unengaged side of the deck, tense with frustration.

With both lines pressing on sail and the French easing downwind, British captains attempting to break through faced difficult problems. Some found it impossible because the ship they were steering for was lasking off almost as fast, or the ship astern of her had closed the gap, others because a British consort had advanced into their track. French commanders were in a worse plight as in their efforts to counter the assault with their unpractised crews their line lost cohesion. Appropriately the first British ship to succeed in breaking the line was Gambier's *Defence*, foremost from the start. She passed astern of the seventh French ship, a 74, raking her as she went by, then rounded up to engage on her lee side. Her next ahead, *Marlborough*, cut through after her – at 9.55 by her log entry – astern of the sixth in the French line, *L'Impétueux*, also a 74, then luffed up and engaged from the lee berth. Meanwhile Graves' flagship, *Royal Sovereign*, ahead of the *Marlborough* in the line, engaged from close on the weather side.

The double assault rendered *L'Impétueux* unmanageable and she fell off the wind, crashing aboard the *Marlborough*'s larboard quarter, where her bowsprit was held over the quarterdeck in the mizzen shrouds. Unable to break free she was subjected to a devastating raking fire from carronades which cleared every soul from her upper deck. Some of the *Marlborough*'s men, caught up in the frenzy of battle, seized boarding cutlasses and tomahawks and leaped into her head rigging and over on to her foc's'le; but having gained the enemy decks, they were called back. Another French 74 from two astern of *L'Impétueux* had passed her to windward and was attempting to work into a raking position across the *Marlborough*'s bow. She was met with such a weight of shot she too became unmanageable and instead fell aboard *L'Impétueux* whose bowsprit had by now carried away. Shortly afterwards all her masts fell. The newcomer was then blown round by the wind against the *Marlborough*'s bow, where she met the same fate as her consort, her upper deck cleared of living men by grape and canister, her rigging severed, her masts cut down.

Ahead of these tangled hulks, the five leading French ships had been forced to leeward by Pasley's and Graves' flagships and two 74s between them in the line, while the *Caesar* remained at a distance to windward. Meanwhile, in the centre the battle reached a climax. As Howe had borne down under a press of sail towards the stern of *Le Montagne* through fire from the two ships in line astern, the commander of the first of these, the 80-gun *Le Jacobin*, had made sail to close the gap between him and his flagship. Almost at the same time Villaret backed topsails for the same purpose. As a result *Le Jacobin*, coming up rapidly on *Le Montagne*, had to sheer off downwind, taking up the very position under Villaret's lee quarter which Howe was intending to occupy. Nevertheless, after a moment's doubt Howe determined to press on to set the example, if necessary running *Le Jacobin* aboard. The sailing master, Bowen, called out firmly, 'That's right, my Lord! The *Charlotte* will make room for herself!'[56]

With the French flagship making little way through the water, Howe swept close under her stern, so close it is said that the *Queen Charlotte*'s rigging brushed *Le Montagne*'s great white ensign with the tricolour in the upper corner. The situation was so tense no one remembered to give the gun decks the order to fire, but the larboard guns' crews did so as their pieces bore, the balls smashing through the stern windows, splintering the elaborate carvings of the galleries, raking the French decks from end to end, scything limbs and men; Villaret's flag captain fell, mortally wounded.

Howe called to Bowen to starboard the helm to round up under the enemy's lee. Bowen replied that that would take them aboard her second – *Le Jacobin*.

'What's that to you, sir!' Howe said sharply.

Bowen gave the order to the quartermasters, muttering audibly, 'Damn my eyes if *I* care if *you* don't! I'll go near enough to singe some of our whiskers!'

'That's a fine fellow!' Howe said to Sir Roger Curtis.

Le Jacobin's commander, seeing the British flagship bearing down on him, paid off the wind, opening a narrow space into which the *Queen Charlotte* swept, her jib-boom almost touching *Le Jacobin*'s mizzen shrouds before she came round. At the same time the *Charlotte*'s fore topmast, whose rigging had been cut during the approach, crashed over the side. She still carried such a press of sail that the sills of the lower gun ports on the starboard side were practically level with the sea; despite which their lids were hauled up one by one as the ship rounded up and the heavy pieces were fired point blank into *Le Jacobin*'s hull. Waves burst in cold green, washing the sand from the deck, and the guns' crews, wading through the tide, lowered the lids before sponging and reloading with flexible rope-handled rammers. Meanwhile as the ship surged up in the lee of *Le Montagne* leaving little space between their yardarms, the larboard guns poured in another murderous broadside.

The ship immediately astern of the *Queen Charlotte* in the line of battle, the 74-gun *Brunswick*, was commanded by one of Howe's favourites, John Harvey. Resolved to vindicate the trust reposed in him by his chief, Harvey steered to break the line two ships astern of *Le Jacobin*. However, the next astern, the 74-gun *Vengeur du Peuple* under Captain Jean-François Renaudin, sailed up to close the gap. Harvey held on, forcing him to bear away, but Renaudin left it so late his fore shrouds and chains hooked the *Brunswick*'s starboard anchor and the two ships, locking together, swung against one another, yardarm to yardarm. The duel that erupted between them was the closest of the day. Where the hulls ground together in the swell neither side's lower deck crews were able to raise the port lids; they simply fired through closed ports directly into the enemy timbers less than a cannon's length away. Not a shot could miss. The British had the advantage of flexible rope sponges and rammers and, soon gaining an ascendancy, began alternately elevating and depressing their pieces to extreme angles, firing up through the deck beams, then down into the hold timbers, tearing breaches in the French ship's structure.

Meanwhile, next astern in the British line, the 74-gun *Valiant* had cut through the gap left by Renaudin when closing up for the *Brunswick*; and two astern of her the 90-gun *Queen*, flying the flag of Rear Admiral Gardner, also went through, rounding up in the lee of the 80-gun *Le Jemappes*. Attempting to escape Gardner's broadsides, *Jemappes* only succeeded in closing the range to 'pistol shot', perhaps 50 yards; while towards the rear the 110-gun *Royal George*, flying the flag of Admiral Sir

Alexander Hood, younger brother of Lord Hood, broke through under the stern of Rear Admiral Nielly's flagship, the 110-gun *Le Républicain*, and engaged close in her lee.

What had been the French line was now in utter confusion. Howe had achieved by intent what had been granted Rodney at the Saints by the vagaries of the wind. Fighting in a formal line – as developed particularly by the English in the seventeenth century in order to dictate a stand-off battle and utilize advantages over the Dutch in weight of shot – had been replaced with mêlée by design to hold French ships to close action in the confidence that British seamanship and gun discipline would prevail. As they did now in short time.

Jeanbon, on the quarterdeck of *Le Montagne*, found the engagement more confused and horrible than he could have imagined. About him Villaret's officers and aides were cut down as suddenly and indiscriminately as the men at the guns; the deck became slippery with blood. Whirling clouds of gunsmoke isolated them for long periods from sight of their consorts, rendering his special signals for the dismissal and replacement of commanding officers redundant; indeed the frigate captains were to report afterwards that the flagship was invisible for two hours. His own recorded impression was of a battle fought 'at the range of a pistol shot with unheard-of ferocity'.[57]

Villaret reported maintaining the duel with Howe's flagship for an hour.[58] However, it appears from the *Queen Charlotte*'s log that *Le Montagne* made sail and went ahead after Howe ranged up with him, the British flagship prevented from following by the loss of her fore topmast and a ball through the leading edge of the main topsail which destroyed its motive power. The French flagship's place was taken by a 74 from the line astern, which was soon dismasted by the *Charlotte*'s tremendous broadsides.

Villaret passed on to the mêlées in the van. Finding the *Marlborough* attempting to back clear of the hulks she had dismasted, he came up under her stern, backed his main topsail and opened a raking fire which completed the destruction of the British 74's rigging and brought her masts crashing over the side. Her captain was wounded in the hail of shot and helped below to the surgeon; the first lieutenant, taking command, had a Union Jack flown from the spritsail yard and a St George's flag nailed to the stump of the mainmast. He soon had this removed as the predominant colour, white, made it appear like a French ensign, and it attracted British fire. Seeing some ships from the French rear sailing towards him, he passed orders to the guns' crews to lie down at their quarters, receive the enemy fire, then up and return it. They did this with much success, losing only two more men as the French passed to leeward.

Near by, Gambier's *Defence* had her mainmast shot down as she engaged these ships. She had previously lost her mizzen, but though unmanageable with her helm lashed a-lee she fought her batteries vigorously as the enemy passed by. The scene on the lower gun deck was described by a young midshipman, William Dillon: the confined space was 'at times so completely filled with smoke that we could scarcely distinguish each other, and the guns were so heated that, when fired, they nearly kicked the upper deck beams'. One reason for the dense smoke was that British guns' crews, with their flexible sponges and rammers, lowered the port lids when the guns had jumped inboard after firing before they began reloading. Some French ships, by contrast, appeared to be using an archaic and clumsy system of sponging and loading from outside the hull. Dillon, peering through an open gun port at one enemy, was astonished to see a man 'riding upon a lower deck gun, loading it. He was stripped from the waist upwards, and had we been sufficiently near, our marines could have picked him off with their muskets.'[59]

Dillon spoke French and in earlier conversations with French officers taken from two corvettes captured before the action he had heard them express astonishment both at the 'cleanliness and good order of the *Defence*' and at the rapidity with which the British ships were tacked, often within five minutes, against a quarter of an hour in their own service; they had let slip apprehensions about Villaret's chances when engaged by this British fleet. As for cleanliness, the French Revolutionary warships had greater difficulties since they carried livestock aboard sufficient to feed the whole ship's company, whereas the British only carried a small stock of animals confined beneath the foc's'le for the captain, officers and the sick. Nonetheless, the Frenchmen's comments on the backwardness of their service as compared with the British precisely echoed Admiral de Grasse's comments aboard Rodney's flagship twelve years earlier.

The result of the encounter fully bore them out. After the last of the stragglers from the French rear had passed and borne away downwind, where they were rallied by Villaret in line on the starboard tack, and the guns had fallen silent and the smoke dispersed, Dillon came up to the quarterdeck – his buckled shoes 'covered with blood . . . face and hands smutched with powder and blood' – and looking out at the ocean about

them counted fourteen of the line without a mast or with only one standing, rolling heavily among the debris; all were French except for the
Marlborough and *Defence*. In the British fleet, now re-forming line ahead
and astern of Howe's flagship, he saw eighteen still with t'gallant yards
across, suggesting they were fit to resume the fight. Everyone aboard the
Defence assumed they would.

Howe was sixty-nine years old. He had been under constant pressure
for five days, his only rests snatched in an armchair wrapped in a greatcoat, and now he had won he was completely played out. He could
barely keep his balance on deck. A midshipman caught him and saved
him from a tumble when the flagship gave a heavier than usual roll; after
which he went below to sleep. It was left to Sir Roger Curtis to direct the
fleet. Curtis had already shown extreme caution by advising against
bearing down to the aid of Gardner's *Queen*, which had lost her mizzen
mast and was falling off downwind towards Villaret's reconstituted line.
He had been overruled as a result of Bowen's insistence that the *Charlotte*,
despite the damage aloft, would still steer. But now he judged that any
attempt to renew the action with much of the fleet, like the flagship,
damaged aloft would give Villaret the chance to turn the tables on them.
He contented himself with bringing the line round together to the starboard tack to conform with ten French ships which had formed about
Le Montagne some three miles downwind, and detailed ships to secure the
dismasted French prizes.

Several of the French escaped nonetheless, either setting spritsails to
carry them downwind or towed off by frigates and corvettes. Seven were
left in British hands, fulfilling Howe's prophecy that as many would be
taken as British ships broke the line. Of these one was sinking. The hull
of the *Vengeur du Peuple* had been holed and shattered during her bilge to
bilge contest with the *Brunswick*. Afterwards the *Ramillies*, four astern in
the line and commanded by Henry, brother of John Harvey of the
Brunswick, had completed her destruction. She was filling fast. Boats from
nearby British ships were taking off survivors, but when she capsized and
sank later that afternoon she left over 100 men crying out and drowning
amongst the wreckage.

The six other prizes were found to be in as filthy a condition as the
prisoners aboard the *Defence* had implied. It was also discovered that for
making up their powder cartridges the French gunners used music sheets
stolen from cathedrals or finely illuminated genealogical tables belonging to the highest noble families.[60]

Despite the failure to take all the disabled French ships or follow up the triumphant opening, the battle, soon christened 'the Glorious First of June', was the most complete victory over a materially equal – in fact superior – fleet achieved by the Royal Navy to that date. It had been won within an hour of the first British ships forcing close action. Long before noon Villaret had been bearing away to gather survivors of his broken line downwind. Isolated skirmishes continued and Renaudin of the *Vengeur* did not haul down his colours until nearly 2 p.m. His opponent, John Harvey, was at that time recovering from having his arm removed by the surgeon after suffering three wounds early on. He was to die a month later of complications. But the action had been decided before 11.30 by the devastating weight of shot thrown horizontally by the British guns' crews into the enemy gun decks. There were more killed and wounded in the seven captured French ships than in the entire British fleet, some 1,270 against 1,156; in all, the French suffered over 2,500 casualties – excluding 2,300 taken prisoner and about 300 who went down with the *Vengeur*.

However, it was Howe's tactics which had brought the British gunners to close quarters and allowed them to inflict such death and destruction. A few days later Collingwood wrote that as seamen they had known of Howe's great professional abilities, but he had surpassed all opinion that day: 'The proceedings of the 1st June were like magic, and could only be effected by skill like his.'[61]

The sailors were of the same opinion. Some time after the battle and after repairs to the damaged spars and rigging, a deputation of the *Queen Charlotte*'s petty officers and seamen asked Bowen if they might congratulate Howe and thank him for leading them so gloriously into battle. Howe received them on the quarterdeck. Visibly moved at their address, his eyes glistened with moisture as he doffed his cocked hat to reply, 'No, no, I thank *you*; it is *you* my brave lads – it is you, not I, that have conquered.'

'The glorious First of June' set a standard in British naval ascendancy that was to endure throughout the years of the French Revolutionary and Napoleonic wars. For all that, Villaret had achieved everything that could have been expected of him. He had diverted Howe from the grain convoy, and his miscellaneous commanders and crews, with a high proportion of barely trained landsmen among them, had inflicted sufficient damage on the British ships to persuade Howe to sail for home with his six prizes rather than pursue him or continue searching for the convoy.

Villaret, on his way home off Ushant, faced off a British squadron of nine of the line and made Brest Roads safely on 11 June. The convoy arrived the following day, enabling Jeanbon to claim that, despite the military reverse, they had achieved a great political victory. They had indeed saved large areas of France from certain famine.

On the other hand, the battle provided a much needed propaganda coup for the British government and a great boost to British morale. In Portsmouth, the toast was 'May the French ever know Howe to be master of the sea!'

As for Howe, he wrote several years later:

> Some occasions in our profession . . . will justify, if not require, more hazard to be ventured than can systematically be defended . . . But admitting the risk of mutual injury to be as great, as I believe many of the officers supposed, the times or peculiar circumstances of the country at that period . . . called loudly, in my opinion, for some conclusive issue of the contest.[62]

4

St Vincent, 1797

HOWE HAD SHOWN the way. Within a few years Nelson would follow and lift naval warfare to greater heights of daring and destructiveness. For the moment, in July 1794, he was still captain of the 64-gun *Agamemnon* under Lord Hood, and feeling undervalued. Hood had embarked on a campaign to seize the island of Corsica from the French in order to establish an advanced base from which to watch Toulon, once again the French Mediterranean fleet base. Nelson had played a vital role, first in command of a detached blockading squadron preventing French arms and supplies reaching the island, more recently as Hood's chief adviser and commander at the siege of the port of Bastia, which had fallen on 23 May. Yet Hood referred to him in his despatch only as directing the seamen landing guns and stores. 'I, only I, am without reward,' Nelson lamented to his uncle, William Suckling. 'Nothing but my anxious endeavour to serve my Country makes me bear up against it; but I sometimes am ready to give all up.'[1]

Despite the oversight in his official despatch, Hood's private congratulations were warm, and he retained absolute confidence in Nelson whom he next entrusted with the naval command of combined operations against the port of Calvi on the north-west corner of the island closest to the coast of France. Nelson's spirits lifted, as always when actively employed. 'I am very busy,' he wrote to his wife, 'yet I own I am in all my glory. Except with you, I would not be anywhere but where I am, for the world.' He could not help adding, 'I am well aware that my poor services will not be noticed: I have no interest [i.e. patronage]; but however services may be received, it is not right in an Officer to slacken his zeal for his Country.'[2] Nor was it in his character.

It was in the morning of 12 July while ashore with the batteries facing the walls of Calvi that he received the first of the wounds that would mark him for life. An enemy shot struck the parapet of sandbags before him and, ricocheting close by his head, drove sand, stones and splinters into his face and chest. Among the lacerations he received was a deep cut in his right brow which penetrated the eyelid and eyeball. He passed it off as 'a little hurt' and returned to duty next day, but he was never to see from his right eye again.

Calvi capitulated in August and Corsica was annexed to the British Crown. In the autumn Hood went home, to be succeeded by Vice Admiral William Hotham; and it was under him the following March – 1795 – that Nelson next found a chance to distinguish himself. The Toulon fleet of fifteen of the line had been ordered out to engage the British fleet and clear the way for an expeditionary force to retake Corsica. Hotham sailed to meet the French with fourteen of the line, coming up with them in the Gulf of Genoa. Although Jeanbon Saint-André had been sent to re-establish discipline at Toulon after his return from Brest the previous July, the French officers were disinclined to engage and contented themselves with holding the weather gage. Next morning, the 13th, Hotham decided to give his captains the utmost latitude to close in order to bring on a general action, and he put out the signal to chase. The wind was in the south-west and squalling. Nelson in the *Agamemnon* was in the leading division to westward of the main body of the fleet and was soon working his way to windward of all his consorts except a frigate, *Inconstant*, when the third ship from the French rear, the 80-gun *Ça Ira*, ran aboard her next ahead, carrying away her own fore and main topmasts, which fell over her lee side, dragging in the water and slowing her.

The *Inconstant* closed as the *Ça Ira* fell off to leeward, and opened fire, but was driven off by the French liner's broadsides. Nelson, who had just had seven live bullocks – acquired out of concern for the health of his men – hove overboard, was far enough to windward to weather the cripple by this time. However, she was now supported close off her weather bow by the 120-gun *Sans Culotte* and a 74. Since Nelson was far in advance of the rest of his division he could not expect support, and he steered into the *Ça Ira*'s wake, intending to come up close under her stern, or as he put it 'touch her stern', before opening his broadside to rake. Long before this, the French ship, now under tow by a frigate and making reasonable progress, began firing from her stern chasers with such accuracy that scarcely a shot missed. With the prospect of his masts and rigging being crippled before he could fetch her close, Nelson bore up while still 100 yards distant, turning his starboard side to the enemy, and opened fire with his main batteries. Directly all guns had fired he had the helm put down, the mizzen yards braced up and stood after her again in her wake until he had made up the lost distance, when he again bore away to give her a raking broadside before following once more, repeating the manoeuvre time after time.

After some two hours of this, shortly before one in the afternoon, the *Ça Ira*'s towing frigate went about, assisting the battleship round with her, and Nelson, holding his course towards them, passed very close on the opposite tack, exchanging broadsides. Fortunately for the Agamemnons the French guns had been laid with too much elevation and nearly all the shot flew harmlessly overhead. Immediately he had passed, Nelson tacked, keeping the enemy under fire from his stern chasers, then the starboard batteries as the *Agamemnon* came round, the hands working the ship with as much exactness, he reported afterwards, as if she had been turning in to Spithead. By this time the *Sans Culotte* and other ships from the French rear had also come about to the rescue of their consort, as a result of which Hotham made the recall signal. Nelson obeyed promptly.

It was a remarkable episode. The little *Agamemnon* was fast and handy; Nelson had reported on her to his wife earlier in the year as 'the finest Ship I ever sailed in'.[3] It is nonetheless puzzling that none of the 74s of the van division had been able to work up to his support during the two hours of his lone sortie. The tactical results were not in doubt: he had damaged more of the *Ça Ira*'s masts and spars, inflicted 110 casualties against a mere seven in the *Agamemnon*, and most importantly prevented her hands from repairing the damage sustained in the collision.

As a result she remained crippled during the night, and although taken in tow by a 74, sagged so far to leeward of her fleet that Hotham was able to cut the two ships off next morning. The French line wore to their support bringing on a brief engagement, but retired after both the *Ça Ira* and the ship towing her had been forced to strike their colours. Nelson immediately went aboard Hotham's flagship and proposed pursuing the enemy, now reduced by accident and battle loss to eleven of the line. Hotham, evidently satisfied that he had frustrated the French, replied: 'We must be contented, we have done very well.' Nelson could do no more. Privately he was exasperated: 'Had we taken ten sail and allowed the eleventh to escape, when it had been possible to have got at her, I could never have called it well done,'[4] he wrote; and in another letter, 'Sure I am, had I commanded our Fleet on the 14th, that either the whole French Fleet would have graced my triumph, or I should have been in a confounded scrape.'[5]

In July Hotham had a second encounter with the French fleet off the coast near Toulon. He now had twenty-three of the line against seventeen French, and in the chase that ensued the rear French ship was taken, although the main body escaped in light and fluky winds. Once again the *Agamemnon* was well to the fore in the action; and again Nelson was highly critical in private of Hotham, who had started the day with formal manoeuvring. One of Nelson's most perceptive biographers, the nineteenth-century US naval historian, A. T. Mahan, a professional sea officer, suggested that this lost opportunity may have inspired the opening sentence of Nelson's celebrated order before the battle of Trafalgar:

> Thinking it almost impossible to bring a fleet of forty sail of the line into a line of battle in variable winds, thick weather and other circumstances . . . without such a loss of time that the opportunity would probably be lost of bringing the enemy to battle in such a manner as to make the business decisive, I have therefore made up my mind . . .[6]

Nelson was next ordered on detached service with a squadron of eight frigates to cooperate with the southern Austrian army which was due to invade France along the Riviera coast. His task was to prevent supplies from reaching the opposing French forces by sea. However, he also had instructions originating in London and circulated by Hotham not to offend neutrals. He resolved the conflict by asking the British Minister at Genoa for an assurance that unless all neutral shipping were stopped the Austrian campaign would fail. When the Minister confirmed this in writing, Nelson issued orders to his captains to let nothing pass. Not for the first time he was, as he put it, 'acting not only without the orders of my commander-in-chief, but in some measure contrary to them'. There is no doubt that, being Nelson, he relished the situation, as he enjoyed the 'consciousness that I am doing what is right and proper for the service of our King and Country'.[7]

*

By THIS time, summer 1795, the French Revolution had undergone another profound change. Robespierre had fallen the previous July, soon after conducting his fantastic Festival of the Supreme Being. In a sense his undoing had been a logical result of the success of the campaign to save the Republic. The prolific arms production and mass army achieved by conscripting so many civilians to the war effort – together with radical reforms in tactics, artillery control and staff work in the years preceding the Revolution – had allowed the army in the north to gain decisive victory over the main Austrian army in Belgium on 26 June 1794,[8] and opened the way to Brussels, which had fallen on 8 July. With the Republic no longer in imminent peril and in the ascendant over its chief continental enemy, the rigid controls imposed by the Committee of Public Safety and the terror that enforced them had begun to seem inappropriate, and Robespierre and his cabal to appear as tyrants. Yet the number of executions was rising as members of the ruling Committee sought to preserve themselves from enemies raised during the year of sacrifice. The surge in bloodletting further increased fear and faction, and a massive programme of expropriation of large estates outlined by Robespierre and his fellow ideologue Louis de Saint-Just alarmed property owners, including the small proprietors who had gained from the sale of church and émigré lands. On 26 July the majority in the National Convention turned against Robespierre; on the evening of the 27th (9 *Thermidor*) he and his close allies were arrested, and on the following day taken without trial to the guillotine on the Place de la Révolution – now the Place de la Concorde – where so many of their opponents had met their end, and to the cheers of the crowd gathered to watch, quickly despatched.

More 'Robespierrists' and radical members of the Paris Commune were guillotined in succeeding days, and some 3,500 'suspects' released from prison, among them the captains of *Le Montagnard* and *Le Jacobin*, whom Jeanbon had sent to face the Revolutionary Tribunal in Paris, the first for deserting the fleet on 29 May, the second for permitting Howe to break through the line on 1 June.[9] The reaction against state violence and 'puritanism' led to abandonment of economic controls and the apparatus of terror and was accompanied by a resurgence of royalist feeling in Paris and the regions; royalist revolts broke out again in their old strongholds in the south and west of the country, whole areas of which reverted to anarchic forms of civil war. Meanwhile the ending of price controls combined with continued expenditure on armaments led to further food price rises, reimposing on the poor the miseries of the worst days before the Revolution, inciting riots.

The great trading ports and industrial cities had already been ruined by the official terrorist purges, price controls on goods, and not least by the British naval blockade around the coast from the Channel to the Mediterranean, which isolated them from overseas supplies and markets. Of course, individuals had gained from the Revolution: industrialists supplying armaments, provisions and uniforms to the army and navy, government contractors and financiers, the inevitable wartime speculators and those who had bought land and property seized from the Church and émigré nobles. But for the rural and urban poor, for widows and single women who had lost their menfolk, for the country as a whole, now cruelly divided by ideological schism so deep it would persist for centuries, with its most dynamic trading cities hopelessly retarded by comparison with the rival across the English Channel, and with its finances in worse state than those of the late monarchy, the Revolution had proved an unmitigated disaster. The legislators of the National Convention were left to debate yet another new constitution while attempting to suppress civil unrest, preserve property, protect themselves from a Bourbon restoration which would cost many their lives as regicides, and prosecute the war. This last was the key, for conquest was the surest way to restore state finances. In a cosmic demonstration of the soundness of Burke's assessment of the limitations of human character and reason, a Revolution intended to bring forth a new moral society had succeeded only in reasserting traditional warrior imperatives.

The first and obvious target was the United Provinces. As noted, the republic had been undermined by years of revolutionary agitation by 'Patriot' societies and French agents of subversion, and when the rivers forming the defensive moat froze over in January 1795 the French army marched in. Advance propaganda and dissatisfaction with an Orange regime imposed with British money and Prussian bayonets leant much of the invasion an air of liberation. The French entered towns already decked out with tricolours and revolutionary posters, to be greeted by welcoming crowds; a British observer likened the mood to a carnival. British forces retreated hastily, to be evacuated from Bremen; William V fled with his family and court to England.

The National Convention had achieved almost peaceably what the Bourbons had failed to gain by war: control of the trading and financial resources and navy of the merchant republic – although, of course, these assets had depreciated since the Dutch republic had been surpassed by Britain. Renamed the Batavian Republic by the 'Patriot' revolutionary committees whom the French supported in the wake of occupation, the former leading maritime power of Europe became a satellite of Revolutionary France, and in May 1795 declared war on Great Britain. Despite this she was required by the Paris government to pay a war indemnity of 100 million guilders – nearly £9 million – and cede Flanders and three small eastern states.[10] Giving up Flanders meant renouncing the historic restrictions imposed on trade on the river Schelde, and thus on Antwerp, as a result of which Amsterdam had gained its commercial primacy.

The loss to the Allies of the whole of the Netherlands, north and south, had much to do with the failure of Friedrich Wilhelm II of Prussia to honour an agreement to send 62,000 troops to the region. The British government had paid over £1 million and the Dutch government rather less for these men, but Friedrich had been too distracted by a Polish uprising to risk his troops in Flanders. In April 1795 he dropped out of the Allied Coalition altogether.[11] In July Spain, too, made peace with Revolutionary France, leaving only Great Britain and Austria to continue the struggle to contain her.

The British government reacted swiftly to the hostility of the new Dutch republic. Before the formal declaration of war two squadrons had sailed with 6,600 troops to seize the Dutch colony at the Cape of Good Hope. The security of the British East India Company's route to India had been an anxiety for years. During the previous American war the directors of the company, regarding the Cape, with reason, as the 'Gibraltar of India', had stressed that whoever, Britain or France, held the Cape, 'the same may govern India'.[12] In 1787 when it had seemed the Dutch 'Patriots' would seek French aid to overthrow William V, Pitt had sent instructions to India that in the event of a rupture with France, an immediate attack was to be launched on the Dutch colony in Ceylon – whose splendid harbour at Trincomalee provided the only secure refitting base on the eastern coast of the subcontinent – while an expedition would be sent from England to seize the Cape.

Both these projects were now executed. The Cape fell to the British force in September; Trincomalee and all other Dutch posts in Ceylon and southern India were in British hands by early the following year, 1796. Dutch colonies in the Indonesian islands and the West Indies were similarly mopped up. In England, William V had been persuaded to sign an order addressed to all Dutch colonial governors instructing them not to resist the British but to hand over their forts, harbours and ships. The governors of Malacca, Amboina and west Sumatra complied; other colonies, split between 'Patriot' and 'Orangist' factions,[13] were soon overcome. Hence the immediate result of the 'Patriot' alliance with France was the devastation of Dutch colonies, trade, shipping and shipbuilding, the bankrupting of the ailing Dutch East India Company and accelerated decline in Dutch industry and the numbers and economic well-being of the urban population.

Since French trading ports and associated industries had already suffered in the same way and the main French West Indian sugar islands, Martinique and Guadeloupe, had been seized in 1794 – although Guadeloupe had been retaken and was to become over the following years a particularly aggravating privateer outpost against British and American shipping – it is clear that the war had settled into the classic shape of a maritime-trading versus territorial-acquisitive contest.

In internal policies, Pitt's government had had to make further responses to the revolutionary emissions from Paris. The Police Act of 1792 and the Alien Act of 1793 which suspended habeas corpus for foreigners, have been mentioned. In spring 1794 government informers infiltrated the London Corresponding Society and produced evidence sufficient to have its leaders arrested for sedition, upon which Pitt had habeas corpus suspended for all British subjects. The removal of this bedrock of English liberties guaranteeing individuals against illegal imprisonment indicates the extent of government alarm.[14] However, the grim response snuffed out any threat of revolution. Corresponding societies were allowed to continue as safety valves for the expression of dissatisfaction but their activities were restricted by a Seditious Meetings Act and they were monitored by Magistrates' or Alien Office agents.

In his war strategy Pitt continued to act in decidedly maritime character, as the seizures of overseas bases and trading posts indicates. In May 1795 a loan to Austria of £4.6 million was raised on the London market to enable the emperor to maintain his armies, and preparations were finalized for landing an émigré force on the Atlantic coast of Brittany to operate with royalists in the region – while in the Channel Islands Captain Sir Sidney Smith pretended to set up a base for the expedition and carried out other feints which convinced the Paris government that the anticipated landing would take place in Normandy.[15] Meanwhile, financial support for the counter-revolutionary groups within France had been stepped up. A new Superintendent of the Alien Office, William Wickham, member by marriage of a powerful Anglo-Swiss banking family, had established residence at Berne in Switzerland, from where he ran communications and intelligence networks and dispersed the increasingly large sums of Secret Service money to Paris and from thence to the principal royalist centres, Lyons, Bordeaux, Nantes, Vannes and the Brittany and Channel ports. Further intelligence and communications lines passed through the commanders of the cruiser squadrons operating round the coasts, from Sir Sidney Smith in the Channel to Nelson in the Mediterranean.[16] The grand plan conveyed through these conduits was for the Austrian attack in the south and the émigré landings in Brittany to trigger royalist risings in Paris and the regions. Great reliance was placed on dissident or mercenary French Republican generals in British pay.

On 17 June 1795, the expeditionary force of 3,500 émigré troops – diluted with French prisoners of war to make up numbers – together with eighty noble volunteers 'of the best blood in France',[17] sailed under escort for Quiberon, covered by the Channel Fleet under Alexander Hood, raised to the peerage as Viscount Bridport for breaking the line after Howe at the Glorious First of June. Although Sidney Smith's prior deceptions had entirely misled the French about the likely destination of the expedition, the Brest fleet under Villaret had come out after another British squadron and was off Belle-Île to seaward of the Quiberon peninsula as the expedition arrived there. The political *représentant* with Villaret, apparently mistaking the transports for the British fleet, ordered retirement to Brest, in the course of which Bridport, alerted by the escort commander, intercepted them off the Île de Groix and engaged, but like Hotham in the Mediterranean with such caution that only three of the line were taken. Villaret and the bulk of his fleet escaped with heavy damage into Lorient.

The émigré force was put ashore a few days later in Carnac Bay at the base of the Quiberon peninsula without opposition. Breton royalists known as Chouans had previously taken Vannes and success was so complete that the British government hurriedly set about raising a far larger expedition to exploit the beachhead. The initial advantage was soon lost; over-cautious leadership brought about by splits between 'Legitimists' anticipating a complete return to the *ancien régime* and 'Constitutionalists' wanting a limited monarchy on the English model, together with difficulties in combining effectively with the Chouan irregulars,[18] allowed the

Republican general Lazare Hoche time to bring his troops down from
the north and retake Vannes; finally the French prisoners of war enlisted
with the émigrés delivered up the base fort on the peninsula to the
Republicans and the entire expedition was routed, survivors only saved
by the ships' boats.

The anticipated uprisings in Paris and elsewhere stalled on similar factional divisions. These had been exacerbated in early July by news of the
death in prison of Louis XVI's ten-year-old son. An inquest determined
the cause as scrofula, or 'the king's evil', known now as tuberculosis of the
lymph gland. 'Constitutionalists', including powerful anti-Republican
generals, had looked forward to having the boy crowned as a constitutional monarch, Louis XVII. Instead his death had provoked Louis XVI's
younger brother, the Comte de Provence, who was unsure of support
from the British or Austrians, to rush out a *Déclaration* proclaiming himself
Louis XVIII of France, pledging a return to the old order and promising
no mercy for those who had murdered his brother. This was worse than
a provocation to the Constitutionalists, who were not in any case prepared to see the social changes of the Revolution reversed. To those many
in and outside the National Convention who had supported or taken part
in the trial and execution of Louis XVI it represented a contingent death
sentence, thus turning many royalists, including the most influential
figures, into even more committed opponents of the 'legitimist' cause;
their lives depended on Louis XVIII not succeeding.

Louis' *Déclaration* might be seen as a turning point when the hopes
entertained by so many within France of closing the Revolution with a
restoration of the monarchy were shattered.[19] Single individuals can
scarcely bear such historical responsibility. Like his elder brother, Louis
XVI in 1789–90, he and the courtiers who surrounded him were repos-
itories of centuries of tradition, culture and privilege at the opposite pole
to the ideas introduced by the revolutionaries. And while there was more
than sufficient despair and revulsion in France after the terror to raise
dreams of a return to remembered stability, there was also a ferment of
lost ideals, altered stations, personal ambitions, provincial jealousies
which had resulted in political fragmentation, nowhere more than in the
royalist groupings within and outside the country. It was these that prevented a restoration; for who would be restored? And it was knowledge
of the schisms that had made the British government wary of sending
substantial forces to aid the Chouans at an earlier stage when it might
have been possible to overthrow the Republic. Yet this was surely at the

margin of consideration; concentration on overseas conquest at the expense of aiding counter-revolution was built in to the commercial-maritime culture of the nation.

Despite the setbacks, Pitt and his Foreign Secretary persevered with efforts to subvert France from within. William Wickham in Switzerland continued to deploy large sums to buy Republican generals, troop commanders and police officials in the Paris region and support his many royalist clients. While paying lip-service to a restoration of Louis XVIII, Wickham's aim was rather to unite all the discordant groups under British patronage.[20] Further funds passed through Sidney Smith's Channel Island network and other cruiser squadrons off the French coast. The escort commander of the expedition to Quiberon, Commodore Sir John Borlase Warren, seized islands in the bay as watering and supply bases and continued to support the Chouan leaders with money, ammunition and hopes that a large British expedition was being gathered to aid them.

It is interesting that on 28 August that year, 1795, Warren wrote to the First Lord of the Admiralty with a request that 'lemon juice with all anti-scorbutics, greens, beer and live stock may be sent us from Plymouth and Ireland',[21] for this was the date – within a day – that lemon juice was officially adopted in the Royal Navy as a cure for scurvy, as will appear.

The British-royalist plot came to a head in Paris in early October. The Revolution had now turned full circle. As a result of mass unemployment and destitution following the ending of price controls and subsequent reckless issues of *assignats*, which lost all value,[22] compounding a vicious, descending economic spiral, popular outrage was directed at the National Convention. Royalists harnessing the mood recruited some 30,000 Parisians, far outnumbering the troops available to the Convention, and once again it seemed the course of the Revolution would be dictated by a popular uprising, this time led by moderates and reactionaries.

Virtually at the last moment before the planned coup one of the leading figures in government and Chief of the Army of the Interior, Paul Barras, a prominent regicide whose life was forfeit if the restoration should succeed – who had nevertheless learned the details of the revolt by pretending support for the royalists[23] – offered command of the defence of the regime to Napoleon Bonaparte. He had first met him while a government *représentant* at the siege of Toulon. Since then the young artillery brigadier general had fallen into obscurity with the loss of his patrons, the Robespierre brothers, and he was even considering offering his services abroad. It took him little time to accept the opportunity presented, huge as the risks were, even less time to specify the solution to lack of troops: artillery. In the early hours of the morning of the uprising, 5 October – 13 *Vendémiaire*, Year IV – guns were hurried into position to command the bridges and approaches to the Convention, and that afternoon the advancing citizen-rebels were routed with grapeshot.

Barras and Bonaparte were made; and the following month the new constitution which had been drafted by the Convention was set up. It provided a tight executive of five *directeurs* with wider powers of appointing ministers and controlling the administration than had been granted the monarch in the constitution of 1791, and two legislative chambers, the Council of Ancients – aged forty years and upwards – and the Council of Five Hundred. The Directory, as the new regime was termed, has been characterized as 'bourgeois' government; certainly its two-tier electoral system admitted to the legislature only men of means and property. It was intended to stabilize politics after the turmoil of the past five years, protect those who had profited, and keep the lid on popular dissent. In its emphasis on the separation of powers – to prevent the tyranny of the previous unitary legislative-executive – it approximated to the early proposals for two-chamber government on the British model, with *directeurs* in place of a constitutional monarch. But the innocence of 1789 had been lost. And in practice the new regime marked the displacement of idealism by cynicism and luxury – epitomized in the way of life of the most influential and longest-serving *directeur*, Paul Barras. The twentieth century has seen odious regimes, but Duff Cooper was probably not exaggerating greatly when in 1932 he described the Directory as 'the most inefficient, corrupt and contemptible [government] with which any great country has ever been cursed'.[24]

In historical terms the most significant feature of the repulse of the royalists in *Vendémiaire* was the re-emergence of Bonaparte at the very centre of the French state. Appointed Commander of the Army of the Interior, he became military adviser to the *Directeurs*, hence privy to intelligence on all external and internal threats to the Republic. He was twenty-seven, small, thin, fired by ambition, radiating energy, with fine eyes and fine features as yet unsoftened by good living. 'What a head he has!' the artist David enthused after meeting him. 'It's pure, it's noble, it's as handsome as anything in antiquity!' Paul Barras' Creole mistress, Josephine, the widow Beauharnais, seasoned by many affairs in a sophisticated milieu Bonaparte had not known, immediately recognized him as a coming man; at all events, she enchanted him in short time and early the following year, 1796, he married her hours before departing Paris for Nice, where he had been appointed commander of the army facing the Austrians and their allies in Italy.

Here he came first to the attention of the world. Inspiring the ill-fed and demoralized troops with the prospect of 'honour, glory, wealth' from the conquest of rich Italian cities and provinces, he led them to a series of stunning victories over an enemy nearly twice their strength in men and guns. He had devised the initial plan of campaign much earlier for the Committee of Public Safety. It relied on surprise and the choice of ground to divide the enemy forces and defeat them in detail; in practice it called for exceptional speed of movement, which he achieved by urging his men to feats of endurance in day and night marches across the Ligurian hills west of Genoa. It also called for the particular qualities of energy, tenacity, eye for the ground and readiness to risk all that defined his military genius: any fool, he observed, could devise an obvious plan; the capacity of the strategist was shown by his power to carry it out.[25]

Over the next twelve months he carried out a series of victorious campaigns against superior forces that made him master of the whole of northern Italy and carried him to within a few days' march of Vienna, forcing the Austrian emperor to an armistice.[26] Greeted as a liberator by Italian intellectuals still sucking at the ideals of the Revolution, he created Italian republican regimes in the image of the French Directory, nominally independent but bound to France by treaty and martial severity; and like all conquerors before and after, he siphoned off the wealth of the Italian cities with forced levies in money and kind, excessive taxation and simple plunder. Art treasures were a particular target – since he had educated himself by reading widely in classical and Enlightenment literature. Convoy after armed wagon convoy crowded with paintings and sculptures was despatched to France. He revealed larger ambitions, confessing that his triumphs were not intended for the aggrandizement of the lawyers and Directory in Paris; nevertheless, the amount of tribute extracted from his Italian satellites would allow the French government to abandon its disastrous paper money and return to a metal currency.[27]

He was also instrumental in saving the Directory from the latest British-funded royalist coup, headed this time by General Jean-Charles Pichegru, former commander of the Army of the North during the Netherlands campaign. First he forced a written statement on pain of death from a royalist diplomat arrested in Trieste which implicated

Pichegru and fellow conspirators, and sent it with supporting evidence to Barras;[28] next he sent him a detachment of the army under one of his most dependable lieutenants, Pierre-Françoise Augereau, soldier son of a Parisian servant who had preserved the oaths and prejudices of a sans-culotte untainted by the sudden wealth acquired from plunder in Italy. On his arrival in Paris in early September – 18 *Fructidor* – 1797, vowing to kill the royalists, the leading conspirators including Pichegru were rounded up in a pre-emptive strike. They were later sentenced to deportation to a penal colony where life expectancy was so short it was termed 'the dry guillotine'.

Once again Bonaparte had preserved Barras and the constitution, but the balance of power had shifted massively in his direction. Moreover, having removed the Austrian emperor's hopes for a restoration in France he was able to force him out of the war on his own terms, which were signed at Campo Formio on 17 October that year, 1797. They included France's retention of the southern, hitherto Austrian Netherlands and – most important to Bonaparte – recognition of the satellite republics he had created in northern Italy from states formerly controlled by Austria. To gain this, he sacrificed the ancient republic of Venice, an outrage which has earned him condemnation over the years. Allowing Austria to take the fabled city and its eastern territories, he incorporated its western-most domains in his Cisalpine Republic and turned Corfu and the Ionian Islands over to France. So the once proud symbol of merchant wealth in the eastern Mediterranean finally lost her independence to the effusions of the Revolution just two years after her successor in mercantile riches, the Dutch republic, succumbed to the same phenomenon; ironically, both were subverted by liberal slogans before falling to naked territorial conquest and pillage. However, the immediate outcome of Bonaparte's justly famous first Italian campaign was that Republican France supplanted Austria as the dominant power in Italy and the Adriatic.

Only Great Britain remained at war with the Revolutionaries. As noted, Spain had defected from the coalition in July 1795; the following year she had resumed her traditional eighteenth-century stance as an ally of France and in October formally declared war on Great Britain, whom she accused of interference with her shipping. Her real fear was that Britain intended using her dominance at sea to seize the Spanish West Indian sugar islands and expanding colonial trade.[29]

*

PITT'S GOVERNMENT now faced a crisis comparable to the worst years of the American war. Spain brought a fleet of seventy of the line, on paper almost equal to the French battle fleet,[30] into the hostile camp; French control of Italy forced the British fleet watching Toulon to abandon Corsica and leave the Mediterranean altogether. Worse, the financial system underpinning the war had become dangerously unbalanced. Despite greatly increased taxes, expenditure since 1793 had exceeded revenue by over £100 million, and borrowing to make up the deficits each year had pushed the national debt to the unprecedented level of £360 million, demanding over £13 million annually in interest.[31] Foreign payments for keeping allies in the field, fomenting insurrection inside France and buying grain and naval stores had drained the country of bullion. Bank of England reserves had fallen from £5.6 million two years earlier to the alarming figure of just over one million. Almost equally disturbing was a shortage of coin in circulation to meet the demands of the expanding economy. The Governor of the Bank had been making increasingly urgent representations to Pitt about both concerns, and in October 1796 Pitt, determined to end a war which seemed to be running out of financial control, had sent a plenipotentiary to Paris to take peace soundings.

The Directory made a pretence of interest for a while, but under cover prepared an expeditionary force for Ireland to aid Irish nationalists under Wolfe Tone in a planned uprising against their British overlords. The force of nearly 15,000 troops sailed from Brest in the late afternoon of 16 December 1796. It was commanded by General Lazare Hoche and escorted by seventeen of the line under Villaret's successor, Rear Admiral Morard de Galles. Lord Bridport, still commanding the Channel Fleet, was maintaining a watch with portions of his force roughly equal to the number of French warships ready for sea and rotated on a two- to three-week cycle, but the easterlies which allowed de Galles out blew the blockading squadron some 30 miles into the Atlantic where the frigates stationed inshore to report French movements failed to find it.[32] This fortunate chance for the French was negated by confusion among their ships as the wind rose and de Galles countermanded his original course instructions. The celebrated frigate captain, Sir Edward Pellew in the *Indefatigable*, compounded disorder by sailing amongst them that night firing off rockets and signal guns and lighting blue flares at random. By morning one ship of the line had foundered on rocks, two had collided and the remainder of the expeditionary fleet was scattered widely.

In the absence of the fleet flagship carrying both de Galles and Hoche, the second in command rounded up the greater part of the vessels and led them to Bantry Bay, south-western Ireland, the intended haven for disembarkation. There, further gales proved too much for the inexperienced crews and after several ships had been blown out to sea, the remaining captains held a council at which it was decided to abandon the venture and sail home. Most arrived back in January 1797 without meeting Bridport. One straggler, the 74-gun *Droits de l'Homme*, was intercepted by Pellew in the *Indefatigable* in company with another frigate, *Amazon*, off Audierne Bay, south of Brest, in the evening of 13 January; both frigates harried the battleship in high winds and seas through the night until she – and the *Amazon* – drove ashore and was wrecked on the Penmarch rocks. The *Indefatigable* narrowly escaped the same fate.

Pellew's legendary feat did nothing to calm public fears of further French invasion attempts, and in February intelligence of plans to concentrate a Franco-Spanish fleet in Brest led the government to order livestock to be driven inland from the coasts. This heightened the general anxiety and provoked a run on the banks; two in Newcastle closed their doors. Alarm in the financial community was reflected in the fall of 3 per cent Consols to a new low of $51^{1}/_{2}$.[33] Such was the situation when on the 22nd a French raiding party landed on the Welsh coast near Fishguard. A small force of some 1,200 ex-convicts and men sentenced to the galleys, commanded by an elderly American adventurer, it surrendered without a fight when confronted by local militia next day, but in the panicky financial atmosphere Pitt was forced into precipitate action. Fortunately it was a Saturday when news of the 'invasion' reached London. He had time before the banks opened again to have the king agree a royal message to Parliament and sign an Order in Council directing the Bank of England to suspend cash payments. The anticipated throng packing Threadneedle Street on Monday morning intent on withdrawing their money from the Bank found copies of the Order posted on the walls.[34]

For the Bank to suspend cash payments was unprecedented. Nevertheless, crisis was averted when later that morning a meeting of leading City men agreed unanimously to continue accepting Bank of England notes. Pitt next brought in a Bill allowing the Bank and county banks to issue low denomination notes of £1 and £2 as an inconvertible paper currency to cover the shortage of coin. In Parliament the opposition criticized him for introducing his own *assignats* – with all that implied in terms of runaway inflation – but commercial activity and confidence returned and the temporary measures were to prove so successful in responding to the needs of the war economy they were continued long after they had ceased to be necessary, and long after the end of the war against France. Whether government credit would have remained so robust had there been a serious uprising against British garrisons in Ireland supported by French troops imbued with Republican fervour under a young and aggressive commander such as Lazare Hoche is another question. It may be that Pitt had only been saved the previous December by gales and French naval incompetence.

The Directory's Irish scheme, like countless Bourbon schemes before it, had been a direct attack on Britain's financial credit. With bases in Ireland complementing Brest and Saint-Malo it had been hoped to extend a blockade across the approaches to the English Channel. Yet the expectation was unrealistic. Whatever effects a successful landing may have had on Pitt's administration, the Royal Navy was simply too strong qualitatively and quantitatively for the disorganized French and Spanish services to have seriously threatened its command at sea, and thus the integrity of the financial system. The proof had been exhibited earlier that month in the Atlantic, although the news had not yet reached London.

It concerned the Spanish element of the Directory's plan to concentrate a Franco-Spanish fleet at Brest – thence sailing up-Channel to Holland to escort another invasion army to Ireland. It was a desperate scheme concocted by soldiers and politicians, reminiscent of Philip II of Spain's disastrous design for the 1588 Armada campaign. The new commander-in-chief of the British fleet which had evacuated the Mediterranean, Admiral Sir John Jervis, had intelligence of the Spanish force preparing to leave the Mediterranean, and waited for them off Cape St Vincent at the south-west corner of the Iberian peninsula – from where he could intercept whether they put in to Cadiz or steered north for Biscay.

By all normal rules of war the odds facing him were insuperable; he had fifteen of the line with him against twenty-seven in the Spanish fleet. But he was a commander of a different stamp to Hotham, even Bridport. Hardened in adversity during his earliest days at sea when so poor he had had to leave the midshipmen's mess and find a berth on the bare deck, he had become a man of iron, notorious for the sternest standards of duty and discipline, irascible temper and tongue. He was also a first-rate judge of men. From the beginning he had gauged Nelson's worth and offered him a larger ship. Nelson had declined, although he had later transferred with reluctance to the 74-gun *Captain* when his beloved *Agamemnon*, as the weakest unit in the fleet and fast wearing out, was ordered home with a convoy.

Jervis was also a tactical innovator in Howe's likeness. On assuming command he had added a new code number 50 to the signal books he issued to the fleet. It was for use when approaching an enemy fleet on the opposite tack and unable to weather it. The action to be taken was detailed in a separate 'Secret Instruction'. This directed the 'weathermost and headmost Ships . . . to decrease Sail and to edge down so as to collect a strong Body of Ships which are to form [line] as they arrive up with each other, and to force through the Enemy's Fleet in the direction, *where they judge the body of our Fleet can fetch thro'*.' When the number of ships which had passed through equalled the number of enemy ships separated by the manoeuvre, the headmost ship was to tack, followed by the others in succession, to engage the section of the van so cut off. Meanwhile the centre and rear would attempt to prevent the enemy centre and rear from rejoining their separated van.[35] Possible enemy responses were listed, together with the action to be taken in each case. The premise, like Howe's and it seems every British officer's, was that if the enemy line could be separated and disorganized British superiority in gunnery and seamanship would ensure victory.

The almost mathematically complex manoeuvres described would have been possible only with a fleet trained to perfect sailing discipline and awareness of the handling capabilities of consorts; over the following months Jervis had worked ceaselessly to ensure this, his piercing gaze even extending to such details as 'the lifts not being boused sufficiently taut when the reefs were in',[36] until the individual ships had been welded, so far as winds and seas and the tolerance of natural materials allowed, into a combined instrument of deadly precision. 'They at home do not know what this fleet is capable of performing,' Nelson had written to his wife towards the end of 1796, 'anything and everything . . . Of all the fleets I ever saw, I never saw one in point of Officers and men equal to Sir John Jervis', who is a Commander able to lead them to glory.'[37]

The transformation Jervis had wrought had come to the notice of the Admiralty. On 1 February 1797 the First Lord had written to advise him that the king wished to honour him for his ability and zeal 'not only in the active operation of the fleet . . . but in the internal arrangements and discipline', and would raise him to the peerage 'as soon as it shall be known what title you would desire to bear',[38] although this letter did not reach him before the battle that was to make his name.

The Spanish fleet under Admiral Don José de Córdova could not have provided more marked contrast: the ships' companies, desperately short of seamen, were filled with landsmen and soldiers of new levies, and many of the officers had little experience. Nelson had had opportunity to judge the Spanish service four years previously when welcomed in Cadiz as an ally. 'The Dons may make fine ships,' he had recorded, 'they cannot, however, make men';[39] he had estimated that if 75 to 100 picked British sailors were to get aboard one of their first rates with a complement of 1,000 they would take her. It is interesting that despite the cruelty of the age and indeed his own care to provide bullocks and other live animals aboard to be butchered for the sake of his men's health, when taken by his hosts to a 'Bull-feast' he was so sickened by the way the beasts were tormented he thought at first he would be unable to sit it out, and noticed from the faces of his fellow officers that they shared his feelings.

The two fleets met in the morning of 14 February some 35 miles south-west of Cape St Vincent.[40] The wind was in the west and Córdova in the magnificent *Santíssima Trinidad* of 130 guns was steering east-south-easterly for Cadiz. Jervis in the *Victory* of 100 guns had been aware of the Spaniards' proximity since the previous day when Nelson, returning from detached service in the Mediterranean, had reported falling in with them during the night. Jervis had the signal made to clear for action and keep close order and that evening at dinner with guests in his quarters toasted 'Victory over the Dons in the battle from which they cannot escape tomorrow!'[41]

The 14th dawned foggy and it was not until 6.30 that the first Spanish ships were sighted to windward. Gradually more appeared from the haze spread wide across the horizon. Jervis' response to the sighting reports entered legend.

'There are twenty sail of the line, Sir John.'
　'Very well, sir.'
　'There are twenty-five sail of the line, Sir John.'
　'Very well, sir.'
　'There are twenty-seven sail of the line, Sir John.'
　'Enough, sir, no more of that: the die is cast; and if there are fifty sail I will go through them.'

Upon which Captain Hallowell, a passenger in the flagship and one of
the previous night's dinner guests, so far forgot himself as to lay his hand
on the admiral's bowed, bulldog shoulders, exclaiming, 'That's right, Sir
John! That's right! By God, we shall give them a damned good licking!'[42]

The British fleet, well closed up in two columns, was steering southerly
towards a point of interception ahead of Córdova's easterly line of
advance. By about 9 a.m. Jervis discerned that the Spanish ships were in
two distinct groups with a space between; and, determined to go through
the space to prevent them uniting – rather as in his 'Secret Instructions' –
he signalled his leading ships to chase. The foremost, *Culloden*, a 74 under
Captain Thomas Troubridge whom Jervis considered the finest officer in
the navy, 'with honour and courage bright as his sword', set t'gallants;[43]
astern of him two three-decker first rates setting royals above their t'gallants and three other 74s stretched ahead as an advanced division. The
Victory followed, leading the main body of the fleet in a tight line close-
hauled on the starboard tack – described by a midshipman aboard the
Barfleur, third astern of the *Victory*, as 'one of the most beautiful and close
lines ever beheld'.[44] This was the essence: a compact line whose concentrated firepower would overwhelm less united enemy ships in detail.

Córdova had been sailing in cruising formation in three columns
when the British were reported to larboard. Wishing to retain the
weather gage, he had signalled for single line on the larboard tack. It was
a complex manoeuvre involving each ship wearing round to a northerly
course, then merging into an evolving line; moreover, Córdova and his
squadronal admirals who had been leading their columns on the starboard tack were left astern of their ships on the larboard tack. It would
have taxed Jervis' captains. It proved too much for Córdova's. As
Troubridge approached they were bunched chaotically, still three deep
in places.

The wind was now veering somewhat to the north of west allowing
Jervis at 11.24 to signal an alteration of course a point to starboard,
towards the enemy. Two minutes later he hoisted Howe's signal number
40: 'the Admiral means to pass between the ships of the line for engaging them to leeward';[45] and two minutes after that number 83: 'to haul
the wind on the starboard tack' – in other words point still closer to the
wind and the enemy. In complying Troubridge headed straight for a
cluster of three ships including a three-decker flagship attempting to join
their consorts of the leeward group. When his first lieutenant pointed
out that they must go aboard one of these, Troubridge replied, 'Can't

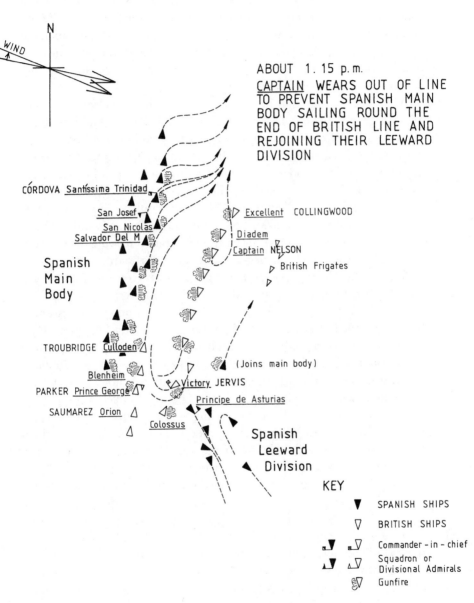

N

WIND

ABOUT 1.15 p.m.

CAPTAIN WEARS OUT OF LINE
TO PREVENT SPANISH MAIN
BODY SAILING ROUND THE
END OF BRITISH LINE AND
REJOINING THEIR LEEWARD
DIVISION

CÓRDOVA Santíssima Trinidad

San Josef

San Nicolas

Salvador Del M

Excellent COLLINGWOOD

Diadem

Captain NELSON

British Frigates

Spanish
Main
Body

TROUBRIDGE Culloden

(Joins main body)

Blenheim

PARKER Prince George

Victory JERVIS

Principe de Asturias

SAUMAREZ Orion

Colossus

Spanish
Leeward
Division

KEY

▼ SPANISH SHIPS

▽ BRITISH SHIPS

◢▼ ◢▽ Commander-in-chief

▲▼ △▽ Squadron or
Divisional Admirals

🌀▽ Gunfire

Battle diagram 2   St Vincent, 14 February 1797

help it, Griffiths! Let the weakest fend off!'[46] The Spaniards tacked independently and minutes later, as the *Culloden* passed close on the opposite course, the action began, spreading quickly down the line astern. Before noon the whole of the British fleet was in action. The midshipman in the *Barfleur*, feeling choking sensations from the smell and smoke of the gunpowder, described the roar of fire as 'like heavy thunder, and the ship reeled and shook as if she was inclined to fall in pieces'.[47]

With the fleets on opposite courses, the *Culloden* soon cleared the rear Spanish group. As his guns fell silent Troubridge had his hands man the braces and bowlines, sheets and tacks, and stared astern at the *Victory*'s halyards for the signal to go about. It came at 12.08, number 80: 'to tack in succession'. Troubridge's acknowledgement and repeating flags were already at the yardarm, rolled up with a stop to prevent them flying. He called out to the signal lieutenant, 'Break the stop!' and to the quartermasters, 'Down with the helm!' Simultaneously the tacks and sheets of the headsails were cast off; as the canvas shivered, removing the pressure forward, the rounded bows began swinging to starboard.

Aboard the *Victory* Jervis exclaimed, 'Look at Troubridge there! He tacks his ship to battle as if the eyes of all England were upon him!'[48]

The ships astern of Troubridge came about after him in succession as he chased northwards after the Spanish rear. It took him more than thirty minutes to catch them and reopen fire. Jervis was on the poop of the *Victory* at about this time, attempting to see through the clouds of gunsmoke astern. What he made of the situation is not known for his subsequent despatch is uninformative and he never talked of his battles; but he must have realized that the leading Spanish ships would soon pass north of the last British ship, Collingwood's 74-gun *Excellent*, after which they would be free to double round and take his rear between two fires, rejoin the detached group to leeward or square off for Cadiz. At all events, soon afterwards, at 12.51, while the *Victory* was tacking to a northerly course after her next ahead, he had signal 41 made: 'ships to take suitable station for their mutual support and to engage the enemy as arriving up with them in succession.'[49] It was a catch-all, allowing initiative to individual captains and releasing them from strict line of battle.

At almost the same moment, give or take differences between different ships' timekeeping, Nelson, flying the broad pennant of a commodore in the *Captain*, third ship from the tail of the British line still heading southwards on the starboard tack, saw the great *Santíssima Trinidad* and her close consorts turning downwind, as is recorded in the ship's log:

'evidently with the intention of joining a division of his fleet of 10 sail of the line which were on the *Captain*'s lee bow'.[50] This is no doubt what Córdova was attempting; having signalled his van to wear to the other tack, without any effect, he was now setting the example himself. Whether Nelson was aware of Jervis' hoist number 41 – whether it had even been made yet – is not clear. It is of small consequence since on Nelson's record there is little doubt he would have acted on his own appreciation of the situation whatever the letter of the signalled instruction. He ordered his flag captain to wear ship, and coming round on the larboard tack, steered northwards between his next astern and Collingwood's *Excellent* – in itself testimony to the remarkable standards of seamanship in the fleet – to place the *Captain* across the line of advance of the *Santíssima* and her seconds, two 112-gun three-deckers and an 80-gun ship. It was an act of brazen daring or reckless self-confidence. An army officer watching from a British frigate thought 'the contrast between the *Captain*, a small 74-gun ship, and the gigantic ships of the enemy, was so preposterous that we could, at the moment, only view the proceedings of Nelson as rash and perilous in the extreme'.[51] Yet, astonishingly, confronted with a two-decker barring his way across the British rear, the *Santíssima Trinidad* and her huge consorts hauled their wind to resume a northerly course, firing as their broadsides opened.

The *Captain* returned fire and maintained the unequal contest for some time before Troubridge worked his way up to relieve her, and shortly afterwards Troubridge's next astern, the 90-gun *Blenheim*, followed in turn by the others of the leading division. The gunfire increased in volume, and it appeared to British observers in the frigate that the 'superiority of the British fire over that of the enemy, and its effects on the enemy's hulls and sails were so evident, that we in the frigate no longer' hesitated to pronounce a glorious termination of the contest'.[52] Jervis, meanwhile, quick to see the value of Nelson's initiative, had made a general signal for all ships to come to the wind on the larboard tack – instead of waiting to tack in succession after their next ahead.

Collingwood promptly put the *Excellent* about and worked northwards to Nelson's relief to windward of several damaged Spanish ships. He was a disciplinarian in Jervis' mould with a particular dedication to gun drill and target practice and had worked his guns' crews up to a rapidity and accuracy of fire probably unequalled at that date. This was now demonstrated. Closing within pistol shot of a three-decker, he poured in such a volume of double-shotted broadsides that her guns soon fell silent and her colours came down. Satisfied that she had struck, he passed on to a damaged Spanish 74, ranging 'so close alongside that a man might jump from one ship to the other. Our fire carried all before it; and in ten minutes she hauled down her colours.'[53] After this he 'pushed up with every sail set to save his old friend and messmate' as Nelson was to put it, arriving up with the *Captain* as she was re-engaging the *San Nicolas* – after the respite afforded by Troubridge and the rest of the leading division. Collingwood interposed between the two within ten feet of the Spaniard – so close 'you could not have put a bodkin between us',[54] as he described it afterwards – and once again drove the raw Spanish guns' crews from their pieces with the rapidity of his broadsides. His cannon were so hot by this time that many shot passed through both sides of the *San Nicolas* into the three-decker *San Josef* which had lost her mizzenmast and fallen aboard her on her unengaged, windward side. Collingwood then moved up the line to support the leading division and came up against the huge *Santíssima Trinidad*, now severely damaged after engaging successive British ships for over two hours. It was approaching 3.30.

Nelson, meanwhile, carried off the second astonishing stroke of the day, one which would establish his fame with the public. The *Captain* had lost her fore topmast, all her rigging was cut, her wheel shattered and she was scarcely manageable; in addition she had expended most of her ammunition. Her opponent was in worse case, locked together with the *San Josef* and drifting downwind. Nelson told his flag captain, R. W. Miller, to summon boarders and lay the ship aboard her. Miller, a New York royalist who had joined the Royal Navy in the American war to fight his rebellious, or 'Patriot', fellow countrymen, succeeded in luffing up and bringing the *Captain*'s bowsprit over the enemy's poop, where the spritsail yard hooked into the mizzen rigging and held as the bows ground against her starboard quarter. Nelson's former first lieutenant, Edward Berry, led the boarders across via the enemy's mizzen chains; Nelson himself joined a diversionary party which dropped into the enemy's quarter gallery, smashed the windows of the captain's cabin and charged through to the quarterdeck, where they found Berry in possession, hauling down the Spanish colours. The Spanish captain, mortally wounded in the onslaught, offered his sword to Nelson, who, after accepting it, summoned more men from the *Captain*, and directed the boarders to the *San Josef* still locked alongside by yards and rigging. Musketry fire was coming from her stern which rose above the larboard side amidships, but as the boarders clambered across and Berry helped

Nelson negotiate the main chains, a Spanish officer appeared at the rail and surrendered the ship. Nelson was soon on the enemy quarterdeck, where he accepted the captain's sword – the rear admiral was mortally wounded below – followed by those of the ship's officers. 'And on the quarterdeck of a Spanish 1st rate, extravagant as the story may seem, did I receive the swords of vanquished Spaniards; which as I received I gave to Wm Fearney, one of my bargemen, who put them with the greatest sangfroid under his arm.'[55]

The sight of the *Captain* alongside her two large prizes moved the men of the *Victory* to line the side and roar huzzas as the flagship sailed by, an act of spontaneous admiration and delight that was repeated by the companies of the ships following as they passed in succession. Two other prizes had been secured by this time, approaching 4.30, and the *Santíssima Trinidad*, which had been engaged after Collingwood by Captain James Saumarez in the 74-gun *Orion*, was a wreck with only the stump of her mainmast standing. Some 200 of her men were dead or wounded, her decks a shambles and her guns were silent. Saumarez saw a white flag hoisted, then the British union flag above the Spanish ensign, upon which he ceased firing into her.

However, several of the Spanish ships which had not been engaged had worn to her rescue, while to the southward ships from the Spanish lee division were sailing towards the 74-gun *Colossus* which had been crippled aloft and was falling off downwind. Jervis recognized the need to concentrate the fleet in order to protect the prizes and his own vulnerable ships. He had made the preparatory signal to bring to much earlier; now he signalled line ahead in close order. It was 4.39. The February day would soon be over. As the British drew into line on the *Victory*, then wore to protect the *Captain* and the *Colossus*, the Spaniards closed around the *Santíssima* and she was taken in tow. Next day the fleets separated, the Spanish making for Cadiz, the British for Lisbon.

Despite the escape of Córdova's flagship, Jervis had won a spectacular victory, hailed when the news reached England as 'in all its circumstances [of numerical inferiority] first and unparalleled in naval history'.[56] Of the four prizes, two were three-decker first rates of 112 guns, one an 80, one a 74; it is notable that all, as well as the *Santíssima* which had so narrowly escaped, had been victims of Collingwood's devastating foray through the already damaged portion of the Spanish fleet. As Nelson had written four years earlier, despite the excellence of the Spanish ships, their scratch crews were no match for the British, whose

rapidity and accuracy of fire had simply overwhelmed them. The casualty figures tell the story. Apart from the *Captain*, which sustained 80
killed and wounded – 17 during the boarding actions[57] – only two other
British ships, the leaders *Culloden* and *Blenheim*, recorded substantial casualty lists, 57 and 59 respectively; nine of the fifteen ships, including the
Victory, did not reach double figures. By contrast 683 dead and wounded
were recorded aboard the four Spanish prizes, an average of 170 a ship;
and of the rest, it is believed the *Santíssima Trinidad* alone suffered over
200 killed and wounded.

News of the victory restored British government credit practically at
a stroke. It was more than ever clear that, however many ships her
enemies might bring against her, they would be no match for British
fleets. As for Nelson, he experienced the fame he had always craved. On
the quarterdeck of the *Victory* immediately after the battle with smoke-
blackened face, his uniform torn and half his cocked hat shot away, he
had been embraced with the utmost warmth by Jervis who told him – as
Nelson described it later – he could not sufficiently thank him. To his
uncle Suckling, he wrote, 'you will receive pleasure from the share I had
in making it a most brilliant day, the most of any I know in the annals of
England. *Nelson's patent bridge* for boarding 1st-rates will be a saying never
forgotten in this Fleet.'[58] He did not forget to send Collingwood a note
thanking him for his 'assistance in nearly a critical situation' for the
Captain. To his wife, he confessed that the more he thought of the action,
the more he was astonished: 'it absolutely appears a dream . . . As to
myself I assure you I was never better, and rich in the praises of every
man from the highest to the lowest in the fleet', adding, 'the Spanish war
will give us a cottage and a piece of ground, which is all I want.'[59]

It was far from all he wanted. An officer who spoke to him about the
honours he might expect to receive from his decisive role in the battle
was left in no doubt from his answer 'that he wished to bear about his
person some honorary distinction, to attract the public eye, and mark his
professional services'. From subsequent acquaintance with Nelson, the
officer concluded: 'The attainment of public honours, and an ambition
to be distinguished above his fellows, were his master passions. His
conduct was constantly actuated by these predominant feelings.'[60]

In the awards showered on the victorious fleet by a grateful king and
Parliament, Jervis became Earl of St Vincent and Nelson received the
Order of the Bath, whose shimmering insignia embracing three golden
crowns graced his uniform thereafter. He had already passed in the

normal course of promotions at the beginning of February from the top of the captains' list to the flag list and was a rear admiral of the blue.

Above all, Nelson's exploits had captured the imagination of the public, whose admiration he would never lose. Over the following years he and Napoleon Bonaparte, another man of small height and slight build who had raised himself through similar extraordinary ambition, flare and audacity to heroic status, would personify the distinctive genius and to a remarkable extent the fortunes of their very different nations.

5

Camperdown, 1797

NEWS OF THE victory off Cape St Vincent revived British spirits, but little over a month later Pitt was grappling with a situation as potentially dangerous as February's run on the banks: mutiny in the Channel Fleet. Unlike the French naval mutinies of 1790 and 1793 this revolt owed little or nothing at the start to revolutionary slogans or rejection of an aristocratic officer class; it was in essence a well-organized strike aimed at bringing long-standing grievances to the attention of the Admiralty, and was conducted with exemplary restraint and respect.

The chief complaints were over pay, which remained at levels set in the middle of the seventeenth century, since when prices had almost doubled. This was exacerbated by feelings of injustice as army privates had had their pay raised to a shilling a day – against 22 shillings and sixpence a month for able seamen, 19 shillings for ordinary seamen. Thus it appeared that a higher value had been placed on soldiers than sailors, who, in their own words, 'for centuries had been recognized as England's bulwark and pride . . . and by whose manly exertions the British flag rides triumphant in every quarter of the globe'.[1] Moreover, merchant seamen fortunate enough to escape impressment into the navy could earn four or five times more, such was the wartime shortage of skilled sailors. Another bitterly resented result of manning difficulties for the hugely expanded wartime navy was the practice of enticing volunteers, usually with no sea experience, with 'bounties' ranging from £20 to £40, more than a sailor was paid over a whole commission.[2]

There were many other festering resentments, including the payment of wages by 'ticket' exchanged for money at the Pay Office in Tower Hill, London, the customs of paying wages six months in arrears and 'turning over' men to another ship without paying them; lack of provision for transferring part of the wages to a sailor's family, and the minute shares of prize money distributed to sailors compared to the captains and officers.

Petitions for an increase in wages were first sent to Lord Howe, nominally in command of the Channel Fleet although Bridport had long been in active command. Receiving no reply – since Howe simply passed them to the Admiralty – the sailors' leaders began organizing a take-over of the fleet to begin at a signal from Howe's former flagship, *Queen Charlotte*. The officers got wind of preparations and on 14 April the admiral commanding Portsmouth warned the Admiralty that ships' companies intended refusing duty until their pay was increased. Despite many indications over the past year of the men's deep-seated dissatisfactions the Admiralty reponse was to order Bridport to split the fleet and put to sea. Bridport knew it would not work, but gave the necessary orders on Easter Sunday 16 April, two days before the scheduled take-over. The men refused, after which the leaders' plans were put into operation with as much smooth regularity as if they had been handed down by Bridport himself.

Two delegates from each ship convened daily in the admiral's great cabin of the *Queen Charlotte* to concert their demands and the fleet's harbour activities. The majority were long-service seaman petty officers, others able seamen. Some of their first acts were to ensure that frigates and smaller craft continued trade protection duties and that a convoy sailed on schedule; and they announced that they would call off the mutiny and sail in defence of the country at the first sign of an enemy fleet. Otherwise normal routine continued: captains coming or going were accorded the full honours of marine guard and bosun's pipe – as indeed were the mutineer delegates – and men continued to be punished for violations. Almost the only outward signs of change were red flags of mutiny in place of the admirals' flags or captains' pennants at the mastheads.

The delegates were equally judicious and moderate in their negotiations with the Admiralty; as a result, all their terms were eventually met: able seamen would receive a shilling a day, petty officers a proportionate rise, and these and other concessions were drafted into legislation for Parliament, while the king signed and sealed a full pardon. Pitt reassured the First Lord of the Admiralty that the expense was 'comparatively of no consequence'.[3] It was a triumph of firmness, tact and shrewdness from representatives of the hard-handed sailors who were truly, as they claimed, the country's 'bulwark and pride'. The Board of Admiralty, who for too long had disregarded the strength of the men's legitimate grievances, did not emerge with such credit.

The only bloodshed occurred after suspicions were aroused by a few newspaper reports and deliberately seditious handbills that the government intended reneging on its promises. The violent consequences of this misinformation were confined to one ship separated from the rest, and the passions aroused when a seaman was shot and mortally wounded by a lieutenant were calmed by two delegates whose eloquence could not have been bettered by defence counsel in a court of law. Finally Lord Howe, revered in the fleet not only as the victor of 'the Glorious First of June' but as 'the sailors' friend', who would visit and talk to every ill or wounded man and provide delicacies from his private store, went aboard each ship in turn to talk to the men. He was forced against his better judgement to agree that 107 unpopular commissioned and warrant officers who had been sent ashore by their ships' companies – among them an admiral, four captains, twenty-nine lieutenants, eight officers of marines, four surgeons and a chaplain[4] – would not be reinstated, but replaced by others. Having conceded this, he was able to seal the men's return to duty in an aquatic procession through the fleet with massed bands playing 'Rule, Britannia!' and 'God save the King!', accompanied by the delegates, one of whose leaders sat at Lady Howe's side. The date was 15 May. Two days later the fleet weighed and sailed for Brest.

Pragmatic as this settlement was, the idea of mutiny had spread in the meantime to other home squadrons in which the sailors' delegates had fallen under the influence of political subversion. France had a network of agents within Britain under the overall control of Lazare Carnot, most powerful *directeur* after Barras. He had several principal targets: one, reminiscent of a better known drive in the twentieth century, was to recruit undergraduates with revolutionary ideals from the universities of Oxford and Cambridge; another with higher priority was to place intelligent agents in all the main ports with the object of encouraging disgruntled sailors to mutiny.[5] Aided by local radical clubs, corresponding societies and United Irishmen, these succeeded in politicizing what had started at Spithead as a simple demand for the redress of grievances.[6]

The most immediately dangerous rising was at Yarmouth, where the North Sea Fleet under Admiral Adam Duncan marked the expeditionary force being prepared in Holland for the invasion of England. Duncan, a huge Scot 6 foot 4 inches in height with breadth to match, whose figure and handsome features made him an object of admiration wherever he went, held the revolt at bay by sheer force of personality and an appeal to patriotism. When mutiny re-emerged in one ship, the *Adamant,* he went aboard her and challenged anyone who dared dispute his or his officers' authority to step forward. One man did, whereupon Duncan seized him by the collar, swung him over the side of the ship and held him dangling with one arm.

'My lads! Look at this fellow – he who dares deprive me of command of my fleet!'[7]

The outbreak ended there, and the Adamants remained loyal thereafter. Duncan appeared to have his fleet so well under control that the Admiralty decided to bring it against a squadron lying at the Nore – the anchorage in the Thames at the mouth of the river Medway – which had become brazen in defiance of authority under the leadership of a formerly disrated warrant officer named Richard Parker, who styled himself admiral of the 'floating republic'. Then intelligence from Holland indicated that the invasion force had embarked and was waiting for a favourable wind to sail; Duncan was ordered to the Texel instead. He had scarcely weighed on 17 May, however, when his ships were taken over by their crews, who either turned them back to the anchorage or sailed them for the Nore to join Parker's 'floating republic'. Only his flagship and the *Adamant* remained loyal.

With these two he sailed for the Dutch coast and carried out a remarkable deception, appearing the first day close in to the entrance to the Texel in the guise of a rear admiral of the red and hoisting a stream of signals as if to a fleet in the offing, the next day as two private ships flying captains' pennants and making more signals, and the third day in his own colours as an admiral of the blue. On the fourth day he was joined by two more ships the Admiralty had despatched, and as the wind went round into the east, allowing the Dutch to sail, he stood in with his little squadron and anchored off the outer buoy of the Texel, instructing his captains to fight their ships till they sank, when their hulks would block the exit channel. The Dutch fleet of seventeen of the line which was to escort the expedition did not attempt to put to sea; contrary to the intelligence received by the British, the army was not yet ready, and it was assumed that Duncan's squadron was bait to lure them out, when they would be set upon by a fleet beyond the horizon. On 10 June Duncan was joined by six more ships detached from the Channel Fleet, and on the 13th by a Russian squadron of five of the line under orders to assist him. The danger was past. It had seemed very real at the time. The self-confidence and moral and physical courage of admirals like Duncan and Jervis elevated their deeds to legend.

In the meantime the Admiralty had isolated the mutinous squadron at the Nore, cut off all supplies and declared the mutineers rebels. Parker and his colleagues had been forced into violent repression to preserve their authority over moderates who saw the hopelessness of their situation. The violence, together with hunger and a patriotic reaction against radical leaders who suggested taking the ships over to the enemy, led to counter-revolution in ship after ship; finally on 14 June Parker's own 'flagship', the *Sandwich*, was last to haul down the bloody flag of mutiny. Irresponsible as Parker's conduct had been, he submitted with grace. Instead of fleeing like many of his colleagues, he took a vote of the ship's company and when this went almost unanimously in favour of the officers, led three cheers for a return to duty and gave himself up. He was tried by court martial the following week, sentenced to death and on 30 June smartly hoisted by his neck to the *Sandwich*'s fore yardarm.

The majority of his fellow leaders who had not escaped to the continent were pardoned by the Admiralty, although 28 were also hanged, 29 imprisoned and 9 flogged. The combination of severity and extraordinary leniency, together with the increased pay and other concessions won by the Spithead mutineers, and a general easing of officers' attitudes towards shore leave and punishment resulting directly from the shock of the mutinies restored the fleet to discipline. Those ships still suspected of containing seditious groups were sent to join St Vincent's fleet blockading the Spanish fleet in Cadiz. He made examples of the disaffected by having their own ship's company hoist them to the yardarm, and the word spread to new arrivals inclined to revolutionary jargon, 'By God, if old Jarvie hears ye, he'll have you dingle-dangle at the yardarm at eight o'clock tomorrow morning.'[8]

Notwithstanding the victory off Cape St Vincent, the few months between February and the end of June had marked Great Britain's nadir, probably the most dangerous period any British government had faced in recent times, with sections of the Royal Navy, the ultimate sanction of the British state, apparently toying with revolutionary ideas. Pitt had steered through this gruelling period with incisive firmness. It would not overstate the case to say that the British parliamentary system itself had been on trial. As a microcosm of the society from which it was recruited, the navy exhibited the characteristics of a representative system of government resting on tacit consent and mediating people's concerns despite their social class – as distinct from the Bourbon French system of hierarchy and regulation by state officials. The French mutinies of 1790 and 1793 were marked by gross insubordination and a purge of noble officers, a large proportion of whom either left because conditions had become insupportable, or were dismissed; eventually discipline was re-established in as harsh a form as before, but the ethos and professionalism of the service had been broken, and remained so for the duration of the war.

By contrast the mutiny at Spithead had been preceded by humble petitions from the sailors to Lord Howe asking him to mediate their grievances with the Admiralty, 'and grant such addition will be made in their pay as in their Lordships' wisdom they shall think meet'.[9] Even at the Nore, which eventually saw more violence, an assistant surgeon present recorded: 'Our men, to their credit, behaved with great moderation, begged pardon of their officers, apologizing for the necessity of their so proceeding.' When an officer said to one man, 'How do you spare me? Did I not get you flogged the other day?' the answer was, 'You did, sir, *but I deserved it.* You are a gentleman and a good officer. You never punished men but when they were in fault, and you did it as an officer ought to.'[10] Certainly brutal and unpopular officers had been sent ashore, but as detested individuals, not as representatives of authority or of a class – indeed British naval officers came from many classes and there were comparatively few aristocrats among them. When it came to refusal of duty, the sailors' grievances had been settled by negotiation; Howe, who concluded them, wrote during his final arbitration that he was having 'to quiet the most suspicious, but most generous, minds he thinks he ever met with in the same class of men'.[11] Above all, however, as the subsequent naval war was to prove beyond doubt, neither the discipline nor the fighting efficiency of the service, nor the essential patriotism of the sailors was affected in any way.

It might be inferred that the very different results of the mutinies in the two navies, and the outcome of the naval war itself, were functions of the differences between parliamentary democracy and absolutism. A recent study of the French navy in the Revolution concludes that 'political stability and sound ideas of government have a direct bearing on naval superiority'; indeed Nelson's subsequent victories 'represented the triumph of British parliamentary government over the French Revolution'.[12]

Off Cadiz that summer, 1797, Nelson hoisted his flag in the *Theseus*, 74 guns, one of the troubled ships sent to St Vincent from the Channel Fleet. He took his flag captain, Miller, with him. Ships' companies always responded to Nelson's leadership, and St Vincent transferred him deliberately to erase residual traces of sedition. The magic worked in short time. His energy and transparent sense of duty, the almost boyish animation which lit his eyes when his mind was engaged, his direct relations with the men based on his sense of natural hierarchy – that in the order of society it was his part to lead, theirs to follow – his genuine respect for them and practical concern for their welfare, his fairness, above all, perhaps, the reputation for reckless courage which preceded him and was soon reinforced in action when St Vincent appointed him to command the inshore squadron watching Cadiz, all proved irresistible. Physical courage was the quality sailors admired before others; embodied in the slight figure of their admiral, it inspired more than admiration – it is not too much to call it love. Within a fortnight of his move to the *Theseus* a note in awkward handwriting and signed in block capitals 'SHIP'S COMPANY', was left on the quarterdeck:

> Success attend Admiral Nelson! God bless Captain Miller! We thank them for the officers they have placed over us. We are happy and comfortable and will shed every drop of blood in our veins to support them, and the name of the *Theseus* shall be immortalized as high as the *Captain*'s.[13]

In the last they were to be proved wrong. That July Nelson's self-esteem was dealt a terrible blow. Ordered by St Vincent with a small squadron to Santa Cruz in the Spanish Canary Islands to capture a Mexican treasure ship, *El Principe de Asturias*, supposed to be there, and to 'take, burn, sink or otherwise destroy all enemy vessels', he launched a surprise assault led by Troubridge under cover of darkness on forts commanding the harbour. An offshore wind slowed the boats' progress and as dawn broke they were still a mile from land. Surprise was lost, and Troubridge turned back to consult Nelson. In the judgement of Nelson's biographer, A. T. Mahan, Troubridge's failure to use his initiative and press on to take the heights behind the forts – as he recommended doing as soon as he reported to Nelson – marked 'the distinction between a really great captain [Nelson] and the best type of a simply accomplished and gallant officer'.[14] Mahan had no doubt that had the positions been reversed Nelson would have assumed responsibility for carrying on without referring back for orders; his whole career illustrated it; indeed he wrote subsequently in a private letter that had he been present the attempt would not have failed. In the event, by the time the party was landed for an assault on the heights Spanish troops were deployed in force and the attempt was abandoned.

Nelson now made a serious error of judgement. Refusing to admit defeat, he prepared a desperate plan for a frontal assault on the town itself, splitting his forces into divisions to create doubt in the enemy's mind, and leading the main body in person to attack the harbour mole. He and other officers taking part composed letters to their families in case they should not return; he also wrote a note to St Vincent containing a characteristic genuflection to fate: 'tomorrow my head will probably be crowned with either laurel or cypress.'[15] His party succeeded in gaining the mole through high seas and a barrage of canister and grape, but found enemy troops massed beyond, barring advance to the town, where they were to rendezvous with other divisions. Nelson himself had his right arm above the elbow smashed by grapeshot as he climbed on to the mole. Josiah, his stepson, with him as ever, saved his life by improvising a tourniquet from a silk scarf, then mustered a boat's crew to row him back to his ship. On the way, hearing cries from men whose cutter had been sunk beneath them by shot, Nelson insisted the boat divert to rescue as many as possible from the water.

When eventually they pulled alongside the *Theseus*, he called for a rope to be thrown down to him and, brushing away assistance, twisted it around his left arm and climbed up the side, then went below and submitted himself to the assistant surgeon, a French royalist refugee, who no doubt administered the customary measure of rum and gave him a leather pad to bite on. Then, in swaying lantern light he sawed through Nelson's upper arm close to the shoulder, and after sewing folds of skin over the stump, gave him opium to dull the excruciating pain.[16] The physical trial and continuing pain affected Nelson less than the failure of the assault. For those sailors and marines from flanking parties who managed to fight their way to the town centre found themselves next morning surrounded by 8,000 disciplined Spanish soldiers and had no choice but to surrender. The Spaniards proved extraordinarily generous, opening their hospitals to the wounded, dispensing bread, fruit and wine to the British and ferrying them back to their ships – for which Nelson sent the governor his sincere thanks and a cask of English beer and a cheese. The governor replied with best wishes for Nelson's recovery and two flasks of the finest Canary wine. Nelson then offered to carry the governor's despatches retailing his own defeat to Cadiz.

In the context of the war Santa Cruz was at most a minor setback. For Nelson it was a humbling lesson. He had allowed his scorn for the crews of Spanish warships to blind him to the fighting qualities of Spanish troops ashore and the need for accurate intelligence of enemy strength; and there is little doubt that the adulation he had received since his exploits off St Vincent had gone to his head and given him a sense that he could not fail. His deflation in the wake of defeat was as profound as his elation after he had found himself a national hero. 'I am become a burthen to my friends', he wrote to St Vincent unsteadily with his left hand, 'and useless to my Country . . . When I leave your command, I become dead to the World; I go hence, and am no more seen . . . I hope you will be able to give me a frigate, to convey the remains of my carcase to England.'[17] He did not forget to recommend promotion for his stepson, Josiah. St Vincent reassured him, 'Mortals cannot command success', and promised he would ask for him again as soon as possible after his convalescence.[18]

Returning to England, Nelson arrived in Portsmouth in early September and travelled to join his wife in Bath, thence to lodgings in London for medical consultations. The stump of his right arm was swollen and continued to give him great pain. The silk ligature used by the French surgeon to tie the artery – instead of waxed thread as used by most British surgeons – had trapped a nerve, and he had to drug himself with opium every night to sleep. In a narcotic slumber in the evening of 13 October neither gun salutes nor revelry in the streets outside woke him, and it was not until the following morning he learned that Admiral Duncan had won a decisive victory over the Dutch in the North Sea.

Duncan had been watching the invasion force in the Texel since flaunting his colours off the coast at the height of the mutiny in June; knowledge of his presence had prevented the force putting to sea, and when it had become clear that neither the Brest fleet, watched by Bridport, nor the Spanish fleet, blockaded in Cadiz by St Vincent, would arrive to clear the way, the expedition was abandoned. The Admiralty had learned of this in late September and ordered Duncan back to Yarmouth. With his disappearance the commander-in-chief of the Dutch fleet, Admiral Jan Willem de Winter, was instructed to put to sea. The aims were vague: to restore morale in the ships, which had been idle too long, perhaps to lure any part of the British fleet he encountered into shoal waters off the coast, or if the size of the opposing force offered 'hope of success', to engage. His departure was observed by two ships stationed by Duncan off the entrance, who sent word to Yarmouth and shadowed. Duncan immediately sailed back for the Texel and, finding the anchorage empty, waited in the offing.

He was rewarded in the morning of 11 October as de Winter returned. The shadowing ships hovering to windward of the Dutch as they sailed easterly along the coast, sighted Duncan to the north and signalled, 'Enemy in sight bearing south by west'. The wind was north-north-westerly, strong and squalling. Duncan at once put his helm up to run down towards them. By 9 o'clock the enemy topsails were in sight and he made number 10, 'Prepare for battle'. He was using Howe's signal book and accompanying instructions.[19] De Winter was also using a numerical code with ten numeral flags and pendants for the 100s. Many of the evolutions prescribed were taken directly from the French navy instructions, although their general sense was aggressive in the Dutch historical tradition of attempting to defeat the enemy rather than defensive in the French tradition of preserving the fleet in order to accomplish the mission. Some of the higher numbered signals envisaged the British attempting to break the line, thus 752: 'Enemy is trying to cut our line: ships to close up and stop them'; 754, 'Close up and stop enemy ships which have cut our line from rejoining main body'.[20] In the event neither Duncan nor de Winter paid too much heed to tactics. Duncan signalled 'Chase' and at 10.24 number 35, 'to engage the enemy as you come up with them'. De Winter ordered a close-hauled line of battle on the larboard tack, heading north-easterly to await the assault.

De Winter had fifteen mostly light ships of the line mounting from 56 to 68 guns although four, including his own flagship, *Vrijheid*, were 74s; he also stationed an obsolete two-decked 44-gun ship in the line. Duncan out-gunned him with sixteen of the line comprising seven 74s, seven 64s and two 50-gun vessels; crucially, all carried wide-bored carronades on foc's'le and poop where the Dutch only had small-bore cannon. Duncan's fleet was organized in two divisions of eight ships each, although as they pressed down under all sail with the wind astern, the *Adamant* from his own weather division – which he led in the *Venerable* – became attached to the lee division led by Vice Admiral Richard Onslow in the *Monarch*. By 11 a.m. the ships were stretched out and he ordered the leaders to shorten sail to allow laggards to catch up, then attempted to dress the line in a north-easterly to south-westerly direction to parallel the Dutch. While doing so, shortly before 11.30, the sun broke through to reveal low land and the villages of Camperdown and Egmont barely nine miles from the Dutch van; realizing there was no time to lose if he were not to be drawn into shoal water, he ordered the fleet to bear up, each ship to steer for and engage her opponent. Five minutes later he signalled Onslow's division to starboard of him to attack the enemy rear. Meanwhile, he led down towards the *Vrijheid*, fifth ship from the Dutch van.

Approaching half a mile from the Dutch line at 11.53, he made Howe's signal number 34: 'the Admiral means to pass between the ships of the line for engaging them to leeward'. His aim, very different from Howe's at 'the Glorious First of June', was to get between the enemy and the shoaling water into which he feared they might draw him. Another difference from Howe's approach, brought on by the same apprehension, was that instead of an orderly line of bearing, his fleet was coming down in two straggling wedges spearheaded respectively by the *Venerable* and *Monarch* with almost a mile between them as Onslow led down for Vice Admiral Reyntje's flagship four from the tail of the Dutch line.

Unlike the French, the Dutch ships held their fire until the *Monarch* and a close supporter, *Powerful*, were within point-blank range, when Reyntje's flagship, *Jupiter*, and his seconds opened their broadsides into the bows of the approaching ships. The guns' crews had been practised almost every day through the summer and had reached high levels of proficiency in the calm waters inside the Texel;[21] it was different outside with strong squalls and lumping seas lifting the sides, and no doubt some of the shot flew high. Onslow, approaching almost at right angles, could not reply; he held on silently, steering for the narrow gap between the *Jupiter* and her next astern, the 68-gun *Haarlem*, passing through about 12.30, when his larboard guns opened, raking the *Jupiter*'s decks through her stern windows as they bore; his starboard guns raked the *Haarlem*. As he rounded up to engage the *Jupiter* on her lee side, the *Powerful*, close on his starboard quarter, surged through the same gap, also raking the *Haarlem* as she passed. Three more of Onslow's division to starboard rounded up to engage the *Haarlem* and the last two ships in the line from windward; another passed through the line and engaged from the lee berth.

Some way ahead of them Rear Admiral Storij in the 74-gun *Staten General*, seconding de Winter's flagship astern, saw Duncan heading to cut the line between him and his chief and closed until his bowsprit was over the *Vrijheid*'s taffrail. This produced a gap astern. Duncan veered to starboard and passed through it, his guns' crews rising from the deck roaring huzzas and opening a raking fire through Storij's stern windows. Duncan's second on his starboard side broke through astern of the next ship while his second to port rounded up opposite de Winter's flagship and engaged from windward, after which successive British ships attacked the Dutch van as they came up.

The almost perpendicular assaults by two separated groups brought superior concentrations to bear on the tail and the head of the Dutch line and took them between two fires, disrupting their formation and leaving five ships in the centre unengaged and temporarily out of the action. These steered towards the mêlées about the fleet flagships, but in the meantime the rear was overwhelmed and all four ships forced to strike; the *Jupiter* hauled down her colours at about half past one. This was the crucial point. It freed many of Onslow's division to set topsails and mainsails and work up to reinforce Duncan in the van. The Dutch fought with desperate courage, as always, but could not recover from the initial disruption, nor match the devastating fire of the British carronades at close range. By 3 o'clock the *Vrijheid* was dismasted and unmanageable with almost half her complement of 550 killed or wounded; de Winter, the only unscathed officer on deck, had no option but to yield. He was mortified, telling Duncan when brought aboard the *Venerable* that he was the first Dutch admiral ever to have surrendered.[22] Four other ships from the van were captured, which together with the four from the rear made a total of nine of the line; in addition two 44-gun ships were taken – in all practically two-thirds of the fleet. In the short October daylight Duncan dared not risk chasing the survivors which were led by Rear Admiral Storij into the shallows. It was nonetheless the most devastating defeat in proportion to numbers engaged in modern naval history and signified the end of the Dutch fleet as a factor in the war. Two years later Storij would surrender the remaining ships without a shot fired after the capture of the Texel by a British expeditionary force.

The moral effect of Camperdown was as important as the strategic result. 'Where shall I find words to convey to you the slightest idea of the enthusiasm created by your glorious splendid and memorable achievements?' the wife of the First Lord of the Admiralty enthused to Duncan.[23] A popular tonic, a great fillip for the government after a grim year, another proof that the Royal Navy was more than equal to all its numerous enemies, so reinforcing confidence in the City of London, it also drew a bloody line under the mutinies of the summer. Seven of the ships in the victorious fleet had refused to accompany Duncan to the

Texel in June, and two of these had suffered the heaviest casualties. The surgeon of one of the latter, the *Ardent*, first to engage de Winter's flagship, who had been employed continuously from the start of the action until 4 the following morning treating ninety men brought down to his cockpit operating theatre with often horrific wounds, described amputees exulting when they heard of the scale of the victory and declaring 'they regretted not the loss of their limbs'.[24]

As for the successful tactic of bringing overwhelming concentrations to bear on the rear and van and leaving the centre unengaged, this was entirely fortuitous, brought about by Duncan's desperate need to close before de Winter drew him into the shallows. There is no doubt that in the open sea he would have completed dressing his ships, afterwards approaching in regular line of bearing parallel to the enemy as Howe had done at the First of June. And while there are many similarities between the approach forced on Duncan and the approach Nelson had to take in very different conditions some years later at Trafalgar, there is no evidence that Nelson pondered the tactics of Camperdown or incorporated the idea of a perpendicular approach into his schemes for annihilating the combined Franco-Spanish fleet.

On 19 December that year the government staged a triumph in the form of a national thanksgiving for the three great naval victories under Howe, Jervis and Duncan. The captured enemy colours mounted on three artillery wagons marked 'June 1794', 'February 1797', 'October 1797' were drawn through cheering crowds from the Admiralty building to St Paul's Cathedral, each escorted by officers and petty officers with drawn swords and cutlasses, followed by bands and large detachments of Royal Marines. A procession of carriages carrying seventeen admirals, including Nelson displaying his glittering star of the Bath, preceded members of the Lords and Commons; state coaches drawn by cream Hanoverian horses carried the royal family from St James's Palace, the king in navy blue uniform, the queen and princesses displaying blue in dress or jewellery. What a spectacle to have witnessed – partially recoverable only through contemporary accounts and the eye of imagination. The pageantry and concluding act of thanksgiving in St Paul's constituted a striking popular promotion of the navy, the government and national unity; viewed in historical perspective, it was also a statement of the nature of the formidable fiscal-naval state Great Britain had become over the past century.

*

THIS WAS exemplified in Pitt's Finance Bill that month. His moves for a negotiated peace had clearly failed; subsequent attempts to buy peace from the notoriously venal Barras had also come to nothing. Forced to contemplate a war to which he could see no end, he had to put government finances on a new footing to prevent the national debt spiralling out of control. Already in the past year the cost of new borrowing had risen from around 4½ to over 6 per cent. Further large rises in the debt would provoke higher rates requiring more borrowing to meet the higher charges. To prevent this vicious spiral he had to reduce the annual deficits by bringing current revenue more into line with expenditure; taxes had to be radically increased. His estimated gross deficit for the fiscal year ahead was £22 million.[25]

He rejected a general increase in indirect taxes which would hit the poorest, already suffering severely from inflation in basic food prices. He also rejected property or income taxes which would require inspectors to pry into personal affairs – always a sensitive issue – electing instead for a threefold increase on existing so-called 'assessed taxes' on inhabited houses, windows, male servants, horses, carriages and equipages, furniture and luxuries, in short on the expenditure of the middling and wealthy classes whose standard of living could be quantified. He designed the increases on a sliding scale, as he explained to the Commons, to fall most heavily on 'those whose state of life rises to opulence', while completely exempting some two to three millions of the poorer classes.[26] Despite a storm of protest from those affected in both Houses of Parliament the need was so evident that the Bill passed with only minor amendments on 4 January 1798. In addition, almost £2½ million was raised by 'Voluntary Contribution', a euphemism for donations which Pitt prised from his Cabinet colleagues, the king, and others in public position by demanding that they pledge one-fifth of their income – double the highest rate of the increased 'assessed' taxes. It was probably the nearest he came to the Bourbon and French Revolutionaries' expedient of forced levies on the rich.

Meanwhile the admiral who would become the personification of the nation's will to win was released from the pain and evil swelling in the stump of his right arm. On 4 December 1797 the silk ligature had finally rotted and come away in the surgeon's hand; Nelson was again able to sleep easily. On the 21st he was appointed to the *Vanguard*, 74, to rejoin St Vincent's fleet off Cadiz.

6

The Nile, 1798

IN THE STRUGGLE for primacy between the two great western European rivals a familiar stalemate had been reached: Great Britain unconquerable at sea, France dominant and apparently unconquerable on land. Neither could grasp the other to obtain a stranglehold. Yet internally and financially Britain held the advantages. After the failure of the Pichegru-royalist coup in Paris in September – 18 *Fructidor* – that year, 1797, and a subsequent rebuff for another delegation sent by Pitt to take peace soundings, one of the British delegates reported on the question mark hanging over France's future: 'The Directory wielding the executive power without a shilling in the Treasury, the two Councils legislating for the nation in defiance of the nation, a minority governing a majority, all parties violating the constitution in the name of the constitution. The people perfectly inert and passive . . .'[1]

Despite revolution caused by the bankruptcy of the Crown and the impossibility under the old regime of attaining necessary fiscal and constitutional reforms, government finances remained in disarray, the new constitution as discredited as the old. Realists who had sought to increase France's strength by transforming her into a modern constitutional state like Great Britain had failed; the only remedies for the weakness of the Directory appeared to be restoration or a military coup. Barras, living in grand and profligate style reminiscent of the salacious libels on the old court, was attempting to secure himself against any eventuality by soliciting the self-styled Louis XVIII for letters patent absolving him from his part in the execution of Louis XVI. But the name on all lips was

Bonaparte, hero of the Italian campaign and the humbling of Austria at Campo Formio. Wickham's deputy in Switzerland reported to the Foreign Secretary, Lord Grenville, that Bonaparte was already referred to as '*le premier homme de l'Europe*'; however, no one understood his motives, only that he had 'ambition and great designs'.[2]

Whatever these were, he took care on his return to Paris in December 1797 to conceal them, going about in civilian dress or a worn old uniform, and when honoured by election to the mathematical section of the Institute of France, formerly the French Academy, giving the impression that his highest ambition had been fulfilled. He had intimate discussions with Barras and with Talleyrand, appointed Foreign Minister after returning from exile that summer, and it appears that he colluded in secret negotiations conducted through two international bankers for a Bourbon restoration funded by the British government.[3] The negotiations came to nothing, but it was a fact of surpassing importance for Bonaparte's career, indeed the future history of Europe, that the British government and Louis XVIII believed that he participated wholeheartedly in these negotiations.

For the moment he was appointed to command an army gathered in northern France for the invasion of England. This accorded with his own strategic appreciation and ambitions. His first-hand knowledge of the intrigues Pitt and Grenville were fomenting in Paris and throughout France left him in no doubt that defeat of Great Britain was the priority, which once accomplished, as he wrote to Talleyrand, would leave Europe 'at our feet'.[4] To help fund the enterprise, one of his commanders in Italy marched into Rome and seized the Papal Treasury, subsequently organizing a central Italian Roman Republic on the lines of the 'sister' republics he had created in northern Italy; and the Directory, protesting that Switzerland was the *foyer* of Anglo-royalist intrigue – as indeed it was – launched an invasion there, seized millions in gold francs from Geneva and created the Helvetic Republic as another French satellite. Bonaparte, meanwhile, on a tour of the northern ports from which the Army of England was to be despatched, concluded that the enterprise was next to impossible while the Royal Navy commanded the Channel and North Sea. Instead, he suggested pushing into north Germany or launching an expedition to Egypt to threaten Britain's position in India.

The conquest and colonization of Egypt had been mooted decades earlier by Louis XV's Foreign Minister, the Duc de Choiseul; the proposal had been resurrected by Talleyrand in July 1797 in a lecture to the Institute of France, following which he had discussed it in correspondence with Bonaparte in Italy.[5] Bonaparte had also been attracted to the idea of occupying Malta, ruled since the early sixteenth century by the Knights of St John of Jerusalem. 'Four hundred Knights and at most a regiment of 500 men are the sole defence of the town of Valetta, whose inhabitants ... are very well disposed to us and thoroughly disgusted with the Knights,' he had written in September, adding, 'I have purposely had all their possessions in Italy confiscated.'[6] Besides the strategic value of the island commanding the central Mediterranean, it had not escaped Bonaparte's attention that the ancient Order had amassed considerable wealth.

In January 1798 Talleyrand had recommended the invasion of Egypt to the Directory, following up in February with a weighty report explaining the ease, comparatively low cost and considerable strategic and commercial advantages of planting a colony there to compensate for the loss of the Cape and islands in the West Indies to the British.[7] On paper it appeared sound: with Italy, Corsica and a strong naval base at Corfu already under French control, the addition of Malta and Egypt would seal French dominance in the eastern Mediterranean and provide an advance position from which to attack British eastern commerce and aid native anti-British forces to expel the British from India. The crucial importance of India in France's future had been stressed in several Foreign Ministry memoranda since the time of the American war.[8] However, the scheme rested on the premise that the British fleet had been permanently expelled from the Mediterranean and could never return, and this was to misjudge the offensive temper of the Royal Navy.

It is often suggested that Barras adopted the proposal and appointed Bonaparte to command the expedition in order to remove his ally and most dangerous rival as far as he could from Paris; however, it appears that Barras argued against the scheme, which was eventually carried by majority vote of the other *directeurs*. No doubt they found Bonaparte's partnership with him dangerous. It is even possible that Talleyrand, who had schemes of his own for altering the form of government, wished to rid Paris of his dynamic protégé. It seems more probable, in view of the immense resources needed to mount the enterprise, that it was a genuine strategic response to British naval mastery around the North Sea, Channel and Atlantic coasts of Europe; the Mediterranean was the one stretch of sea where it appeared that France could navigate in safety and strike a blow at Britain's eastern empire by an interior line shortcutting the sea route around the Cape.

This was certainly Bonaparte's vision when he was appointed to command the expedition with instructions to seize Malta, invade and take possession of Egypt and drive the English from all their Oriental possessions he could reach, notably their settlements in the Red Sea. His mind filled with images of glory and dominion in the east. He pictured himself as a modern Alexander entering India on an elephant with a turban on his head; even, according to later remarks, founding a new religion. He read all the books he could find on the region, heavily scoring passages that interested him, and gathered a cohort of archaeologists, artists, astronomers, mineralogists, surveyors, engineers and leading scientists to accompany his army, and administrators to rule the new territories he would bring into the orbit of European civilization. More remarkably, he instructed Vice Admiral François Paul Brueys d'Aigailliers, who was to command the escorting fleet, who his chief of staff was to be and how to dispose his ships,[9] conceits which would not have been tolerated by a British fleet commander – another symptom of the profound difference between a territorial and a maritime power.

On 10 May he arrived in Toulon, the base for the operation, and addressed troops assembled there, many of whom were veterans of his Army of Italy. Reminding them of past triumphs, he promised them each sufficient on their return to France to buy six acres of land; and significantly he told them they were 'one of the wings of the Army of England'.[10] Preparations were completed over the following days and on the 19th the fleet weighed early and put to sea. It was joined by transports from other ports as it headed east around Corsica and steered southerly for Malta. All told, over 30,000 troops were embarked, together with 1,230 cavalry and draught horses for 171 field guns; it was believed numbers of horses would be seized in Egypt. Bonaparte sailed in Brueys' flagship, formerly the *Sans Culotte*, and in Louis XV's day *La Dauphine Royale*, now renamed *L'Orient*; he amused himself during the slow days at sea quizzing the scholars of his 167-strong academic brigade or lying in his cot while his secretary read to him from books selected from the library he had brought. He had no inkling of British warships in the vicinity.

NELSON, FLYING his flag in the *Vanguard*, had joined the fleet blockading Cadiz on 30 April. St Vincent had been awaiting him impatiently, and immediately sent him into the Mediterranean in command of a small squadron of observation consisting of two other 74s, the *Orion* under Sir James Saumarez and the *Alexander* under Alexander Ball, and three frigates. His instructions were to ascertain the real object of the 'considerable armament preparing at Toulon . . . destination according to some reports Sicily or Corfu, and according to others Portugal or Ireland'.[11] To the First Lord of the Admiralty, St Vincent wrote, 'I do assure your Lordship that the arrival of Admiral Nelson has given me a new life; you could not have gratified me more than in sending him.'[12]

By 17 May Nelson's squadron had taken station some 70 miles south of Toulon, but on the 20th, as their target began its passage east around Corsica, a gale struck with such violence that the *Vanguard* lost her main and mizzen topmasts and foremast, which hung over the foc's'le, beating against the bilge as the ship rolled. The potentially fatal disaster was probably due to the inexperience of Nelson's flag captain, Edward Berry. A Norfolk man like Nelson, he had served under him as lieutenant in both the *Agamemnon* and the *Captain*, from where he had led the boarders into the *San Nicolas* and *San Josef* at the battle of St Vincent. Made post in the subsequent promotions, the *Vanguard* was his first command. Nelson never criticized him directly; and it is good to record that after the flagship had been towed off a lee shore by Ball in the *Alexander* and found safety to refit in Sardinia, he was able to write self-mockingly to his wife: 'I ought not to call what has happened to the *Vanguard* by the cold name of accident: I believe firmly that it was the Almighty's goodness to check my consummate vanity. I hope it has made me a better man.'[13] Nelson believed in God as firmly as he loathed the Revolutionaries who had profaned Him, and by extension all the French.

The intervention of the storm prevented Nelson gaining any intelligence of Bonaparte's route since his frigates expected him to make for Gibraltar to refit, so sailed there themselves. It also prevented Bonaparte and Brueys from learning of his presence. Nor was it guessed at on Malta. Consequently, when Bonaparte and Brueys arrived at Valetta on 10 June and landed assault parties, the Knights saw no hope of relief and quickly capitulated. They were an anachronism, certainly by the ideals of the Enlightenment, and they and the Maltese people they ruled had been infiltrated in the usual way prior to the assault by French agents of subversion promoting the slogans of the Revolution. Bonaparte appointed a governing council and ordered all coin, gold, silver and precious stones belonging to the Order seized and placed in his treasury aboard *L'Orient* before departing for Egypt.[14]

Meanwhile the British government had decided that the navy must re-enter the Mediterranean. The Austrians, with whom they were already in negotiation for a second coalition against Revolutionary France, demanded it to sustain their client kingdom of Naples, or the Two Sicilies. Above all, the British government was exercised about the destination of the Toulon expedition. Ireland was under martial law: a revolutionary and Catholic uprising against a Protestant government imposed and held in power by London was suppressed only by the most brutal methods. Should the Toulon expedition break out of the Mediterranean into the Atlantic on the way to support armed rebellion in Ireland it might not be intercepted before reaching its destination. On 29 April the First Lord of the Admiralty had written to St Vincent advising him that 'the appearance of a British squadron in the Mediterranean is a condition on which the fate of Europe may at this moment be stated to depend', adding that it was 'almost unnecessary to suggest to you the propriety of putting it under the command of Sir H. Nelson, whose acquaintance with that part of the world, as well as his activity and disposition, seem to qualify him in a peculiar manner for that service'.[15] Nelson was, of course, in the Mediterranean by the time the letter reached St Vincent, although with a much smaller squadron than envisaged.

The letter had been followed by formal Admiralty instructions to St Vincent to detach 'twelve sail of the line and a competent number of frigates' into the Mediterranean in quest of the Toulon armament 'to take or destroy it'.[16] In compensation he was sent eight of the line from Bridport's fleet watching Brest. St Vincent selected ten 'choice' 74s from his inshore squadron off Cadiz, placed them under the command of his favourite Troubridge in the *Culloden*, and on 24 May, as the sails of their replacements appeared over the horizon, made the signal for him to depart. Troubridge found Nelson on 7 June back on station off Toulon, as over 400 miles to the south-east Bonaparte neared Malta.

Nelson organized his enlarged squadron in three divisions under himself, Saumarez and Troubridge, each with a distinguishing triangular flag – red, white with a red stripe, and blue – and next day issued general orders for battle. These enjoined divisional commanders to 'keep their ships in the closest order possible, and on no account whatever to risk the separation of one of their ships' and stressed that 'the destruction of the enemy's armament is the sole object'. He further emphasized that divisional commanders were under no circumstances to separate in pursuit of the enemy unless by signal from him, 'and the ships are to be kept in that order that the whole squadron may act as a single ship'.[17] As the authority on naval tactics and signals, Brian Tunstall, has remarked, this makes nonsense of the idea, recently resurrected, that Nelson believed in allowing his captains wide discretion in all circumstances. In case they found the enemy at anchor, he issued another memorandum recommending that each ship prepare a cable from the stern for the sheet anchor, together with springs, and added two new signals: 'number 182. Being to windward of the enemy, to denote that I mean to attack the enemy's line from the rear towards the van, as far as thirteen ships, or whatever number of British ships of the line may be present . . . Number 183: I mean to press hard with the whole force on the enemy's rear.'[18]

He now knew the French had sailed three weeks before, but still had no idea of their destination. It was not until the 13th, while steering down the Italian coast, that he spoke a Tunisian vessel which had seen the French expedition off north-western Sicily on the 4th, steering easterly. He wrote to the First Lord, 'If they pass Sicily I shall believe they are going on their scheme of possessing Alexandria, and getting more troops into India – a plan concerted with Tippoo Sahib, by no means so difficult as might at first be imagined.'[19] Four days later, by which time he had learned of Bonaparte's occupation of Malta, he was off Naples and sent Troubridge in with a note for Sir William Hamilton requesting free use of Sicilian ports and provisions 'to enable us to starve the French in Malta . . . The King of Naples may now have a part of the glory in destroying these pests of the human race.'[20] To St Vincent he wrote, 'I will bring the French fleet to action the moment I can lay my hands on them.' The next day he wrote again to Sir William lamenting his lack of frigates and presenting his 'best respects to Lady Hamilton. Tell her I hope to be presented to her crowned with laurel or cypress.'[21]

He pressed on southwards through the Strait of Messina and on the 22nd, off south-eastern Sicily, learned that the French, having taken Malta, had departed with their fleet and transports on the 16th for an unknown destination. Since the wind had been blowing from the west and they had evidently not landed in Sicily, this seemed to confirm his suspicions that they were making for Egypt. He called a council with Saumarez, Troubridge, Ball of the *Alexander*, Darby of the *Bellerophon* and Berry, which soon arrived at the conclusion he clearly wanted: to

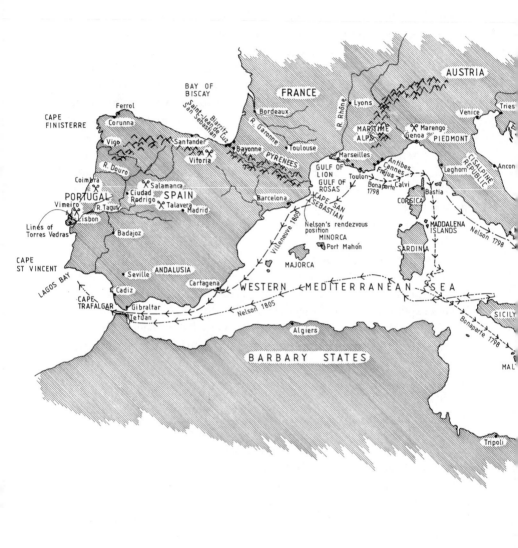

Map 1   The Mediterran

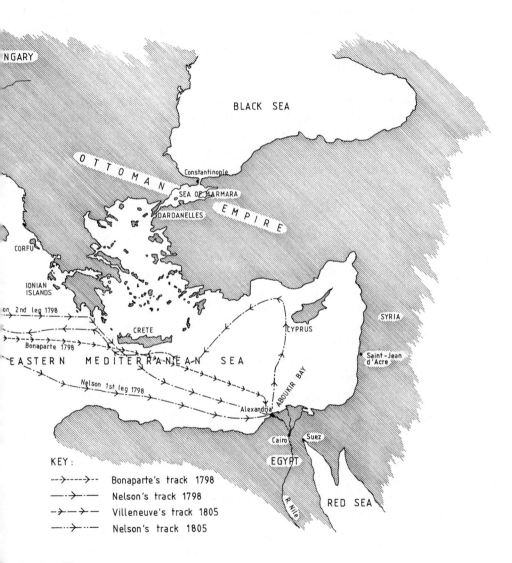

NGARY

BLACK SEA

OTTOMAN

Constantinople

SEA OF MARMARA

DARDANELLES EMPIRE

CORFU

IONIAN
ISLANDS

on 2nd leg 1798

Bonaparte 1798

CRETE

CYPRUS

SYRIA

EASTERN MEDITERRANEAN SEA

Nelson 1st leg 1798

ABOUKIR BAY

Saint-Jean
d'Acre

Alexandria

Cairo Suez

EGYPT

R Nile

RED SEA

KEY:

--->-----> -- Bonaparte's track 1798

———>—·— Nelson's track 1798

->—>—·— Villeneuve's track 1805

—···>···— Nelson's track 1805

Peninsular Theatres

leave out Malta and steer for Egypt. He bore up for Alexandria before a still strong west-north-westerly wind. Four days later, some 200 miles from Alexandria, he sent a note to the British consul there to say he thought the French object was 'to possess themselves of some port in Egypt, and to fix themselves at the head of the Red Sea, in order to get a formidable army into India; and in concert with Tippoo Sahib, to drive us, if possible, from India'.[22] By then he was actually ahead of the French, who had departed Malta on the 19th, three days later than he had been led to believe. Without the great armada of heterogeneous transports Brueys was shepherding, he had made much faster time. Consequently, when Alexandria's Pharos tower and the ancient harbour city came in sight on the 28th there was no sign of the enemy.

Deeply depressed by what he judged his wrong guess, Nelson waited only a day before setting off again to search northwards towards Turkey. Next morning, 1 July, the French expedition arrived at the anchorage he had just vacated. Bonaparte, at last aware of the British squadron and its close proximity, lost no time landing the troops and by evening on the 2nd had taken the city. Brueys' strong inclination, after stores and artillery were landed, was to remove his fleet from the open coast to the protected naval base at Corfu where it would be safe from attack yet able to exert pressure on any British attempt to blockade the army in Alexandria. Bonaparte, for reasons not entirely clear but no doubt connected with the treasure and reserves of ammunition aboard the flagship, wanted the fleet at hand and ordered Brueys to bring it inside the harbour. Surveys soon revealed that, once inside, the ships could only emerge one at a time, and thus could be blocked in by even a single enemy commanding the main entrance channel. The only alternative anchorage near by which offered some natural protection was Aboukir Bay, 12 miles to the east, so Brueys led his ships there, anchoring them in a slightly convex line in five to six fathoms of water, heads towards Aboukir Island and a surrounding shoal which extended from a low sand spit forming the western point of the bay. At the end of the spit beyond a small fishing village stood a somewhat dilapidated fort – quite useless as a protection for the ships which lay outside the range of its old cannon.

The anchorage was in fact indefensible from a determined enemy in any winds but southerly or south-westerly; yet Brueys wrote to Bonaparte on 13 July claiming that he had taken up a strong position in case he should be forced to fight at anchor. That he had doubts is clear from his further comment that he had 'less to fear at the head of the line than at the rear, where the enemy is most likely to direct his efforts'.[23] By this date Bonaparte was advancing up the Nile towards Cairo, where the army of the Mameluke rulers of Egypt had gathered to oppose him. They were a mounted martial order more anachronistic even than the Knights of St John of Jerusalem and when the forces met near the Pyramids on the 21st they were routed by the disciplined firepower of the French infantry. Next day Bonaparte crossed the Nile and entered Cairo as the new ruler of Egypt.

Nelson had by now circled the eastern Mediterranean and was back in Sicily at the port of Syracuse taking on fresh fruit and vegetables and live bullocks. He still had no firm news of Bonaparte, but reasoned that if the French had sailed west from Malta Sir William Hamilton – who knew that he, Nelson, had gone east – would have relayed the news for him to every port in Sicily. Evidently he had not done this; so they must have gone east.[24] He weighed on the 24th and steered for the Greek archipelago, and finally on the 28th received confirmation of his original hunch from a Turkish governor in the Peloponnese: the French were in Egypt. Favoured with a westerly wind, he crowded sail for Alexandria again.

On the 31st, nearing the port but lacking frigates, he sent two 74s, *Alexander* and *Swiftsure*, ahead as scouts. They raised the now familiar Pharos tower in the middle of the morning of 1 August, and soon after noon had approached sufficiently close to see the harbour filled with French transports, but only two ships of the line amongst them. Receipt of this news must have caused Nelson the blackest despair. He had been fretting for weeks and for the past days had scarcely eaten. Saumarez, who recorded his own feelings at this moment, could not recall 'ever to have felt so utterly hopeless or out of spirits'.[25]

All was changed at 2.30 when from the most easterly of Nelson's ships, *Zealous* and *Goliath*, the masts of Brueys' battle line were sighted over the low land bordering Aboukir Bay, and the *Zealous* made the signal for sixteen sail of the line at anchor; in fact there were thirteen and four large frigates. Amid the surge of elation throughout the squadron Nelson's pleasure and relief were noticeably intense.

He was now confronted with the most vital decision of his career to date: whether to give battle that day, risking his ships in an unknown bay with at best an hour or two of daylight remaining by the time he could reach the enemy; and if so, whether to gather his ships together first. They were at present stretched over several miles, with the *Alexander* and *Swiftsure* well to the south-west – although he had recalled them a quarter of an hour earlier – and Troubridge's *Culloden* far astern towing a prize. Alternatively, should he wait until morning and attack in the closest formation – as his general orders stressed – with the whole day in which to ensure a decision?

Like Drake two centuries earlier off Cadiz he determined to sail straight in. No doubt, as with Drake, the judgement formed intuitively; all his experience told him time and a favourable wind once lost could never be recovered; all his instincts required him to seize the initiative and strike before the enemy could prepare. The wind was north-north-westerly – what Berry described as a 'topgallant breeze'[26] – blowing into the bay and directly down the anchored line of Brueys' ships from van to rear. He hauled round on the larboard tack and steered easterly towards the bay, and shortly before 3 o'clock made number 53, 'Prepare for battle',[27] followed almost immediately by a signal to the *Culloden* to cast off her prize.

In the event his decision was fully justified. Brueys was lamentably unprepared. Despite expecting the British squadron to return, he had no scouts to seaward; his first intimation of strange ships was a signal from the ninth ship in his line when her lookouts sighted Nelson's mastheads at about the time his own masts were seen from the *Zealous* and *Goliath*. It was not until 3 o'clock that he was sure they were British; he ordered his ships prepared for action and all shore parties recalled, but it was another two hours, when Nelson's leading group began rounding the shoal off Aboukir Island, before he realized he was about to be attacked that evening.

Ever since taking up his position he had been undecided about the merits of fighting at anchor or weighing to meet the enemy in open sea. His first instinct now was to weigh, and he had his t'gallant yards swayed aloft. Almost immediately he saw the confusion that must result from the inexperienced, short-handed crews attempting to work out of the bay against an onshore wind while engaging the enemy, and he made the signal to fight at anchor, following it with instructions to each ship to let go another anchor with a spring attached – to enable them to heave round to bring the guns to bear – and to pass a cable to the next astern with a hawser attached for use in the same way. He also ordered the frigates to send their best guns' crews to the ships of the line. How completely these orders were followed in the short time available is not known; they had little discernible effect.

Nelson had by now signalled his intention to his squadron: at 4.22

when the *Vanguard* had advanced far enough for him to see past the fort at the end of the land into the bay and the anchored enemy line, he had made the signal to prepare for battle and for anchoring with springs and anchor cable taken in at a stern port. Half an hour later he hoisted numbers 45 and 46 together: engage the enemy's centre; engage the enemy's van.[28]

Brueys' assumption that the British would attack his rear was about to be proved disastrously wrong. He had made provision for the van to weigh and come to the support of the centre or rear if attacked, but none for the rear to come to the aid of the van[29] – which would in any case have been impossible with the wind from its present direction – and he had placed his two oldest and weakest ships, *Guerrier* and *Conquérant*, at the head of the line. Moreover, it seems clear both from the course of events and from recent archaeological discovery of the French warships' anchors in the bay that he had not placed his leading ship hard up to shallow water.[30]

As the foremost British ships passed Aboukir Island and ran on to clear the long shoal extending eastwards, the *Zealous* and *Goliath* were in the lead abreast of one another, with the *Vanguard* on the *Zealous*'s weather quarter, close enough for Nelson to hail her captain, Samuel Hood, to ask whether he thought they were far enough to the east to bear up around the shoal. Hood told him he was in 11 fathoms and had no chart, but if Nelson would allow him, he would bear up and try with the lead and lead him as close as he could with safety. Nelson said he would be obliged to him and swept off his hat. Hood swept off his own in reply, but it slipped from his fingers and sailed into the sea. He turned to his first lieutenant, 'Never mind, Webley! There it goes for luck! Put the helm up and make sail!'[31] To leeward of the *Zealous*, Captain Thomas Foley of the *Goliath*, anticipating the turn, immediately put his own helm up and set studding sails; as he came round on the inside he edged into the lead. This may have been fortunate since he had a French atlas which marked the depths; on the other hand both leaders sounded continuously.

Shortly after rounding the shoal the *Vanguard* backed her main topsail in order to pick up a boat from a brig attached to the squadron which had taken local sailors from a vessel out of Alexandria to act as pilots. As she lost way the *Theseus* went past, but Berry hailed her captain with an order from Nelson to act as his second ahead, a post of honour; upon which she hove to. The *Audacious* and Saumarez's *Orion* sailed past to take the third and fourth positions but a good way astern of the two leaders.

The *Vanguard* shortly filled her sails again and Nelson made the signal to form line of battle ahead and astern of the admiral as most convenient, following it with number 34: 'Alter course one point to starboard in succession' – towards the enemy van.

Aboard the *Goliath*, leading down under a press of canvas towards the head of the enemy line and almost within gunshot, Foley was listening from the forward quarterdeck rail to the leadsman calling the depths, wondering whether there was sufficient water to steer across the bows of the leading French ship to attack her from inside. The anchor buoy was visible about a cable's length ahead of her stem, and he decided there was room to pass between it and the end of her bowsprit. Resolving on it, he said to the master beside him that he would not be surprised to find the Frenchman unprepared for action on her inner side. Nelson, according to Berry, saw the opportunity at about the same time, exclaiming that where there was room for an enemy's ship to swing there was room for one of theirs to anchor.[32] But whether Foley's decision was the result of plans for attacking an enemy at anchor laid by Nelson and explained to his captains long before the action – as Berry asserted – or whether Foley acted on his own initiative is not clear; certainly Hood, just astern of him, was surprised when he realized what he intended.

It was after 6 o'clock. The sun hung low in the western sky. Ten British 74s had rounded the shoal and formed an unevenly spaced line following Foley. Three other 74s, together with a 50-gun ship, *Leander*, which Troubridge had attached at Gibraltar before joining Nelson, were still on an easterly course north of Aboukir Island and the long shoal stretching from it: first Troubridge's *Culloden*, then the *Leander*, followed by the *Alexander* and *Swiftsure*. The odds should have favoured the thirteen French at anchor. Brueys' great three-decker, *L'Orient*, seventh in the line, was seconded ahead and astern by 80-gun ships and each of these three at the central elbow of the French formation was more powerful than any ship in the British squadron. Moreover, by hauling on springs attached to their anchor cables, the leading seven French should have been able to bring their broadsides to bear on the British coming down one after the other practically at right angles, and to inflict sufficient damage to masts and rigging to make it difficult for at least Foley and Hood in the lead to handle their ships with the precision required to keep out of the shallows close on their starboard hand. But Brueys' men held their fire as the enemy leaned towards them.

The silence was palpable, broken only by the rising and falling

cadences of the leadsmen calling the depths. The British 74s stood on across the ruffled blue-green water, yellow sides horizontally banded or chequered with black along double rows of gun ports, guns run out below the red of raised port lids, white canvas stretched above in tapering tiers against a clear blue sky. On both sides men waited with tense brows; ten thousand urgent private images hung suspended before the act.

As the *Goliath* came within 500 yards of her target the suspense broke. The French ships ran up their colours and opened fire, the *Conquérant* first, followed by the *Guerrier* at the head of the line, the thunder and smoke spreading to ships astern, some of which had heaved themselves round with hawsers to bring their broadsides to bear. Most of the shot went high. Foley, steering for a point just beyond the end of the *Guerrier*'s jib-boom, reduced sail as the soundings decreased towards the danger mark of five fathoms, and gave the order to fire when the guns bore. Passed to the guns' crews by the officers of the quarters below, it drew full-throated cheers, which were repeated from Hood's *Zealous* close astern. Two minutes later the *Goliath*'s foremost guns, angled to their extreme forward bearing, erupted, followed successively by the other pieces down the decks as the ship swept past the Frenchman's bows and raking jib-boom. Once inside his opponent, Foley wore round to engage on his larboard side, and the master gave the order to cut the lashings on the anchor cable through the stern port. These proved obstinate and it was not until the *Goliath* was almost abreast of the *Guerrier* and pounding her with another broadside that the anchor dropped; Foley had to run on paying out cable until he could bring her up on the *Conquérant*'s larboard quarter. His guess that the French might not be prepared for action on the inner side proved correct. Neither the *Guerrier* nor the *Conquérant* had their larboard guns run out, and stores and lumber obstructed the upper deck gun ports. His guns' crews were able to make practically unopposed practice. One of the men stationed in the powder magazine making up cartridges for the 'powder monkeys' – the boys and some of the women carried aboard, chiefly the wives of responsible petty officers, who distributed the charges to the gun decks – recollected years later that 'the women behaved as well as the men'.[33]

Hood, following close in Foley's wake, dropped his anchor directly he had passed inside the French line and brought up where Foley had intended on the *Guerrier*'s larboard bow, from where his double- and treble-shotted cannon and upper deck carronades broke in the timbers between the French gun ports, swept the decks with splinters and grape, overturned cannon, severed rigging and cut through the foremast, which crashed over the side by both Hood's and his first lieutenant's accounts within seven minutes – at which the bay rang with cheers from the British ships following. The first of these, *Audacious*, now swept past Hood's stern, dropped her anchor and fetched up off the larboard bow of the *Conquérant*, adding her fire to the *Goliath*'s. Following her, Saumarez's *Orion* made a wider sweep and came under fire from a frigate further inshore. Replying with her starboard broadside, she drove the frigate on a shoal and brought all her masts down, then briefly touching ground herself, veered back towards the French line, dropped her stern anchor and brought up opposite the fifth French ship. She was followed across the *Guerrier*'s bows by the *Theseus* whose captain described reserving his fire until he saw the *Guerrier*'s remaining two masts in a line and her jib-boom about six feet clear of his rigging: 'we then opened with such effect that a second breath could not be drawn before her main and mizzen masts were also gone.'[34] He wore round between the now mastless hulk and Hood, whose men ceased firing and cheered. The cheers were answered by the company of the *Theseus* as she passed on, steering close outside the *Audacious* and *Goliath*, and brought up to a stern anchor opposite the third ship in the French line.

The sun had now set. The western sky was a fiery red. Nelson and Foley between them had taken Brueys completely by surprise. The two leading French ships were thoroughly beaten, although neither had struck yet; the third and fifth were under heavy fire from the *Theseus* and *Orion*. Nelson, possibly because of the fading light, probably because he wished to double the enemy and bring his whole force as he had signalled against the van and centre, did not follow the *Theseus* inside the French, but had Berry bring the *Vanguard* round to engage the third ship from outside the line. The *Theseus* was already engaging her from inside, and to avoid firing over her into the *Vanguard* her captain redirected his after guns' crews to the *Conquérant*, the forward guns' crews to the fourth French ship.

The captains of the two ships following the *Vanguard* divined Nelson's intentions exactly, and passing him on the outside, brought up successively opposite the next two vessels in the enemy line, which was now enveloped by an overwhelming concentration on both sides down to the fifth ship. The next British ship, *Bellerophon*, made for the sixth, so far unengaged Frenchman, but paid out too much cable and brought up off the starboard bow of Brueys' flagship, *L'Orient*, seventh in line, whose three tiers of great guns were soon wreaking heavy damage and casualties. In the smoke and failing light the last of the British main body, *Majestic*, also overshot; her jib-boom became entangled in the rigging of the ninth French ship, where for a time she was trapped between her fire and that of *L'Orient*'s 80-gun second ahead of her.

Meanwhile Troubridge, crowding sail to reach the fighting, had rounded into the bay too early and grounded on rocks at the eastern extremity of the entrance shoal. Despite laying out kedge anchors to heave her off and lightening ship by opening up water and wine casks and throwing provisions and a great quantity of shot overboard, the ship held fast. Her flag signal that she was aground served as a warning to the *Leander*, *Alexander* and *Swiftsure*, still heading easterly outside the bay, and enabled them to avoid her fate.

By the time these had rounded the shoal and approached the embattled lines darkness had fallen, but moonlight from a clear sky and constant gun flashes illuminated the scene and even made it possible to distinguish colours through brief gaps in the clouds of gunsmoke. The five leading French ships had by now struck or been reduced to wrecks, but the French centre around *L'Orient* was more than holding its own, and it was here the captains of the three new ships placed themselves with sure judgement and exceptional skill: the *Alexander* across *L'Orient*'s quarter, the *Swiftsure* between the French flagship and her second ahead to engage both, and finally the little *Leander*, which had attempted to assist Troubridge off the shoal, across the bows of *L'Orient*'s second ahead; she was able to attain this superlative raking position in which any shot missing its target flew into the French flagship beyond because the fifth French ship engaged by Saumarez's *Orion* had drifted out of the line, her cable cut and all her masts gone.

The *L'Orient*'s weary guns' crews suffered immediately from the fresh onslaught, and Brueys himself, already wounded in head and arm, was almost cut in two by a round shot through his middle; he asked not to be taken below, but to be allowed to die on his own quarterdeck. His flag captain was knocked unconscious by flying wrack and carried below. Shortly afterwards a fire started in Brueys' quarters. The captain of the *Swiftsure* immediately directed his forward guns and musketry at the affected area and succeeded in making it impossible for the fire-fighting parties to extinguish the flames, which burnt through the deckhead and up the mizzen mast and horizontally along the deck, apparently feeding on oil and paint jars which had not been stowed below. The flames spread downwards as well as up the masts and before long the three-decker had become a giant flaming beacon, lighting adjacent ships and hulks and wreckage in the water. The heat was intense. Men leaped from gun ports into the sea. Captains of nearby British ships ordered fire buckets hoisted aloft to douse the sails and had gunport lids and magazines closed; the nearest cut or veered their anchor cables to distance themselves from the blast anticipated when the flames reached the magazines. Nelson, who was below in the *Vanguard* after being wounded above the right eye by a metal fragment, was escorted on deck to witness the sight and immediately gave orders for boats to be sent to rescue survivors.

L'Orient blew apart at 10 o'clock. The roar was ear-splitting. Flaming wreckage soared to vast heights in all directions. Between decks in nearby ships and in cockpits and magazines below the waterline the blast felt as if a giant had seized and shaken the vessels bodily. Then burning spars and timbers and red hot embers rained down, starting fires on friend and foe alike. The jib and main royal of the *Alexander* were set ablaze and had to be cut away to prevent the flames spreading. Above, a blanket of black smoke obscured the moon. Recent underwater archaeology suggests that there were two almost simultaneous explosions, forward and aft, which fragmented both ends of the ship, leaving the middle section open to the sea and sinking. Cannon above the seats of the explosions were shattered, others blown more than 150 yards through the air.

After the blast the guns fell silent. Momentary cheers rose from some of the British ships, but the eruption had been so stunning the primary feeling was shock; some guns' crews were so exhausted they fell asleep at their posts. A few of *L'Orient*'s survivors were rescued by boat; others who swam to nearby British ships were hauled in shivering through the lower ports and given clothing by the sailors.

The battle was now decided. Although fighting resumed for a while around *L'Orient*'s second ahead, two-thirds of her crew were already killed or wounded, and, beset from both sides, she soon succumbed. Spasmodic firing continued through the rest of the night between some of the French rear and the *Majestic* and *Alexander*, which two were joined at dawn by the relatively little damaged ships from the van, *Zealous*, *Goliath*, *Audacious*, *Theseus* and the little *Leander*. Together they forced the submission of all but two of the surviving French ships of the line and two frigates. These four, led by the commander of the rear division, Rear Admiral Pierre Villeneuve, succeeded in beating their way out of the bay, frustrating a brief chase by Hood in the *Zealous*. Otherwise the French Mediterranean fleet had ceased to exist. It was victory on a scale Nelson had longed for, achieved partly in consequence of Brueys' failure in reconnaissance and inability to envisage an assault on the head of his line, but chiefly owing to Nelson's decision to attack at once while the wind held, and to Foley's bold initiative in sailing inside the enemy; indeed, all the British captains had positioned themselves with extraordinary judgement and skill in surrounding and crushing the enemy van. Nelson was later to describe his commanders, in a Shakespearian phrase which entered legend, as 'a band of brothers'.

For the French, Aboukir Bay presented a sight as mournful as the aftermath of a great battle on land. The shattered or burned hulks flying British colours on their few remaining masts or stumps were surrounded by floating wreckage intermingled promiscuously with the bodies of the slain, some 1,700 French against only 218 British, described by a participant as 'mangled, wounded and scorched, not a bit of clothes on them except their trousers'.[35] In terms of battleships taken and destroyed it was the worst French defeat since Barfleur–La Hougue over a century earlier; in the proportion of the fleet lost to an equal enemy it was the worst ever French defeat and unprecedented in naval history. Strategically, it was decisive. France had lost control of the Mediterranean. Bonaparte's army was imprisoned in Egypt and, cut off from sea-borne reinforcements or supplies, Bonaparte's dream of entering India on an elephant dissolved. In grand strategic terms, France's enemies were encouraged, and in the following months Pitt was able to fashion a second coalition, consisting this time of Austria, Turkey and Russia, but without Prussia.

The effects on Nelson were less happy. The blow from flying metal which he had received at the height of the battle had bared his forehead to the bone for a full inch above his right eye and caused him to fall, believing he was mortally wounded:[36] he had asked Berry, who caught him, to remember him to his wife. The wound had been excruciatingly painful and he complained of a splitting headache for weeks afterwards; he had probably been concussed. This may be considered the generous explanation. More likely the plaudits, honours and gifts showered upon him from all sides, and the popular adulation manifested in songs, prints, porcelain and pottery likenesses and every type of souvenir of the Naval Hero produced for sale, simply turned his head. But having left Samuel Hood to continue blockading Alexandria and returned to Naples in the *Vanguard*, he appears to have undergone a change of character. Elevated as Baron Nelson of the Nile and Burnham Thorpe, he famously lost himself in mutual admiration with Emma, Lady Hamilton, lapsed from his former standards of duty to king and country, hazarded the larger struggle against the French 'pests of the human race' to his perception of the interests of the court of the Two Sicilies and disobeyed the orders of a new commander-in-chief who replaced St Vincent the following summer. At the same time, what had been a thirst for glory and personal distinction, far from being satiated by worldwide renown since 'the Glorious First of August', grew so inflated he became a caricature of vanity, according to Sir John Moore, 'covered with stars, medals and ribbons, more like a Prince of Opera than the Conqueror of the Nile'[37] – an opinion endorsed by other observers.

Notwithstanding his temporary eclipse, British forces in the Mediterranean recaptured Port Mahón, Minorca, as a base from which to watch Toulon, took Malta from the French – a vital acquisition which would serve as a base for the British Mediterranean fleet for over 150 years – and contained the Brest fleet when it was sent south to join the Spanish fleet.

BONAPARTE'S EGYPTIAN foray was finally closed by Captain Sir Sidney Smith. Since commanding the Channel Island squadron and operating a clandestine network of agents with the Chouans in northern France, Smith had been captured while chasing a privateer too far up the Seine, and held subsequently as a state prisoner in the Temple in Paris – where the Bourbon royal family had been imprisoned. Here he had lived in great style, meeting and corresponding freely with whomever he chose, including the Foreign Secretary's spymaster, William Wickham, and apparently acting as intermediary with the Parisian counter-revolutionary plotters.[38] He was as original and confident in his own judgement as Nelson – too confident, in the opinion of superior officers; even fellow captains found him showy and boastful. Yet those who served under him recorded his courtly manners, great good humour, kindness and infinite variety: 'He was the life and soul of the ship, composed songs and sang them; full of anecdote, so well told that you lost sight of the little bit of egotism they smacked of.'[39]

In appearance he was described as more like a Turk than an Englishman, with dark curly hair and penetrating black eyes. At sea he cultivated ferocious moustaches; homeward bound he shortened them each day and stepped ashore in England clean shaven. He had been made post captain at the exceptionally early age of eighteen – two years younger than Nelson – during the American war when his dash and ability had brought him to Rodney's attention. Unusually for a naval officer, he was also socially and politically well-connected, a first cousin to the Prime Minister and nephew of the Foreign Secretary's wife, Lady Grenville, and no doubt he owed his involvement with the secret service and Lord Grenville's funds for the Paris counter-revolutionaries to these relationships. While in the Temple at the pivot of negotiations for a Bourbon restoration, he must surely have been aware of Bonaparte's involvement.[40] At all events, after Bonaparte was appointed to the Egyptian expedition hopes for a restoration faded and Smith had been spirited out of prison and home to England with the aid of secret service funds.[41]

Directly news of Nelson's victory at the Nile reached London Smith was sent to Constantinople where his brother, Spencer Smith, was chargé d'affaires at the British Legation, and the two were given plenipotentiary powers to sign a treaty of alliance with Turkey with the aim of removing Bonaparte from Egypt. He was also empowered to take British warships in the area under his command, and was given secret instructions to infiltrate agents of subversion into Bonaparte's army, for which purpose he took a group of French royalists with him in his flagship, *Tigre*.

His appearance in the Mediterranean early in 1799 armed with such diplomatic and independent naval authority so outraged St Vincent and Nelson that the Admiralty moved quickly to reassure them the normal chains of command applied, and he was instructed to take his orders from Nelson. Yet, as he made clear in writing to the First Lord, he intended carrying out his mission for the Cabinet, agreed with the Turkish government, by which Bonaparte and his army would be allowed to lay down their arms and return to Europe as unexchanged prisoners of war, ineligible to fight again.[42] This was quite contrary to Nelson's aim of keeping them locked up in Egypt. It was also contrary to the First Lord's ideas, since he did not trust Bonaparte to adhere to the terms; but he had not attended the Cabinet which had approved Smith's commission in the first place, nor did he know of Bonaparte's involvement in Barras' intrigue to restore Louis XVIII. Smith, on the other hand, had been convinced by his French royalists aboard the *Tigre* that once back in France Bonaparte would take action to restore the monarchy.[43]

Bonaparte had no intention of surrendering his arms. News of the treaty concluded by the Smith brothers with the Turkish government, followed by a Turkish declaration of war against France, rekindled all his original visions of eastern glory. He had already subdued Egypt; now, in early February 1799, he struck north along the coast through Palestine with 13,000 picked troops intending to march on Constantinople – and return to Europe over the ruins of the Ottoman empire – or possibly strike east for the Persian Gulf. Smith learned of his plans through intercepted letters and agents already infiltrated into the French army, and resolved to halt him where the coast road passed the old crusader fortress of Saint-Jean d'Acre jutting into the Mediterranean above a bay providing good anchorage. Sending a trusted lieutenant who had been incarcerated with him in Paris to open negotiations with the Turkish governor there, together with an engineer from amongst his émigrés to renovate the decayed fortifications, he sailed north and hired a force of Bosnian, Albanian, Turkish and other mercenaries to reinforce the small Turkish garrison at Acre and purchased a flotilla of gunboats to augment the firepower of the *Tigre* and one other 74 which he had attached to his command from the squadron blockading Alexandria.

He brought this polyglot force to Acre and began sending naval guns and marines ashore and organizing the defences on 15 March, just three days before Bonaparte arrived. They were a crucial three days. Bonaparte could not continue northwards and leave the enemy at his back; he was obliged to halt and lay siege to the fortress, yet he lacked battering guns to break down the walls since Smith's forces had captured his siege train which was following in boats up the coast. The morale of his army was also running low; provisions were short, uniforms ragged and men beginning to go down with bubonic plague, which had appeared first the previous autumn. The émigré agents helped to augment disaffection and reported the causes to Smith, enabling him to compose a letter as from Bonaparte to the Directory in Paris detailing the army's distresses. Copies of this were then distributed amongst the French troops. They appeared so authentic that one was sent to the Turkish ambassador in London, who forwarded it to the Foreign Office.[44] Meanwhile, under Smith's personal leadership Bonaparte's assaults were repeatedly thrown back; and owing to Smith's command of sea supply routes the normal conditions of siege warfare whereby the besieged were starved into submission were reversed. It was Bonaparte's men who suffered lack of food and supplies. Finally, on 20 May, after sixty-three days, with his men's discontent reaching mutinous levels, Bonaparte raised the siege and began a retreat to Egypt.

To the end of his life he maintained that Smith had denied him his destiny in the Orient. 'In that miserable fort', he claimed, 'lay the fate of the east.'[45] In view of the distances and hostile terrain involved, and the constant attacks his comparatively small army would have been subjected to if his ambitions were to be realized, it seems as likely that Smith saved him from a later and greater humiliation. The reverse certainly assisted Bonaparte's career in Europe. Having brought the remnants of his army back to Cairo through the most gruelling desert conditions, harassed by Turkish partisans, he staged a victory parade for his conquests in the Holy Land, and the following month routed a 15,000-strong Turkish army which Sidney Smith had landed in Aboukir Bay. Thus he preserved his victorious and romantic reputation for those in France who could not know the hopeless realities of his situation.

Soon afterwards he sent a lieutenant to parley with Smith in the *Tigre*. What was said is not known, but the result was that Smith promised to open a door in the blockade for Bonaparte's escape.[46] The inference must be that Bonaparte played the royalist card, reinforcing Smith's belief that if allowed to return to France he would lead a coup to place Louis XVIII on the throne. This was Pitt's primary war aim.

As a result of the meeting, on 22 August 1799 Bonaparte, taking five generals and what remained of the money in the army chest, abandoned his hapless second in command and the depleted and demoralized men to whom he had promised so much, and slipped away from Aboukir Bay after dark in a French frigate. It was a shameful betrayal; had the full facts been known in France, no doubt his reception would have been different. As it was, when he landed at Fréjus on the Provençal coast on 9 October he was acclaimed as a saviour by crowds who mobbed his coach all the way to Paris. After years of revolutionary disruption, shortages, brigandage, anarchy and civil war all the French people wanted was a return to peace and normality and an end to political corruption; this young general with an invincible aura seemed the man to provide it.

Members of the Directory had also been searching for a strong man to bring stability to government, and within weeks of Bonaparte's arrival in Paris a coup had been engineered,[47] largely by Talleyrand and the Abbé Sieyès, recently elected as a *directeur*, which swept away the constitution, the Directory and elected councils and installed Bonaparte as First Consul with virtually unlimited powers; his two fellow Consuls were little more than advisers. So France turned full circle from absolute monarchy, in theory rather than practice, through revolution and ruinous internal strife to military dictatorship, in practice rather than theory.

Whether Nelson or Sir Sidney Smith had the larger hand in curbing Bonaparte's eastern ambitions and so, indirectly, bringing him to power in France, the overall cause was French naval inferiority. Once Pitt's Cabinet decided that the Royal Navy must re-enter the Mediterranean Bonaparte's schemes were doomed. Nelson and Smith simply used this marvellously flexible instrument to lock the door on French overseas adventure. As for Smith's motive in unlocking the door briefly for Bonaparte to escape, he told his brother later that he had intended him to be captured at sea. This would have been an uncertain way of securing a general in an already hopeless situation; it is an unlikely story. However, Smith's true reason – his belief that Bonaparte had signed a pact with royalists to place Louis XVIII on the throne in return for becoming lieutenant general of the royal armies[48] – was a considerable underestimate of the man's boundless vision.

7

Copenhagen, 1801

BONAPARTE CHOSE TO consolidate his power by striking at the Austrians who had advanced into the north Italian plain, scene of his early victories. Nothing better illustrates the contingent nature of events, as opposed to the deep underlying tides of history, than the battle he fought there on 14 June 1800 around the little village of Marengo, south of Alessandria. Had he lost, as he should have done since he misjudged his enemy and divided his force, the chances are that the name Napoleon would be unknown to history. As it was, within a short time of the start of the battle he realized his error and sent desperate messages to his two dispersed corps commanders, 'For God's sake come, if you still can!'[1] One was too far away; the other, General Louis Desaix, marched his force over ten gruelling miles, arriving in the early evening as Bonaparte was preparing to concede defeat and leave the field. The Austrian commander, confident of victory, had left two hours earlier to write his despatches. Desaix's new but weary troops halted the Austrian advance and a cavalry charge on the Austrians' flank created disorder which turned into rout. Next morning Bonaparte was able to negotiate an Austrian withdrawal from northern Italy.

Marengo completed his glorification and secured his authority by the popular will; thenceforward Bonaparte was France. The battle also hastened the dissolution of Pitt's second coalition. Tsar Paul of Russia, annoyed by the treaty negotiated by Sidney Smith with the Turkish government and representatives of the French army in Egypt,[2] had already signalled his intention of withdrawing his troops from the coalition. Marengo made him an ardent Bonapartist and convinced him of the desirability of a Franco-Russian alliance. He was reinforced in this attitude when the British government refused to give him Malta after it was retaken from the French. He was Grand Master of the Knights of St John of Jerusalem, former rulers of the island, for whom he had a mystical obsession; he also wanted a naval presence in the Mediterranean. Consequently he readily fell in with Bonaparte's suggestion that he should revive the Armed Neutrality formed by the Baltic powers against Great Britain in 1780 during the American war. As then, it was British naval interference with neutral ships carrying French or French colonial goods or contraband of war to French ports that provided the motive. British pretensions to stop and search neutrals for enemy goods had always provoked hostility; but commercial blockade aimed at crippling the enemy's commerce and industry and preventing vital commodities reaching his naval arsenals had always been a prime British strategy, as well as acting as a spur to Royal Navy officers.

When Paul raised the old cry of the freedom of the seas, invoking the seventeenth-century Dutch claim that a neutral flag protected the goods aboard, and in December 1800 persuaded Denmark, Sweden and Prussia to join him in a new League of Armed Neutrality[3] to deny the Baltic to British ships – and impounded some 300 British vessels and British goods in Russian ports – Pitt's government reacted promptly and predictably. Baltic supplies of tar, hemp, flax and timber, especially masts and spars from the tall, straight firs and spruce trees whose slow growth in the forests of northern Germany, Russia and Sweden endowed them with particular toughness and flexibility, were essential for the maintenance of British naval mastery; denying them to the enemy was almost as essential. A fleet of twenty of the line and supporting frigates was hastily gathered for the Baltic to back diplomacy, or if necessary destroy the Danish, Swedish and Russian fleets in detail, and placed under the sixty-one-year-old Admiral Sir Hyde Parker, who had grown rich from prize eighths garnered while commanding the West Indies station, but was otherwise undistinguished. In case it came to fighting, Nelson was appointed his second in command.

Nelson had returned to England in November after crossing the continent in company with Sir William and Emma Hamilton – as she put it, a 'Tria Juncta in Uno'. Certainly the frail and aged Sir William was devoted to Nelson, regarding him as his best friend in the world; Nelson adored Emma, his mistress for many months, with all his ardent nature and she, in the words of one young widow who saw much of them, was 'totally devoted to the same object', yet obviously committed to her naval hero, 'a little man without dignity' according to the same widow.[4] Her comment echoes other descriptions of Nelson's unremarkable physical appearance.[5] His fascination derived from the liveliness of his features when his mind was engaged, and his direct intelligence, although this was not a quality the young widow was able to discern as he submitted himself completely to the once-ravishing, now overblown Emma, calling on her in the evenings for songs in his own praise or acclaiming her famous *tableaux vivants* with whoops and cries of 'Mrs Siddons be damned!'[6]

Reunited with his wife in London, Nelson maintained his close relationship with the Hamiltons, and continued to display his passion for Emma without regard to his wife's feelings or the disapproving talk of society and of his fellow officers. By mid-January 1801, Lady Nelson was able to bear it no longer and told him he must choose between her and Emma. The result was never in doubt, particularly as Emma was carrying his child. He left his wife, writing later that he had made her a very liberal allowance and wished to be left to himself without any enquiries from her. On 28 January Emma bore twin girls; one she christened Horatia, the other was probably stillborn.[7] Nelson received the news in February after hoisting his flag in the 98-gun *St George* with orders to join Hyde Parker's fleet preparing for the Baltic.

The situation of the country had altered radically by this date. Pitt, in seeking to solve the dangerous unrest in Ireland, had united that country politically with Great Britain,[8] but failed to persuade his Cabinet or the king that Irish Catholic emancipation was an essential condition of the union, and resigned. A new administration had been formed under Henry Addington, who had appointed St Vincent First Lord of the Admiralty.

On the continent the Austrians had been defeated decisively by the French in southern Germany, forcing the Emperor once again to the peace table; by the Treaty of Lunéville, signed on 4 February, Bonaparte had extended French borders to the Rhine, gaining the southern Netherlands (Belgium) and Luxembourg, and obtained formal recognition of the satellite republics in Holland, Switzerland and northern Italy. Dutch, Spanish and north Italian ports were already closed to British ships; now he bullied the kingdom of the Two Sicilies into closing Neapolitan ports,[9] shutting out British trade from the whole of Italy. It was this same policy of barring British merchants from European markets, and thus ruining Britain's economy and her ability to wage war

– forerunner of his later 'continental system' – that had led Bonaparte to encourage Baltic armed neutrality. The ambition was stupendous. As the eminent historian and educator, H. A. L. Fisher, put it, the strategy could not work in part: 'It must either succeed entirely or not at all . . . drawn by the mirage of a universal blockade, he [Bonaparte] was condemned to the pursuit of a universal empire.'[10] His Foreign Minister, Talleyrand, recognized this, and had already sent a peace envoy to London. But for the present Great Britain was again fighting alone, this time against a France reinvigorated under her charismatic young general and dominant in Europe. Again, survival seemed to depend upon the Royal Navy which now needed to destroy the Baltic coalition and at the same time keep a tight enough watch on Brest to ensure that the French fleet could not emerge to support an invasion.

So it appeared on the surface of events. Significant counter-currents played beneath. Talleyrand's envoy found Addington and his new Foreign Secretary so eager for peace they were ready to give up practically every overseas conquest made during the course of the war, including the French West Indian islands, the important Mediterranean bases of Malta and Minorca, and the Cape of Good Hope, key to the east. Below this, in subterranean depths still not entirely fathomable, a conspiracy was shaping to overthrow Tsar Paul I. It had begun with members of the Russian imperial family and high military and government officials who were both antagonized and alarmed by Paul's aberrant, even crazed rule. His recent destruction of the balance of power in Europe by switching loyalties towards France while still formally at war with her had provided the final impetus. Diplomats of Louis XVIII's Agence de l'Extérieur had joined the conspiracy since Paul had rejected Louis when adopting Bonaparte; and because Louis was dependent on British funding, Pitt and his Foreign Secretary were deeply implicated. The international conspiracy was hatched in the castle of Bialystock in Lithuania, hard by the Russian border, although those chosen to do the deed were Russian nobles and army officers whom Paul had exiled or disgraced.[11]

How much Hyde Parker was told of the probable or possible overthrow of the tsar is impossible to know because the instructions he received from the Foreign Office, as opposed to his official Admiralty instructions, are missing. Since two other crucial documents concerning the Baltic situation are also missing, the recent historian of British secret service operations during this period, Elizabeth Sparrow, concludes that the papers were deliberately weeded.[12] However, if Sir Hyde was advised to hold his hand until the situation in St Petersburg clarified, it might explain his dilatory behaviour, first in Yarmouth Roads where he delayed for a ball arranged by the eighteen-year-old he had recently married, then after St Vincent had warned him that further procrastination would do him 'irreparable injury' and he had cancelled the ball and sailed, in the Kattegat while a British mission in Copenhagen attempted to detach Denmark from the neutral coalition. Nelson burned with impatience, writing to Troubridge, now a Lord of Admiralty, that the fleet should be off Copenhagen: 'it would be a bold Dane who put his name to a paper which would in a few moments involve his master's navy and I hope his capital in flames', and 'to keep out of sight is to seduce Denmark into a war'.[13]

Three days later, on 23 March, the British mission headed by Nicholas Vansittart reported to Sir Hyde in his flagship that negotiations had failed. Nelson, who until then had been kept largely in the dark, was called aboard to a council. He questioned Vansittart in detail about defensive preparations made by the Danes over the past days and finding that the most formidable were concentrated about the Trekroner fort commanding the Copenhagen entrance channel, proposed outflanking these and attacking the rear of a line of ships and floating batteries extending southwards, insisting that not an hour should be lost in bringing the fleet off the Danish capital and beginning the attack. Having crushed the Danes, they should then sail to confront a Russian squadron at Revel directly the ice broke – the tsar being the root of the trouble. Sir Hyde would have preferred to remain in the Kattegat and await events – probably in accordance with his Foreign Office advice – but Nelson's advocacy of immediate attack before the ice melted and allowed the Russian and Swedish fleets to join the Danes was so compelling that he carried the council. His arguments have been accepted by historians ever since. It is evident that his lapses of military and political judgement while serving the court of the Two Sicilies had been temporary aberrations, and this was the essential Nelson again bringing clarity, eloquence and daring to a problem. He had not, of course, been told of the impending coup in St Petersburg.

The fleet was delayed by contrary winds and it was not until the 30th that it came to anchor some eight miles off Copenhagen. Nelson now prepared a plan whereby he would lead a detachment of ten of the lighter ships of the line – augmented by Sir Hyde to twelve – together with the frigates, gun brigs and bomb vessels down an outer channel beyond the shoal off the harbour in order to round up and attack the weaker, southern end of the Danish defences while the heavy ships under Sir Hyde made a demonstration off the Trekroner at the northern end. As at the Nile it was an attack on an anchored line, but on this occasion Nelson had time to have his intended approach sounded by night and buoyed. He transferred to the 74-gun *Elephant* commanded by Thomas Foley, who had led at the Nile, and on 1 April took his squadron down the newly buoyed channel to anchor in the evening some two miles from the southern end of the Danish line. That night further soundings were taken of the approaches and Nelson dictated instructions detailing the sailing order and precise position each ship was to take in the attack; these were then copied and distributed. By morning the wind, which had been in the north the previous day, enabling the squadron to sail south, had gone round to the south-south-east, blowing directly up the Danish line, the ideal direction for the intended assault. Nelson had the signals made to prepare for battle and for anchoring with cables from stern ports and springs attached to the cables, followed at 9.45 by the signal to weigh in succession.[14]

At first all went to plan. Danes crowding every vantage point atop and behind the battlemented walls of the city saw the leading British vessels stand on through the fire of their armed hulks, low floating gun platforms, converted transports and warships until they reached their allotted positions and brought up to a stern anchor. However, the intended fifth British ship had anchored too far north of the middle ground shoal to weather it, despite every attempt to work southwards with kedge anchors, and the sixth, while passing outside the ships ahead of her and already engaged, ran on to a spur of the middle ground shoal and stuck fast. Nelson, the stump of his right arm working restlessly as it did when he was excited or agitated, had the *Elephant*'s helm starboarded to pass inside her and directed others to take the places of the stranded vessels. Eventually, after one more had run on to the middle ground, he had nine of the line disposed in approximately the positions he had intended with frigates extending the line north in place of the three stranded ships of the line. Possibly he had underestimated his opponents, more probably he considered his force too small to attempt concentrations to overwhelm sections of the far more numerous but generally inferior units of the defence; whatever the reason, his ships were spaced evenly along the line about 100 yards apart and often faced by more than one opponent; consequently as the Danes fought stubbornly to defend their capital, the

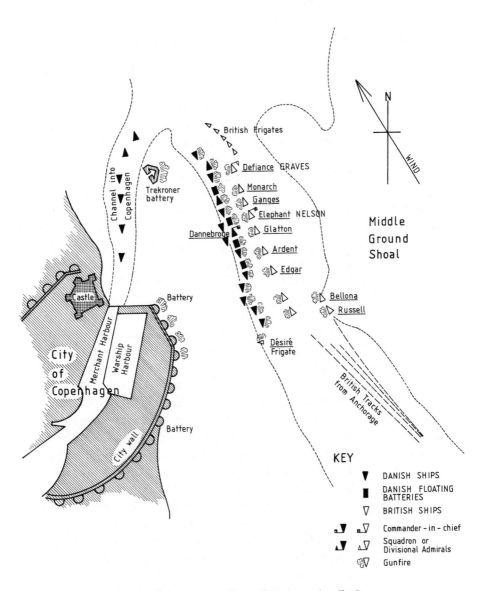

Battle diagram 5   Copenhagen, 2 April 1801

battle developed into static gunnery duels of a more equal character than he could have wished. Casualty figures and the journals and letters of those who took part testify to the destruction and carnage wrought on both sides. His second in command, Rear Admiral Thomas Graves, was to write afterwards:

> Considering the disadvantages of navigation, the approach to the enemy, their vast number of guns and mortars on both land and sea, I do not think there was ever a bolder attack . . . In short it was worthy of our gallant and enterprising little hero of the Nile. Nothing can exceed his spirit.[15]

The hero of the Nile, pacing the starboard side of the *Elephant*'s quarterdeck in cocked hat and a green sheepskin greatcoat with Colonel the Hon. William Stewart, commanding the expedition's troops, was in that state of intense animation always induced in him by battle. A shower of splinters struck from the mainmast by a ball evoked a smile and the comment, 'It is warm work. And this day may be the last to any of us at a moment.' As he stopped to turn by the forward rail, he added, 'But mark you, I would not be elsewhere for thousands!'[16] Stewart would never forget his expression or the emotion in his voice as he said it.

Meanwhile Sir Hyde was attempting to bring the heavy ships down towards the Trekroner fort, but making little progress against the southerly wind and a wind-induced current. By noon he was still over four miles away, well outside long gunshot, and apparently discussing with his flag captain, Robert Otway, whether he should order Nelson's division to break off the engagement. Otway advised strongly against this: indeed it is hard to understand why the question should have been raised so soon after the last of Nelson's ships had come into action – firing had commenced at the leading ship at about 10.30 a.m. Sir Hyde was still a long way from the battle; his view was obscured by clouds of gunsmoke blowing up the lines towards him; two British ships were visibly aground flying signals of distress and they would be at the mercy of the Danes if their consorts broke off action and retired. What had possessed Sir Hyde? In the event, Otway obtained permission to take a boat to visit Nelson to find out how things were, but before he returned, or even reached the *Elephant*,[17] Sir Hyde had number 39, 'Discontinue the action', hoisted and enforced with two guns to make it general to all ships. This was about 1.15 p.m., or 1.30 by his journal entry, which went on, 'and sent Captain Otway aboard the *Elephant*'. According to Otway's account he had already been sent away at noon. Discrepancies of this sort are normal for logs and journals of the day, but Sir Hyde's signal seems so incomprehensible that there may be more to this anomaly than mere differences in time-keeping, as will appear.

Nelson's response to the order is well known. When asked by his signal lieutenant whether he should repeat it, he answered, 'No, acknowledge it.' He then asked whether their own number 16 – for engaging the enemy more closely – was still flying. When told it was, he said, 'Mind you keep it so.' After one or two turns up the quarterdeck, the stump of his arm working in more than usual agitation, he said to Stewart, 'Leave off the action! Now, damn me if I do!' And turning to Foley, 'You know, Foley, I have only one eye – I have a right to be blind sometimes.' Stewart's account of this episode continues, 'and then, with an archness peculiar to his character, putting the glass to his blind eye, he exclaimed, "I really do not see the signal!"'[18]

The gesture Stewart described as 'arch', Nelson's biographer, A. T. Mahan, considered 'a profound moral allegory. There is a time to be blind as well as a time to see.' Nelson knew that to retire through enemy fire by an unmarked channel in shoaling water with ships already damaged aloft would be 'to convert probable victory into certain, and perhaps overwhelming disaster'. More than that, he was able 'to shut his eyes to the perils and doubts surrounding the only path by which he could achieve success, and save his command from a defeat verging on annihilation'.[19] Mahan was surely right to view this as a supreme moral achievement.

It is also true that from Nelson's vantage point at the centre of the battle it was apparent the balance had tipped towards him. This is clear from a less well-known comment he made to Stewart shortly after placing the telescope to his blind eye:

These fellows hold us a better jug than I expected. However, we are keeping up a noble fire, and I'll be answerable that we shall bale them out in four, if we cannot do it in three hours. At least I'll give it them till they are sick of it.[20]

The rear Danish armed hulks and converted transports were already beaten and firing their few remaining pieces only slowly; several other units had been abandoned or struck their colours and the Danish flagship *Dannebroge*, opposite Nelson's next astern, Captain William Bligh's *Glatton*, had been set alight by incendiary shells and was burning uncontrollably. The *Glatton* was remarkable for having an all-carronade armament, ideal for such close-range pounding; it demonstrates that besides well-trained guns' crews – against many untrained volunteers aboard the Danish vessels – the British had a decided technological edge. The Danes were still feeding fresh men and powder out to those units continuing the struggle and their shore batteries were still inflicting damage, especially on those ships near the head of the line, but the Danish commander-in-chief, like Brueys at the Nile, had been surprised by the direction of Nelson's attack and had made no arrangements to reinforce endangered sections with fresh ships – difficult as this would have been against the southerly wind.

When Sir Hyde's signal was reported to Rear Admiral Graves at the northern end of the line, he asked whether Nelson had repeated it; on being told he had not, Graves said, 'Then we have nothing to do with it.'[21] He had the signal repeated, but kept number 16 for closer action flying in a superior position at the main topmast head and continued in action, as did all the ships of the division except the frigates at the head of the line, whose senior officer, unable to see the *Elephant* through the smoke, ordered the cables cut and retired north-eastwards through the fire of the Trekroner fort. Almost his last words before he was cut in two by a ball were, 'What will Nelson think of us?'[22]

Within half an hour of Sir Hyde's disregarded order the Danish defence line south of the Trekroner had been broken. The blazing *Dannebroge*, her cables cut, was drifting northwards, men leaping from her ports, whilst boats from several British ships were rescuing survivors. However, parties sent to secure those hulks and floating batteries no longer in action were repulsed by small arms, and guns ashore and from the fort were still firing. To cut through the confusion and continuing slaughter, Nelson called the purser and, retiring with him into the stern gallery, had him copy a note he wrote in his own hand using the rudder head casing as a table. 'To the Brothers of Englishmen, the Danes', it ran:

Lord Nelson has directions to spare Denmark, when no longer resisting; but if the firing is continued on the part of Denmark, Lord Nelson will be obliged to set on fire all the Floating-batteries he has taken, without having the power of saving the brave Danes who have defended them.[23]

He dated and signed it, 'Nelson and Brontë, Vice Admiral under the command of Admiral Sir Hyde Parker', and had a man sent below to fetch his seal, sealing wax and a candle from the cockpit. On the way the man's head was taken off by a ball. When this was reported Nelson had another man sent; he was determined the letter should bear no trace of haste or confusion. Finally, sealed with a clear imprint of his coat of arms, the letter was taken ashore under a flag of truce and handed to the Danish crown prince in overall charge of the defence of the city. The prince sent an aide to ascertain Nelson's precise object. 'Humanity,' Nelson replied, detailing this as a cessation of hostilities until he had taken his prisoners from the prizes, landed all wounded Danes and removed or burnt his prizes, which although unable to resist were still caught in the crossfire. The prince thanked him for his humanity and both Nelson and the Danes hoisted flags of truce, variously recorded in the ships' logs as at some time between 3 and 3.30 p.m. The fighting had lasted some four and a half hours at scarcely over point-blank range, something under 200 to 250 yards in most cases. The damage and very balanced casualties reflected it: a total of 1,035 Danes against 944 British killed or wounded. In addition 1,770 Danes were taken prisoner.[24]

Whether Nelson's note which brought an end to the fighting was a genuine humanitarian gesture to spare wounded and survivors aboard the disabled and surrendered Danish units or a ruse to rescue his own battered ships from disablement while the wind held has been a matter of dispute ever since. Danish historians generally take the latter view. It is true that Nelson was able to withdraw his own damaged and grounded ships with his prizes during the truce; it is also clear from ships' logs and other accounts that he had won a partial victory and the city's floating defence line south of the Trekroner fort had been demolished. A neutral observer ashore, the Swedish liaison officer, Vice Admiral Cronstedt, had reported before 2 o'clock that the greater part of the Danish line was totally ruined and he doubted whether the remaining vessels to the northward had any chance.[25] Moreover Parker's heavy ships were unscathed and approaching the northern end of the defences. However, the formidable Trekroner and other shore batteries had not been silenced, and thus Nelson's objective – to clear the way for his gun brigs and bomb vessels to bombard the city – had not been achieved, except perhaps at the southern end of the channel out of range of the Trekroner. In these balanced circumstances Nelson, according to his companion that day, Colonel Stewart, 'resolved to push his advantages no further . . . for victorious as we were, the narrowness of the channel in which our ships were engaged & the commanding batteries on shore had left our ships, six of which were grounded, in a most perilous situation'.[26] Nelson's flag captain, Thomas Masterman Hardy, who was also privy to Nelson's thoughts that day, gave a similar interpretation in a letter to his brother-in-law, concluding, 'The more I see of His Lordship the more I admire his great character, for, I think on this occasion, his political management *was, if possible*, greater than his Bravery.'[27]

Whatever the tactical reasoning, there is no doubt that Nelson was always moved by humanitarian considerations, as much for the enemy as for his own men, as his immediate reaction to the fire aboard *L'Orient* at the Nile illustrates. An excellent summary of his motives in writing 'To the Brothers of Englishmen, the Danes', is provided in a recent study by Ole Feldbaek, who concludes that his note was 'an impenetrable mixture of humanity and cynical threat'.[28]

There is another mystery surrounding the circumstances at the time the note was sent. The coup against Tsar Paul I had been executed on the night of 24–25 March: he had been strangled while resisting conspirators let into his private apartments by suborned members of his guard, and early in the morning of the 25th his elder son had acted swiftly to establish himself as Tsar Alexander I. The news had been despatched to London and other European capitals, and according to the Swedish ambassador at St Petersburg the Russian Minister in Copenhagen was instructed to visit the British Baltic fleet flagship to inform the admiral and so prevent a battle.[29] It is not known when this instruction reached the Danish capital, and it has not come to light in the archives. However, Elizabeth Sparrow has pointed out, 'There is considerable evidence in the log of Admiral Parker's flagship and in Captain Otway's memoir of the arrival of a boat which caused him to send Otway with an urgent message to Nelson.'[30] If the boat carried the Russian Minister or a British agent privy to the conspiracy with news of Paul's death and Alexander's new posture, it would explain Sir Hyde's otherwise unaccountable signal to break off the action – which had been rendered unnecessary. It would also explain the opening to Nelson's note: 'Lord Nelson has directions to spare Denmark, when no longer resisting . . .' Captain Otway had reached the *Elephant* by this time and the directions could only have come from Sir Hyde.

In their reports of the battle neither Nelson nor Sir Hyde Parker made any reference to news of Paul's death – which is not supposed to have reached Copenhagen until 6 April, a very long time even by the standards of the day – nor did either refer to Sir Hyde's signal to break off the engagement. It has been supposed that Sir Hyde did not want to publicize an order that would have snatched defeat from the arms of victory, nor Nelson to have made his disobedience known. However, since the publication of Elizabeth Sparrow's work, there is an alternative explanation: Sir Hyde's signal was a response not to Nelson's tactical position but to news of the altered international situation, and his instructions to Nelson by Captain Otway were made with this in view. As to why, if this was the case, he never mentioned it, perhaps British government involvement in the Bialystock plot and his own instructions from the Foreign Office were so sensitive that no hint could be allowed to surface, even to Nelson. But large questions remain over this interpretation.

Having arranged the truce, Nelson was deputed by Sir Hyde to negotiate with the Danes. He did so by landing, braving the hostility of the people – who in the event turned out in crowds to see him as much from curiosity and admiration as from anger – and dealing directly with the crown prince. Using the combination of flattery and threat that had distinguished his note, he eventually achieved an armistice for fourteen weeks during which Denmark would suspend her membership of the armed neutrality and make no naval preparations, and the British Baltic fleet could supply itself from Danish ports. It was a skilful passage of diplomacy, giving the commander-in-chief all that he needed to press on into the Baltic to deal with the Russians and Swedes: an advanced supply base and secure communications; and Copenhagen was spared bombardment. It is true that by the date of the agreement, 9 April, the crown prince, although apparently not Nelson, was aware of Paul's death, and consequently did not have to fear his wrath. Nonetheless, the treaty and the battle together constitute one of Nelson's highest achievements, very much more hazardous and demanding than the victory in Aboukir Bay and at least comparable in its geopolitical effects. St Vincent wrote congratulating him: 'all agree there is but one Nelson.'[31] That Nelson had come to the same opinion is indicated by letters of this date in which he refers to himself in the third person.

He was burning to rejoin Emma Hamilton and his new daughter; instead on 5 May despatches arrived appointing him commander-in-chief in place of the dilatory Sir Hyde, who was ordered home. It was a bitter shock to both men. But in effect Nelson's work in the north was done: the assault on Copenhagen and the assassination in St Petersburg together had put paid to the armed neutrality. Nelson paraded ten of the line and two frigates off Revel, ostensibly as a courtesy to the new tsar, but given his reputation for sudden destructive action it was perceived as a threat and he withdrew. Shortly afterwards he received word that

British ships, goods and men caught in Paul's embargo were to be released, confirming his belief in British warships as the best negotiators. Returning to Denmark, he was disgusted to see the court under French influence violating the terms of his armistice by masting and arming warships and preparing floating batteries. He lodged a complaint, but the armed neutrality had been formally abandoned by this time and the British government let it rest.

In June he was relieved on health grounds, only to be posted almost immediately on his return to command a squadron of frigates and smaller craft to protect south-east England from invasion. Bonaparte was promoting fears that troops and small craft gathering along the Channel coast from Flushing to Boulogne were intended for a surprise raid on London. Nelson was told that only his reputation would calm fears in the country and at the same time indicate to France that she might have subdued Europe, but not Great Britain; as St Vincent put it to him, 'Our [peace] negotiation is drawing near its close . . . and I need not add, how very important it is that the enemy should know that *you* are constantly opposed to him.'[32]

During this command he deputed Emma Hamilton to buy a house for him. She settled on Merton Place, Surrey, a substantial red-brick building set in extensive grounds an hour's drive south of the centre of London, which she bought and furnished to be a home for him, herself, their daughter Horatia and the ageing Sir William.

8

Warriors and Merchants

PRELIMINARY ARTICLES OF peace were signed in October and ratified at
Amiens in March 1802. Outmanoeuvred by Talleyrand, Addington's
government agreed to hand back all Britain's overseas conquests except
Trinidad (from Spain) and Ceylon (from the Dutch); Malta was to be
returned to the Knights of St John, Egypt to Turkey. After nine years of
war both sides were in desperate need of respite; both rejoiced, although
France had most to celebrate: she had consolidated and legitimized the
Revolution, extended her borders to the Rhine and Alps, her hegemony
to Holland (the Batavian Republic), Switzerland (the Helvetic Republic)
and virtually the whole of Italy; and her patronage and influence
extended to the central German states. Moreover, she had prised Great
Britain from the naval bases she had acquired in the Mediterranean east
of Gibraltar and could hope to regain command over that sea, and even
over Egypt and the interior route to India.

In gratitude for peace with triumph the French people in a referen-
dum voted Bonaparte First Consul for life with the right to designate a
successor. Inside two years he would proclaim himself Emperor with
rights of succession for his heirs, and in December 1804 legitimize the
claim by having Pope Pius VII officiate at his coronation, during which
he pledged himself to govern in the interests not only of the happiness
but of the 'glory' of the French people. Other trappings of the old order
would soon be reinstated, princely titles and an imperial nobility,
outward manifestations of a regime which had returned to France's
roots – although the new nobility was not legally differentiated from the

ordinary citizenry. He had already created the Order of the Legion of Honour in 1802 to reward outstanding military bravery or civil service irrespective of birth or rank. It was an effort to restore to French society disoriented by Revolution an incontestable standard of distinction, and it was designed to affirm the martial values dominating the culture. As Grand Master of the Order, he presided at the first investiture in 1804. The same year, as Emperor, he created eighteen Marshals of France, endowing them with princely titles and lands and salaries, making it 'strikingly evident', as Louis Bergeron has pointed out in his study of France under Napoleon, 'that military men were to be at the top of the social hierarchy'.[1]

Like his Bourbon predecessors Bonaparte, or as he became the Emperor Napoleon, appointed ministers, generals, senior civil servants and members of the Council of State – equivalent to the Bourbon Conseil d'État du Roi – through which he ruled. His writ was enforced uniformly throughout France by *Préfets* appointed by and answering to the Council, each administering a *département* as Bourbon *Intendants* had governed a province. An elected legislative assembly was retained as a gesture to the ideals of the Revolution, but deprived of authority. The Senate was composed at first of fifty members: he appointed thirty-one; the others were coopted by these. Just as in the seventeenth century the young Louis XIV, having seen his country ravaged by the internal wars of the Fronde, had seized all reins of power to himself, so after the convulsions of the Revolution the young Napoleon Bonaparte, as if guided by historical laws, took it upon himself to unify and oversee every aspect of his country's life. It would also be true to say that, after the turmoil, French politicians and people were happy to empower him to do so. Thus France returned naturally and thankfully to the absolute rule of a monarch through a centralized administration which emptied all remaining representative institutions of meaning.[2]

One legacy of the Revolution was belief in rationality. Yet, of course, the great Bourbon ministers had been supremely rational managers, defeated only by the established orders and civic and provincial interest blocs into which France had been divided by her social and military history. It was these the Revolution had cleared away, leaving Bonaparte – Napoleon – a clean slate on which to exercise his intellect. He did so with prodigious energy, bringing reason to bear and codifying every area of French life.

The vital questions of restoring state credit and stabilizing the currency had been addressed in the wake of the coup which had brought him to power. A Banque de France had been set up in Paris along the lines of the Bank of England, but funded by state as well as private capital; the government, besides being a major shareholder, provided the governor and two deputy directors. This was wholly in line with attempts by Bourbon ministers to imitate the instruments of capitalism while ensuring government control; and Bonaparte echoed their sentiments when he declared, 'The Banque does not solely belong to its shareholders; it also belongs to the state which granted it the privilege of creating money.'[3] He allowed it to issue high denomination banknotes, the least worth 500 francs (*c. £*22), thus confined to commercial and financial use. There was to be no mass circulation of paper money, no repeat of the infinite inflation of the *assignat*. The favoured coinage was silver which, like the banknotes, was tied to gold. Pre-Revolutionary livres continued to circulate with the new francs; copper coins were minted for workers' needs.

He retained the tax system bequeathed by the Revolution which relied heavily on a land tax, indirect taxes on tobacco, salt and other consumer items, and customs duties, but did not upset those who had gained from the Revolution by increasing the rates of tax on real estate in line with inflation or increasing rates on luxuries; nor did he introduce an income tax. He did reform methods of collection. He also began the presentation of orderly public accounts.[4]

The financial reforms and his personal prestige restored French government credit, although not to the level the British had won over a century of scrupulously transparent management of the national debt in Parliament. Military victories were to bring the interest rate on French government borrowing down from over 12 per cent in 1802 to under 6 per cent within four years, but it would remain on average 2½ per cent higher than the interest on British government bonds.[5] Initially this difference was more than made up by squeezing taxes from the satellite republics, and in the coming great war, as in the Revolutionary war, extracting indemnities and taxes from subjugated enemies; yet, as noted, this was ultimately self-defeating, destroying prosperity and the sources of capital creation, leading inevitably to the need for further conquest, ever the issue for warrior nations.

That France under Napoleon retreated from Enlightenment ideals to the certitudes of her warrior past is shown in most other spheres: police organization was strengthened; judges were appointed by the government, not elected as they had been during the Revolution, and while

their tenure was for life their advancement was controlled by the government. Crimes were investigated in secret by a *juge d'instruction*; jurors for
a trial were nominated by the *Préfet*: these and other measures undermined the protection of the innocent and facilitated local political or
state intervention. Later Napoleon would even decree the militarization
of schools under a government-controlled University of France, established in 1806 to organize and oversee all branches of education
throughout the empire with the object of directing the 'political and
moral opinions'[6] of young people to fit them for serving and dying for
La Patrie.

His most impressive monument was the codification of civil law which
became known as the *Code Napoléon*. The process had begun in the immediate aftermath of the Revolution (1790); as First Consul, he energized,
supervised and pushed it through to completion in 1804. The result was
a brilliantly clear and succinct harmonization of the laws of old France
with those Revolutionary enactments which he endorsed. It laid the basis
for a secular society constructed on the Enlightenment values of equality
before the law, individual liberty and freedom of conscience, incorporating traditional concerns for the sanctity of private property and discipline
in family life – where the wife was subject to her husband. Bonaparte's
own views could not have been more rigidly patriarchal, but he reluc-
tantly accepted the institution of civil divorce; otherwise the suppression
of women's claims for property, education and other rights, begun in the
later stages of the Revolution, was formalized. It was not entirely a reflection of Bonaparte's own views. A substantial strand of Enlightenment
writing had presented women as on the one hand sexually voracious and
intellectually inferior to men,[7] on the other as fitted exclusively for moth-
erhood and family with the responsibility of passing on the culture to the
next generation. Moreover women, who had frequently been to the fore
in rioting and certainly foremost in support for the Church against anti-
clerical Republicanism, provided an easy scapegoat for the failure of the
Revolution; as Olwen Hufton puts it in her history of women in western
Europe: 'Without ever naming her, the figure of Eve was resurrected to
explain why man was kept out of earthly paradise.'[8]

The *Code Napoléon* formalized the civil gains of the Revolution, bringing to the French people those legal freedoms for which Enlightenment
intellectuals had so envied the British and Americans. What was not
specified in this or any other Napoleonic Code was a political structure
to preserve those freedoms. All tendencies were in the opposite direction.

Since established checks on the absolute powers of the Bourbons had been cleared away, Napoleon and his centralized administration enjoyed a new dimension of unfettered, theoretically total power. It was a reverse image of the British model envisaged by the practical statesmen of 1789. It did accord, however, with the strong current of physiocrat thought and with the tradition and experience of the legally trained state functionaries who had been elected in such numbers to the Revolutionary assemblies. The centralized Bourbon state had resurrected itself in purer form. This was to be demonstrated in succeeding years by what Louis Bergeron has called the 'gigantic correspondence with all parts of the empire' conducted by the Minister of the Interior through the *préfets*, 'a mass of paperwork that was constantly fed by the growing minuteness of the regulations',[9] and by an increasingly rigorous censorship of the press, the suppression of intellectual freedom by the central University of France and the activities of the secret police against dissidents of every description, arbitrary arrest, detention without trial, torture and indeed murder.[10]

Napoleon was a logical outcome of the Revolution, but there is no doubt that he conspicuously betrayed the Enlightenment consensus on the evils of the slave trade. A Société des Amis des Noirs, inspired by the British abolitionist movement, had been founded in Paris just prior to the Revolution, its membership including the Abbé Sieyès, one of the chief conspirators responsible for bringing Bonaparte to power. As in Great Britain, West Indian planters and merchants from the great slave trading ports formed a powerful opposition; Société members were represented as British agents and threatened with death, and the transshipment and employment of plantation slaves was depicted as essential for national prosperity. Thus, although the Assembly condemned slavery in principle in early 1791 no practical steps were taken to end it, and the Republican government continued to subsidize the trade with a bounty for each slave landed in the islands.[11]

Frustration felt by slaves whose hopes had been raised by the humanitarian rhetoric of the Revolution and the Declaration of the Rights of Man erupted the following year in Saint-Domingue, the French colony on the island of Hispaniola, and in the only completely successful slave revolt in history the blacks won freedom and independence for the territory under the native Indian name, Haiti. The shock this caused, particularly in the former slave-trade capital of Nantes, where several of the biggest slaving merchants were ruined, was followed in February 1794 by the Jacobin-dominated National Assembly ending the bounty on slaves landed. The same year Guadeloupe, which had been seized by the British in 1794, was retaken by a French expedition whose government representative, a committed Jacobin named Victor Hugues, fulfilled the Assembly declaration by abolishing slavery on the island. In addition he had a large number of white planters massacred, earning himself the sobriquet 'the colonial Robespierre'. He attempted to spread the doctrine of emancipation to neighbouring islands until prevented by a British expedition, when he directed his formidable energies into a highly successful privateer campaign against British and American shipping; by 1798 he had helped bring the United States to the brink of war with France.[12]

Bonaparte rescinded the emancipation of slaves shortly after peace was signed in 1802. Convinced by deputations from Nantes, Bordeaux and Marseilles that slave labour in the plantations was essential if the flourishing pre-war commerce with the sugar islands were to be re-established, he had legislation enacted for the continuation of the slave trade under the rules in force before 1789 and despatched expeditions to retake Saint-Domingue–Haiti and restore order and the plantation economy in Guadeloupe. His ambitions were boundless. His goals, despite the peace, were to prevent British goods entering the large area of western Europe dominated by France, to extend that dominion to the central German states, and at the same time to expand the French West Indian empire and recolonize mainland north America – although the Royal Navy had thus far blocked his every overseas move. He also retained aspirations in India and the east. It is impossible to distinguish between his desire to win a universal empire and his perception of the prior need to break British industrial supremacy and crush the island kingdom; they were twin aspects of the same demon which drove him.

France had lost her north American colonies in the mid-eighteenth century, in the Seven Years War; the greater part had been taken by Great Britain in the peace settlement of 1763, but Louisiana west of the Mississippi had been ceded to Spain. In October 1800 Bonaparte had prevailed upon Charles IV of Spain to sell this vast area back to France. When the news reached Washington, nascent capital of the United States, Thomas Jefferson, the third President, instructed his ambassador in Paris to negotiate the purchase from France of at least the New Orleans region at the mouth of the great river complex. American settlers had been pushing west along the valleys of the Ohio and Tennessee rivers which fed the Mississippi; their commercial livelihood depended on unconstrained use of the waterways and the ocean trans-shipment port of New Orleans. Talleyrand procrastinated over a year until the ambassador made allusion to a possible rapprochement between the United States and Great Britain. By this time it was evident that war between Britain and France was about to be resumed; both the expeditions to Saint Domingue–Haiti and Guadeloupe had failed, and Bonaparte, evidently taking a more realistic view of his strategic possibilities, and anxious not to push the United States into the arms of Britain, offered the whole of Louisiana for sale. Jefferson could not refuse.

On 2 May 1803 a treaty was signed – backdated to 30 April – whereby the United States bought the Louisiana territories, which extended from the present state of Louisiana up the Mississippi basin to embrace what are now Arkansas, Missouri, Iowa, Nebraska, North and South Dakota and parts of neighbouring Minnesota, Montana, Wyoming, Colorado, Kansas and Oklahoma, a total of over 800,000 square miles for what became in the final analysis just over $27 million – approximately five cents an acre. Undoubtedly the best bargain in American history, it was also the most significant single act of territorial aggrandizement in the history of the world: it removed the chief international obstacle to the westward expansion of the United States, allowing it to spread without serious opposition to the Pacific coast. It is, of course, doubtful if such a powerful commercial and demographic force could have been contained in any case in the long run; that is another question. As for Bonaparte, there is equally no doubt that he made a historic error when he passed up his American ambition for the mirage of European hegemony and the defeat of Great Britain. The history of the eighteenth-century struggle between Britain and France was there to confirm it for those with eyes to see. Few had. Most in France had been blinded by the Enlightenment. Talleyrand had not; he attempted to steer Bonaparte into pacific channels and partnership with Great Britain, but in vain.[13]

IF BONAPARTE's France displayed all the territorial characteristics of Bourbon France in more absolute form, Great Britain ended this phase of the struggle as a magnified version of the antithesis, the merchant empire. It was little over a hundred years since she had attained this state at the Glorious Revolution. Then she had been a lightly taxed country with limited government unencumbered by permanent debt. She had

since fought six great wars against France during which she had borrowed chiefly on long-term loans to cover the difference between tax
revenue and war expenditure. This 'national debt' had approximately
doubled during each war in spite of ever higher taxes. The latest struggle had been no exception. Despite Pitt's steady increases in tax, despite
burgeoning customs receipts from expansion in trade, the debt now
approached what would have been regarded at the beginning of the
financial revolution as the unimaginable figure of £600 million.

The worst suspicions of the old landed classes had been realized in
full. Moneyed men had taken hold of government for their own ends
and transformed Britain into the most heavily taxed and indebted nation
in the world. This was so because the wars against France – and Spain
and others – had been in essence armed contests for world trade; and
the finance to fight them had come in great part from customs receipts
on trade and taxes on trading wealth and subscriptions to war loans from
merchants and moneyed men – assisted by foreign, especially Dutch sub-
scribers – who benefited from the investment offered. The system rested,
as it had in the Venetian and Dutch models, on confidence in sound
money. Pitt, whose inheritance came from profit made in India, was
merely the latest in a line of Treasury ministers who understood their
primary role as that of preserving confidence in government finance.

This was where British practice differed so radically from the French
– Bourbon or Revolutionary. In order to clear the huge debt inherited
from Louis XV's government, the Revolutionary Constituent Assembly
had, as noted, simply nationalized the Church, whose property had
become the security for the new government 5 per cent bonds known as
assignats. Burke had considered this 'an outrage on all the rights of property' and wondered why it was the Church's estates which had been
stolen to repay government creditors, not 'those of the long succession
of ministers, financiers and bankers who have been enriched whilst the
nation was impoverished by their dealings and their counsels'.[14] He had
supplied the answer himself: because the literary cabal – the Enlightenment establishment – had 'rendered hateful, by every exaggeration, the
faults of courts, of nobility, and of priesthood'.[15]

But *assignats*, instead of being used simply to buy expropriated property, had begun to change hands as paper money, and subsequent
Revolutionary governments had printed more to pay for their war; the
bonds had depreciated accordingly. By February 1796, 40 billion livres'
worth had been issued, equivalent at face value to £1.6 billion, and their

value had sunk to virtually zero. Besides plunging the economy into crisis, provoking shortages and food riots – and effectually wiping out the Bourbon debt – the result had been to destroy French government credit and implant distrust of paper money in the French psyche,[16] all of which Bonaparte's new Banque de France was designed to correct. Of course, the other arm of Revolutionary financial policy had been to milk conquered territories; by 1800 levies and taxes imposed on the Netherlands alone accounted for about a quarter of total French government revenue.[17] And this was the way, despite the new Banque, that Bonaparte, the Emperor Napoleon, would pay for his wars.

Pitt's handling of national finances stood in complete contrast to these cavalier attitudes. Having found that his threefold increase in 'assessed taxes' on expenditure failed to meet the anticipated target, he had replaced them with a tax on income. This was graduated from 5 to 10 per cent on incomes from £60 to £200 and above, but had a large voluntary element since taxpayers were not required to itemize sources of income. As a result, yields had again fallen short of expectation. The next year, 1800, he had introduced itemized tax returns, but met the traditional protest against government interference in personal and commercial transactions which he had always anticipated, and had to modify his proposals before he could get them through Parliament. Despite this inauspicious start, income tax was to prove a vital factor in reducing annual deficits, and thus borrowing requirements, throughout the later war with Napoleon. In the meantime he kept additions to the long-term debt to a minimum by increased use of short-term borrowing, chiefly bills on the Exchequer.[18]

At the same time the inconvertible paper money forced on him by the invasion scare of 1797, together with the reform of the mint required to make a greater volume of coinage available, had proved so successful in meeting the needs of an expanding economy, that he had allowed it to continue. Thus, with few precedents to guide him, he steered the country through the most expensive war she had ever fought, tapping her growing wealth to reduce the borrowing requirement, yet not so excessively as to stunt investment and enterprise, while increasing the money supply, yet not by so much as to provoke inflation. All parts of the system were interlinked and increasingly recognized to be so by bankers, parliamentarians and economists whose publications at this time began to lay the theoretical basis for modern economic management. Meanwhile, Pitt's system of taxes, his sinking fund for the long-term debt and his close contact with the Bank of England over the circulation of notes and coins carried the country through without further financial crises; the arrangement would continue under his successors with only minor modifications until the end of the war against France.

It was not only the unique system of public credit that enabled Britain to survive and ultimately prevail: the system was primed by the increases in trade, and thus of customs revenue, derived from her war gains over-seas – which might be loosely compared with the tribute France drew from her land conquests. In past conflicts growth in trade had been offset by losses and disruption from enemy commerce raiding, the *guerre de course*; in the early eighteenth century and the recent War of American Independence these had caused a small decline in trade figures. In the spectacularly successful Seven Years War in mid-century, however, when the Royal Navy had imposed a tight hold on French naval bases, British trade had increased by over 25 per cent. In the latest struggle with Revolutionary France, commerce raiding squadrons and individual pri-vateers like the Saint-Malouan Robert Surcouf had again taken a heavy toll; even so, trade had grown by 90 per cent between 1793 and 1801 to an aggregate figure for imports, exports and re-exports of over £75 million a year.[19] Imports of grain, sugar, tea, wine and timber had doubled, imports of raw cotton had trebled and coffee imports had expanded by a factor of almost seven, while exports of woollen and worsted yarn and manufactures had doubled and most significantly exports of cotton yarn and manufactures had expanded fourfold. This was a sign of more than simple trade growth; it was an indication that incremental changes in technology over the last quarter century had transformed textile manu-facture into a mass-production factory process; and since cotton, the fastest growing of the textiles, was, in Paul Kennedy's words, 'a catalyst or "multiplier" in itself, demanding ever more machinery, steam power, coal and labour',[20] it was pulling other British trades and industries into what would become known as the 'industrial revolution'.

It was this technological advance, and the fact that Britain had crushed French overseas commerce and won a virtual monopoly for her own mer-chants, that underlay the extraordinary growth in trade; and it was the trade figures that bolstered Pitt's confidence despite the alarming increases in public debt over which he had presided. As he told Parliament in 1800: 'If we compare this year of war with former years of peace, we shall in the produce of our revenue and in the extent of our commerce behold a spectacle at once paradoxical, inexplicable and astonishing.'[21]

Underpinning all these necessary attributes of merchant power, expansive trade, low interest rates on public borrowing, prosperous industry and merchant shipping and a supreme navy, was the Constitution of 1689 that had subordinated the royal prerogative to Parliament in most important areas, crucially in that of finance. Radical corresponding societies, the United Irishmen, Tom Paine and other polemicists had promoted revolutionary republican forms of government; inflation and food shortages – although usually mild by comparison with the French experience – had caused distress, pauperization, starvation and in extreme cases food riots, but the government had borne down harshly. The law and the Constitution had been preserved; the navy had returned to duty and triumph, celebrated in popular song and verse. By contrast France had suffered a catastrophic decline in the morale and efficiency of her navy, the virtual annihilation of the overseas shipping, trade and industry of her great Atlantic ports, unprecedented inflation, default on her public debt and a succession of new constitutions and *coups d'état*. And having failed in every area important to merchants, she had ensured the triumph of martial over merchant values by handing absolute power to a soldier, Bonaparte.

The outward symptoms have been noted: centralization and bureaucracy, the regimentation of society by codes handed down from above, the rejection of women's claims for rights, the subjugation of women within the patriarchal family, the reimposition of slavery – although the latter was at the request of merchants. In Great Britain the picture was very different. Centralization was practically confined to revenue collection; elsewhere, as de Tocqueville would learn, 'each county, each town, each parish looks after its own interests'.[22]

More subtle but real differences showed in women's lives. It was scarcely apparent in legal theory: a wife was as much the property of her husband in Britain as in France; for the purposes of law a married couple formed a single person, the husband, who had absolute control of the wife's property and the children of the marriage. Nonetheless, among the professional and merchant classes and the landed elites law was being used to raise the wife's autonomy. Increasingly marriage contracts stipulated an allowance, 'pin money', for the wife's personal use; increasingly women protected their property in trusts before marriage so the husband could not touch it.[23] Divorce was too expensive for all but the wealthiest, yet increasingly private separations were agreed, the husband contracting to pay the wife an assured annual allowance, generally about a third of his income or less.[24] Nelson, with typical generosity, settled half his annual income on his wife.[25] Increasingly, also, husbands, wives and lovers colluded in so-called 'criminal conversation' suits, from which the husband won damages – later to be returned in secret – entitling the couple to an uncontested parliamentary divorce. This had become so common as to demonstrate, in the words of the social historian Lawrence Stone, 'how far elite opinion had moved in favour of full divorce by 1790, sixty years before serious moves towards statutory reform'.[26] And increasingly in cases of separation courts were allocating custody of children to the mother in equity, that body of law complementary to the common law in Britain and the United States.

The patriarchal society had been undermined in even more fundamental ways by the individualism bred in a merchant society whose values were based on freedom to pursue personal goals, particularly as the opportunities for women had expanded hugely by this time. Amanda Vickery, in a study of women's lives in Georgian England, claims that it is 'hard to overestimate the impact of what has been termed the English urban renaissance on the scope of privileged women's social and cultural lives'. The presence in towns up and down the country of assembly rooms, theatre companies, concert series, sporting events, circulating libraries, clubs and pleasure gardens had 'inaugurated an entirely new public, social terrain which celebrated, indeed depended upon active female involvement'.[27] Women also took prominent roles in the many charitable and benevolent institutions founded towards the end of the eighteenth century.

And there was shopping. What is now termed 'consumerism' was in full tide in Britain. Stores in London's West End streets displayed materials and produce from every corner of the trading world arranged alluringly behind large plate-glass windows, lit until late in the evening by oil lamps.[28] No continental city could match the dazzling range of choice. Similar spectacles on a smaller scale occupied the central thoroughfares of cities and market towns throughout the country. In this domain women were paramount. Taught from girlhood to appraise quality and judge prices, they managed both the household budget and necessities of fashion; husbands were not expected to interfere.

Women's domestic circumstances had changed as much as their social and public horizons. Education in a growing number of private girls' schools had been broadened to include history, geography, literature and current affairs in addition to the social accomplishments. Placing women on a more equal intellectual footing tended to subvert absolute male authority; it undoubtedly aided the development of the companionable marriage, a trend complemented by other cultural phenomena: the civilizing effects on manners and morals of market exchange in a commercial society, discussed earlier, the idealization of romantic love, as portrayed in a large number of novels and stories by British women for women published at this time, and an upsurge of moral sensitivity expressed particularly as distaste for cruelty and injustice. The outstanding example of this was the countrywide movement for the abolition of slavery. Interestingly, women led boycotts on slave-produced West Indian sugar in the shops.[29] The vogue for romantic love, together with the greater social opportunities for young women to meet men, had led to the love match becoming an acceptable, even usual basis for a union, while arranged marriages for reasons of property were to an extent falling into disrepute.[30] The climate of sensibility to the sufferings of slaves and animals was conducive to happier relationships between husband and wife, parents and children; indeed the child-centred family had evolved in the professional and landed classes.[31] The heroine of Jane Austen's *Emma* grew up in one, 'the youngest of the two daughters of a most affectionate, indulgent father', the only drawbacks in her situation being 'the power of having rather too much her own way, and a disposition to think a little too well of herself'.[32]

These changes generally to the advantage of women were as much products of merchant society as the manufactures of British workshops. They had occurred first in the wealthy urban middle classes, thence spreading gradually among the landed gentry and to lower economic levels of the middle classes, although they would take a long time to reach the labouring poor. Precisely the same transformation had occurred earlier in the great days of the Dutch republic, Britain's predecessor as supreme maritime and mercantile power. Then foreign visitors had been astonished, often shocked at the liberties women and girls enjoyed; married women had legal rights to property unknown elsewhere and the affectionate, companionable marriage and delight in children had been celebrated on luminous canvases.[33]

The comments of foreign visitors to England towards the end of the eighteenth century are strikingly similar to those made by travellers to Holland in the mid-seventeenth century: thus in 1788 the Duc de la Rochefoucauld expressed his surprise at the opportunities open to young people in England to become well-acquainted before marriage: 'they go with their parents everywhere. Young girls mix with the company and talk and enjoy themselves with as much freedom as if they were married.'[34] He put this down to the companionable marriage, which he thought peculiar to England, suggesting that three out of four marriages were based on affection, and the couples remained far closer than in France. On an earlier visit he had been struck by the way English husbands and wives were always together in society; he found it very rare to meet one without the other, 'and the wife in particular has an air of contentment which always gives me pleasure'.[35]

The difference between women's expectations in Britain and France was expressed in literature: both countries produced radical polemicists for women's rights. In England Mary Wollstonecraft's *A Vindication of the Rights of Women* (1792) insisted that women were made, not born; that is to say, if given the same education and career opportunities as their brothers they would prove as rational and capable as men. In France Olympe de Gouges' *Les Droits de la femme* (1791) claimed statutory rights to bring women equality with men, significantly including the right to own property within marriage. Both were too radical for their age. It was in fiction that the real differences in national cultures were expressed: British novels from the mid-century, culminating in Jane Austen's brilliant evocations – the first three written in the 1790s although not published until many years later – were concerned with moral responsibility and love as the only valid guides to marriage. 'In marrying a man indifferent to me, all risk would have been incurred, and all duty violated,'[36] Anne Elliot declares to her naval captain in *Persuasion*. French writers, by contrast, men and women, showed the influence of Rousseau, in whose two novels the education and role of women was limited to that of pleasing a man and being a good mother; in effect French novelists colluded in the Revolution's suppression of any form of female emancipation.[37]

Émigré women returning to France from England, stimulated by the heady mood of female independence, found they had to limit themselves to the part assigned them in post-Revolutionary society. Some, like the portrait artist Élisabeth Vigée-Lebrun, removed themselves again; Germaine de Staël, most powerful of the liberal voices for women, was censored, then exiled by Napoleon. But most settled for their traditional dependent role as wives and mothers at home.[38]

Just as the trend towards emancipation for women in England emerged from the individualism and variety of opportunity in a commercial society, so the movement for the emancipation of slaves – once the barbarities involved had been publicized – was driven by individual moral concern. It was the same in the former British north American colonies. In both cases the Puritan religious sect of Quakers – who were equally concerned to promote the rights of women – provided the initial impetus. The first legislative results were to be seen in north America. Pennsylvania, originally colonized by Quakers, passed an Act in 1780 granting freedom to Negroes and mulattos born after that date; by 1789 most of the northern and central states of the recently formed United States had passed laws abolishing slavery and prohibiting the slave trade, although these had little practical effect since the trade remained legal in the southern states: southern plantation owners continued to import slaves and northern merchants continued to supply them. The Federal government was prevented by the constitution from legislating on the issue before 1807 – a compromise agreed in order to prevent the southern states leaving the union.

In Britain the Quaker campaign had inspired John Wesley, founder of the Methodist evangelical Christians, to write what proved the most influential early onslaught on the slave trade, *Thoughts on Slavery* (1774) – although numerous earlier authors had attacked the system. Two years later the Quakers provoked the first debate on the subject in the British Parliament. After the American war the beacon was taken up by James Ramsay, a Scottish naval surgeon with first-hand experience of the horrors of slave ships and of the treatment of slaves on the sugar island of St Kitts. He had spent fifteen years there as surgeon and vicar – after having himself ordained in the Anglican Church – and had documented the savage cruelties inflicted on plantation slaves. In 1781 he returned to Britain to take up an appointment as secretary to Sir Charles Middleton, now Comptroller of the Navy, former commander of a ship in which he had served. Middleton's home, Barham Court, Kent, had the living of Teston village church attached, and as this had fallen vacant, he offered it to Ramsay, who became vicar; the rectory adjoined Barham Court. Teston and Middleton's London home had then become centres for a circle of literary, philanthropic and political figures who were to launch the final, ultimately successful assault on the slave trade. One of that circle, the playwright Hannah More, correctly predicted: 'Teston will be the Runnymede [site of the signing of Magna Carta] of the Negroes.'[39]

Ramsay's own distillations of his experiences in St Kitts, *Essay on the Treatment and Conversion of African Slaves in the British Sugar Colonies* and *An*

Inquiry into Putting a Stop to the African Slave Trade, both published in 1784, made a crucial contribution to the campaign, inspiring Thomas Clarkson, a young Cambridge graduate, to devote his life to researching and publicizing the abominations of the trade, and persuading both William Wilberforce, Member of Parliament for Hull, and the Prime Minister, William Pitt, to carry the abolitionist cause to Parliament.[40] Clarkson and a Quaker member of the Teston circle, Granville Sharp, took the lead in 1787 in setting up a Committee for Effecting the Abolition of the Slave Trade – pattern for the Paris Société des Amis des Noirs – and in what Hugh Thomas, historian of the slave trade, has identified as 'the first major public campaign in any country for a phil-anthropic cause',[41] the Committee's speakers and publications awoke the conscience of the nation. By the following year abolitionists were even holding meetings in Liverpool, headquarters of slave shipping. In Manchester, whose industries contributed to the goods supplied in exchange for slaves, petitions demanding an end to the trade were signed by two-thirds of the male population.[42]

It was against such a background of humanitarian concern in the country that Pitt and Wilberforce in May 1789 – coincidentally the month the Estates General met in Paris – launched the campaign in the House of Commons for the abolition of the trade. The assumption was that, if successful, this must lead to the end of slavery itself, at least in the western colonial system. Both had first-class minds and were fine speakers; both were completely sincere about the degradation the traffic brought to all in any way party to it; and as Wilberforce pointed out, this included every Member of Parliament. They were backed by giants of oratory in the cause of liberty, Edmund Burke and the opposition leader, Charles James Fox. Nevertheless, the alliance of West Indian and com-mercial interests in Parliament and the sheer inertia of custom and received opinion defeated them. The institution of slavery was, after all, as old as recorded history and widely practised in Africa itself. Fundamentally, slaves constituted property; to interfere with the trade with the aim of eventual emancipation would be to strike at the indi-vidual's right to unmolested enjoyment of his property, one of the key freedoms for which, according to political theory, government was insti-tuted. In commercial terms, it was argued, ending the trade would bring low the colonial trades, particularly sugar and cotton, on which the nation's prosperity and the livelihoods of tens of thousands depended.

It was also argued that the sailors who manned the slaving ships formed a nursery of seamen for the Royal Navy in time of war; if the trade were to be abolished, a Liverpool slave ship owner declared, 'the naval importance of this kingdom is abolished with it'.[43] This was a view shared by naval officers, who in general supported the status quo. Nelson, hardly a friend of the planters of Nevis and St Kitts, nevertheless regarded himself as 'bred in the old school, and taught to appreciate the value of our West Indian possessions', which he vowed to defend against 'the damnable doctrine of Wilberforce and his hypocritical allies'.[44]

All hard-nosed commercial arguments favoured continuing the trade; all moral considerations combined against it. That Pitt, the Prime Minister of a merchant power dependent on trade, nonetheless took the moral part against all established interests and indeed the king who had called him to office, and who supported the slaving interests, is the measure of his character and the flexibility of the British parliamentary system which produced him. Refusing to accept defeat, he and Wilberforce and their allies, Burke and Fox and others, pleaded the case for abolition in the Commons year after year. They were matched by abolitionist agitation in the country. In 1792 women initiated the boycott against slave-produced sugar and 500 petitions were prepared against the traffic; and that year Pitt put the abolitionist case in a speech that Fox and others in the Commons accounted 'one of the most extraordinary displays of eloquence they had ever heard'; it left them with the feeling they had been present at one of the supreme moments of parliamentary democracy.[45]

Despite this the House voted for a compromise amendment that the trade ought to be 'gradually abolished'. Obstructive tactics in the Lords, aided by the Crown and bishops of the Church of England, suggested that 'gradually' meant a period of indefinite duration. The following year war broke out with Revolutionary France. Fears that radical republicanism would spread to Britain aided the slaving interests: they could represent abolition as another manifestation of the claimed 'Rights of Man' – which of course it was – the abolitionists as friends of France, just as French slaving interests had represented the Amis des Noirs as British agents. Nonetheless Wilberforce continued his parliamentary campaign, bringing the subject before the House of Commons year after year, whilst Pitt, despite preoccupation with the war, and Burke and Fox continued to support him. Ironically, perhaps, these were the years of spectacular increases in slave-powered colonial trade and industry, which produced the additional revenues that allowed Pitt to borrow so heavily for the war. By 1800 British ships were carrying over 50,000 slaves a year from Africa to the West Indies and America and, partly because of the acquisition of enemy colonies, the slave population of the British empire had grown by about a quarter.[46]

Yet it was precisely in these years that the argument was won in the House of Commons and the country.[47] The legislation abolishing trade in humans would not be enacted until 1806, after the war with France had been resumed, but during this period of unparalleled growth in colonial trade and profits and while Britain was engaged in mortal struggle with Revolutionary France, Parliament and people were converted. Wesley, Ramsay and the Teston circle, Clarkson, the Quakers and non-conformist Churches, Wilberforce, Burke and Fox, above all William Pitt were the heroes of this unprecedented victory for moral principle over profit. It was also a defining time in the history of merchant empires. In his last speech in reply to tributes to his leadership in war, Pitt famously said, 'Europe is not to be saved by any single man. England has saved herself by her exertions, and will, as I trust, save Europe by her example.'[48] He was referring to the often lone struggle against Revolutionary France, but his words could be equally applied to the genuine humanitarian achievement of those years which laid the foundation for the end of slavery in the western world.

A parallel debate in the United States would lead to a similar result in early 1807, the passage of an Act in Congress making it illegal to bring any person into the country as a slave, or to equip, finance or operate a slave ship. In France there had been no lack of opposition to slavery among enlightened circles – as noted, the Jacobin Assembly had declared universal emancipation for slaves in 1794. Yet the movement never penetrated the French people so deeply, and finally the institution and the traffic was resumed on the say of a single man. This marked the difference between the British and French political systems as much as between Pitt and Bonaparte. Between these two the comparison is to the eternal advantage of the civilian statesman guided by moral principle in defiance of the commercial interests of the country he led.[49]

9

Bonaparte's Army of England, 1803

THE PEACE OF Amiens was a brief interlude in the mortal struggle between the opposing systems of Britain and France. Both sides continued to plot the destruction of the other. Bonaparte, in the year the peace was signed, 1802, inaugurated a great fleet-building programme with one 80-gun ship of the line and six 74s.[1] In London the peace-loving Addington and his ministers reviewed all clandestine intrigues to bring down the French government by Pitt's administration since the start of the Revolutionary war and decided to weld the surviving insurrectionary leaders and agents into a new grand conspiracy to topple Bonaparte.[2] British funds also supported insurrections against the French-controlled authorities in Switzerland. In October 1802 a revolt broke out there in the canton of Vaud;[3] Bonaparte ordered General Ney to march in and occupy the whole country. He had already made himself President of the north Italian Cisalpine Republic, practically incorporated Piedmont into France and strengthened French garrisons in the Dutch Batavian Republic, all actions contrary to the provisions of his treaty with Austria.

More serious from the British view was his commercial policy. Despite the remarkable growth of British overseas trade during the Revolutionary war, all outlets in western Europe had been gradually stopped up. Following the French occupation of the Low Countries in 1795 and the subsequent defection of Spain to the French camp, Bonaparte's victories in Italy had closed the traditional British trading marts in the western Mediterranean and Adriatic, Leghorn (Livorno) and Ancona; British goods had been confiscated and local merchants required to

repudiate debts to British houses. Finally, in 1801 the last western loopholes had been closed when both Portugal and the kingdom of Naples
had been forced by military threat into treaties which stipulated they
deny their ports to British shipping.[4] With the return of peace British
merchants anticipated normal trading. Instead it became evident that
Bonaparte intended keeping all continental ports under his control
closed to British commerce. British merchant houses found it impossible
to re-establish themselves in French-dominated Europe or even to obtain
payment of debts or compensation for wartime confiscations. As a
result, those British commercial interests which had welcomed peace
soon came to recognize the inevitability of renewed war.

Bonaparte's commercial policy served both as an attack on the sources
of British wealth and a protection for French industry, which could not
compete with the produce of British factories. Since his territorial aspirations served the interests of army officers, for whom conquest was the
road to glory and riches, and the contractors, industrialists and financiers who supplied the armies, it is evident it was not only Bonaparte's
ambition, but large sections of a new establishment created by the
Revolutionary war which drove France in directions inimical to Britain's
vital interests – in Talleyrand's view against France's best interests too.

By early 1803 Addington's government recognized that there could be
no accommodation: peace was allowing Bonaparte to consolidate his
position and create the conditions for French hegemony over a European continent from which Great Britain would be excluded politically
and commercially. A further danger signal appeared in the official
Moniteur that January – a report by a French military agent suggesting
how easily Egypt might be reoccupied. It had already been decided, in
view of Bonaparte's menacing posture, that Malta would not be evacuated as it should have been under the terms of the Treaty of Amiens –
although evacuation of the Cape of Good Hope was already under way.
Preparations to bring the reduced peace navy back to a war footing were
put in hand and in April the Foreign Secretary sent Talleyrand a deliberately unacceptable ultimatum requiring the withdrawal of French
troops from Holland and Switzerland, recognition of Malta as a British
possession and an explanation of the *Moniteur* report. Talleyrand tried to
temporize, but on 18 May Britain declared war.

A squadron of the Channel Fleet under Vice Admiral Sir William
Cornwallis had already sailed to take station off Brest; at the Nore that
day Admiral Lord Keith hoisted his flag in command of the North Sea

Fleet to watch the Dutch; Nelson was on the coach to Portsmouth with orders to sail for the Mediterranean to take command of the fleet watching Toulon. In secret session clandestine networks had been reactivated as channels of intelligence, communication and funds for the new internal conspiracy to overthrow Bonaparte. This depended heavily on dissident French generals headed by Jean Victor Moreau – who before Bonaparte's surprise landing at Fréjus in 1799 had been canvassed by the Abbé Sieyès to lead the coup against the Directory – and Jean Pichegru, whom British agents had spirited from his south American penal servitude. Sidney Smith, under Lord Keith's command, would organize a principal line of communication through Boulogne.[5]

The pre-emptive declaration set Bonaparte aback. He had anticipated stringing the British along for another year at least. His fleet preparations and the replenishment of the naval arsenals had scarcely begun, his warships were scattered abroad; French merchantmen on the high seas were to fall easy prey to British captains.[6] However, his main focus for destroying the British government and bringing the island empire into his design for Europe was invasion. A preliminary study of the military force required had been completed in the War Ministry in April; he had decided that the army should go by the shortest route across the Strait of Dover; Boulogne was to be the principal port of embarkation. Work had begun in early May to extend the quays there bordering the river Liane and excavate a large artificial basin to increase capacity. In the week after the British declaration the first contracts were awarded for over 1,000 vessels to form an armed invasion flotilla. Orders for a further 2,400 were added in July. For speed of assembly they were to be built not only at the usual naval building yards but in coastal and up-river towns throughout France.[7]

The designs for the vessels – which ranged from 110 feet long, three-masted *prames* armed with twelve 24-pounder cannon on a single deck and intended to carry 120 soldiers, down to open 60-foot *péniches* carrying some 65 soldiers – illustrate the fatal flaws in Bonaparte's system. The Conseil de la Marine and its minister, Rear Admiral Denis Decrès, were employed in most important matters simply as conduits for his own decisions. He had formidable energy, a formidable memory for detail and utter confidence in his own judgement. What he lacked was naval or shipbuilding experience; against the advice of Decrès and all professionals, he had had the invasion craft designed by an engineer whose previous experience in naval architecture was confined to barges on the river Seine; the results were flat-bottomed, shallow-draught vessels without proper keels devised for beaching in shallow water, yet rigged like conventional warships of their size. Decrès and naval officers generally declared them monstrously unsuited to the Channel; Bonaparte would not listen. In the event they were to prove disastrously unstable, unhandy and in many cases impossible to steer.[8] In addition some 700 existing coastal and fishing craft were bought for conversion to pure transports without armament.

This vast building and purchasing programme, together with equally ambitious engineering works enlarging harbours and creating new ones near Boulogne and eastwards along the coast, and the construction of fortifications to protect them from bombardment by inshore divisions of Lord Keith's fleet, was enormously expensive. Bonaparte applied much of the proceeds from the sale of Louisiana to the project, demanded a contribution from his Italian republic and, like the Bourbons in times of need, requested patriotic contributions from French *départements*, cities, corporations and wealthy individuals. In addition, he obtained a bank loan for 20 million francs (*c.* £870,000). In June he forced an agreement from the Batavian Republic to provide, arm and man at their own cost five ships of the line, five frigates, 100 armed brigs, 250 gunboats and transports to carry some 40,000 men together with artillery and horses. For participation in the successful invasion they were to regain Ceylon, which Britain had been allowed to keep at Amiens. Spain was prevailed upon to provide 6 million francs a month from her American treasure and open her dockyards to French warships.

By early September 1803 Bonaparte had fixed on sites for the main encampments of an invasion army 150,000 strong: Saint-Omer, 30 miles east of Boulogne, as headquarters of the overall commander, Nicolas-Jean Soult, one of those Revolutionary generals who had risen through the ranks; Montreuil, 20 miles south of Boulogne; and on the right wing Bruges inland from the Netherlands embarkation ports of Flushing, Ostend and Nieuwpoort. In addition General Augereau would assemble troops, including Irish volunteers, at Brest for a simultaneous landing in Ireland. It was not obvious how these forces were to evade the British navy. Bonaparte came up with his first plan the following spring, 1804: the Brest fleet was to come out and sail *away* from Boulogne, drawing Cornwallis after it, while the Toulon fleet, having avoided Nelson, would sail into the Atlantic, attach additional warships from Rochefort, then enter the Channel to command the Strait of

Dover and southern North Sea for sufficient time to enable the flotillas to cross.

The scheme was as impractical as the types of craft he had ordered to convey the army across. Through the eighteenth century the Royal Navy had evolved an infinitely flexible system of blockading squadrons around the coasts of France and Spain which divided or concentrated as necessary to meet the shifting threats on intelligence from frigates and smaller craft at sea or agents ashore; it was unlikely that in face of Bonaparte's massed invasion craft and blood-curdling threats, Cornwallis, Nelson, Keith and the Admiralty Board would allow the Toulon fleet to slip up-Channel unnoticed. Beyond this was the unpredictability of wind and weather and the tides which ripped through the Dover Strait and the shoals off the north French and Netherlands coast. The embarkation of troops, guns and horses would take at least four days. Conditions favouring boats departing Flushing or Ostend might be impossible for those sailing from Boulogne and nearby ports of the Pas de Calais, and vice versa. A gale could disperse and destroy all the light craft, as one did in July 1804, wrecking a flotilla which Bonaparte had ordered out into Boulogne Roads for inspection, against the categoric objections of the commanding admiral, whom he dismissed on the spot.

But the basic error repeated by Bonaparte in a series of subsequent plans for winning temporary command of the Channel was the failure to recognize the virtual impossibility of coordinating fleets and flotillas drawn from the Mediterranean to the North Sea coast – and dependent on winds and tides – with the precision necessary both to evade the enemy and concentrate. Moreover, given the prevailing south-westerlies, if his fleet did manage to evade the main British fleet under Cornwallis and enter the Channel, it would find itself bottled in, with the enemy in a position of advantage to windward. On the other hand, of course, he could not hope to gain command through victory in battle since his fleet was numerically and qualitatively inferior.[9]

On paper, the chances would improve if he could harness Spain to the design. She had constructed a magnificent battle fleet since the American war including some of the best sailing ships and largest first rates in the world. The greatest of these, the *Santíssima Trinidad*, had been given an extra gun deck at her latest refit, making her the only four-decker in any navy. Yet behind these magnificent vessels built to protect her American, West Indian and Pacific possessions, trade and treasure, the navy remained in a worse state even than the French, still suffering chronic shortages of men and money. There were not enough deep-sea sailors in the country to man even the reduced peacetime squadrons, and ships' companies could only be completed with high proportions of soldiers and pressed landsmen.[10]

The service was also technically backward. In 1793, the year Nelson had visited Spanish ships in Cadiz and judged the crews so poor 'much service cannot be expected of them',[11] a Spanish report on the British navy emphasized the superiority of British gun carriages and method of firing by flintlock, concluding that these gave the British great advantages over other navies in ease and speed of handling and firing the great pieces.[12] Also, like their French counterparts, Spanish officers and men lacked the constant employment at sea which gave British ships' companies their sharp edge in ship-handling. Above all, health was not made the priority it was under British commanders. Nelson's correspondence was peppered with references to his men's physical and mental well-being. Perhaps partly because of his own frequent periods of debilitating illness, he considered 'the great thing in all military service is health'.[13]

He followed a long British tradition of care for the men. Since at least the sixteenth century, individual captains had protected their crews from scurvy, the age-old scourge of long-voyage sailors, by providing them with lemons and fresh vegetables. The particular efficacy of citrus fruit had been proved by a British naval surgeon, Dr James Lind, in controlled experiments from 1747, and he had published his conclusions in *A Treatise on Scurvy* in 1753. This had been overshadowed by James Cook's practical success in warding off scurvy by other means during his long voyages of discovery, but Lind's disciples continued to press the case for 'those fruits abounding with an acid such as the citrus class' as 'more effectual than others',[14] and at the start of the Revolutionary war the commander-in-chief in the East Indies had been persuaded to issue lemon juice regularly to his crews. It kept his squadron free from scurvy over a nineteen-week voyage, and this practical demonstration was used to prevail on the Admiralty Board to make anti-scorbutic policy official. On 27 August 1795 they issued orders to the Victualling Board to supply rob (syrup) of lemon to all large blockading fleets; it was to be added to the men's daily issue of 'grog' – watered rum.

In a scientific age it had taken an inordinate time to find the specific for by far the most debilitating and eventually fatal sickness afflicting all navies. More surprisingly, although French and Spanish naval surgeons and officers were aware of Lind's work and the recent British practice, neither service adopted the use of citrus fruit.[15] Whether this was because they spent less time at sea or their victualling departments were disorganized or lacked funds, or whether it arose from different attitudes to the welfare of common sailors and soldiers in martial societies – as discussed in the Introduction[16] – is not clear. What is certain is that, aside from ship design, the French and Spanish navies were far behind the British in all vital disciplines.

The Royal Navy had also moved ahead in signalling practice. A new 'Vocabulary Signal Book' allowed British admirals who adopted it to say whatever they wished to their ships instead of being confined as fleet commanders had been throughout history to the set phrases in their signal books. This was the work of Captain Sir Home Popham, another of the brilliant individualists who illuminate the period. He had recognized the inefficiency of existing signal books during the American war when an admiral wishing to convey particular orders not in the book had to summon frigates under the flagship's stern and shout instructions through a speaking trumpet, whereupon the frigate made sail to the ships or divisions affected to repeat the orders. In his 'vocabulary' code Popham represented the letters of the alphabet by signals one to twenty-five – 'I' and 'J' sharing the same number – so that any word could be made by a combination of one- and two-flag hoists. To shorten the process, he also produced a 'dictionary' of the commonest or most useful words for naval purposes numbered from 1 to 999; each of these words could thus be made with a single two- or three-letter hoist. In 1803 he produced a second 'dictionary' of another 999 words, and a third with 'sentences most applicable to military or general conversation'.[17] The dictionary in use was denoted by the presence and position of a ball or pendant in the hoist. The system allowed British fleet commanders unprecedented tactical flexibility and although it was not officially endorsed by the Admiralty until the closing stages of the war, by then it was in common use. Nelson adopted the system when he took command of the Mediterranean fleet in 1803.

Bonaparte, who believed that battles were decided by the resolution of commanders and the morale and bravery of the troops, never comprehended the scale of technical inferiority of his own and the Spanish fleet. The Spanish were very aware of it and when hostilities were resumed, fearing for their ships and transatlantic possessions, tried desperately to avoid being drawn in. For a while they succeeded, despite flouting their neutral status by subsidizing Bonaparte and allowing the French to sell prizes and fit out their warships in Spanish ports.

To Pitt, who was returned to power in May 1804 after pressure for a stronger direction to the war than Addington could provide, it was evident that Bonaparte could call upon the Spanish fleet the moment he needed it; nevertheless he took no action until September, when it was reported that Spanish warships in Ferrol were fitting out for sea and French troops were marching to Ferrol through Spain to man five French warships there. Combined action to promote the invasion of England seemed imminent, and he sent instructions to the British ambassador in Madrid to demand an explanation and the immediate demobilization of the Spanish fleet, failing which he was to leave the capital. And orders were sent to Cornwallis off Brest to prevent the French or any Spanish ships from leaving Ferrol, and to intercept and detain Spanish frigates expected with the annual treasure from Mexico.

The frigates were sighted on 5 October but resisted 'detention'. During a brief engagement one blew up, the remaining three were captured with over 3 million silver dollars aboard as well as gold ingots, copper, tin and general merchandise.[18] This pre-emptive strike at the source of Spain's subsidies to France was followed by a blockade of Cadiz. Spain replied with an official declaration of war against Great Britain on 12 December, yet she still had no intention of surrendering her fleet completely to French designs. In November most secret instructions had been sent to Admiral Don Federico de Gravina, conducting alliance negotiations in Paris, stating that it was not in Spain's interest for her forces to go to Brest: 'this must be avoided with the double object of not leaving our coasts unprotected and of preventing our allies from succeeding in their much desired landing in England'.[19] In the event, the convention which Gravina signed with France in January 1805 permitted complete military cooperation and stipulated that Spain would provide thirty of the line by the end of March for combined action with a French expeditionary force whose destination was, for the moment, a secret. All knew the destination was England.

By THIS date Bonaparte had transformed himself into the Emperor Napoleon. Early in 1804 the extent of the British-funded internal conspiracy against him had been revealed by captured agents under prolonged torture, and Moreau, Pichegru and over 350 others connected with the plot had been arrested. During Moreau's trial there were extraordinary displays of public hostility to Bonaparte and it was at this point, on 28 May, he had himself proclaimed Emperor by his tame Senate with rights of succession for his heirs, ostensibly to forestall further attempted coups by the Bourbons or by Jacobins wanting a return to the principles of the Revolution. His coronation in Notre Dame when he pledged himself to the 'glory' as well as happiness of the French people followed in December.

With the Spanish battle fleet now available, he drew up new invasion plans in the early months of 1805. They involved the Brest and Toulon fleets escaping past their British blockaders, releasing Spanish squadrons and sailing with them to the West Indies to ravage British colonies, so drawing the British after them, thence returning across the Atlantic as a huge combined force to command the Channel for sufficient time to permit the troop transports to cross. The initial problem was Cornwallis. Following the example of St Vincent, who had relieved Bridport in 1800 and instituted a rigorously close and continuous blockade of Brest, he allowed the new commander-in-chief of the Brest fleet, Vice Admiral Honoré Ganteaume, no opportunity of escape.

His ability to cling to his station west of Ushant with a chain of signalling ships connecting him to inshore frigates flaunting themselves close off the French fleet base month after month in all weathers has been ascribed to the daily issue of lemon juice so recently introduced; otherwise ships' companies would have dropped with scurvy. However, Lord Hawke had maintained an equally continuous blockade of Brest during the Seven Years War half a century earlier. The health of Hawke's crews had been preserved by fruit, vegetables and live cattle brought out from Plymouth by convoys of supply ships and transferred at sea.[20] The same system kept Cornwallis's men in good health. The demands on the victualling organizations in London and Plymouth were immense, but they were met. In addition cattle and fresh provisions were bought from the inhabitants of the islands off the Brittany coast and provisions of all types from entrepreneurs who sailed out to the fleet in private ships from Britain. There were, besides, abundant fish to be caught in the coastal waters.[21] The chief enemy was tedium.

Towards the end of March Ganteaume informed Napoleon by direct telegraph to Paris that he was ready to sail but there were fifteen English ships off the port and it was impossible to leave without risking a fight – in which he had no doubt of success. Napoleon's reply was unequivocal:

'A naval victory under these circumstances serves no purpose. You have but one objective, that of fulfilling your mission. Sail without fighting.'[22]

Up to this point the invasion of England was his first priority. He had sunk immense resources in constructing the flotillas, new harbours and roads leading to them and new fortifications to protect them, and spent so much of his own time and energy driving the project forward that his commitment to the scheme cannot be doubted.[23] Yet he was very aware of efforts Pitt was making to harness Austria, Russia and Prussia into a third coalition against him, and had to consider switching his invasion army to a campaign on the continent directly the combination came together. In January he had told his Conseil d'État that he anticipated a general European war but had assembled the strongest army in Europe. To do this without alarming the other powers, he had needed a pretext; he had found it, he said, by letting them think he was going to invade England.[24] This is likely to have been a double bluff. Certainly, through-out the spring and early summer he continued devising new schemes for bringing the combined Franco-Spanish fleets into the Channel, and issued fresh orders to their commanders.

In April Pitt came to an agreement with Russia, to which it was hoped Austria would accede. The aims were to set bounds to Napoleon's ambi-tions by driving France from Holland, Switzerland, Italy and the German states, afterwards establishing a concert of powers to settle European rela-tionships within a mutually agreed system of law.[25] In July the coalition became reality when the tsar ratified the treaty. Russia and Austria engaged themselves to provide armies which Great Britain would subsid-ize at the rate of £1,250,000 for each 100,000 men in the field to a maximum of 400,000, thus £5 million. Sweden had already signed a treaty with Britain allowing the use of Rügen Island and the adjacent for-tress of Rostock in Swedish Pomerania as bases for an Anglo-Russian descent in northern Germany; later that year she signed a convention agreeing to provide 12,000 troops for offensive operations – for which double commitment she extorted the extravagant sum of almost £250,000 from the British Exchequer. This third coalition of three great powers and one minor power was joined shortly by the Neapolitan kingdom of the Two Sicilies. Of the significant powers, only Prussia had failed to come in, despite the usual offer of subsidies from the British government. This was to prove a fatal default, allowing Napoleon to deploy the magnificent mili-tary machine he had created on the Channel coast in a rapid strike against Austria knowing his northern flank was secure.

That same July Pitt received intelligence from an agent in Paris citing Talleyrand, General Augereau and the United Irishmen's leader, Arthur O'Connor, all dismissing the prospect of invasion: 'there is no serious intention at present – whatever there may have been formerly – of doing anything . . . Nothing has been done lately at Boulogne, nor is it likely there will be soon.'[26]

One part of Napoleon's convoluted naval plan had been partly accomplished, though. The Toulon fleet under Vice Admiral Pierre Villeneuve had evaded Nelson's 'open' blockade – as will be described – escaped into the Atlantic, attached a small Spanish squadron from Cadiz under Admiral Gravina and sailed to the West Indies. Some weeks after his arrival Villeneuve heard that Nelson had arrived in the islands in pursuit and immediately returned across the Atlantic. A British force of fifteen of the line under Vice Admiral Sir Robert Calder was positioned to the west of Finisterre to intercept him and did so on 22 July, but the resulting action in fog was inconclusive with only two Spanish ships captured. Villeneuve was allowed to slip away into Vigo, and from thence to Ferrol, where he attached a further five French and nine Spanish ships of the line to his flag.

He also found a letter from Decrès containing Napoleon's latest orders. These allowed him unusual latitude: the first option was to unite with a squadron in Rochefort, subsequently with Ganteaume in Brest, preferably without fighting, but if forced to fight he should do so near Brest so that Ganteaume could support him. Having attached Ganteaume, he was to press straight into the Channel without anchoring at Brest, and proceed to Boulogne. Alternatively, having attached the Rochefort squadron, he might bypass Ganteaume – and Cornwallis – and sail northabout around Scotland and down the North Sea to unite with the Dutch squadron off the Texel, thence making himself master of the Strait of Dover, if only for the four or five days Napoleon needed.[27]

It was a fantasy. Cornwallis and Calder with thirty-one of the line between them, Nelson still seeking him with eleven of the line, and other smaller detachments would concentrate against him, but it was the state of his own ships and crews which had crossed the Atlantic twice that rendered the orders unrealistic. Decrès knew this, and added:

The execution of the project conceived long ago by the genius of the Emperor is not absolute. In his wisdom the Emperor has anticipated the case in which from incalculable events, the situation of the fleet would not allow our carrying out his designs which would have so great an influence on the fate of the world; and in this case alone the Emperor wishes to assemble an imposing array of forces at Cadiz.[28]

Probably Napoleon too realized the moment had passed and was ready to switch his naval forces to the southern flank against Austria. Certainly Villeneuve and Gravina knew the project was hopeless. The men of the transport flotillas and the troops massed on the Pas de Calais no longer believed in it either. Napoleon went to Boulogne nonetheless, arriving on 3 August, and made a great show of preparations for embarking; on the 7th he issued a manifesto promising the troops the pillage of London. On the 13th came news of Villeneuve's action with Calder. His admiral's lack of offensive spirit filled him with impotent rage, but he contained himself sufficiently to address a last appeal to Villeneuve to rendezvous with the Rochefort squadron and sweep all before him to reach the Channel. 'March straight at the enemy!'[29] The same day he dictated a detailed plan for a strike against Austria, the precise route of march, halts and dates.[30] He was a master of keeping several schemes in the air at once; it is more probable he was now engaged in a major deception similar to one which would be practised by another continental dictator 136 years later.

At all events, by the end of August the Army of England was on the march towards the Rhine.[31]

10

Trafalgar, 1805

NELSON'S COMMAND OF the Mediterranean squadron from July 1803 to
August 1805 was as extraordinary as his achievements in battle. Lacking
a suitable base from which to watch Toulon – since Malta and Gibraltar
were both too far and Minorca with its ideal harbour at Port Mahón had
been restored to Spain at the peace – he remained at sea, never putting
into port or setting foot ashore himself until the end of the period, shel-
tering for provisioning and making what repairs could be made in open
roadsteads, chiefly on the coast of Sardinia. His favourite anchorage was
in the Maddalena islands off north-eastern Sardinia, which he considered 'the most important island, as a naval and military station, in the
Mediterranean'.[1]

He made his summer station and rendezvous in the Gulf of Lion 30
to 40 miles west of Toulon, sufficiently far, he hoped, to entice the French
out, yet in position to prevent a Spanish squadron joining them, with one
or sometimes two frigates off the base itself. He was very aware of the
importance of keeping the French from Egypt, Sicily and Naples and,
for his own purposes, Sardinia, and ensuring the safe convoying of
British merchantmen and supply ships throughout the Mediterranean
and past the Strait of Gibraltar as far as Cadiz, but his prime object, as
he put it, was 'to keep the French fleet in check, and if they ever put to
sea, to have force enough to annihilate them'.[2] Annihilation was a
curious concept for an officer brought up in the eighteenth century; it is
doubtful if any other fleet commander in any navy thought in this way,
let alone formulated the idea, but Nelson meant it, and was to repeat it

constantly. It sprang from his deep hatred of the French, intense patriotism and craving for personal glory – and a realistic appraisal of the weakness of his enemy. He knew it was possible. He had proved it at the Nile, the first true naval annihilation. As the eminent nineteenth-century French admiral and naval historian, Jean-Baptiste Jurien de la Gravière, summed it up later: '*Le génie de Nelson c'est d'avoir compris notre faiblesse.*'[3]

Rather than send single ships or detachments off in turn to replenish or water, he kept his small squadron of nine, later ten of the line concentrated at all times in case the French should come out; thus the whole squadron sailed to water or take on provisions together. And, unlike Cornwallis, who could rely on convoys of supply ships sent out by the Victualling Board, Nelson had to organize his own provisions from wherever he could find them. Some indication of his difficulties appears in a letter he wrote to a medical friend affirming his belief in health as the 'great thing in all military service' and that it was easier to keep men healthy than for a physician to cure them once they had gone down with sickness. He did not neglect mental health:

> Situated as this fleet has been without a friendly port, where we could get all the things so necessary for us, yet I have, by changing the cruizing ground, not allowed the sameness of prospect to satiate the mind – sometimes by looking at Toulon, Ville Franche, Barcelona and Rosas; then running around Minorca, Majorca, Sardinia and Corsica; and two or three times anchoring for a few days, and sending a ship to the last place for *onions*, which I find the best thing that can be given to seamen; having always good mutton for the sick, cattle when we can get them, and plenty of fresh water . . . but shut very nearly out from Spain, and only getting refreshments by stealth from other places, my command has been an arduous one.[4]

Dedicated as he was to organizing convoys and supplies, and to his self-imposed mission of destroying the French fleet, his days were not entirely filled with cares. The Gulf of Lion was notoriously stormy, but there were weeks of Mediterranean sunshine and fair breezes when he could contemplate from the stern gallery of his flagship, *Victory*, the majesty of his command, ship after ship following with swelling sails and hulls painted yellow in the Nelson fashion, chequered with black gunport lids, 'the lofty and tremendous bulwarks of Britain' as the physician to the fleet described them.[5]

He took much exercise on the quarterdeck, generally walking six or seven hours a day according to the *Victory*'s surgeon, wearing a green shade attached to the brim of his cocked hat to shield his good eye from the brilliance of the sun, his coveted four orders of chivalry sewn into his faded blue coat.[6] In the afternoons the ship's band played. At 3 o'clock he took dinner in his quarters with his captain of the fleet, or chief of staff, the captain of the *Victory*, Thomas Masterman Hardy, ever devoted to him, several ship's officers and in good weather admirals or captains from other ships of the squadron invited in rotation by seniority. As in his previous Mediterranean command before the Nile, he discussed tactical contingencies with each individually and impressed each with his own conceptions. His dinners were convivial: champagne and clarets were served; he was affable, interested and attentive, 'as free from stiffness and pomp as a regard to proper dignity will admit', the physician observed; 'If a person does not feel himself perfectly at his ease it must be his own fault, such is the urbanity and hospitality which reign.'[7] The attraction of his personality and transparent longing to meet and annihilate the enemy welded his captains and with them the squadron as a whole into a committed instrument; the continuous cruising in all weathers ensured the instrument was perfectly tuned. 'We are healthy beyond example', Nelson wrote in October 1803, 'and so sharp-set, that I would not be a French Admiral in the way of our ships.'[8]

The French, by contrast, were never at sea as a fleet, only leaving harbour in ones or twos from spring 1804 for training just outside. Nelson tried to lure them further by showing himself with only half his squadron, the other half waiting some 50 miles beyond the horizon, but without success. That August the French fleet commander died. His replacement, Vice Admiral Pierre Villeneuve, arrived in December, hoisting his flag in the new 80-gun *Bucentaure*. He was an *ancien régime* noble, forty-one years old – thus five years younger than Nelson – who had entered Louis XVI's navy at the age of fifteen. His rapid rise had been due both to ability and the thinning of the ranks during the Revolution. At the battle of the Nile he had commanded the rear division and led the only two surviving ships of the line and two frigates from the bay the following morning. The shattering experience is said to have instilled in him a fear of Nelson – a story that derives, as will appear, from the jaundiced opinion of a military officer who sailed aboard his flagship and probably had as little concept of naval operations as Napoleon. It is true that Villeneuve had a realistic attitude to the Royal Navy's superiority: 'It is utterly impossible for us to defeat the enemy when both sides are [numerically] equal,' he wrote to Decrès early in 1805; 'indeed they will beat us even when they are a third weaker than we are',[9] a ratio more than confirmed by subsequent historical analysis.[10] And, like the majority of professional officers, including Decrès, he regarded Napoleon's naval schemes as madness.

On 18 January 1805 he took advantage of fresh north-westerly winds to get under way with the fleet in compliance with Napoleon's latest orders. Outside a gale blew up when, as he reported, 'The few sailors were lost among the soldiers, who were seasick and . . . encumbered the decks. It was impossible to work the ships. Spars were broken and sails carried away both by clumsiness and inexperience and through bad materials supplied by the dockyards.'[11] He limped back inside Toulon and wrote to Decrès offering his resignation, pointing out that 'all one can expect from a career in the French navy today is shame and confusion', and he did not intend becoming the laughing stock of Europe by involving himself in further disasters.[12] Napoleon considered him a defeatist and wanted him replaced, but Decrès could find no one he trusted with such a vital command, and Villeneuve remained.

Nelson, meanwhile, learning from his frigates that the French had sailed, and knowing from prior intelligence that they carried troops, assumed they intended landings in the Mediterranean. Finding they had not gone to Sardinia, he fell back on Sicily and when there was no sign of them there convinced himself that Napoleon was making a second attempt on Egypt and, as in 1798, sailed to Alexandria. After a fruitless search he arrived back off Sardinia on 26 March.

Four days later Villeneuve took his fleet of eleven of the line out for a second time in more moderate weather and, avoiding Nelson's known rendezvous off the Spanish coast, succeeded in escaping detection and making his way through the Strait of Gibraltar to Cadiz. Here he was to attach a Spanish squadron under Admiral Gravina. Lately ambassador in Paris, Gravina had returned in February to find a dire situation: a poor grain harvest had made it impossible to manufacture sufficient biscuit, which formed the basis of the seagoing rations; there was no money for other provisions and stores, and the seafaring population of the region had been decimated by yellow fever.[13] When Villeneuve arrived off the harbour, therefore, instead of the fifteen of the line Gravina had promised in his negotiation with Napoleon, he could only join him with six manned largely by soldiers and pressed landsmen. One French 74 also joined, bringing the combined fleet to eighteen of the line. With these on 9 April Villeneuve set course for the West Indies.

Nelson had only learned of his departure from Toulon five days earlier. His destination was unclear and as before Nelson covered Sardinia, then fell back to Sicily, spreading frigates for intelligence. None came and he worked westward again. It was not until the 18th, nine days after Villeneuve had departed Cadiz, that he learned that the French had been seen off the Spanish coast east of the Strait of Gibraltar; concluding that they must have left the Mediterranean, he decided to follow through the Strait. On 4 May he heard the first rumour that they were bound for the West Indies, but it was not until the 9th, while anchored in Lagos Bay, east of Cape St Vincent, to take off provisions from supply ships, that he received the first definitive confirmation of their destination. Completing provisioning on the 11th, he set off in pursuit, more than four weeks behind and, as he put it in a letter to the Admiralty, 'running after eighteen sail of the line with ten'.[14]

He gained ten days on the combined fleet on the run across the Atlantic, arriving at Barbados on 4 June, and but for intelligence that the French had sailed south at the end of May – which he could not disregard since it came from the general commanding British troops on St Lucia – he would probably have caught Villeneuve a few days later; for the same day the combined fleet, which had gained two battle ships, bringing the total to twenty of the line, sailed from Martinique, northward. Four days later Villeneuve met and captured a small convoy of British merchantmen out of Antigua, from which he learned that Nelson had arrived with fourteen of the line at Barbados; and assuming he would be joined there by the British West Indies squadron of five of the line, he decided to abandon a planned attack on British islands and return to Europe. His reasoning is clear. He had been shocked by the poor quality of the Spanish crews, but more importantly they and his own men had been going down with sickness in alarming numbers.[15] Nelson's squadron was virtually free from sickness, although he could not know that. What he did know, as he had written in January, was the utter impossibility of defeating a numerically equal British fleet; against the nineteen he believed Nelson to have, he thought his twenty faced inevitable disaster.

Nelson learned of his departure on 12 June and, assuming he was bound for Europe, set off after him, despatching a brig to England to inform the Admiralty of his intentions. Anxious as always that his forecast of the enemy destination might be wrong and that he was again staking all on his own judgement without orders, he nevertheless believed Villeneuve to be making for the Mediterranean, and steered for Gibraltar. To the captains he invited aboard to dine, he confided that he thought the enemy had twenty of the line; 'therefore do not be surprised if I should fall on them immediately; we won't part without a battle.'[16]

However, Villeneuve had received orders in Martinique which directed him, after capturing British possessions in the islands, to return to Ferrol and attach a Spanish squadron there. The courses of the fleets diverged and once again Nelson missed his prey. His despatch brig on the way to England did sight Villeneuve though, and kept company for long enough to determine his course, which her commander reported at the Admiralty early in the morning of 9 July; hence Villeneuve's reception by Sir Robert Calder off Finisterre on the 22nd.

Nelson had made Gibraltar on 19 July and had gone ashore on the 20th, as he recorded in his diary, 'for the first time since the 16th of June, 1803'.[17] On the 22nd he was replenishing with fresh vegetables and live bullocks at Tetuan just inside the Straits; the following day he decided to take the first easterly into the Atlantic to hunt up the Spanish coast and if necessary as far as Brest or even Ireland. He was baulked by head winds above Cape St Vincent and did not reach Cornwallis off Ushant until 15 August. He was immediately given permission to proceed with the *Victory* to England for leave, which the Admiralty had granted him before the outbreak of war with Spain, and he parted the same day.

It will be recalled that when Villeneuve arrived at Ferrol after his encounter with Calder, he had found new orders with a final clause that if 'from incalculable events' he was not able to carry them out 'in this case alone the Emperor wishes to assemble an imposing array of forces at Cadiz'.[18] On 15 August, as 300 miles to the north Nelson's squadron joined Cornwallis, Villeneuve availed himself of this release and bore up for Cadiz.[19] No doubt Gravina's advice had weighed when he came to his decision. The Spanish crews had been much depleted by sickness and the fresh ships had not been to sea for years. Moreover, as Gravina had written to Decrès, the English had been warned of their return and all surprise had been lost.[20] Since Spanish policy was not to allow their fleet to be bottled up in Brest, nor to assist with the invasion attempt, Gravina was in any case strongly opposed to the orders to make for Brest, and thence the Channel; while Villeneuve himself still despaired of the seamanship of his own ships' companies and knew he could rule out any possibility of cohesive fleet manoeuvres in action. His decision seems inevitable.

The *Victory* dropped anchor in Spithead on 18 August and the following morning Nelson went ashore at Portsmouth, greeted by cheering crowds at every vantage point. Early the following morning he was reunited with Emma and Horatia at Merton Place. The same day Villeneuve put in to Cadiz.

NELSON'S TACTICAL ideas for destroying the French fleet had been maturing during the two years' watch on Toulon and from long before. Whether they owed more to the study of John Clerk's *An Essay on Naval Tactics*[21] or to Howe's practical demonstrations of the use of an advanced squadron and of cutting through the enemy line to engage from to leeward in the campaign of the Glorious First of June,[22] or to Duncan's two-pronged perpendicular assault at Camperdown[23] is impossible to know. All formed part of the tactical vocabulary of the day. His overriding principle is clear, and it was the same as Howe's: if his ships could get close alongside the enemy and hold them to action they would inevitably prevail. His part was to enable them to do so in the shortest time so as to leave the maximum period of daylight to crush the maximum number.

As noted, his mind was fixed not on victory, but annihilation. Called to give advice to government ministers during his leave that August and early September, he used the word many times; we know he used it with the First Lord of the Admiralty, Lord Barham, formerly Sir Charles Middleton,[24] host to the Teston anti-slavery circle, and when talking to the Cabinet – 'only numbers can annihilate'[25] – and with the Prime Minister. After a meeting on 5 September, he recorded, 'Mr Pitt knows . . . [it is] annihilation the country needs, and not merely a splendid victory.'[26] Pitt was so impressed with Nelson's sound judgement and self-belief that he insisted, after it was learned that Villeneuve had taken the combined fleet in to Cadiz, that Nelson and no one else must command the fleet being concentrated off the Spanish base. Barham had already reached the same conclusion.

Nelson's other main tactical ideas were concentration against parts of the enemy line – as at the Nile – and deception about which sections he intended attacking. As he explained to one of his most trusted captains, Richard Keats, who visited him at Merton in August, he would form the fleet into three divisions, one composed of twelve or fourteen of the fastest two-deckers, which he would always keep to windward to throw into battle at whatever point he chose.

'With the remaining part of the fleet formed in two lines, I shall go at them at once, if I can, about one-third of their line from their leading ship. What do you think of it?'

Before Keats had time to give a considered reply, he went on, 'I'll tell you what I think of it. I think it will surprise and confound the enemy. They won't know what I am about. It will bring forward a pell-mell battle, and that is what I want.'[27]

This was, indeed, the essence of his approach.

In the three and a half weeks before the *Victory* was ready for sea again and he was called away, he tasted brief fulfilment. The Cabinet hung upon his words; Pitt, at the end of their interviews, rose and escorted him out of doors into his carriage, a compliment Nelson doubted the great man would have paid a prince of the blood. His movements were detailed in the gossip columns. On the streets of London he was immediately recognized and mobbed, not only as the victor of the Nile and Copenhagen, but as the hero who had chased Villeneuve to the West Indies and back again and, unlike Calder, would undoubtedly have drubbed him had he found him. Lord Minto was caught with Nelson in one of these mobs and wrote afterwards, 'It is really quite affecting to see the wonder and admiration, and love and respect of the whole world; and the genuine expression of all these sentiments at once, from gentle and simple, the moment he is seen. It is beyond anything represented in a play or in a poem of fame.'[28]

At Merton he was master in his own country house which Emma had decorated in his honour with paintings of the two of them, prints of his victories and battle trophies. Horatia, now four and a half years old, was bright and 'uncommonly quick'. His mother and father and Sir William Hamilton were dead, but his elder brother and favourite sister and their spouses and children were house guests, and naval friends and colleagues visited frequently. Before breakfast he walked his estate. The dining table was set with Worcester china decorated with oak leaves and laurel and his coat of arms as Viscount Nelson – to which he had been raised after Copenhagen – and Duke of Brontë, the title and Sicilian estate he had been awarded by the King of the Two Sicilies.

Enjoyment of all he had desired and unsparingly earned was shadowed by the sense that this blessed interlude might be his last. No one was ever more aware of his mortality than Nelson. After the battle of the

Nile he had been presented by the captain of the *Swiftsure*, Benjamin Hallowell, with a coffin made by his carpenter from timber from the mainmast of the French flagship, *L'Orient*. Whether Hallowell had meant it as a reminder amidst all the adulation after the victory that he was mortal, or whether, more probably, he had discerned his fatalism, Nelson prized the macabre gift. He kept it in his quarters and when he left his ship had it taken to London and stored. It is said he visited its custodian on this last leave and observed that he might have need of it on his return. A light-hearted remark perhaps; alternatively, as his biographer A. T. Mahan wrote, 'Life then held much for him; and it is when richest that the possibility of approaching loss possesses the consciousness with the sense of probability.'[29]

He took the coach to Portsmouth in the evening of 13 September, at one stop while the horses were changed, writing in his private diary: 'Friday night, at half past ten, drove from dear, dear Merton, where I left all which I hold dear in this world, to go to serve my King and Country . . . May the great God whom I adore, enable me to fulfil the expectations of my Country.'[30] The following afternoon he went aboard the *Victory* after scenes of popular acclamation similar to those that had greeted his arrival twenty-five days earlier, and sailed early on the 15th.

Delayed by head winds in the Channel and off the Atlantic coast, it was not until the 28th that he reached the fleet off Cadiz and took over from his old friend, Collingwood, who now became his second in command. To prevent Villeneuve knowing of his arrival he had sent a frigate ahead with orders that no salute should be fired when he joined. Next day was his forty-seventh birthday; he invited junior admirals and half the captains to dine, the other half on the following day.

A new mood animated the fleet. Collingwood was a distant disciplinarian, described by an officer who served with him as 'iron, and very cold iron' in body and mind;[31] by contrast Nelson appeared to one captain who had not met him before as 'so good and pleasant a man that we all like to do what he likes without any kind of orders'; another wrote, 'Lord Nelson is arrived, and a sort of general joy has been the consequence.'[32] Nelson was very aware of the impression he created:

The reception I met with on joining the Fleet caused the sweetest sensation of my life. The officers who came on board to welcome my return forgot my rank as Commander-in-Chief in the enthusiasm with which they greeted me. As soon as these emotions were past, I laid before them the Plan I had previously arranged for attacking the Enemy; and it was not only my pleasure to find it generally approved, but clearly perceived and understood.[33]

To Emma, he wrote that he believed his arrival was most welcome to almost every individual in the fleet, 'and when I came to explain to them the *"Nelson touch"*, it was like an electric shock. Some shed tears, all approved – "It was new – it was singular – it was simple!" '[34]

For Vice Admiral Calder, though, who had been sent to join Collingwood after Villeneuve had brought the combined fleet into Cadiz, Nelson had an unpleasant message: he was required to return home to account for his conduct in the action of 22 July, especially his subsequent failure to keep touch with the enemy. When Calder learned he was to make the passage in a frigate he broke down, and Nelson, against his military judgement, agreed that, provided an expected three-decker arrived, he could return in his 90-gun flagship – which two weeks later he did. To let one of his most powerful ships go on the eve of the anticipated battle of annihilation simply to save an officer from humiliation showed extraordinary compassion or culpable soft-heartedness. Nelson feared the censure of the Admiralty Board for the latter and for disobeying orders, and wrote to Barham, 'but I trust that I shall be considered to have done right as a man, and to a brother officer in affliction – my heart could not stand it, and so the thing must rest.'[35]

It is relevant, however, that he had been promised substantial reinforcements, and in a memorandum on 9 October setting out the schemes of attack which he had explained to the captains with such dramatic effect shortly after his arrival, he assumed a British fleet of forty of the line. At this time he had only thirty-three.

The memorandum opened famously:

Thinking it almost impossible to bring a fleet of forty sail of the Line into a line of Battle in variable winds, thick weather, and other circumstances which must occur, without such a loss of time that the opportunity would probably be lost of bringing the Enemy to Battle in such a manner as to make the business decisive; I have therefore made up my mind to keep the Fleet in that position of sailing (with the exception of the First and Second in Command) that the Order of Sailing is to be the Order of Battle; placing the Fleet in two Lines of sixteen Ships each, with an Advanced Squadron of eight of the fastest-sailing Two-decked Ships *which* will always make, if wanted, a Line of twenty-four Sail on whichever Line the Commander-in-Chief may direct.[36]

The memorandum went on to prescribe modes of attack if the enemy were to windward or to leeward; in both cases the second in command's line of sixteen ships was to concentrate on the rear twelve of the enemy, Nelson's own line and the advanced squadron taking on the enemy centre 'so as to ensure getting at their Commander-in-Chief, on whom every effort must be made to capture. The whole impression of the British Fleet must be to overpower from two or three ships ahead of their Commander-in-Chief, supposed to be in the Centre, to the rear of their Fleet', after which he looked 'with confidence to a Victory before the Van of the Enemy could succour their Rear'.

A distinctive feature of the schemes outlined was that after Nelson had given his initial signal for the second in command – Collingwood – to lead through the enemy rear, Collingwood was to 'have the entire direction of his Line to make the attack upon the Enemy and to follow up the blow until they are captured or destroyed'. And from what Nelson had said to Captain Keats in the grounds at Merton, he intended the commander of the advanced squadron to be similarly independent after the initial signal, and to employ his ships 'perhaps, in a more advantageous manner than if he could have followed my orders'.[37]

Another feature, unstated but implied, was deception. While Collingwood overpowered the rear twelve ships, Nelson would keep the enemy commander-in-chief guessing about precisely where he himself would attack: 'The remainder of the Enemy's Fleet, 34 Sail [of an assumed 46] are to be left to the management of the Commander-in-Chief, who will endeavour to take care that the movements of the Second in Command are as little interrupted as possible.'[38]

Equally important and entirely novel was the principle of haste; it was apparent in the opening paragraph quoted above, and was palpable in the directions for attack from to windward: after the signal for Collingwood's line to bear up together, they were 'to set all their sails, even steering [studding] sails, in order to get as quickly as possible to the Enemy's Line, and to cut through, beginning from the 12 Ship from the Enemy's Rear'. No doubt this was to shorten the dangerous period when the ships would be heading into the raking fire of the enemy, liable to mast and rigging damage and unable to reply, and to maximize the likelihood of breaking through and creating confusion. However, it was bound to lead to gaps and an uneven impact as the sluggish sailers lagged far astern. It would not have been contemplated by Howe at the beginning of the Revolutionary war, nor by Duncan in 1797 but for the shoal water he glimpsed to leeward of the Dutch. The need for haste arose from Nelson's thirst for complete victory, his willingness to take risks and his very poor opinion of French and Spanish ships' companies. If it marked an advance in tactics, this was only because of the imbalance in professional competence. It was akin to tactics of contempt.[39]

One phrase in the memorandum would provide inspiration for generations of Royal Naval officers to come: 'in case Signals can neither be seen or perfectly understood, no Captain can do very wrong if he places his Ship alongside that of an Enemy.'

As with his long watch on Toulon, Nelson kept a deliberately open blockade, moving the main fleet some 50 miles west of Cadiz in order to keep Villeneuve in ignorance of his strength and entice him out, with frigates keeping a close watch on the harbour and connecting ships to repeat their signals. At the same time the need to send ships to Gibraltar and Tetuan in rotation to take on fresh water and provisions, and also to protect a merchant convoy threatened by a Spanish squadron preparing for sea at Cartagena, forced him to part with what had been Collingwood's inshore squadron of six fast 74s, thus reducing his force to twenty-seven of the line and leaving him without the numbers to form the 'advanced squadron' described in the memorandum.

Villeneuve had by now received fresh instructions from Napoleon: they required him to 'seize the first opportunity of sailing with the Combined Fleet', passing into the Mediterranean, attaching the Spanish ships at Cartagena, thence proceeding to Naples and landing troops to join the French commander there, afterwards sailing to Toulon to refit; should he meet the enemy in inferior force he was to attack without hesitation and obtain a decision.[40] However, he had earlier received a general instruction, conveyed as usual in a letter from Decrès, not to hesitate to attack equal or superior forces and to fight them to the death: 'This is His Majesty's [Napoleon's] wish: he accounts the loss of his ships as nothing, if they are lost with glory.'[41] In view of the known presence of a powerful British fleet outside Cadiz, neither this exhortation nor the instructions to land a handful of troops on the extreme southern flank of Napoleon's new campaign against Austria made military sense. In the light of his ambitious naval construction programme, the appeal to 'glory' made no sense unless perhaps in the context of the warrior ethic.

Villeneuve ordered the fleet to prepare for sea, but Gravina requested a council of war before sailing. It seems extraordinary that Villeneuve did not initiate this himself, if only as a courtesy to his ally; it may be that he

'Those far-distant storm beaten ships upon which the Grand Army never looked' (A. T. Mahan), which broke France: (*above*) the blockade of Brest, 1800; (*below*) 'A first rate taking in stores' by J. M. W. Turner captures the ominous power and solidity of a three-decked ship of the line

Charles-Maurice de Talleyrand, French statesman of genius who survived the Revolution and Napoleon

Edmund Burke, political philosopher who predicted the evils of the Revolution

Charlotte Corday, who stabbed the Revolutionary leader, Marat, through the heart

Maximilien Robespierre, idealist of the Revolution

William Pitt, the Younger, who steered Great Britain through extreme hazards in the French Revolutionary War and set the course which his successors would follow against Napoleon

Left: Richard, Earl Howe, one of the great tacticians of fighting sail

Below: Howe in the *Queen Charlotte* breaks through the French line, dividing the enemy fleet from to leeward, 29 May 1794, preliminary to his victory on the 'Glorious First of June'. Painting by Thomas Whitcombe

Admiral John Jervis, Earl of St Vincent

The young Horatio Nelson; although wearing a captain's uniform, Nelson's features remain those of the seventeen-year-old lieutenant whom the artist, Francis Rigaud, had begun painting three years earlier

Rear Admiral Sir James de Saumarez in 1801; a distinguished fighting captain, Saumarez went on to command successive British fleets controlling the Baltic during the economic struggle against Napoleon

The brilliant fighting commander, spy and raconteur, Captain Sir Sidney Smith, seen here as he would no doubt have wished to be remembered: successfully defending the walls of Saint-Jean d'Acre against Napoleon

Above and below: Vice Admiral Brueys, commander of the fleet escorting Bonaparte's Egyptian expedition, who lost his life when his flagship, *L'Orient,* blew apart during the battle of the Nile

Above: Vice Admiral Pierre Villeneuve, commander-in-chief of the Franco-Spanish fleet at the battle of Trafalgar

The hero of the Nile: the forty-two-year-old Nelson after annihilating Brueys'
fleet in Aboukir Bay at the mouth of the Nile. Painted in Vienna by Friedrich
Heinrich Füger during Nelson's overland return to England with Sir William
and Lady Hamilton

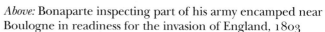

Above: Bonaparte inspecting part of his army encamped near Boulogne in readiness for the invasion of England, 1803

Left: Sculpture of the young Bonaparte

Right: Nelson's flagship, *Victory*, pushes through the enemy line at Trafalgar. Painting by William Clarkson Stanfield

Below: Carronades, the Royal Navy's short-barrelled, wide-bored guns deadly to enemy men and rigging at short range

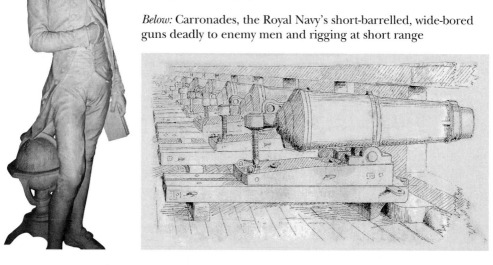

Looking forward from the quarterdeck of the *Victory* as Nelson falls to a shot from a trained marksman in the mizzen top of the *Redoubtable* alongside.

Note at both sides the guns' crews serving their pieces, and the marines beyond firing over the hammock nettings. Painting by Denis Dighton

Arthur Wellesley, 1st Duke of Wellington, 1814. Hailed after his triumphant campaigns against Napoleon's marshals in the Spanish peninsula as the liberator of Europe, he would defeat Napoleon himself the following year at Waterloo. Painting by Sir Thomas Lawrence

'Napoleon crossing the Alps at the St Bernard's Pass, 29 May 1800' by Jacques Louis David, painter successively to the Revolution, the Consulate and the Empire. The propaganda intent of this portrait foreshadows the heroic representations of twentieth-century dictators

Above: Scene below decks in a slaving ship

Left: Thomas Clarkson, leading spirit in the British movement for 'Effecting the Abolition of the Slave Trade', who gathered advice at slaving ports, often at peril of his life

The US 44-gun super-frigate *Constitution* reduces the British frigate *Guerrier* to a wreck in the opening bout of the Anglo-American war in August 1812

Two US naval heroes of the war on the Great Lakes. *Left:* Oliver Hazard Perry, promoted captain after his victory on Lake Erie, September 1813. *Right:* Lieutenant Thomas Macdonough, victor of the battle of Plattsburg Bay, September 1814

Above: New York *c.* 1848: view from St Paul's Church by Henry Papprill. Broadway leads southwards (to the right) towards Trinity Church by Wall Street and the commercial hub of the city; shipping lines the quays of the East River on the far shore

Left: Captain Stephen Decatur of the USS *United States,* victor over HMS *Macedonian* in October 1812. Painting by Asher Brown Durand who, with his friend Thomas Cole, became a pioneer of American landscape painting

knew the inevitable result. Gravina had already confided that, as the King of the Two Sicilies was a brother of the King of Spain, he could not join him in operations designed to boost French forces in southern Italy. He had an even more powerful personal reason: he was the son of a Neapolitan nobleman himself and had been born in Sicily. He had made it clear he would not fight against what he still considered his own kingdom.[42]

Villeneuve convened the council of senior French and Spanish officers aboard his flagship, *Bucentaure*, on 8 October. All agreed that because of the acute shortage of seamen, lack of training at sea or fleet evolutions and the fact that some Spanish ships, including the three-deckers *Santa Ana* and *Rayo*, had only just left dock after refitting, the British fleet outside was far more powerful than their own. It appears that members of the French contingent were nevertheless prepared to obey the orders and fight for glory, but after some warm exchanges a compromise was agreed: to await a more favourable occasion for sailing when the British fleet abandoned its station owing to bad weather or divided its force to protect merchant convoys in the Mediterranean from the Cartagena squadron.[43]

Villeneuve took the opportunity to explain his tactical ideas. They had scarcely changed since he had taken command of the Toulon fleet the previous December, when he had predicted Nelson's mode of attack with uncanny accuracy. Nelson would not, he had stated, engage in a traditional artillery duel in parallel lines, but would 'endeavour to envelop our rear, to break through our line and to direct his ships in groups upon such of ours as he shall have cut off, so as to surround and defeat them'. Villeneuve did not attempt to outline tactics to counter such an assault, probably because he did not believe his ships capable of any more complex manoeuvre than simple fleet line ahead close on a wind; he merely enjoined his captains, once the line was broken, 'to go to the assistance of the ships assailed and to close on the flagship which will set the example'. And he exhorted them in Nelsonic style to have regard to their own daring and love of honour far more than to signals from the admiral, who might be shrouded in smoke; in summary, 'Any captain who is not under fire is not at his post.'[44] Now, at Cadiz, with a greater number of ships assembled in the combined fleet, he was able to detail a squadron of observation organized in two divisions and led by Gravina, to be stationed to windward to reinforce threatened portions of the line. And in compliance with Napoleon's instructions, he intermixed Spanish and French ships alternately throughout the line. Otherwise he repeated his previous analysis and exhortations, which were issued as instructions later in the month.

Several French captains prepared their own answer to the anticipated British tactics by training their men in boarding and entering – a tactic reminiscent of the early seventeenth century, to which it might be said Nelson's intended mêlées and confusion returned naval warfare.

It is generally agreed that the trigger which forced Villeneuve to sail from Cadiz was a decision to replace him as commander-in-chief. This was provoked by a letter Napoleon received from the general commanding troops carried by the fleet; he had been out to the West Indies and back aboard the fleet flagship, and had formed a contemptuous view of Villeneuve's competence and courage, accusing him of being afraid of Nelson and a coward who had never intended to carry out his orders.[45] It struck a chord with Napoleon who needed a naval scapegoat for his invasion fiasco, and he ordered Decrès to send Admiral François Rosily – who had not been to sea for many years – to take command of the fleet with instructions for Villeneuve to return to France to account for his actions to him personally.

Villeneuve's first intimation that he was to be superseded came on 18 October with rumours of Rosily's imminent arrival in Cadiz. At about the same time he received reports from the coast that a British convoy had sailed from Gibraltar escorted by four of the line; one other British battle ship was in Gibraltar and another in the Straits. Evidently Nelson had made a detachment from his fleet: an essential condition for sailing agreed at the 8 October council had been met. And that evening the wind went around to the south-east, the perfect quarter for leaving harbour, and freshened.

Villeneuve went aboard Gravina's flagship, the 118-gun three-decker *Principe de Asturias*, and told him that the new circumstances compelled him to order the fleet to sea; Gravina replied that his ships were 'entirely ready to follow the movements of the imperial fleet'.[46] Whether the two discussed Villeneuve's impending replacement is not known, but a recent authority on the Spanish side of the campaign is in no doubt that the prospect of Villeneuve's humiliating dismissal must have influenced Gravina since it would have reflected adversely on his own reputation: 'he preferred to fight a desperate action rather than to have his honour tarnished.'[47] So, it seems it was Napoleon's disgust with a navy he never understood and an admiral he despised that finally led to a purposeless fleet action which both Villeneuve and Gravina knew could not be won.

It took the 19th and most of the 20th for the combined fleet of eighteen French and fifteen Spanish ships of the line and seven French frigates and brigs to work out to sea. Gravina was still woefully short of deep-sea sailors, but Spanish complements had been made up above normal establishment with soldiers and pressed landsmen. Those of his ships only recently out of dock had not exercised at sea and since there was only one representative of the squadron he had taken to the West Indies with Villeneuve none had sailed together; in consequence rates of sailing had not been established, nor stowage and rig adjusted for station-keeping.[48] Struck by squalls outside, they were soon in difficulties holding formation; these were increased as the wind went round to the west and Villeneuve signalled the fleet to wear together and form the order of sailing in three columns on the starboard tack, heading southeasterly towards the Strait of Gibraltar, Gravina's squadron of observation in two lines to windward.[49] The coming of night made confusion worse. Signal guns, blue lights, rockets and flares erupted from the darkness to windward – the British fleet, it was assumed. Counting the seconds between gun flash and report put them no more than two miles distant. Anxious to avoid night action, Villeneuve used flares to signal fleet line astern of his lee division, but it was as much as most captains could do to avoid collision with one another.[50]

Nelson was a good deal further away than the pyrotechnics implied. He had been alerted to the emergence of the enemy by the chain of signalling ships from the inshore frigates at 9.30 in the morning of the 19th. Not wishing to show himself and frighten them back to harbour, and realizing that Napoleon, having failed in his invasion attempt, must move his fleet to the Mediterranean, he had run south-east to place himself between Villeneuve and the Strait of Gibraltar. His frigates under Captain Henry Blackwood remained in close contact with Villeneuve, signalling his progress and position; these were the lights and flares seen from the combined fleet through the night of the 20th. So effective was Blackwood's liaison that as dawn broke on the 21st the enemy could be seen downwind from the *Victory* grouped along the eastern horizon some ten to twelve miles distant.[51] Beyond, as the early haze lifted, it was just possible to distinguish the far outline of Cape Trafalgar.

Nelson had achieved an ideal attacking position; the whole day lay before him. Villeneuve could not retreat to Cadiz without a fight, and if he ran for the Strait he would be forced to action in more unfavourable circumstances as the British chased and overwhelmed his more sluggish sailers in detail. In any case, the imperial instructions and his honour, impugned by Napoleon, demanded he accept the challenge. He signalled line of battle on the starboard tack, heading southerly; Gravina directed his squadron of observation to form in the van.

The real anxiety for Nelson, watching the irregular mass of the enemy attempt to spread in line, was that the wind, which had dropped away during the night and was now light and variable from the northwest, might die completely. A long and heavy swell rolling in from the Atlantic presaged a violent storm later. The sky was heavy with cloud. His first signal was to form the order of sailing in two columns, which all understood from his memorandum as the order of battle; his next at 7.0 a.m. was number 13, 'Prepare for battle', and shortly afterwards number 76 with compass signal ENE, to bear up from the present northerly course and steer east-north-east, towards the enemy. Reefs were shaken out of the topsails as helms went up; royal sails were set above the t'gallants and studding sails extended either side to catch every slant of wind. The ships in Nelson's own line steered to follow in the *Victory*'s wake while those designated for the lee line manoeuvred to follow Collingwood in his three-decker flagship, *Royal Sovereign*, to the south of the *Victory*.

Villeneuve's frigates reported the enemy as twenty-six of the line – one of Nelson's twenty-seven having become detached to the north – advancing in groups on their rear division. Villeneuve formed the same impression, and to protect his rear from massed assault made the signal for all ships to wear together and form line of battle on the larboard tack in reverse order. The signal was made executive at 8.15. Under normal circumstances the manoeuvre took a long time since in order to avoid collision each ship waited for her next astern to complete her turn before going round herself; with the ships bunched and a light and fluky wind, heavy swell and unpractised companies it lasted interminably and provoked worse confusion. Collingwood seems not to have become aware of the change of direction until 10 o'clock.

With Villeneuve now heading northwards the two British lines were in the correct relative position to carry out the attack outlined in the memorandum, Collingwood to the south with fifteen ships to overwhelm the enemy rear, Nelson, reduced to eleven, to tackle Villeneuve in the centre and ensure Collingwood's movements 'were as little interrupted as possible'. No further instructions were necessary.

As always at the prospect of action, Nelson was in a state of height-

ened animation. His first care after his initial orders directing the fleet at
the enemy was to draw up a codicil to his will in which he left Emma
Hamilton 'a Legacy to my King and Country, that they will give her an
ample provision to maintain her rank in life'; similarly, he left his
'adopted daughter', Horatia, to the 'beneficence' of the country, and
desired she use the name Nelson only. 'These are the only favours I ask
of my King and Country at this moment when I am going to fight their
Battle.'[52] He had Captain Blackwood summoned aboard the *Victory* and
took him with his flag captain, Hardy – he had no captain of the fleet at
this time – to witness his signature on the codicil. Afterwards he summoned the other frigate captains to give instructions particularly on
dealing with captured prizes and disabled enemy ships attempting to
retire to Cadiz; the frigates must join in preventing them. Annihilation
was his aim. And he gave Blackwood authority, unprecedented in a fleet
action, to issue orders to the rearmost ships in his, Nelson's, name.
Quizzing Hardy and Blackwood and the others repeatedly on the
number of prizes they anticipated, he always added that personally he
would not be satisfied with less than twenty, and wondered aloud what
Villeneuve would make of his novel approach in two columns.

The assembled captains, together with the *Victory*'s senior lieutenants
and midshipman aides, accompanied him as he toured the gun decks
reinforcing the men's impatience to come to grips with the enemy. A
fragment of the scene survives in a letter written by one of the able
seamen, John Brown:

> So we cleared away our guns whilst Lord Nelson went round the decks and
> said My noble lads this will be a glorious day for England who ever lives to
> see it I Shan't be Satisfied with 12 ships this day as I took at the Nile So we
> piped to dinner and ate a bit of raw pork and half a pint of Wine . . .[53]

Similar scenes of enthusiasm were played out in the French and
Spanish line. Aboard the *Bucentaure* the Imperial Eagle was paraded
before Villeneuve as he toured the decks, drawing roars of '*Vive
l'Empereur!*' Placing their hands in the admiral's the men renewed their
oath to fight to the last. In the flagship's second astern, the 74-gun
Redoubtable, one of the best trained of the French ships, her passionately
aggressive captain, Jean-Jacques Lucas, preceded on his rounds by
drums and fifes and a standard bearer with the Imperial Eagle, met
equal enthusiasm. He believed in boarding and entering and had drilled

his boarding parties and sharpshooters constantly in Cadiz; now his men reminded him to lay the ship aboard the enemy.

It concerned the *Victory*'s officers that Nelson with his four orders of chivalry sewn into his coat would be a conspicuous target for riflemen known to be among the troops with the French fleet, but Hardy had not yet found an appropriate moment to suggest he cover them or change the coat. Blackwood had proposed he might shift his flag to his frigate in order to gain a better overall view free from the smoke of battle, but Nelson had brushed the suggestion aside with a remark on 'the force of example'. Now Blackwood proposed allowing one or two ships to overtake the *Victory* so that Nelson would not immediately be in the thick of the action. He agreed, but kept the flagship under such a press of canvas that the next astern, the 98-gun *Temeraire*, was unable to pass.

So the *Victory* and the *Royal Sovereign* with piled sails led their separate columns down the smooth Atlantic swell towards the combined fleet awaiting them. The normally aloof Collingwood was so stirred by the scene that he said to the officers about him, 'Now, gentlemen, let us do something today which the world may talk of hereafter.'[54]

But the pace was desperately slow, barely two knots in the fitful airs. It was the opposite of the swift descent Nelson had planned and he grew increasingly fretful. His lines were straggling, the more sluggish sailers wallowing several miles astern of the leaders as the wind dropped to near calm in patches. Instead of the crushing concentrations he had planned to bring against sections of the enemy line, it was his own foremost ships that risked being overwhelmed one by one as they drifted into the enemy. And the very conditions that robbed him of momentum worked to place the combined fleet in the best defensive posture to meet such an attack. Instead of a single line to be pierced, Villeneuve's force of intermixed French and Spanish vessels lay jumbled in a hollow arc, the leading ships close on the wind heading to the west of north, the centre trailing to leeward, two or three deep in places, and the rear, which had been Gravina's squadron of observation, to windward of the rest, heading north-easterly in an attempt to form on the main body. Collingwood believed the formation – reminiscent of the defensive crescent adopted by the Duke of Medina-Sidonia during the 1588 Armada campaign – was deliberate; but it was the fortuitous result of the fickle airs combined with straggling during the night and lack of skill.

There was no lack of resolve. Nelson, observing the manner the enemy held the wind, all sails set for steerage way, preparing to receive the charge without retiring, remarked frequently on the good face they were presenting, always adding quickly, 'I'll give them such a dressing as they never had before!'[55]

Shortly before 11 he had his signal lieutenant, John Pasco, make to Collingwood, 'I intend to push or go through the end of the enemy's line to prevent them from getting into Cadiz'. The *Victory's* helm was put down briefly to alter her course a point more northerly, towards the enemy van. He then went below to what had been his quarters, now bare of partitions, pictures or furniture save for his writing desk, the guns run out through open ports either side and handspikes, rammers and sponges arranged on the sanded deck beside them. He knelt at the desk and made what was to be the last entry in his journal, following on without a break from an earlier observation that the enemy was wearing:

> May the Great God whom I worship grant to my Country and for the benefit of Europe in general a great and glorious Victory and may no misconduct in anyone tarnish it and may humanity after Victory be the predominant feature in the British Fleet. For myself individually I commit my life to Him who made me and may His blessing light upon my endeavours for serving my Country faithfully. To Him I resign myself and the just cause which is entrusted to me to defend. Amen. Amen. Amen.[56]

The enemy line was scarcely over two miles off when he returned on deck. The clouds had dispersed. The band was playing. He announced his intention to amuse the fleet with a signal, and after a moment's thought came up with, 'Nelson confides that every man will do his duty.' Someone, probably Blackwood, offered 'England' in place of 'Nelson'. He was pleased with this and called on Pasco to make it, adding, 'You must be quick, for I have one more signal to make – which is for close action.' Pasco suggested replacing 'confides' which was not in the vocabulary signal book and would have to be spelled out letter by letter, with 'expects' which was in the book and could be made with a single hoist.[57] Despite the subtle change in emphasis, Nelson agreed. So the flags went up: 'ENGLAND EXPECTS THAT EVERY MAN WILL DO HIS DUTY'. Presently a rolling tumult of cheering carried across the water as the men on the different ships were apprised of the meaning.

A midshipman in Collingwood's flagship later recalled the scene as the British columns closed the enemy:

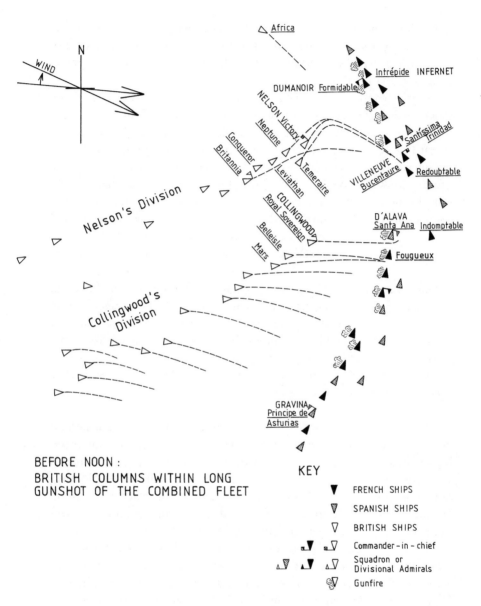

△ Africa

Intrépide INFERNET

DUMANOIR Formidable

NELSON Victory

Santíssima Trinidad

Conqueror
Britannia
Neptune
Leviathan
Temeraire

VILLENEUVE
Bucentaure
Redoubtable

Nelson's Division

COLLINGWOOD
Royal Sovereign

D'ALAVA
Santa Ana Indomptable

Belleisle
Mars

Fougueux

Collingwood's
Division

GRAVINA
Principe de
Asturias

BEFORE NOON :
BRITISH COLUMNS WITHIN LONG
GUNSHOT OF THE COMBINED FLEET

KEY

▼ FRENCH SHIPS

▽ SPANISH SHIPS

▽ BRITISH SHIPS

▪▼ ▪▽ Commander-in-chief

▵▽ ▪▼ ▵▽ Squadron or
Divisional Admirals

▽ Gunfire

Battle diagram 6   Trafalgar, 21 October 1805

There is now before me the beautiful sunshiny morning of the 21st October, the sea like a mill pond, but with an enormous ground swell rolling in from the Atlantic. The noble fleet with royals and studding sails on both sides, bands playing, officers in full dress, and the ships covered with ensigns in various places . . . dear old Cuddie (as we called Collingwood), walking the break of the poop with his little triangular, gold-laced cocked hat, silk stockings and buckles.[58]

Nelson made two more signals, first, in view of the threatening storm, 'Prepare to anchor', and finally, as one then others of the enemy rear opened fire on the *Royal Sovereign* and the whole enemy line ran up their colours to rolls of drums and volleys of musketry, number 16: 'Engage the enemy more closely'.

The *Royal Sovereign* had only recently joined the fleet after re-coppering and was well ahead of the rest of her line. Whether Collingwood had originally been steering for the twelfth ship from the rear according to the instruction in Nelson's memorandum, he was now heading for a worthier target for his flagship, a magnificent black-painted Spanish three-decker, *Santa Ana* of 112 guns, flying the flag of Vice Admiral Don Ignatius Maria de Alava, who commanded the van, but since the order to go about was sixteenth from the rear. Collingwood had also departed from the letter of the memorandum by ordering his column to form the larboard line of bearing. This entailed fanning out into almost a line abreast while still steering easterly. The intention was evidently to align his column, so far as possible, with the enemy formation in order to bring his ships into action together, but like Nelson, he refused to reduce sail and so made it impossible for the vessels following him to comply. They seem merely to have spread somewhat to starboard of the wake of his flagship which was for many minutes the sole focus of the broadsides of the *Santa Ana*, her second astern, the French *Fougueux*, and two other 74s astern of her. The *Royal Sovereign*'s own guns remained silent except for occasional shots fired to cover the ship with smoke. The men were ordered to lie on the deck. 'What would Nelson give to be here!' Collingwood exclaimed to his flag captain.

Watching from the *Victory* more than a mile to the north on her slightly divergent course, Nelson pre-empted him by remarking admiringly to the officers with him on the poop, 'See how that noble fellow Collingwood carries his ship into action!' Now the enemy colours were flying he made out Villeneuve's flagship to starboard of his course and had Hardy bear up and sail directly for her. Whether he had been steering towards the van to prevent Villeneuve retiring to Cadiz as intimated in his signal, or whether his movement northwards had been more in the nature of a feint to prevent Villeneuve from instructing his van to go about and come to the support of the threatened rear and centre is unclear; in the light of recent evidence of a signal Nelson added to the signal book, the explanation for which foreshadowed just such a feint, the latter seems more likely.[59]

Had French and Spanish gunnery been up to British standards, the *Royal Sovereign* must have been crippled during the last 500 yards of her approach. But it was neither so rapid, nor because of the method of firing by slow match rather than flintlock could it be so accurate if there were any motion; and since all vessels of the combined fleet were rolling beam on to the steep swell with scarcely sufficient breeze to maintain steerage way, conditions could hardly have been worse for the guns' crews in the vital matter of elevation for range.[60] Collingwood was able to press through the broadside fire of four ships into point-blank range of the *Santa Ana* with masts and rigging damaged, severely in places, but not disabled.

As his intention to break the line astern of Alava's flagship became clear, Captain Louis Baudoin of the *Fougueux* moved his ship up to close the gap. Collingwood instructed his flag captain to steer straight for his bow and carry away his bowsprit, but as he bore down on her Baudoin backed his main topsail to take off way and the *Royal Sovereign* headed through the narrow space left under the *Santa Ana*'s stern, the main yard briefly catching the Spaniard's gaff vangs. Collingwood had permitted fire from the starboard guns as they bore on the *Fougueux* and ships astern of her; now as the ship passed within yards of the *Santa Ana*'s stern galleries his larboard guns' crews came into action, from forward aft. The pieces were double-shotted. Erupting in pairs, the balls broke up the rich black carvings, passed through the windows of the admiral's and captain's quarters and the relatively weak stern timbers, smashed down the length of the gun decks, overturning cannon, swathing paths of lethal splinters, leaving torn limbs and bodies. Above, grapeshot and langridge from the upper deck carronades maimed and killed troops at the bulwarks, cut rigging and pulverized a great timber cross displayed, as with all the Spanish ships, from the spanker boom over the taffrail. At the same time the starboard guns' crews fired into the *Fougueux*'s bows, raking her also from end to end.

The studding sails were cut away as the *Royal Sovereign* ranged through; they fell in the sea or on deck. The helm was put down, the head sheets and braces loosed and the ship rounded up on the *Santa Ana*'s starboard lee quarter, so close that the yards of both vessels locked together. Collingwood's former flagship had been capable of firing three aimed rounds in three and a half minutes;[61] no doubt the *Royal Sovereign*'s men approached this remarkable proficiency. The larboard pieces were fired as soon as they had been recharged and run out, again from so close they could not miss; thunder and smoke spread down the deck. These first broadsides put an end to the *Santa Ana* as an effective fighting unit. Her officers continued rallying the surviving members of the guns' crews and they maintained a sporadic fire from a few pieces, but she had been broken as a first-rate battle unit. Well over 100 of her complement of 1,089 had been killed or wounded by the initial raking fire, and casualties and damage mounted under the *Royal Sovereign*'s repeated double-shotted bombardment.

Meanwhile an 80-gun French ship to leeward of the *Santa Ana* had opened fire on Collingwood's flagship from off her starboard bow; the *Fougueux* was firing on her from her starboard quarter and one or two ships ahead to leeward also joined in. Entirely surrounded, she suffered heavy damage and loss for some minutes before her leading consorts reached the enemy line and worked up to her support. And gradually the ships following these came into action against Gravina's rear, which broke into separate mêlées shrouded in gunsmoke.

By this time, to the north, the *Victory* was under fire from Villeneuve's flagship and the group of ships ahead of her. At the first ranging shots Nelson had despatched the frigate captains back to their ships, instructing them to hail the battle ships astern to say it was his intention to cut through the enemy line about the thirteenth or fourteenth ship, afterwards making sail for their van; he depended upon them to get into action as soon as possible by whatever means, provided it led them quickly and closely alongside an enemy. In parting, Blackwood had said he trusted on his return to find Nelson in possession of twenty prizes. 'God bless you, Blackwood,' was the reply, 'I shall never speak to you again.'[62]

No sooner had they gone than the *Victory*, like the *Royal Sovereign* earlier, became the focus of concentrated fire. The range was over a mile and most of the shot splashed short or whirred overhead, but a significant number cut rigging or spars, holed sails or struck the hull. One of Nelson's secretaries was almost cut in two as he talked to Hardy on the quarterdeck; his remains were heaved over the side. Soon after him the captain's clerk was killed. Aloft the slender studding-sail spars were cut away by shot one after another; at the same time the breeze dropped until the ship was ghosting at under two knots, impelled as much by the long westerly swell, it seemed, as by the reduced and perforated canvas aloft.

The *Temeraire* came up along her starboard side as if to pass. Nelson hailed from the poop, 'I'll thank you, Captain Harvey, to keep in your proper station, which is astern of the *Victory*.' She fell back on his quarter. The three-decker *Neptune* came up on the larboard quarter, the three first rates forming an arrowhead leading the column at a broad angle towards the enemy centre. Approaching within some 500 yards shortly after noon, the *Victory* opened fire with her larboard guns at extreme forward bearing at the group ahead of the *Bucentaure*. Most conspicuous was the four-decker, *Santíssima Trinidad* of 136 guns, flagship of Rear Admiral Don Hidalgo de Cisneros; painted in four bands of vermilion divided by ribbons of white with a colossal group of white carved figures under her bows representing the Holy Trinity from which she took her name, she towered above Villeneuve's two-decked flagship astern of her.

The *Victory* suffered increasing damage as she closed agonizingly slowly. The mizzen topmast was shot away; a ball shattered the wheel; steering was transferred to parties below hauling on tackles to move the tiller. Another ball felled eight of a group of marines drawn up on the poop; another passed between Nelson and Hardy as they paced the quarter-deck, striking a cloud of splinters from bitts on the way. 'This is too warm work, Hardy, to last long,' Nelson said. The fore topsail yard was broken by one of the first shots from Captain Lucas' *Redoubtable*, seconding Villeneuve from close astern. Soon afterwards the fore topmast was shot down and the main t'gallant. Already twenty men had been killed, thirty wounded.[63]

They were steering to cut between the *Santíssima Trinidad* and *Bucentaure* but these two and the ships ahead and astern were bunched so close Hardy saw no possibility of breaking through without running one of them aboard. It did not signify which, Nelson told him, 'Go on board which you please!'

Deciding on the smallest of the group, Hardy bore up to bring the *Bucentaure* on the larboard bow. Off her quarter, he ordered the helm down and headed straight for the bow of the *Redoubtable* which Lucas had advanced until the jib-boom was over Villeneuve's taffrail; and like the *Royal Sovereign* with the *Santa Ana* earlier, the *Victory* surged on the swell so close under the French flagship's stern that her yards caught the mizzen rigging; below, her foc's'le carronade discharged a 68-pound roundshot and a cask of 500 musket balls through Villeneuve's poop windows, while cannon, double- and treble-shotted,[64] pierced the gilded carvings of the after quarters beneath and ravaged from end to end of the gun decks. Clouds of choking black smoke blew back through the ports, and dust from the shattered timbers settled on the clothes of officers and marines and guns' crews on the upper deck.

At the same time the *Victory* collided with the bow of the *Redoubtable*; her weight urged the smaller vessel round until the two ground together side by side, the French ship's stern under the *Victory*'s quarterdeck, yards above interlocking. Lucas had his grapnels ready aloft; they were dropped to hold the two ships together and bugles summoned his practised boarding parties. Seizing muskets with bayonets, cutlasses and pistols from nettings between the great guns, they rushed the ladders to the upper deck while the lids of the lower gun ports were closed to prevent the British boarding through them. Sharpshooters in the tops fired down on the marines in scarlet lining the *Victory*'s hammock nettings, others lobbed grenades from the deck. But the boarders gathering on *Redoubtable*'s gangways and clambering into the nettings and up the rigging were cut down by grape and musketry. And from the lower decks the *Victory*'s starboard guns' crews, unopposed, fired as soon as they could run their pieces out, muzzles striking against the enemy timbers in places. Reloaded with rope-handled sponges and rammers, they were soon hauled out to fire again.

The *Temeraire*, following close on the *Victory*'s starboard quarter, had now ranged up on the *Redoubtable*'s far side, simultaneously engaging her and a French 80-gun ship to starboard, while the *Neptune*, following the *Victory* across the stern of the *Bucentaure* and raking the French flagship, rounded up in her lee and loosed another broadside before passing on to tackle the mighty *Santíssima Trinidad*. These were shortly followed by two 74s and the 100-gun *Britannia*, bringing an overwhelming superiority against Villeneuve's already crippled centre. While the ships following them scrambled into action where they could, Villeneuve's ten leading ships maintained their northerly heading, away from the fighting. Villeneuve was flying number 5 flag on his fore and mizzen masts as a signal to all ships not engaged to take up any position that would bring them into action as speedily as possible;[65] together with the instruction issued before sailing that any captain not under fire was not at his post, this should have brought them down to his relief. But the flags could not have been easy to see: the *Bucentaure* was cloaked by the giant bulk of the *Santíssima Trinidad* and shrouded in smoke, and the wind blowing down the line away from the van was too light to do more than ripple the bunting. For whatever reason, the leading ships did not put about.

It was exactly the situation Nelson had intended to provoke: mêlées at murderously close range with the enemy van out of the action. By the time they came round – should they do so – it would be too late: it was already too late for much of the embattled rear and centre. It was at this point in the early afternoon, 'About 1.15' by the *Victory*'s log – less than an hour after she had run the *Redoubtable* aboard – that a marksman in the latter's mizzen top some 50 feet above the *Victory*'s quarterdeck fired a shot which struck Nelson's left epaulette, passed down carrying fragments of gold lace and silk with it through his shoulder and lung, puncturing the left pulmonary artery, fracturing two ribs and his spine between the sixth and seventh vertebrae before lodging in the muscle below his shoulder blade.[66] Hardy, pacing beside him, turned as he fell and leant over him.

'They have done for me at last,' Nelson said. 'My backbone is shot through.'

He was carried below with a handkerchief covering his face and the stars on his chest so the men would not be discouraged by the sight of their fallen chief, testament to his abiding presence of mind, and delivered to the surgeon treating the wounded in the cockpit below the waterline; laid against the ship's side in the shuddering gloom, pierced with groans and the cries of amputees and detonations and the clatter of gun-carriage trucks on the deck above, his life ebbed with the blood pulsing from the wounded artery into his chest cavity. His first thoughts were for Emma and Horatia; his next for the progress of the battle, and he called frequently for Hardy.

Hardy could not come. The *Victory*'s upper deck had been practically cleared by grenades and musketry from the *Redoubtable*'s tops and Lucas had had his main yard cut down to lie across the two ships as a bridge for his boarders. But even as he sensed the wild hope of taking the British flagship by storm his own ship drifted down on to the *Temeraire*, whose three tiers of guns erupting against his starboard side and sweeping his upper deck with grape and langridge at pistol-shot range extinguished his command as an organized entity. 'It would be difficult', he wrote later, 'to describe the horrible carnage caused by the murderous broadside of this ship; more than 200 of our brave lads were killed or wounded. I was wounded at the same instant.'[67]

While the destruction of the French ship continued from both sides – the *Victory*'s cannon depressed so the balls did not plough straight through into the *Temeraire* – and Nelson lay deprived of sensation or movement in his legs and lower body, but feeling the repeated shock of the guns above through the frames at his back, a short distance to the north Villeneuve paced his quarterdeck protesting audibly at a fate which had left him of all men alive. A lonely figure in uniform tailcoat with a high, flat collar, greenish corduroy pantaloons and half boots, sword and gold watch-chain, he had been preserved without a scratch amid the devastation visited on his flagship by successive British ships across his stern. His chief of staff, flag captain and first lieutenant were below among many more wounded than the surgeon and his team could cope with, and an extraordinary number of his men had been killed outright. And still – and this must have contributed greatly to his despair – despite the number 5 flag flying at his fore and mizzen and a more recent signal he had made for the van to 'wear together',[68] his leading ships were standing away to the north.

His final humiliation came shortly. A broadside from the latest antagonist, the 74-gun *Conqueror*, brought down his main and mizzen masts, which fell to starboard, shrouding his guns on that side. With unbalanced canvas aloft and masts and sails dragging in the swell, the ship's head fell off to leeward and the bowsprit lurched into the *Santíssima Trinidad*, so parting and loosening the forward rigging, and the foremast fell, also to starboard. Powerless either to fight his starboard guns or to run from the enemy bombarding him, unable even to transfer his flag since all the ship's boats had been smashed, Villeneuve had no option but to prevent further senseless slaughter by instructing a lieutenant to strike the colours which had been attached to the stump of the mainmast; he turned away as it was done.

The marine officer who boarded the *Bucentaure* to take possession was horrified by the scenes he encountered below: 'The dead, thrown back as they fell, lay along the middle of the decks in heaps and the shot passing through had frightfully mangled their bodies . . . An extraordinary proportion had lost their heads.'[69]

The *Conqueror* passed on to engage the *Santíssima Trinidad*, already under fire from the *Neptune* ahead of them, and from the far, weather bow, by the 64-gun *Africa*. The Spanish ship attempted escape but within minutes of the *Conqueror* opening fire from her starboard quarter her main and mizzen plunged spectacularly into the sea with topsails set, described by a British observer as one of the most magnificent sights he had ever beheld;[70] and shortly afterwards the foremast fell. A party was sent from the *Africa* to take possession. They and others who came later to assist in heaving more than 200 dead bodies into the sea found the decks slippery with gore, and the beams 'covered with blood, brains and pieces of flesh, and the after part of her decks with wounded, some without legs and some without an arm', none of whom had been properly attended.[71]

By this time, around 2 o'clock, the battle in the centre was decided: besides the two beaten flagships, the *Redoubtable* had struck half an hour before, her mainmast across the *Temeraire*, her hull reduced to wreckage. Lucas reported later:

> all the stern was absolutely stove in . . . the decks were all torn open . . . all the guns were shattered or dismounted by the shots from these two ships having run us aboard . . . all the lids and bars of the ports were utterly cut to pieces; four out of our six pumps were shattered, as well as our ladders in general, in such sort that communication between the decks and the upper works was extremely difficult; all our decks were covered with dead, buried beneath the debris.[72]

An extraordinary proportion of her company, some 300 out of 643, had been killed, 222 wounded; most of the survivors had been employed below the waterline in the magazines.

The *Fougueux* had also struck. Disabled by successive British ships following the *Royal Sovereign*, she had been unable to move clear when the interleaved mass of the *Victory*, *Redoubtable* and *Temeraire* drifted from the battle in the centre and fell aboard her – so forming a spectacle probably unique in fleet actions, four ships of the line aboard one another side by side. The *Temeraire*'s broadsides completed her destruction; with fore and main masts gone and three-quarters of her complement killed or wounded, her colours had been lowered.[73] A little further south the mastless hulk of the *Santa Ana* had ceased resistance, as had others from the rear, while several attempting to retire downwind were being followed by British vessels.

Meanwhile the van was coming about. The movement appears to

have begun with the leading ships, including the 80-gun *Formidable*, flag-ship of the van commander, Rear Admiral Dumanoir le Pelley, attempt-ing to tack in response to Villeneuve's number 5 flag, which had been made out shortly before the *Bucentaure*'s masts fell. The wind was so light that boats had to be lowered to tow the ships' heads around – despite which two ships ran aboard each other. Dumanoir had then repeated Villeneuve's final signal for the van to wear. Consequently, instead of coming down as a concerted force, two or even three groups were formed, one led by Dumanoir heading to windward of the centre, from which Captain Louis Infernet of the *Intrépide*, followed by the Spanish *Neptuno*, bore up for the *Victory*. Another group to leeward which had worn round bore away towards those ships retiring from the rear mêlées.

At the same time the last two ships of Nelson's line were pressing all sail to reach the action. These crossed close ahead of Dumanoir as he came down and raked the *Formidable*, then rounded up to engage her and the three ships following in succession. Dumanoir's flagship was so severely damaged he continued on his southerly course at long gunshot from the rear. Only Infernet and Commodore Don Cayetano Valdés y Flores Bazán following him in the *Neptuno* were prepared to seek honour in defeat, pressing on towards the *Victory*, which Hardy had now managed to work free from the wreck of the *Redoubtable*.

Hardy called the fresh ships which had intercepted Dumanoir to the flagship's defence, then, shortly before 3 p.m., at last felt able to leave the deck to visit Nelson below. He found him wrapped in a sheet, attended by his steward and his secretary for foreign correspondence supporting his shoulders. To the first question about the course of the battle, Hardy replied that they had twelve or fourteen enemy ships in their possession. Nelson told him he was sinking fast. 'It will be all over with me soon. Come nearer,' and in a low voice catching with pain, 'Pray let dear Lady Hamilton have my hair, and all other things belonging to me.'[74]

Hardy came down to see him about an hour later, having sent a message to Collingwood to warn him of Nelson's impending death. This time he congratulated him on a brilliant victory: it was impossible to see how many of the enemy had been taken, but fourteen or fifteen were certain.

'That is well,' Nelson replied, 'but I had bargained for twenty', and with sudden animation, '*Anchor*, Hardy, *anchor!*' He reiterated the order to anchor, and then asking him to take care of Lady Hamilton, said, 'Hardy, kiss me.'[75]

Hardy knelt and kissed his cheek.

'Now I am satisfied; thank God I have done my duty.'

Hardy stood and gazed down for a few moments at the slight figure he revered, so evidently close to death, then knelt again to brush his forehead with his lips before leaving him for the last time to return to the quarterdeck.

'Hardy!' Nelson called after him, 'If I live I'll anchor', and repeated it several times after he was out of earshot. His pain increased. Within half an hour he was dead.[76]

BLACKWOOD TOOK boat to the *Victory* as soon as he could after hearing that Nelson was wounded, but arrived just too late. 'In my life I never was so shocked or completely upset,' he wrote to his wife in the early hours of the following morning; the victory had come at such expense 'in the loss of the most gallant of men, and best of friends', it was one he never wished to have seen.

> His unfortunate decorations of innumerable stars, and his uncommon gallantry, was the cause of his death; and such an Admiral has this country lost, and every officer and man so kind, so good, so obliging a friend as never was. Thank God he lived to know that such a Victory, and under circumstances so disadvantageous to the attempt, never was before gained.[77]

Hardy was in equal distress, so too the usually unemotional Collingwood, who shed tears, and wrote to his father-in-law, 'I cannot tell you how deeply I was affected; my friendship for him was unlike anything I have left in the Navy.'[78] And such was the spell Nelson had cast on the fleet that even those officers and men who had not known him personally felt an echo of the loss suffered by his friends: 'all the men in our ship are such soft toads they have done nothing but Blast their eyes and cry ever since he was killed,'[79] one sailor wrote home.

The ambivalent emotions were shared by the country at large when news of the victory reached England. Pitt was woken in the middle of the night to read Collingwood's despatches; he had scarcely known Nelson before his consultations with him in September, but as he told a friend later, although he had often been called up at various hours by the arrival of news of different shades, he had always been able to sleep again afterwards; this news, however, 'brought with it so much to weep over, as well as to rejoice at, that he could not calm his thoughts, but at length got up, though it was three in the morning'.[80]

THE TOTAL of ships lost by the combined fleet in the battle was eighteen, one of which burned to the waterline and blew up. More had been shattered but managed to get away. One such was Gravina's flagship from the rear, the 118-gun *Principe de Asturias*. Gravina himself had been seriously wounded at 2.30 and taken below – he was to die four months later. At 4 o'clock his second in command, Rear Admiral Don Antonio de Escaño, also had to be taken below and the men considered surrender, even it seems lowering the colours. However, Escaño returned to the deck in a chair and 'not seeing the national flag, ordered it to be hoisted at once'. Then, realizing that further resistance was hopeless, he made a general signal for the surviving ships to join his flag, and steered north-westerly for Cadiz;[81] five Spanish and five French ships followed. Together with Dumanoir's four French ships, which escaped southwards, these were the only survivors from Villeneuve's thirty-three of the line.

All firing had ceased by 5.30. The *Royal Sovereign* had lost her masts, so Collingwood transferred his flag to Blackwood's frigate, which had taken him under tow. He sent her boats away with instructions for all captains to take the disabled ships and prizes in tow and signalled the fleet to come to the wind on the starboard tack, heading southerly, away from Cape Trafalgar, visible in the south-east only eight miles away. At 9 p.m. he made the signal by gun to prepare to anchor. Few ships were in any condition to do so, and as the wind backed to the south of west threatening to force them into shoaling water off the Cape he fired three guns for the fleet to wear to the larboard tack, and steered south-westerly up the coast towards Cadiz.

Next morning the wind freshened and blew up into the expected gale from the southward. With all the prizes under tow and water gaining on the pumps in their shattered holds it became a desperate struggle to claw off the land. Collingwood wrote that in his life he 'never saw such exertions as were made to save those ships'.[82] In addition to the violence of the storm, he had to contend with a small force emerging from Cadiz in a brave attempt to cut out the prizes. They succeeded in retaking two, but lost three of their own ships. The following day, the 24th, Collingwood seeing 'no prospect of getting the captured ships off the shore' made the signal to quit and destroy the remainder. According to Rear

Admiral Escaño – by then in Cadiz with Gravina's flagship – these ships were lost because of deficient pumps. He ascribed the survival of even the most battered British ships to the introduction of double-acting pumps in the Royal Navy in 1793.[83]

At all events, Collingwood, provided with a fresh flagship and strengthened by the return of the detachment Nelson had sent to the Straits to provision and water, was able to resume the blockade of Cadiz before the end of the month. In early November Dumanoir's four ships were intercepted. They were making for Rochefort when Rear Admiral Sir Richard Strachan with a squadron of four of the line and two frigates gave chase. The ensuing action was notable for the initiative shown by the frigates which sailed ahead of Strachan and engaged the rearmost French ship, forcing Dumanoir to come up into the wind and form line of battle, after which, most unusually, the frigates joined in the battleship action. All four French ships were taken. Thus, in a sense, Nelson's desire for twenty prizes was fulfilled, although few survived to be commissioned into the Royal Navy.

No mention of the momentous allied defeat was permitted in the French press until the following year when the *Moniteur* reported several ships lost after an imprudently delivered battle. Villeneuve was also erased from the record. He was carried to England in Blackwood's frigate, impressing the officers with his quiet good manners, and repatriated in April 1806. Napoleon, who had created the defeat through his fatal combination of a dictatorial command structure, egotism, ignorance of naval affairs and disregard even for his own campaigning principle of avoiding attempts to concentrate separate corps from widely divergent routes, ordered him not to come to Paris. From a hotel in Rennes he wrote to his wife saying his life had become a disgrace and death a duty, adding, 'What an honour that I have no child to receive my horrible heritage and bear the burden of my name.' Afterwards, according to official accounts, he took his own life. Since six deep stab wounds were discovered in his chest, this is unlikely.[84]

TRAFALGAR WAS the only major sea battle of the Napoleonic war. It was also the last major battle under sail, and the most decisive. It did not end Napoleon's naval ambitions; three three-decker first rates, an 80-gun ship and six 74s had been laid down for the French service that year, and over the eight years following the keels for a further fifty-nine French battle ships would be laid.[85] How much this was a serious naval programme, how much an attempt to break Great Britain financially by forcing her to compete in the building race is not clear.

Nor, except in the short term, did Trafalgar banish British fears of invasion. Naval opinion had never taken Napoleon's plans too solemnly: Pitt's First Lords were fond of quoting St Vincent, 'I do not say the French will not come; I only say they will not come by sea.'[86] Nonetheless a programme authorized by Pitt for a chain of 'Martello tower' forts to command every feasible landing beach along the southern and eastern coasts of England, and the construction of the Royal Military Canal as a secondary line of water defence behind Romney marshes in Kent and Sussex, went ahead as planned despite Trafalgar; and it was not until these were complete that British governments felt truly secure.

For Spain, Trafalgar did mark the end. Her fifteen of the line in Villeneuve's fleet were fought as the French ships were, with great courage against fearsome point-blank fire, but nine were lost and were never replaced; indeed no Spanish ship of the line was launched after 1798, no frigate after 1800. She had never been able to man her magnificent ships with a full complement of sailors. Trafalgar not only broke her pretence to major naval status, but broke her will to pretend. Jan Glete, in his comparative study of naval power, has noted that after Trafalgar 'it is difficult to find [in Spain] any coherent naval policy'.[87] Her fleet withered and the British blockade severed her trade and communications with her overseas possessions, ruining her already weak economy and encouraging her American colonies to declare independence – as from 1810 they did. So she finally dropped from the ranks of the great powers.

Trafalgar was equally decisive in the struggle for supremacy between Great Britain and France. British naval officers had assumed their service superior to the French – and all others – since at least the mid-eighteenth century. Trafalgar provided final proof. In terms of the war it meant that Napoleon could neither break out from continental Europe, nor because of British commercial and political interference could he subject the continent to his will. His efforts to resolve this stubborn irregularity drew him into ever more hazardous adventures, and final disaster. This was the true measure of Trafalgar, and of the British naval dominance that produced the victory.

For Great Britain it meant even freer use of the seas for trade and the transport of troops and military supplies. Through the rest of the nineteenth and early twentieth centuries French naval strategists took it as an axiom that after Trafalgar the oceans passed into British hands. As expressed by Paul Fontin of the French Ministry of Marine in 1902: 'The English fleet which owns the empire of the seas places its frontiers at the enemy's coasts, and will dispose of all commerce behind that frontier, just as an army disposes of the resources of a conquered province.'[88] Guerrilla attacks by privateers and small squadrons fitted out for the *guerre de course* continued, but their depredations were contained; more than ever the creation of wealth by trade on the high seas proved superior to pillage. In the longer term, for well over the century during which Great Britain's trading empire grew to encircle the world, Trafalgar and Nelson stood as symbols of the invincibility of the Royal Navy.

In tactical terms the inheritance is far from clear. Nelson's achievement was to provide maximum scope for his ships to display their superiority in seamanship and great gunnery. For this purpose he gave his second in command complete freedom of action after pointing him in the desired direction and so brought two overwhelming concentrations to bear on two portions of the enemy line. He and Collingwood effected this by example, coolly bringing their flagships into murderous range of the enemy flagships and practically extinguishing them with their initial raking broadsides. The captains who followed placed their ships with marvellous skill in the very light breeze off the stern or quarter or bow of their opponents and, crucially, supported their colleagues. Villeneuve, as a prisoner afterwards in Blackwood's frigate, said he had never seen anything like the irresistible line of the British ships.[89] The technical superiority of flintlock over slow match, the speed of loading and precision of horizontal aim attained in the British ships by continuous drill over months at sea did the rest. The wrecked hulks of the French and Spanish vessels, swept clear of masts or with only one mast left standing, and the disparity in casualty figures, some 5,860 against 1,695 in the British fleet – although the French figures included many later drowned – provide the proof. Only three British ships were totally dismasted; none was lost.

Yet it is evident that bearing down at a large angle to the enemy exposed the leading British ships to a destructive fire which they could not subdue with their own broadsides; and as Lieutenant Humphrey Senhouse of the *Conqueror*, fifth in Nelson's line, put it, 'an enemy of equal spirit and equal ability in gunnery would have annihilated the ships one after another in detail', particularly as they approached so slowly. Both the *Victory* and the *Royal Sovereign* suffered heavy casualties, but many of these were sustained after they had broken through the line, and neither was disabled during the long approach. Then again, if the enemy had possessed equal skill his van would have tacked directly it became clear that Nelson had altered course towards Villeneuve in the centre. It could then have doubled the leading group of Nelson's ships and brought a superior concentration to bear before his rear ships reached the scene.

None of this implies criticism of Nelson's design. His genius, as Jurien de la Gravière put it, was to recognize the enemy's weakness. He adapted his tactics accordingly and had the nerve to execute them despite the light and fitful wind, and the naked courage to lead down almost perpendicularly into Villeneuve's fire until aboard his second astern. It was a rare fusion of experience, planning, genius and audacity combined with resolution and the physical bravery he had always displayed. As such it was unique. Had this form of attack been copied by another officer commanding a less well-honed fleet or against a more equal enemy, it should have led to disaster. It might be said that Duncan had triumphed at Camperdown with just such an assault in two groups; but Duncan had brought his fleet into line just outside long gunshot, the wind had been strong, ensuring a swift descent and above all his ships had been individually more powerfully gunned than those of his Dutch opponents, and had spent a long time at sea while the Dutch had been blockaded in harbour. All in all, Nelson's – and Duncan's – tactics were not the culminating achievement of the sailing era, but an anomaly induced by their enemy's decline. They were tactics of disdain.

11

The Empire of the Oceans

On 19 October, two days before Trafalgar was fought, Napoleon gained the first of a series of victories against Pitt's new continental alliance. An Austrian advance guard under General Karl von Mack had moved across Bavaria towards France unaware that Napoleon had left Boulogne and was leading what had been the Army of England, renamed the Grande Armée, across the Rhine into Germany. Napoleon's speed of march, averaging over 14 miles a day over the routes and to the timetable he had dictated on 13 August after learning that Villeneuve had put into Vigo, was such that Mack was unable to extricate himself from an exposed position at Ulm on the upper Danube. Outnumbered and outmanoeuvred, Mack surrendered with the greater part of his men.

Napoleon pressed on to Vienna, which was undefended, entering on 13 November. The main Russian and Austrian armies were now united and marching on the city and he moved north to meet them in a situation of his own choice, finding it on a long plateau of high ground to the east of Brunn overlooking the villages of Rausnitz and Austerlitz. Encouraging the Allies to believe he was standing on the defensive there, he lured them into an encircling movement, so drawing troops from their centre, opposite which a force under Marshal Soult approached unseen along a cleft in the plateau. Soult then fell on the weakened centre, splitting the Allied army, while a reserve under Marshal Louis-Nicolas Davout, which Napoleon had kept out of sight, surprised the Allied forces attempting to drive round his southern flank. By then Napoleon knew the day was his. His opponents had done everything he wished. It was 2 December – by chance the anniversary of his coronation as Emperor.

In conception and precise execution, the battle of Austerlitz was Napoleon's masterpiece. Strategically, it forced Austria from the alliance. Talleyrand advised generous terms on the grounds that the Habsburg empire must be the future ally of France to preserve the peace of Europe and act as a bulwark for western civilization against Russian expansion.[1] Instead Napoleon instructed him to extract the most humiliating terms:[2] the cession of Venetia and other territories containing some three million subjects and contributing considerable revenues to the empire, recognition of Napoleon as master in northern Italy and the payment of an indemnity of 40 million francs – thus transferring to Napoleon's war chest a great part of the money Pitt had supplied for putting Austrian troops in the field.

It is said that Austerlitz turned Napoleon's head and gave him delusions of invincibility. Yet his ambition had always been limitless and this was not the first time he had rejected Talleyrand's proposals for building a stable balance in Europe. Of course, he needed the money. After the vast costs of his preparations to invade England French finances were again in crisis and the Banque de France faced collapse. It was only rescued in January 1806 when a Paris banker agreed to guarantee loans against the security of south American gold promised by the Spanish government.[3]

Meanwhile, even before the Austrian treaty Napoleon had brought Prussia into the French camp by offering her Hanover, hereditary domain of George III of England.[4] The twin blows meant the collapse of Pitt's policy: only Sweden and Russia, whose defeated troops were retiring eastward, remained of the coalition he had constructed. His health had been causing anxiety before news of Austerlitz reached London; afterwards he sank further, appearing 'much worn out', his eyes 'almost lifeless', his voice hollow, and on 23 January 1806 he died, his last lucid words, 'Oh, my country! How I leave my country!'[5] One of his close colleagues wrote that he had sacrificed his life to his country 'as much as Lord Nelson did'.[6] His great parliamentary opponent, Charles James Fox, expressed the general feeling of shock after hearing the news: he found 'something missing in the world – a chasm or blank that cannot be supplied'.[7]

Fox became Foreign Secretary in the succeeding administration and initiated peace talks. The most radical of politicians, he had welcomed the French Revolution and never ceased criticizing the war against

France as a crusade against freedom by the forces of despotism. In office his eyes were opened. Napoleon was exerting the influence he had gained over Prussia and the north German states to extend the scope and severity of restrictions on British trade with the continent, and on 16 May 1806 the government of which Fox was a leading member retaliated as no doubt Pitt would have done by proclaiming a blockade of northern France and the Low Countries over a thousand miles of the coast from the Elbe to Brest. Neutrals might trade here providing they were not carrying enemy goods or contraband of war, but ports from Ostend to the mouth of the Seine were put under a complete blockade through which nothing was permitted to pass. Whatever slim chances of peace there might have been ended with the proclamation. Fox died six months later; by then he had come to recognize the depth of Napoleon's hostility to Britain and the duplicity of his negotiations.[8]

Prussia had now changed sides again. Recognition of French double-dealing played a part here too – since Napoleon had held Hanover out as a bait for Fox during the British negotiation. In July Prussia had signed a secret alliance with Russia and the following month mobilized her army. In September she demanded the withdrawal of French troops from Germany and without waiting for the Russians advanced south-westerly, joined by Saxon troops, to threaten the Grande Armée's lines of communication. Napoleon had not expected this, but he moved with his customary speed to meet the threat and on 14 October gained a decisive victory at Jena. It was not military genius that brought his success on this occasion so much as the over-formal tactics of the Germans and a remarkable feat of arms by Davout's corps, which withstood repeated attacks by the main Prussian force with over twice its own numbers at the village of Auerstadt a dozen miles north of Jena, and finally routed them.

As remnants of the Prussian army fled, a substantial portion heading east to join the Russians, Napoleon entered Berlin in triumph. From the Prussian capital on 21 November he issued his response to the British blockade. Termed the 'Berlin Decree', this placed the British Isles under blockade, banned all commerce and correspondence between Britain and continental ports under French control or influence, declared all British and British colonial property or produce lawful prize and barred any vessel which had visited a British port from any port under French control or influence.[9] Napoleon's obsession with Britain is reminiscent of William III of Orange's fixation at the close of the seventeenth century on preventing Louis XIV of France from gaining continental hegemony.

Lord Halifax's comment on William's seizure of the English Crown in 1689, 'he hath such a mind to invade France that it would incline one to think he took England only in his way',[10] might be paraphrased for Napoleon's conquests: he had such a mind to destroy England it would incline one to think he took Vienna, Berlin, Moscow only in his way.

This is not to deny his ambition to bring the anarchic system of European nations under French tutelage and unify them under his own post-Revolutionary legal and civil codes. Yet Great Britain stood in the way, and the destruction of her financial, naval and commercial dominance was the necessary corollary of his drive for continental mastery: the two were indivisible. Even so, the scale of his design was astonishing. In Berlin that winter, whilst concentrating his corps against Russian armies gathering to liberate Prussia, he was also planning the subjugation of Denmark and Portugal to stop up gaps in his barrier against British trade, and the invasion of Spain to replace the Spanish Bourbon monarchy with a regime headed by his own brother.[11] And in order to draw off Spanish troops before his projected coup against their king, he planned to use them to occupy Denmark.

The British government learned of his Danish project in December that year, 1806, and by the following June had intelligence of his intention to march into Spain and place his brother Lucien on the throne – indication of a very high level source, since this was Napoleon's most closely guarded secret. In the meantime, on 7 January 1807 Britain responded to Napoleon's Berlin Decree with an Order in Council prohibiting trade between French-controlled ports from which British ships were excluded: 'any vessel coming from such a port . . . which shall be found proceeding to another such port, shall be captured and brought in and, together with her cargo, shall be condemned as lawful prize.'[12]

In turn, on 27 January, Napoleon ordered the seizure of all British goods and colonial produce in the north German and southern Baltic ports. This was potentially highly damaging for British exports and re-exports and for naval and merchant shipbuilding, reliant as it was on Prussian oak; it was equally damaging for continental suppliers and merchants and for neutral shipping caught between the belligerents. And as the British government issued further Orders in Council designed to influence friendly or deter unfriendly neutrals and secure the passage of strategic materials from the Baltic, the situation became extremely confusing for British naval commanders.

Meanwhile, early in February 1807 the Russians and the rump of the

Prussian army which had retired from Jena held Napoleon to a bloody stalemate at the east Prussian town of Eylau (Bagrationovsk) south of Königsberg. The commander of the Russian main army, Count Leonty von Bennigsen, had launched a surprise thrust between the separated elements of the Grande Armée after they had settled into winter quarters, but he was detected and to avoid encirclement fell back on Eylau, where on 7 and 8 February the two sides fought to exhaustion in driving blizzards, each leaving some 20,000 or more dead or dying in the snow together with the carcasses of thousands of horses, abandoned guns and broken carriages. That night French reinforcements appeared and Bennigsen withdrew. Napoleon made no serious pursuit, instead falling back to the line of the rivers Passarge (Pasłęka) and Omulew midway between Königsberg and Danzig, north of Warsaw.

Through the spring of 1807 Napoleon brought up fresh troops and drilled them in preparation for moving forward once the ground was firm in June. Again Bennigsen stole the initiative, attempting to cut off an advanced corps in the centre. Again the French were alert and he fell back, first to Heilsburg, which he had fortified with redoubts and entrenched batteries, and when Napoleon began to move around him, to Friedland (Pravdinsk) on the river Alle 27 miles south of Königsberg. The river would have provided a defensive barrier, but the appearance of the French advance guard under Marshal Jean Lannes well ahead of the main body tempted Bennigsen to stay and fall on the small force before crossing the river. His artillery preparations were too deliberate and Napoleon, informed of Lannes' predicament, rushed up reinforcements until Bennigsen's own men were outnumbered; moreover, contravening a cardinal principle of war, they had their backs to the river. Napoleon launched his main assault in the late afternoon of that day, 14 June, and drove them into the river or the narrow streets of the town already burning from artillery fire, where they were mown down with grape and canister at close range. Scarcely more than two-thirds of Bennigsen's 58,000-strong army survived. The French and German, Dutch, Italian and Polish troops with Napoleon lost only some 9,000.

In moral terms Friedland was a greater victory than Austerlitz, for Bennigsen's Russians had shown at Eylau that they could hold the Grande Armée; yet now they too had been routed. Napoleon appeared invincible. The Prussian survivors of Jena and Eylau, who were holding Königsberg, abandoned the city after Friedland and retired eastward. Tsar Alexander I, bowing to the inevitable, agreed an armistice.

Napoleon famously met him on a raft decorated for the occasion, moored in the middle of the river Niemen at Tilsit in East Prussia hard by the border with Russia, and dictated his terms. Alexander could hardly refuse and quickly agreed to an alliance and the division of Europe between them. The first and public part of the treaties eventually signed in early July had the purpose of reducing Prussia to impotence as Austria had been reduced after Austerlitz. In the east a great part of the territory she had acquired from Poland was stripped away to form a new Polish state, the Grand Duchy of Warsaw, under Napoleon's ally, the King of Saxony, whilst another part went to Russia. In the west her lands were taken to create a kingdom of Westphalia. She was left with little more than her Brandenburg heart, Silesia and the strip of Pomerania and East Prussia bordering the Baltic. She was to be limited in the number of troops she could raise and was occupied by French troops as surety for payment of a colossal war indemnity of 120 million francs (over £5 million). Looking back from his later years, Napoleon regretted his leniency.[13] Talleyrand, whose advice he continued to reject, knew that Prussia, humiliated as she had been, could never be a reliable partner for France, but would harbour a spirit of vengeance which would break out in action directly an opportunity presented itself. From this time onwards he opposed Napoleon and did all in his power to hasten his downfall.[14]

In secret articles of the Tilsit agreement Napoleon promised to support Russian expansion into the Turkish-held Balkans, and Alexander was given a free hand to conquer Swedish Finland. In turn, he acknowledged French hegemony over western and central Europe. Napoleon exercised this as President of a Confederation of the Rhine, formed from the remaining German states as a counterweight to Austria and Prussia, and placed members of his own family on the thrones of the French dependencies: Jerome as King of the new kingdom of Westphalia; Louis as King of Holland, formerly the Batavian Republic; Joseph as King of Naples, while he himself reigned over the north Italian kingdom of Italy. Reforms already under way in the earlier satellites, designed to break down the privileges of the nobility and the grip of the Church and introduce Napoleonic codes, spread throughout central Europe. So did liability to conscription and financial impositions for the imperial wars, lighting the fuse of resentment.

Britain was, of course, Napoleon's target, and the most significant of the secret clauses signed at Tilsit tightened the continental blockade against British trade: both Prussia and Russia were obliged to close their ports to British ships and Alexander bound himself to coerce Denmark, Sweden, Portugal and Austria into joining the blockade – so completing the continental barrier – and to form a northern alliance to regain naval mastery in the Baltic.

In Britain a new administration included two of Pitt's most able disciples in key posts, Viscount Castlereagh as Secretary for War and the Colonies – a significant duality – and George Canning as Foreign Secretary. They detested each other, but shared their former mentor's recognition of the need to fight Napoleon to the death. First news of the armistice arranged at Tilsit arrived at the Foreign Office on 5 July 1807, and suggested that the tsar was preparing to make peace; this was confirmed on the 12th in a letter from a British envoy in Memel: 'the Emperor of Russia and Bonaparte [the British did not recognize Napoleon as Emperor] have, it is said, embraced as friends.'[15] Further despatches received on the 16th reported that the two had agreed terms.

It was desperate news. The Cabinet's reflex response was to raise a fleet for the Baltic. Canning drafted 'Most Secret' instructions for an envoy to sail with the fleet to Copenhagen to reassure the Danes; if asked to explain the purpose of the fleet, it was to support Sweden.[16] At the same time he despatched a messenger to another experienced diplomat, Francis Jackson, then on holiday, summoning him urgently to London. Arriving in the early afternoon of the 18th, Jackson was instructed to sail with the fleet for a special mission to Kiel to negotiate with the Crown Prince of Denmark for the surrender of the Danish fleet to Britain. In return Denmark could have an alliance and an annual rent of £100,000.[17] The same day the Admiralty ordered the preparation of fifty-one ships, eventually to include twenty-five of the line, for a 'particular service' under Admiral Lord Gambier – who as a captain under Howe had been first to break through the enemy line at the Glorious First of June. Castlereagh ordered troops to Yarmouth to sail with the fleet and sent orders for a British force already in the Baltic on Rügen Island to join the expedition off Copenhagen.

Three days later Canning received intelligence 'directly from Tilsit' confirming the government's worst fears: 'On the 24th or 25th June, Bonaparte brought forward a proposal to the Emperor of Russia at Tilsit for a Maritime League against Great Britain, to which the accession of Denmark was regarded as certain as it was essential.'[18] Canning immediately sent additional instructions for the envoy to Copenhagen to 'require from the Danish Govt., a direct and official explanation on this important point'.[19]

The source of this intelligence has proved a historical puzzle. No official despatches were recorded at the Foreign Office that day, 21 July, and Canning never divulged who revealed what was to become one of the secret protocols of the Tilsit treaty. Talleyrand has been suspected, but such direct treachery is discounted by his biographer.[20] Bennigsen is another suspect – indeed, almost any member of the generally Anglophile Russian aristocracy might have provided the information.

The sums spent by the British government on secret service had expanded dramatically with her increasing isolation, and there was a clandestine network of high diplomats of all nationalities working against Napoleon's domination of Europe and for a return to pre-Revolutionary certainties, among them the one-time Russian Foreign Minister, Nikita Panin – who was close to Alexander – and the Comte d'Antraigues, who would be Canning's informant early the following year when Alexander made the decision to execute the secret articles of the treaty and invite Sweden to join a northern maritime league and declare war on Great Britain.[21] However, a recent study of British secret service during this period suggests that the information came from the British diplomat, Sir Charles Stuart, who was at Alexander's headquarters throughout the Tilsit period and could have learned it from Alexander or a close confidant, possibly Bennigsen, although Talleyrand is not entirely ruled out given his revulsion at his master's policies. The probability is that the courier was Sir Charles' 'confidential' servant, William Wood, 'who was by family tradition, the bearer of the news that there were proposed secret clauses to be added to the Treaty of Tilsit'.[22] The most Canning ever revealed was that 'this information came from a British Minister', but together with his reference to receiving the intelligence 'directly from Tilsit',[23] this provides strong support for believing it came from Sir Charles.

Gambier sailed from Yarmouth Roads on the 26th and anchored off the Skaw at the northern tip of the Danish peninsula on the 31st. From there he moved into the Sound off Copenhagen, detaching a squadron into the Great Belt to seal off Zealand Island – on which the capital lies – from the Jutland peninsula where the Danish army was concentrated against the threat of French invasion. The troop transports from Yarmouth joined on 8 August and those from Rügen with the commander-in-chief of the land forces, Lord Cathcart, on the 12th. By this time the Danish crown prince, who was pro-French and had just been threatened by Napoleon with the choice between war or an alliance with him, had rejected Jackson's proposals for the surrender of the Danish fleet.

The first troops went ashore early on the 16th under Colonel Sir Arthur Wellesley, an elegant thirty-eight-year-old from the Anglo-Irish ascendancy with a serious mind, outstanding notions of honour and duty, and soldiering qualities honed in campaigns which had extended British power in India. After covering the disembarkation of the main body and artillery, Wellesley advanced and laid siege to Copenhagen. Towards the end of the month a hastily levied Danish force attempted to raise the siege but was routed. The Commandant of the city nevertheless refused to surrender the Danish fleet and on the evening of 2 September Cathcart ordered the batteries ringing the walls to open fire. Red-hot shells and rockets devised by Sir William Congreve with casings over three feet long and 16-foot stabilizing sticks traced glowing arcs over the battlements to rain fire and destruction on the buildings within the walls. Ships from Gambier's fleet, chiefly bomb vessels firing high-angle mortars, joined in. There was no difficulty in seeing the target: the sky over the spires of the city was soon lit by flames and as bright as day.

By the 7th fire damage was so extensive that the Danes agreed to negotiations, which resulted in Gambier removing the entire fleet Denmark had constructed since Nelson's assault six years earlier: this included seventeen of the line, although only four were afterwards considered fit for service in the Royal Navy, no doubt because Denmark was in the process of reducing her sailing battle fleet, instead building vast numbers of oared gunboats for defence of her territory against Napoleon.[24] British ministers discussed occupying the country but Wellesley advised against this and his good sense prevailed; the object had been achieved. Once the Danish warships had been taken out and the dockyards stripped of materials the troops were re-embarked. It was as devastatingly swift and successful a pre-emptive strike as could have been hoped for. Castlereagh's secretary was probably not exaggerating when he wrote, 'There never was an expedition of such magnitude so quickly got up, so secretly sent off and which was conducted from the beginning to its termination with greater ability or success.'[25]

It was also an unprovoked assault by a great power on a small neutral. As such it provoked outrage in Europe and on the opposition benches in Parliament. Ministers defended the action as dictated by an extreme national emergency. Indeed, the freedom of the Baltic was a vital national interest. As for international morality, Napoleon had massed 30,000 troops under Marshal Bernadotte for the occupation of Denmark. He had simply been outmanoeuvred. He erupted in fury when he heard the news. The coup not only removed the Danish fleet from his grasp, it encouraged Sweden to reject Alexander's call for a maritime league against Great Britain. Canning and Castlereagh had proved reliable successors of their late master.

GREAT BRITAIN had kept the Baltic open, but Napoleon still bestrode the continent. Yet in retrospect it can be seen he had already made the decision that would undermine that mastery and lead to his eventual downfall: in a secret conversation with Spain in October, he gained agreement for the partition of Portugal between them, and to effect this, the passage of French troops through Spain from Bayonne to Lisbon. His ostensible motive was to bring Portugal into line with his continental blockade against British trade, but underlying this was another grand design which he had divulged to Talleyrand the previous December: to overthrow the Spanish monarchy and impose his brother on the throne. Gaining agreement for French troops to enter Spain unopposed concealed a policy of dominating the entire Iberian peninsula.[26]

Since this was to prove the turning point in his career of conquest, it is appropriate to ask what drove him: those elements in his character which had brought him his victories, chiefly determination to seize the initiative at whatever risk and the complementary habit of minimizing difficulties and disregarding negative counsel? Unlike European dictators who followed him, he was not surrounded entirely by sycophants. Talleyrand was a dissenting voice who had foreseen the disasters which limitless ambition must bring; Talleyrand resigned as Foreign Minister after Tilsit, but Napoleon promoted him to the senior imperial position of Vice Grand Elector where he remained an important figure in foreign affairs. How much the ambition that alarmed him was induced by Napoleon's need to master others or bring order and uniformity to a chaotic world, symptoms of personal insecurity, how much by belief in his infallible genius after his string of triumphs can never be calculated; all that can usefully be said is that without the need to dominate he would not have achieved his position, and the achievement of his position reinforced the characteristics that brought him there in a cycle of ever-increasing self-belief.

There were, nonetheless, powerful strategic and financial motives for taking over the Iberian peninsula: the treasure that flowed from Spain's American empire – provided it could be brought in through the British naval blockade – and Spanish and Portuguese naval, shipbuilding and manpower resources would significantly enhance his power; above all, however, he needed to stop up the leaks in his continental barrier against British trade. Britain had important trading links with Portugal and maintained a large clandestine trade with Spain through Gibraltar. He was drawn into the Iberian peninsula as much by his determination to ruin Great Britain as by hubris.

Which poses a question: the French Revolution had been prepared by subversive ideas of equality before the law imported from Great Britain and was precipitated by bankruptcy after participation in the American war against Britain and the vain attempt to construct a fleet to rival the British fleet. Was Napoleon – a product of forces released by the Revolution – similarly a necessary result of Britain's maritime and industrial dominance? And was Talleyrand misguided in his belief that France could lead a stable European balance of powers with such an expansionist financial, naval and industrial system just across the Channel?[27]

Rapacious as British capitalism was, this same year, 1807, saw the British Parliament outlawing one of its principal motors, the trade in slaves. It was not the first to do so. Denmark had banned slaving to her West Indian islands four years earlier, largely it seems because too many sailors died on slaving ships and the government was convinced that Britain was about to ban the trade.[28] Even before that most of the northern and central states of the United States had abolished both slavery and the slave trade. The Federal government had been prevented from considering the matter by the constitutional compromise that had held the southern plantation states in the union, but directly the limitation ended in January 1807 a Bill was introduced to Congress to make it illegal to bring a Negro into the United States as a slave or equip, finance or operate a slaving ship from a US port. By 11 February it had been passed by the Senate and the House of Representatives, and it was signed into law on 2 March.

By extraordinary coincidence the British Bill to abolish slaving went through Parliament at the same time. The efforts of the Quaker Church, Wesley, Ramsay and the Teston circle, Thomas Clarkson and others who had woken the public to the evils of the trade have been noted, together with the persistence of Wilberforce, Pitt, Burke and Fox in Parliament.

Before he died in September 1806 Fox had had the satisfaction of piloting a resolution through the House of Commons pledging Parliament to abolish the trade 'with all practicable expedition';[29] the Lords made a similar resolution, as a result of which a Bill prohibiting the purchase, sale or transfer of slaves in or from Africa passed both Houses in January and February 1807 – with a majority in the Commons of 283 to 16 – and became law in March.

Great Britain had the largest stake in the trade: her ships were carrying some 50,000 slaves a year across the Atlantic; the slave population of her West Indian islands had expanded dramatically during the war and sugar production with it. Jamaica had increased her exports of sugar by over 50 per cent to some 100,000 tons in 1805, making her the largest sugar exporter in the world.[30] Abolitionists expected Britain's voluntary renunciation and the humanitarian feeling that provoked it – in the face of continuing opposition from West Indian, slaving and banking interests – to encourage other slaving nations to follow her example. The reverse happened. Perhaps stung by fear that Britain might use her naval strength to enforce the ban across all nationalities, Portuguese, Spanish and other slavers increased their activities, transporting more Negroes to the Caribbean and Latin America in subsequent years, and even to the southern states of the United States where no special means of enforcing the American ban had been established. Nor, of course, did the British or American bans have any effect in Africa itself except to increase the number of Negroes available for the trans-Saharan slave trade to Egypt and the Mediterranean, or for domestic and agricultural employment within the country itself: the practice of slavery was integral to native tradition and culture.

Nonetheless, March 1807 remains one of the most significant dates in the history of the West. It marks the point when two aggressively commercial nations, Great Britain and the United States, passed laws on essentially moral grounds against their own economic interests. Subsequently both were to expend much diplomatic effort attempting to persuade other governments to follow suit, and the Royal Navy was to spend the rest of the century attempting at great expense in sailors' health and lives to suppress the seaborne trade in slaves from both west and east Africa. Such a sustained national philanthropic mission was unprecedented. Significantly the movement, like the prior legislation in the northern and central United States, was initiated in consultative assemblies dominated by commercial interests. It is true that the Jacobin

National Assembly in Paris had decreed the universal abolition of slavery in 1794 on the grounds of 'the Rights of Man', and the Jacobin Victor Hugues had put the policy into practice on the island of Guadeloupe. However, Bonaparte had rescinded the decree, as noted, shortly after assuming dictatorial power and no monarchical, despotic or bureaucratic government in Europe or Asia showed any interest in ending either the institution of slavery or the trade in slaves. This indicates a superior moral potential in open, consultative government – not necessarily democratic government since Great Britain was far from a true democracy at this time. For it cannot be said that the British or Americans engaged in slaving, whether financiers, plantation owners or shipowners and masters, showed any moral superiority to their counterparts in other countries; their depravity or self-delusion in pursuit of profit at the expense of fellow humans was incorrigible.

WHILE NAPOLEON made himself master of Europe, the Royal Navy exercised control of the seas. The traditional policy of blockading enemy naval bases – although relaxed immediately after Trafalgar – combined with the organization and escort of large convoys of merchantmen past enemy cruisers and privateers operating from the smaller ports and in the West Indies and Indian Ocean, was augmented by cruiser patrols which could reinforce convoy escorts in focal areas, and by a system of signal stations around the British coasts manned by naval personnel and able to pass warnings of enemy raiders and convoy information rapidly in either direction. Losses could not be entirely prevented since there were some 20,000 British ships alone to be protected, and numbers were rising year by year; and such French sea-going effort as there was after Trafalgar was concentrated on the *guerre de course* – as was Danish naval effort against British merchant shipping after the bombardment of Copenhagen. Merchants and underwriters complained to the Admiralty about losses, but these were kept within acceptable commercial limits, some 500 to 600 vessels a year, or less than 3 per cent of the merchant fleet in numbers and tonnage.[31] Insurance premiums had risen to more than twice their peacetime level and they were to rise much more than that for the Baltic after Tilsit; but ships and cargoes remained insurable. This was not so in France: French merchants continuing to trade overseas had to carry their own risks.[32]

The Royal Navy's comparatively straightforward duty of protection had been transformed by Napoleon's Berlin Decree and the British Orders in Council into an infinitely complex attempt to control the destinations of all shipping, British and neutral, since it was only by providing British vessels with false identities or using neutral carriers provided with bogus bills of lading, their crews coached in false accounts of the voyage, that British products could be pushed into ports under Napoleonic control and vital raw materials brought out, especially from the Baltic. The French were forced to use the same ruses to evade the British naval blockade.

In practice the Orders in Council gave rise to such difficulties of interpretation and legal dispute that on 11 November 1807 the British government issued a comprehensive Order placing all ports controlled by France or her allies under the same restrictions as if they were 'actually blockaded by His Majesty's naval forces in the most strict and rigorous manner' and declaring trade in goods produced or manufactured by France or her allies unlawful;[33] any ships trading to or from French or allied ports would be captured and condemned as prize. As explained by an Admiralty circular early the following year, this established a 'principle of capture to a degree new': officers were advised that when visiting and searching neutrals the cargo was in many cases immaterial, 'the *destination* having now become the principal ground of Prize'.[34] This was as far as it was possible to get from the principle upheld in Dutch maritime law in the seventeenth century and espoused by the French that a neutral flag covered the goods aboard.

To enforce the Order the Admiralty established a licensing system: every neutral was required to call at a British or British-controlled port to obtain, after payment of charges, a voyage 'licence' before proceeding; without one, ship and cargo were deemed lawful prize. The ship was then directed into one of the regular convoys organized in liaison with merchants for different destinations, and had to stay with the convoy until arrival lest the master slip off into a French-controlled port.

Napoleon countered on 17 December 1807 with a decree from Milan, stating that ships calling at British ports (for a licence) or submitting to British search thereby lost their own nationality and became British property; as such they were lawful prize. Vessels entering French-controlled ports had to prove that they had not called at a British port and that their cargo had not originated in Britain or her possessions.

Neutrals were now in theory in an untenable position, unable to trade with either belligerent without becoming liable to be seized as lawful prize by the other. In practice the Royal Navy could enforce the British writ at sea while the French navy was generally locked up in its bases and French privateers were unable to exert more than local disruptive influence. Neutral shipowners and merchants had little choice but to throw in their lot with the British; consequently Britain acquired a huge pool of foreign shipping with which to break Napoleon's continental embargo and ensure strategic supplies from the Baltic.[35]

Ships proceeding from Britain to the Baltic were provided with expertly forged papers showing they had come from a port in the French or neutral sphere; ships loading at Baltic ports with Prussian oak, pine or fir masts or other materials vital for the navy and merchant shipping declared their destination to the authorities as Norway or the Low Countries, but once at sea and boarded by a British officer they would show a British licence and join a convoy for escort to England.

Besides directing shipping for the benefit of British trade and denying essential strategic materials to the French – who were forced to convey them laboriously by land and river transport – the Royal Navy advanced British merchant interests by taking and holding offshore entrepôts where goods could be stored and trans-shipped. The tiny island of Heligoland in the German bight was one. Taken in September 1807 by the 74-gun *Majestic*, it served both as a base for suppressing enemy trade from the Elbe, Weser and Ems and as depot and forwarding station for clandestine British trade into the German rivers. British companies established branches there with warehouses and facilities for gathering market intelligence and forging the necessary papers. Heligoland also served as a political listening post and way station for secret service correspondence; a packet service ran from there to Harwich.

The Channel Islands served a similar function off the northern coast of France,[36] and on the southern flank of the continent Gibraltar and Malta doubled as naval bases and commercial entrepôts through which British goods were passed illicitly into Spain and through Trieste to northern Italy and central Europe.

On the oceanic routes the most important gain in the period immediately after Trafalgar was the Cape of Good Hope. The Dutch had been reinstated at the Cape at the Peace of Amiens, but an expeditionary force under the naval command of Commodore Sir Home Popham – of vocabulary signal fame – took it back in January 1806. Long recognized as the key to the security of the trade routes to India and the east, it was to be held until British decolonization in the twentieth century.

The month after reclaiming the Cape the Royal Navy had gained a small but important victory in the West Indies. A detachment of eleven of the line and frigates had broken out from Brest when close blockade was lifted after Trafalgar. The force had split into two squadrons, one of which under Vice Admiral Leissègues carried troops to a French garrison at San Domingo, Hispaniola, and was ready to proceed from Ocoa Bay on orders to cruise against shipping off Jamaica when a British squadron was sighted in the offing; Leissègues put to sea at once and formed line of battle. The British pursued. The squadron was commanded by Vice Admiral Sir John Duckworth, who had crossed the Atlantic on his own initiative after sighting but losing touch with the other half of the Brest ships. He had six of the line to Leissègues' five, and the advantage of the wind, and signalling his intention to cut off the three leading enemy, he bore down in Nelsonic style in two divisions of three ships each. The casualty figures in the ensuing action reflected the gunnery disparity between the two navies at this period: some 1,500 French against about 340 British killed and wounded. Two of the French ships of the line, including Leissègues' 130-gun flagship, were so shattered they ran aground and were lost; the other three were captured. The victory removed a potentially dangerous threat to British trade in the Caribbean.

Meanwhile, Popham, having accomplished his mission at the Cape of Good Hope, decided to take his squadron to south America. Prior to sailing he had discussed with Pitt plans for aiding the Spanish colonists to break free from the mother country so that their legendary markets could be opened to British trade. His immediate motives were more personally predatory. Borrowing a small force of troops from the commander of the land forces with the promise of making both their fortunes,[37] he sailed to the river Plate, forced the surrender of Buenos Aires, port city and capital of the Spanish colony there, and took over a million silver dollars from the treasury and a far greater value of merchandise from the warehouses, and sent it home. The colonists he came to liberate were not impressed and he was soon turned out by a force from Montevideo on the opposite bank. Retiring to the mouth of the river he took the town of Maldonado and its adjacent island and proclaimed a blockade. It is interesting that the Admiralty Court, when adjudicating later on one of the prizes he took, held his blockade lawful since, although he had acted without authority, a naval commander possessed 'a portion of sovereign authority'.[38]

Popham was recalled and severely censured by the Admiralty for quit-
ting his station at the Cape without orders, but the City of London presented him with a sword of honour for attempting to open new markets
and the government followed up his initiative with an official expeditionary force for the Plate the following year, 1807. The colonists were prepared; the expedition was repulsed with heavy loss of life and compelled
to withdraw from the region. It was to be less than a year, however, before
events precipitated in Spain by Napoleon fulfilled the dreams of generations of merchants by opening much of Latin America to British trade.

Failure in the river Plate was matched earlier that same year, 1807, by
failure in the eastern Mediterranean. Napoleon was courting the Sultan
of Turkey as an ally against Russia – before Tilsit – and orders were sent
to Collingwood, still maintaining a wearisome blockade off Cadiz, to
detach Duckworth to Constantinople to demand the surrender of the
Turkish fleet before it fell under French influence. Collingwood instructed
Duckworth not to negotiate for more than half an hour and to meet a
Turkish refusal with a bombardment of the city or the fleet. On passage
east Duckworth attached the Malta squadron under the egregious Sidney
Smith, who achieved the only success of the mission once past the
Dardanelles entrance forts by driving a small Turkish squadron ashore
and burning it. Arriving in the Sea of Marmara Duckworth failed to use
a southerly wind which would have taken him up to Constantinople, so
limiting himself to distant negotiation without the backing of his guns.
He then allowed Collingwood's 'half an hour' to turn into a week, during
which time the Turkish fleet was warped into defensive posture and the
forts were strengthened. The victor of San Domingo finally made a futile
demonstration before retiring the way he had come. Equal embarrassment attended a British expeditionary force sent to attack the Ottoman
dependency of Egypt. After capturing Alexandria, it was bottled up in
the city and eventually forced to retire with heavy losses. Meanwhile
Russian squadrons succeeded in blockading Constantinople and finally
destroying the Turkish fleet.

These were peripheral humiliations only. The Royal Navy's ability to
direct seaborne trade in the British merchant interest and use the seas as
strategic lines of communication while denying them to the French for
anything but fleeting plunder was the overall reality. Never in modern
history had such complete dominion at sea opposed such absolute
command of the continent. In spring 1808 Collingwood, now off
Toulon, wrote to his wife: 'At sea there is no getting intelligence, as there

used to be on former occasions, for now there is not a trading ship upon the seas – nothing but ourselves. It is lamentable to see what a desert the waters are become.'[39] It is one of the features of the convoy system that the seas between the great concourses of ships become empty.

NAPOLEON'S DOWNFALL was spawned at opposite ends of his continental domain: in the Iberian peninsula and the Baltic. In both cases the Royal Navy's control of the sea was crucial: in the south in strategic support of a land commander of rare genius, Sir Arthur Wellesley, in the north by enabling mercantile forces to drive fissures into Napoleon's continental system and crack it open.

It began in October 1807. Napoleon despatched an army of 30,000 men across the Pyrenees under General Andoche Junot, ostensibly to enforce demands that Portugal close her ports to British ships, confiscate British property and intern British subjects. As noted, Napoleon had already signed a secret convention with Spain to partition Portugal between them, and his ulterior motive was the overthrow of the Spanish Bourbon monarchy itself. The British ambassador in Lisbon, Lord Strangford, urged the Portuguese prince regent, Dom John of the House of Bragança, to remove his government and fleet to the Portuguese colony of Brazil and from there continue the struggle as Britain's ally against Napoleon; Sidney Smith was despatched with a powerful squadron to Lisbon to escort him there. However, British prestige was undermined by news of the humiliation of the Buenos Aires expedition, and with Junot advancing, Dom John threw in his lot with Napoleon. This was changed at the last moment by the arrival of Sidney Smith. He blockaded the Tagus, and Strangford finally managed to persuade Dom John to flee with the Portuguese fleet. Junot's advanced troops were only hours away and he had little choice if he were to preserve his House. The contents of the treasury were transferred to the Portuguese flagship and he and the court and government officials embarked and on 29 November slipped down-river with the rest of his fleet to Sidney Smith's squadron, which saluted with twenty-one guns and escorted them into the Atlantic. It was the third time that year that potential additions to Napoleon's battle fleet had been removed from his grasp.

Junot entered Lisbon the following day, and soon afterwards the Russian squadron that had destroyed the Turkish fleet, now allies of the French, put in to the Tagus. Sidney Smith, leaving a detachment with the Portuguese fleet to escort them to Bahia, Brazil – which they reached on 6 December – returned to find the Russians in the Tagus, and blockaded them. They were to remain locked up until the admiral, unable to obtain provisions from Junot and, like so many of the Russian aristocracy, an Anglophile, turned over his ships to Sidney Smith's successor.

The real campaign in the Iberian peninsula began in 1808. Napoleon used internal splits between the Spanish king, the crown prince and the prime minister, the effective ruler of the country, to lure them all over the border into France and trick the royal family into abdicating and renouncing all claim to the monarchy. Meanwhile, French troops allowed into Spain for the campaign in Portugal had occupied key Spanish fortresses, and a column under his brother-in-law, Joachim Murat, had entered Madrid where the populace, perceiving their country had been sold out to France, had risen against the government. The prize had, it seemed, fallen into Napoleon's hands like an overripe plum. He named his older brother, Joseph, as King of Spain – since his original choice, Lucien, had grown to distrust his ambition and parted with him.

The Spanish people had other ideas. Outside the capital and great port cities, Barcelona, Seville and Cadiz, the majority of Spaniards were untouched by material prosperity or the slogans of the Enlightenment; loyal to their king they lived much as the rural population of France had before the Revolution, following time-honoured customs governed by the soil and the seasons, the fierce sun and the observances of the Catholic Church. The mantras of the 'Rights of Man' had no resonance, the supposed invincibility of Napoleon's armies no significance. Foreign soldiers had occupied their land and deposed their king and they rose to throw them out. The first open revolt was in Madrid on 2 May; it was extinguished with fearful severity on 3 May, but insurrection flared in the provinces and soon spread to every corner of the country. Similar risings against Junot's troops swept Portugal.

Both Spanish and Portuguese were quick to enlist British aid. Two representatives from an Asturian junta arrived in London as early as 4 June and within ten days Sir Arthur Wellesley, recently promoted Lieutenant General, was appointed to command an expeditionary force to cooperate with the Spanish armies. He sailed on 12 July for Portugal, followed by transports carrying some 9,000 troops collected originally for another assault on Spanish America. They made an unopposed landing 100 miles north of Lisbon during the first week of August, and joined by a small British force in the area and an even smaller Portuguese contingent, Wellesley marched south towards the capital. Junot moved north to intercept him.

They met on 21 August about 30 miles north of Lisbon. Wellesley posted his men on steep hills either side of a gorge enclosing the village of Vimeiro. Junot attacked in Napoleonic style in columns preceded by skirmishers whose purpose was to undermine the enemy before the main impact. Wellesley had thought out his answers to French tactics and deployed skirmishers armed with rifles behind cover in front of his positions; these prevented the French skirmishers coming within range of his lines. His batteries, meanwhile, opened on the advancing columns with shot and a new type of shell invented by an artillery lieutenant, Henry Shrapnel; filled with lead shot and a charge which exploded in flight, the shot and fragments of burst shell casing continued on the original trajectory as a scything hail of projectiles. Finally, as the columns pressed up the slope the British infantry in scarlet tunics emerged from behind the crest in line abreast, two deep across their path, as one French veteran described it 'like a long red wall',[40] and waited silent and motionless, their muskets ordered. Like the great guns' crews on British ships of the line, these mostly very young men were the battle-winning factor. They were better drilled in musketry than probably any other troops and steady in the face of a charge. As deployed by Wellesley in lines across the thrust of French columns so that every man had an unobstructed field of fire, whereas only the foremost French could reply, their disciplined volleys from inside 100 yards took a terrible toll. The same French veteran described the shock:

a volley of simultaneous precision and deadly effect crashed upon us like a thunderbolt. Decimated by it we reeled together, staggering under the blow and trying to recover our equilibrium. Then three formidable *Hurrahs* terminated the silence of our adversaries. With the third they were down upon us, pressing us into disorderly retreat. But to our great surprise, they did not pursue the advantage for more than some hundred yards, and went back with calm to their former lines, to await another attack.[41]

This was not a specific description from the battle of Vimeiro, but can serve for it since Wellesley's tactics against the French never changed. His eye for position and the thin red lines of his infantrymen waiting in ominous silence for the order to fire were the constants of his campaigns throughout the peninsula. At Vimeiro they ensured Junot's defeat.

Wellesley was unable to follow up his victory as he was overruled by senior generals sent out over him; instead a convention was signed whereby Junot gave up all forts, arsenals and stores in Portugal and his men were repatriated to France in British ships.

Wellesley was not prepared to suffer the bunglers who superseded him and went home. The senior generals soon followed, called to account for their actions. Command of British forces in Portugal was given to another young general of ability, Sir John Moore, who was ordered to enter Spain to cooperate with the Spanish forces. The regular Spanish armies were defeated, however, and as he moved to strike at French lines of communication north of Madrid Moore found himself hopelessly outnumbered by reinforcements poured into the country by Napoleon to stamp out the challenge to his rule; Moore was forced to withdraw towards Corunna, where he ordered transports to be assembled to take off his army. There he directed a successful defence of the port to allow his men to embark for England, during which, on 16 January 1809, he lost his life. In his last despatch, disillusioned by lack of cooperation from the Spanish, the inadequate equipment of his force and the indiscipline of the men, 'except when there was prospect of fighting' when they were orderly and determined, he concluded, 'I cannot think . . . that there can be any intention of sending a British force again into Spain.'

Wellesley, in England, took a lateral view of the situation. In a memorandum to Castlereagh of 7 March he stated his belief that with an army of 20,000 well-trained and equipped British troops, 30,000 newly trained and equipped Portuguese troops and 40,000 militia Portugal could be held against any force the French could maintain at that distance along their supply lines. The essential premise was that the British and Portuguese would be supplied by sea through Lisbon. By holding Portugal he would tie down large numbers of French troops in the peninsula and with the Spaniards conducting partisan warfare against the French occupation, the British army might 'eventually decide the contest'.[42] It was to prove a visionary paper. It convinced Castlereagh at the time and won over the Cabinet, and Wellesley was given command of his proposed force with specific orders: the defence of Portugal was to be his 'first and most immediate object'.

Napoleon had given his marshals instructions to drive the remaining British in Portugal into the sea. By the time Wellesley arrived in Lisbon on 22 April Soult had entered the country and reached Oporto some 160 miles north of the capital, while Marshal Claude Victor was about the same distance east but still in Spain. Wellesley immediately moved on Soult, surprised him by crossing the river Douro above the city where he had neglected to post sentries and caused his precipitate retreat, to the great joy of the citizens. Wellesley next marched east into Spain to link up with a Spanish army under General Gregorio Cuesta to attack Victor and march on Madrid. Cuesta proved an unreliable ally; the French were allowed time to bring up reinforcements and Wellesley was compelled to fight a defensive battle at Talavera. Although Victor retired, leaving him the field, Wellesley was desperately short of provisions and new French forces were converging on him; now as distrustful as Moore had been of the Spanish generals and juntas who failed to supply him, and fearing encirclement by superior forces, he withdrew to the Portuguese border.

The government trumpeted his victory at Talavera, raising him to the peerage as Viscount Wellington. It was as Wellington that he conducted the critical phase of the war in the peninsula. He took the crucial step in September that year, 1809: leaving the army at the frontier, he returned to Lisbon and spent days riding about the mountainous country north of the capital, afterwards issuing specific orders for the construction of a system of linked hill forts and walls, redoubts, escarpments, batteries and semaphore signals posts to create a virtually impregnable three-tiered defensive barrier above Lisbon from the coast to the river Tagus, known to history as the Lines of Torres Vedras.

At home the British government fell: after the withdrawal of Sir John Moore's army and the prospect of a similar end to the latest adventure in Spain, it was unable to survive the failure of a grand expedition to the Schelde to destroy warships under construction for Napoleon at Antwerp. In addition Austria, encouraged by the Spanish rising to avenge her recent humiliations, had again been crushed on the battlefield by Napoleon and forced into yet another ignominious peace,[43] losing further territories and population. That same month, October 1809, a new British administration was formed under Spencer Perceval, in which Castlereagh was succeeded as Secretary for War by Lord Liverpool and Canning as Foreign Secretary by Wellington's eldest brother, the Marquess Wellesley; his younger brother, Henry, was despatched as British ambassador to the central Spanish junta. Between them, the Wellesley brothers now had enormous leverage on policy concerning Spain and the peninsula.

Wellington's own influence was decisive. He steadied the government after two catastrophic defeats for Spanish armies in the field in November, although early the following year, 1810, he himself wavered briefly when French forces under King Joseph and Soult struck south to plunder the wealthy province of Andalusia and occupied Seville. Cadiz was only saved for the Allied cause at the last moment. Depressed by the lack of effective Spanish opposition, Wellington asked Lord Liverpool whether he had to defend Portugal 'to the last' or turn his mind seriously to evacuation.[44] The reply returned the decision to him: 'the safety of the British army in Portugal is the first object', but he should not evacuate it until 'absolutely necessary'.[45] By the time he received this he had recovered confidence. Napoleon, freed from the Austrian threat, was pouring yet more troops into Spain, yet paradoxically the defeat of the regular Spanish armies, the consequent release of Spanish soldiers into irregular *'guerrilleros'* – bands harassing French garrisons and striking at their supply lines – increased the level of resistance, for the Spaniards were as effective in this mode as they had been ineffective under their army commanders. Moreover, both the Allied garrison at Cadiz and Wellington's own army in Portugal were receiving troop reinforcements and supplies by sea, and the fortifications of Torres Vedras were progressing steadily, as was the training of Portuguese regulars to fight alongside the British.

Napoleon uncharacteristically allowed him the most precious military commodity, time. Preoccupied with founding a dynasty by divorcing Josephine, who had failed to bear him a child and was now too old, and engaging himself to the Austrian emperor's daughter, the Archduchess Marie-Louise – niece of the late French queen – he delegated the task of driving the British from Portugal to Marshal André Masséna. Arriving in late May, Masséna attempted to lure Wellington forward. Wellington refused, and by the time Masséna began advancing with Marshal Michel Ney into Portugal in July the fortifications of Torres Vedras had been completed. Thereafter all went as Wellington had planned: he retired through a countryside which under his direction was emptied of inhabitants, crops, provisions, livestock, carriages or carts; and as the French advanced through deserted towns and villages their stragglers, sentries, couriers and supply columns came under constant attack from Portuguese partisans. Wellington, using the utmost caution to avoid being outflanked, pausing to give battle at one carefully prepared defensive position on a ridge by the convent of Busaco north of Coimbra – where the French lost 4,500 men to only 1,250 British and Portuguese – drew Masséna towards his prepared lines above Lisbon.

Masséna's astonishment when he came upon the integrated defensive system, secured at either end by gun vessels of the Royal Navy, was equalled by the respect he had learned for British and Portuguese musketry at Busaco, and he did not attack, instead preparing positions into which he withdrew for the winter. Wellington resisted pursuit, confident that hunger and disease would do his work for him, as they did. Masséna could see convoys bringing constant supplies to Lisbon for the Allied forces while his men dropped from starvation. By February 1811 he was losing over 500 men a week[46] and in early March he began a retreat to Spain; by the time he reached the frontier he had lost over 25,000 men, more than a third of his original army.[47]

Wellington had fulfilled the aims of his original memorandum to the letter. His strategic genius and the iron resolve with which he had carried out his plan, refusing to be drawn into battle unless on his own terms, and the steadiness of the troops his officers had drilled to perfection, both British and Portuguese, had given Britain an impregnable bridgehead in the peninsula. Besides creating a vast drain on French resources, this kept alive the fires of resistance in Spain, which in turn acted as an incitement to nationalism in European states feeling the increasing weight of Napoleon's yoke, particularly Prussia. In this way the British army under a commander of brilliance with supply lines guaranteed by the dominance of the Royal Navy[48] exerted a continental leverage out of all proportion to its modest size.

Napoleon had miscalculated the character of the Spanish and Portuguese peoples, if not of their governments, and underestimated British ability to support them. He also failed to foresee the effects that the Anglo-Spanish alliance would have on British commerce. For centuries British merchants had coveted access to Spanish-American markets. Now – with local exceptions – most were opened to them, and Spanish-American treasure was diverted from Napoleon to London. Moreover, Spanish forces aided British expeditions to conquer the last French islands in the Caribbean. Martinique had fallen to the British in February 1809; Saint-Domingue fell to an Anglo-Spanish force in June that year, and the final French island, Guadeloupe, surrendered in February 1810. The small Danish islands had already been captured, and the remaining Dutch island entrepôts, St Martin, Eustatius and Saba, were quickly taken. The same year British expeditions took the French Indian Ocean island privateer bases, Bourbon and Réunion, renaming the latter Mauritius, and in the Dutch East Indies Amboina and Banda were seized in a campaign that would soon roll up the entire Dutch eastern empire. With the sugar islands of the Caribbean in exclusively British or Spanish control, the opening of Spanish-American markets to British merchants, a virtual monopoly of eastern commerce, increased trade with the United States, particularly the import of raw cotton and export of cotton manufactured goods, British trade increased by millions,[49] boosting the customs receipts which backed the national debt and relieving some of the distress in manufacturing areas hit both by the continental blockade and inflation resulting from the over-issue of paper money whose convertibility to gold had yet to be restored.

More than two centuries earlier the Elizabethan adventurer, Sir Walter Ralegh, had pronounced a simple rule, 'Hee that commaunds the sea, commaunds the trade, and hee that is Lord of the trade of the world is Lord of the wealth of the worlde.'[50] Great Britain was nearer to attaining this goal than any nation before her, not excluding the Dutch in the seventeenth century. Her navy had grown from the largest in the world with 30 per cent of total world tonnage at the start of the Revolutionary war into an overpowering force with 50 per cent of world tonnage, the only navy in the modern era, probably in any era, to possess half the world's warships.[51] She had over a hundred 74-gun ships of the line in a battle fleet of 152 sail, against forty-six French ships of the line, and the number of frigates on the active list had grown, in response to the demands for trade protection, to 199 with an aggregate tonnage greater than the entire French navy;[52] besides these were scores of unrated gun brigs, sloops and lesser craft also largely employed on trade protection. This unique preponderance had been achieved, not by large construction programmes but by capture. In the five years from 1806 to 1810 alone, 101 enemy ships had been commissioned into the Royal Navy.[53] In view of the superior sailing skills and great gun discipline of British ships' companies as evinced over the years of the wars it is no exaggeration to say that there was no combination of powers which could conceivably have wrested back her prized command of the oceans.

Despite this and absolute control of the colonial trades, west and east, and her supremacy in manufacture, Napoleon's continental blockade was hurting, especially in the Baltic. It was here the decisive campaign was to be waged. The admiral commanding has never received due recognition, yet the five successive seasons in which his fleet dominated the Baltic proved strategically and diplomatically the end for Napoleon.

The Continental Blockade

VICE ADMIRAL SIR James Saumarez had a distinguished career: he had fought under Rodney at the Saints in 1782, received the highest commendation from Jervis for his part in command of the *Orion* at St Vincent in 1797 and been second in command of Nelson's fleet at the Nile in 1798; and after hoisting his own flag in 1801, he had defeated a Franco-Spanish squadron off Cadiz which outnumbered his own force by nine to five. Like Jervis and Nelson he took great care of the well-being of his men, was never afraid to act on his own initiative and similarly allowed discretion to his junior flag officers whom he encouraged to develop their own solutions. In addition his new post demanded and brought out high diplomatic skills.

He was first ordered to the Baltic in command of a fleet of thirteen of the line together with frigates and smaller craft early in 1808. His tasks were to support Sweden, Great Britain's only remaining ally at the time, against in the east Russia, which had invaded Finland, in the west French and Spanish troops – before the Spanish rising – who were poised to cross from Denmark into Norway to attack Sweden from the west; but above all he had to keep the narrow entrances to the Baltic, the Sound and the Belt, open to British and neutral shipping, protect shipping once inside and counter the effects of Napoleon's Milan Decree of December 1807 as applied in the Prussian and Russian ports along the southern Baltic.[1]

By the time he arrived in early May Sweden was virtually past saving. Her fortress of Sveaborg commanding the northern shore of the Gulf of Finland had been taken by the Russians, together with up to 100 of the

oared gunboat flotilla developed for operations among the inshore channels and islands of the Finnish coast. Saumarez could not provide comparable craft. He was, in any case, drawn to the western end of the Baltic
by news of the uprising in Spain and the consequent need to extricate
Spanish troops from the Franco-Spanish force in Denmark. While
engaged in this, he sent Rear Admiral Sir Samuel Hood with two of the
line to reinforce the Swedish battle fleet. Hood's ships played a leading role
in a subsequent engagement with a Russian squadron from Cronstadt.
They were faster than either the Swedish or Russian ships and were instrumental in forcing one Russian 74 ashore, where she was burned, and
chasing the rest into Port Baltic (Batiski) near Revel (Tallinn) on the southern shore of the Gulf of Finland, where they were blockaded. The clear
superiority of Hood's little detachment in sailing and fighting their guns
was regarded with 'awe and amazement' by the Swedes[2] and no doubt the
Russians; at all events, the Russian Baltic fleet never troubled Saumarez
again, although it is doubtful if the prestige Hood had won for the Royal
Navy in the running engagement was the sole reason.

It is interesting that the British ships' companies were also far health-
ier than their Swedish and probably their Russian counterparts. By the
time Saumarez joined the blockade off Port Baltic the Swedish crews
were seriously depleted by sickness. His surgeon inspected and reported
that '*scurvy* of the most obstinate and dangerous nature threatens the
safety of the whole fleet . . . already 1,200 men have been sent to hospital and it is painful to remark no less than 400 have died on board one
ship since yesterday'.[3] Equally interesting, lime juice, which is inferior to
lemon juice in the essential anti-scorbutic vitamin C, was already in use
in the British Baltic ships in place of lemon syrup, no doubt because it
was easier and cheaper to procure limes in the Caribbean, now virtually
a British lake. Saumarez had the Swedish fleet supplied with lime juice
and sugar from his own ships.[4]

The most serious threats to trade at this juncture came from swarms
of Danish gunboats in the Sound and Great Belt, reported by Saumarez
as 'above 60 sail of large gunboats, exclusive of smaller vessels',[5] and
Danish, Prussian and French privateers operating from southern Baltic
ports and often taking their captures in to the Baltic islands of Bornholm
and the nearby Ertholms; sales of prize goods here were such that merchants from Denmark, Prussia and Sweden had taken up residence.
Saumarez was advised to capture the islands to root out the privateers
and use their bases as entrepôts from which British merchants might

Map 2   The Baltic, 1800–1814

smuggle goods into the German ports under French control. He had them reconnoitred but concluded that their capture would need troops, which he lacked. Instead, he convoyed shipping past and had the privateer ports patrolled by cruisers.

His command extended outside the Baltic into the Kattegat. Shipping which had come across the North Sea under escort gathered in Vinga Sound on the Swedish shore near Gothenburg. From there one of Saumarez's junior admirals organized their convoy for the most hazardous stretch of the voyage past the Danish islands. At first they were escorted through the Sound between Sweden and Denmark since this offered one friendly shore, but the navigable channel became so narrow off Malmö that ships were unable to manoeuvre, and on the frequently calm days of summer lay strung out in line at the mercy of the Danish oared flotilla. Their vulnerability was exposed shockingly as early as 10 June 1808, when seventeen merchantmen and an escort were captured. After this the more difficult and longer but broader passage through the Great Belt between the Danish islands was tried, and soon adopted for all convoys. The 'shuttle service' that evolved both ways through the Belt employed six of the line and a number of smaller craft. One battle ship was stationed at each end to receive the convoys and conduct them in; four of the line were stationed at mid-length of the passage near the chief Danish gunboat bases; their boats armed with long guns reinforced the escorting gun brigs and sloops through this most dangerous section. The system was successful enough for Saumarez to report 'very trivial losses';[6] indeed the following year between mid-June and early November 2,210 merchantmen were escorted through without loss.[7]

The smaller escorts which had picked up the inbound ships at Vinga Sound continued with their charges until 150 miles east of Bornholm, after which they made for Karlskrona in southern Sweden, the assembly point for outward-bound shipping, where they would gather another convoy for the westbound transit of the Belt. Individual merchantmen dispersing to or from their destinations in the eastern Baltic relied for safety on the cruiser patrols off the privateer ports.

Apart from the defence of merchant shipping against physical attack, Saumarez was engaged in a campaign of charade and deception. Since the beginning of the Revolutionary war British trade with the Baltic had increased tenfold,[8] owing partly to the vast demand for timber and other naval stores for the expanded navy and merchant shipping, but chiefly to the re-routing of British exports and re-exports for the continent which were barred from French and French-controlled ports. The Baltic had become the main channel through which British products entered continental Europe, and although the Prussian and Russian governments had pledged themselves to Napoleon's blockade, their merchants were dependent on the trade continuing, as indeed were the governments since they were not in any condition to accept the widespread distress that must follow loss of trade. The Russian government after Tilsit was no longer in receipt of British subsidies to keep troops in the field and had lost the use of the London money market for loans; her national debt was rising dangerously and the exchange rate of the rouble falling.[9] Prussia was in a similar situation, bled by Napoleon's huge war indemnity. Thus, while both were formally at war with Great Britain, they were also dependent on maintaining trade relations with her. As Saumarez reported at the end of his first year, the war with Russia and Prussia was maintained in a previously unprecedented manner:

> An immense trade is carried on by British merchants under H.M.'s licence with the different ports of these countries. Both nations are known to be amicably disposed towards Great Britain and openly avow their earnest desire to be on terms of peace and amity with England as well as their abhorrence of their alliance with France.[10]

In his attitude to Russia, which alone had a fleet capable in theory of disputing command of the Baltic, Saumarez had two options: as described to him by the British envoy to Sweden, Russia had only been driven to war against Britain by terror of the French, so might be brought back to amity by a better system of terror; or alternatively, because the war was unnatural for her, especially for her trading community, nothing should be done to offend them. Saumarez leant heavily to the latter view: he blockaded the Russian squadron in Port Baltic but made no preparations to attack the fleet base at Cronstadt or any Russian forts; nor did he blockade the commercial ports. He even initiated a peace feeler by sending a letter to the tsar via the admiral he was blockading enclosing papers relating to the uprising in Spain and events in Portugal. Rebuked strongly by the Admiralty for exceeding his authority, he replied that he had considered it a favourable opportunity to inform the tsar of events in the peninsula 'with a view if possible to detach Russia from her alliance with the French nation and to return her to her former ties of friendship with Great Britain'.[11]

In November he took his fleet home before ice closed the Baltic. In his absence during the winter the Russians attempted a three-pronged invasion of Sweden from Finland over the frozen Gulf of Bothnia and were only narrowly foiled by the break-up of the ice. Returning in May 1809, Saumarez took most of his heavy ships to the head of the Gulf to disrupt Russian supply lines to their armies and support a Swedish landing in Finland. The Russian Baltic fleet of thirteen of the line refused the challenge and remained in defensive posture inside Cronstadt. The Swedish landings were repulsed nonetheless and in September, with little prospect of withstanding the next Russian winter invasion, Sweden concluded peace with the tsar at Frederikshamn, ceding Finland to him and all Swedish territory east of the Gulf of Bothnia together with the strategic Åland Islands at the head of the Gulf. She also had to pledge to adhere to Napoleon's continental blockade of British trade.

Without a single ally on any Baltic shore Saumarez's situation now seemed bleak, but of course Sweden was as dependent on trade as Russia and Prussia; the Swedish government also hoped to enlist British aid in seizing Norway from Denmark as compensation for the loss of Finland, and Saumarez was assured that neither their friendship nor access to their ports and supplies would alter in any way. As for Napoleon's continental system, he was told, it had been mentioned only because the tsar insisted; but Russian interest in it was not the same as French.

British trade with the Baltic had leaped during the year; imports had more than doubled and exports and re-exports trebled to a value of £13.6 million, a quarter of total British exports to all regions.[12] Much of this trade was carried by neutrals, US ships in particular, under the system of British licences, forged papers and false declarations by the crew noted earlier. It seems remarkable nonetheless that such huge volumes of goods were shipped in and out under the noses of port authorities and French consuls ostensibly seeking to exclude British and British colonial produce. Obviously Baltic merchants colluded; organized smuggling took place; some or many officials were bribed; French consuls went 'native' – Napoleon had them changed frequently. It still remains surprising.

The difficulties for port officials and privateers alike are illustrated by instructions issued to a Danish privateer captain by his promoter. He was told that ships from Russian harbours were generally bound for England and cleared for Norwegian or other Allied ports.

The lading of these ships must be signed and accompanied with a certificate from the French consul in Petersburg. All these vessels have English licences on board which you must find, or else you cannot take them as prizes. You can obtain them by promising the ship or money to the Captain. You must promise the men the same; and everything you promise in order to get these licences I will keep quite faithfully.[13]

He was told to look out particularly for vessels inward bound for Russian or Prussian ports which were generally carrying valuable colonial wares. As soon as he went aboard a ship he was to take possession of all papers and examine the whole crew to see if they had anything concealed about their bodies or clothes, after which he was to examine each man individually.

Show him the decree of the Emperor Napoleon of January 11th in which a third part of the prize money is promised to anyone who will declare that the vessel has been examined by the English, or that she sailed from England or has an English licence. Tell the men that everything will be kept silent and they will not have a better opportunity of making their fortunes.

If he met a vessel with a French licence he was to search for an English licence aboard, which he could not fail to find; captains hid their papers under the hearths or about their body. Swedish vessels were to be examined very carefully; all Swedish vessels from Gothenburg, Carlshamn or Stockholm carried colonial produce but under another name. Finally, he was exhorted to remember: 'if you fulfil everything you will make your own and my fortune off Colberg, Pillau, Memel and Libau.'

Swedish Pomerania on the southern Baltic shore was vulnerable to Napoleon and in January 1810 the Swedish government was forced into a peace treaty with France in which she undertook to observe the continental blockade strictly against British trade and to ban British ships from her ports. Privately, Saumarez was again assured that the Swedish government would indirectly afford him every facility and he could continue to use Swedish anchorages provided they were not military bases. For his part Saumarez did not molest Swedish coastal shipping or trade and mail packets between Sweden and Pomerania. The previous year he had seized the Danish island of Anholt in the Kattegat just outside the entrance to the Baltic; this now proved a valuable anchorage for merchantmen excluded from Swedish ports and a depot for British and colonial produce to be smuggled through the blockade; it also provided a constant supply of good water for the fleet. Inside the Baltic the naval base Karlskrona was now barred to him, but he found an excellent anchorage and collection point for the outward trade a few miles west in Hanö Bay, where again a supply of good water was readily obtainable.

Towards the end of July, he was able to report to the First Lord of the Admiralty:

> The best understanding is continuing to be maintained with the Swedes who seem desirous to afford the supplies of fresh provisions required by the squadron, although not openly by the government of the country.
>
> Every possible exertion is used in forwarding the trade to the ports of England . . . and the supplies of grain from Danzig and other ports will I hope arrive seasonably to prevent the apparent scarcity [in England] being too severely felt.[14]

Imports of grain from northern Europe did indeed rise that year, 1810, from a value of £1.1 to £2.7 million; timber imports also rose as dramatically from under £0.5 to £0.8 million.[15]

In August Saumarez learned that Napoleon's marshal, Jean-Baptiste Bernadotte, had been elected Crown Prince of Sweden. The king was failing and it was hoped that Bernadotte would enable Sweden to conquer Norway. As noted, British help was envisaged, and Saumarez was once again assured by the Swedish government that nothing would change in their relationship; their new crown prince would resist Napoleon and his agents. Towards the end of September Saumarez reported to the First Lord his belief that the Swedes 'dread nothing so much as to be in hostility with England'.[16]

This period in the autumn of 1810 marked the beginning of the critical phase of the campaign: Napoleon, having resolved the first stage of his dynastic design by marrying the young Archduchess Marie-Louise, now pregnant with his first child, turned his energies to stopping up the vast leakage of British trade through the Baltic, despatching troops to occupy the Baltic ports of Mecklenburg and Prussia, annexing Holland, Oldenburg and the Hanseatic ports, and in October issuing a decree from Fontainebleau ordering the seizure and destruction by fire of British goods and property. He also forced Sweden to declare war against Britain. The Swedish government delayed the declaration until 17 November when Saumarez had to leave the Baltic for the winter, and again he was assured that there would be no change in their fundamental friendship; neither his fleet nor the trade would be harmed.

The actions of French troops and paid agents in the southern Baltic ports were far more serious than Sweden's pretence of hostility. Insurance rates rose to unheard of levels, 40 per cent in some cases,[17] and merchants in the ports were terrorized, many ruined by wholesale confiscations and destruction of British and colonial goods. As reported to Saumarez the following year:

> The measures adopted at Hamburg against the intercourse with Great Britain and which under the eye of [Marshal of France] Davout extend up to Königsberg are enforced with the most barbarous severity. In the neighbourhood of the former place scarcely a family anyway formerly employed in the British trade is free from apprehension. Several have been transported in chains to Paris, and many have abandoned their home from the insinuations they have received of their names being upon a list of prescription.[18]

This was the inevitable culmination of the war originally launched by Napoleon against the sources of British wealth. It had grown into a war against virtually all seaborne trade, hence against all merchant houses dealing in overseas goods, the industries dependent on them, their bankers and governments and indeed all the peoples of Europe needing or wanting colonial produce and high quality, low cost British manufactured goods. The task of Napoleon's troops and police and spies was to repress the innumerable streams of self-interest fed from the port cities and smuggling harbours. In a direct sense the warrior, bureaucratic ethic was pitted against merchant dynamics, an epitome of the struggle between territorial and maritime systems; in the event it was to prove the final round in the Franco-British contest for world power.

IN ATTEMPTING to keep out British goods by internal repression in his dependent or allied states Napoleon raised protean forces of resistance. The symptoms were evident before the end of 1810. Tsar Alexander I refused Napoleon's request to seize hundreds of neutral ships lying in Russian ports with cargoes suspected of originating in Britain or her colonies and on the last day of the year issued a *ukase* permitting the import of colonial goods into Russia under neutral flag. It was the first overt crack in the Tilsit agreement, caused as much by cumulative complaints from merchants against the continental system as by alarm at the spread of Napoleon's troops through north Germany and Prussia, ostensibly to enforce the blockade. But there were other disagreements between them, and Napoleon was already anticipating another war to enforce his will.[19]

Resistance to French bullying was as strong or stronger in Prussia among merchants and the humiliated military elite. Encouraged by the Spanish war of liberation and Wellington's feats in Portugal, a 'war party' was preparing in secret for a national uprising, and looking to Britain to supply money and arms. One of the prime movers in the army, Count August von Gneisenau, wrote to Saumarez early in September 1811 apprising him of their plans and requesting arms: 'Rumour has it that your government, foreseeing an early rupture between France and Russia, has taken steps to put aboard your fleet an abundant stock of weapons . . .'[20] Saumarez was able to reply before the end of the month that two vessels laden with arms and ammunition were being despatched to the Baltic and he would lose no time in having them escorted to the Prussian fortress of Colberg.[21]

The spirit of resistance to Napoleon was not confined to the Baltic powers whose trade was directly affected by the continental blockade, but was widespread throughout Europe from Austria and Germany to Switzerland, northern Italy and even in France itself, aroused as much by bureaucratic efforts to enforce standardization in all areas as by extortionate taxes and the conscription of young men for French imperial service. As in Pitt's time, liberation movements were funded, armed and kept in touch by British agents. The most influential agent based in Vienna but travelling constantly was J. M. Johnson, who saw himself as William Wickham's heir and had set out to raise insurrection from the Balkans and the Alps to northern Germany. He also maintained a correspondence with Paris, and in March 1811 reported 'disaffection and hostility to the Emperor' in many parts of France affecting both the levying of taxes and conscription for the army: 'Throughout Poitou, Anjou, the Maine, Part of Brittany . . . that tract of Country formerly called the Vendée, the Catholic clergy have steadfastly refused to read the prayers for the Emperor and the Imperial family.'[22]

Of course the most significant resistance leader in France was Talleyrand himself; as early as 1808 he had advised Tsar Alexander in a series of covert meetings that it was in his, Alexander's power to save Europe, and he would only do so by refusing to give way to Napoleon[23] – counsel that must at least have stiffened Alexander's resolve to admit colonial produce through the continental blockade. Subsequently Talleyrand had allied himself with Napoleon's Minister of Police, Joseph Fouché, in order to unite internal opposition. In 1810, however, Napoleon discovered Fouché in a convoluted intrigue to depose him, make peace with Britain and place Ferdinand of Spain on the Spanish throne, and dismissed him.[24] Like the host of other plots to unseat Napoleon and the Revolutionary leaders before him, this too had been funded by the British government.

More significant than internal opposition, the tsar's alienation, Prussia's hostility or British promotion of revolt throughout the empire, French finances were moving into deficit.[25] Up to this point Napoleon had succeeded both in stabilizing the French currency after the ruinous inflation of the Revolutionary years and in making his defeated enemies pay for his wars. However, the vast indemnities and confiscations could not continue indefinitely and his foray into the Iberian peninsula had resulted in a drain on resources and manpower, as well as depriving him of Spanish-American treasure. Moreover, the increasingly heavy taxes levied on satellites tended to their impoverishment, and the continental blockade had stunted and in many cases ruined the formerly dynamic commercial-industrial areas associated with overseas commerce.

Holland was an extreme example. Dutch trade and dependent industries had been utterly broken on the blockade. In Zaandam, the ship-building centre to the north of Amsterdam whose productivity in the seventeenth century had merited its description as Europe's first industrial zone,[26] one shipyard alone remained. Amsterdam, former commercial and financial hub of Europe, had lost its entrepôt and staple functions and suffered such a collapse of market operations and industry that half the population had been pauperized, kept alive only by soup kitchens and free distribution of fuel. French reports of 1811–12 speak of '*misère hideuse et générale*'.[27] Several Dutch financiers had fled to England early in the Revolutionary war and it seems Dutch capital followed, helping to fund British government debt instead of reinvigorating the home economy.[28]

There were areas, chiefly in Belgium and the Rhineland, which had benefited from military orders and from a continental market protected to a large degree from British imports;[29] the effects have not been quantified, but these gains did not make up for the lost dynamism of the overseas trades and industries. What is not in doubt is that tax receipts from France and the empire amounted to little over half Napoleon's revenue, and in 1811 with military expenses rising to meet the needs of the war in the peninsula, control the southern Baltic ports, prepare for the coming war with Russia, the naval building programme, naval mobilization in the Schelde and the Texel and a concentration of troops at Boulogne to frighten England, his outgoings exceeded his revenues by almost 50 million francs.[30]

It is interesting that he was not prepared to sacrifice his fleet-building programme; indeed it was accelerated that year: no less than four great first rates of 110 to 118 guns, six 80-gun ships and a record total of nine 74s were laid down in French and satellite yards.[31] Just as the development of a huge battle fleet to rival the British fleet had contributed to the financial crisis which precipitated the Revolution in 1789, so the cost of Napoleon's programme, which amounted to over 150 million francs annually (some £6.5 million), made a substantial contribution to his financial difficulties from 1811.[32] Whatever his long-term goal, the immediate aim seems to have been to force Britain to build more and so add to her national debt, which he considered dangerously high. He was later to say:

> The debt of England is a gnawing worm ... for in order to sustain this immense weight, it will be necessary to continue, during peace, the levy of these extraordinary taxes imposed during the war; this will, necessarily, lead to an increase in the price of provisions, and insensibly bring the people to the most frightful misery.[33]

He had attempted to model French financial institutions on London's without understanding the necessity for freedom from central control, and he had failed to interpret the financial lessons of the eighteenth-century Anglo-French wars: that Britain, despite virtually doubling her debt over the course of each war, raising taxes to back it, had always retained the ability to borrow more on better terms than her more populous Bourbon rival; subsequent trade expansion had reduced the debt as a proportion of her economy. Instead of seeing the debt as a necessary investment in the struggle for world markets, Napoleon regarded it, like English kings before the Glorious Revolution of 1689, as an index of overspending, and with the example of Louis XVI clearly before him, an agent of disaster. If his aim in the fleet-building programme was indeed to force Britain to overextend herself financially, he was challenging her on her point of greatest comparative advantage.

Similarly Adam Smith and the liberal economists – to whose doctrines Talleyrand subscribed – and the whole feverish panoply of British industrial progress seem to have passed him by. He remained fundamentally a physiocrat, regarding agriculture as 'the soul, the foundation of all national prosperity', foreign trade as merely 'the profitable employment of the surplus of the national products . . . but of much inferior interest to the others, to which it is subservient, and not they to it'.[34] His views reflected the natural predilections of warriors in possession of fertile lands of great extent. He had not, like the Confucian rulers of fifteenth-century China, banned foreign trade, yet curiously his continental system had produced the same result.

Holding these views, it is not surprising that he refused to cover increased military spending by borrowing. He might easily have done so in 1811 at rates only a point or two higher than those on British government loans.[35] Yet during his whole reign he only raised official French public debt from 45 to 63 million francs, scarcely over half his annual expenditure in these later years.[36] Instead he was driven to huge increases in direct taxes, hitting the very class on which he relied for support, reducing consumer demand further and exacerbating a major financial crisis affecting Paris and the other financial centres of Europe.

Simultaneously his campaign against the sources of British wealth at last achieved striking results. Although Saumarez was still supplying and watering his fleet at Swedish anchorages and trade was flowing as before by courtesy of Bernadotte, now in effective control of that country, and the tsar was admitting neutral ships to Russian ports with British colonial produce, French military occupation of the southern Baltic ports, extending to Swedish Pomerania, and the system of terror visited on Baltic merchants had completely disrupted trade: imports from the Baltic as a whole had dropped from almost £7.5 million in 1810 to £2.6 million in 1811, exports and re-exports from £11.2 million to £2.3 million.[37]

This coincided with a ban by the United States of America on the entry of British ships and goods – largely in response to an undertaking by Napoleon of more guile than substance, as would appear. The US was the major single importer of British manufactures, taking over a quarter of those sent overseas, and the almost complete collapse of this market – worth £9.3 million in 1810 and dropping to £1.9 million in 1811[38] – on top of the drastic decline in exports to the Baltic precipitated an industrial slump threatening both the economy and the social cohesion of the country, particularly as a poor harvest that year together with reduced imports of Baltic grain led to higher food prices. The resulting widespread unemployment, part-time working and even famine in some areas provided radicals and opposition politicians hostile to the seemingly endless war against Napoleon with ripe conditions for agitation. And towards the end of the year rioting and machine-smashing by bands of handcraftsmen calling themselves 'Luddites', who saw their livelihoods destroyed by factory mechanization, particularly in the textile and metallurgical industries, seemed to suggest the existence of an organized revolutionary or 'Jacobin' movement. It has been argued that a 'revolutionary situation existed in 1811–12, as in no other year of the entire period of the [French] wars'.[39] At all events, ruthless suppression and the hanging or transportation to the colonies of many Luddite leaders testify to the government's continuing fear of the slogans of the French Revolution. Meanwhile, as warehouses filled with stocks of unsold goods and colonial produce an adverse balance of trade caused the pound to fall on the foreign exchange.

13

The American War, 1812

THE UNITED STATES had become a nation with a government and a President only in the year of the French Revolution, yet as former partners in the British imperial system her merchants, shipbuilders and seafarers had nothing to learn about oceanic trade, and as American neutrality in the war that broke out between Britain and Revolutionary France gave her shipping enormous advantages her merchant marine developed into a dangerous rival for European, particularly British shipowners. The British government, acting in the interests of shipowners, sought to counter these advantages by stringent application of the prize laws. The 'rule of 1756' making a trade illegal if it had been prohibited by the Navigation Laws of a belligerent in peacetime, and commercial blockades of the French West Indies and French Atlantic and Mediterranean ports, hit American shipowners and merchants. As an added insult sailors were impressed into the Royal Navy from American ships.

Feeling against Great Britain was exacerbated by popular sympathy with the expressed ideals of the French Revolution. Even in New York, whose merchants and shipowners were intimately bound up with and dependent on trade with Britain, everything French became suddenly fashionable: men had their hair cut short and brushed forward and wore bloused shirts and baggy pantaloons in imitation of the Revolutionaries; boarding houses became *pensions françaises*, taverns *restaurants*.[1]

Determined to prevent the nation slipping into a second war with Britain, President George Washington sent a mission to London under the Chief Justice, John Jay, who negotiated a trading agreement known as the Jay Treaty, which was signed in June 1795. In return for allowing American ships not exceeding 70 tons to enter British West Indian ports, and some other minor concessions, the United States agreed that her ships would not engage in the international carriage of the staples of the West Indies and southern states, sugar, molasses, cotton; granted Great Britain most favoured nation trading status and agreed to ban foreign privateers from her ports. No mention was made of the most glaring source of dispute, the impressment by Royal Navy captains of British sailors serving in American ships, nor of the 'rule of 1756'. The principle of the freedom of the seas and the neutral flag was thus abandoned to *force majeure*, the overwhelming might of the British at sea. The treaty was highly unpopular. Nonetheless, as American merchants and shipowners exploited wartime opportunities and the dislocation of the belligerent powers' shipping, both US trade and her merchant fleet grew at a prodigious pace.

Since a major part of the trade was with Great Britain, the United States came to be viewed in France as almost an arm of the British maritime-commercial system, and when the Directory took power from the Jacobins in late 1795 there was immediate retaliation: an embargo was placed on US ships in French ports, American property was confiscated, debts to American merchants were repudiated and a privateer offensive was launched against US merchantmen on the high seas, particularly in the West Indies. The island of Guadeloupe under Victor Hugues, the committed Jacobin who had abolished slavery in his territory, became the most virulent centre of the campaign. Hugues disliked the Directory, but he viewed the Americans who had taken over much of the trade of the eastern Caribbean as blatantly supportive of British interests, and thus France's enemies, and converted his island and its populace into the dedicated scourge of Anglo-American commerce – as described in one study, 'a sort of Barbary [pirate] State transposed to a Caribbean setting'.[2] Between mid-1796 and the end of 1798 over 700 vessels were seized and taken before Hugues' Tribunal de Commerce et des Prises, where the vast majority were condemned. At this time his privateer fleet, according to US estimates, numbered between sixty and eighty vessels, chiefly armed schooners, excluding oared craft and craft operating from other islands with privateer licences obtained in Guadeloupe,[3] and he had brought the United States and France to the brink of open war.

To the US administration the French *guerre de course* came as a wake-up call. An Act authorizing the construction of six frigates, the founding charter of the US Navy, had been passed in March 1794 in response to attacks on American shipping by the corsairs of the north African Barbary coast. Before independence US ships in the Mediterranean had enjoyed the protection of the Royal Navy. Now they were on their own and their British and other European rivals were happy to encourage the corsairs to prey on them. Since the Barbary states were known to have 44-gun ships, three of the six US frigates were to carry 44 guns, the other three 36 – rerated to 38 while building; and since their numbers were so limited in comparison with the major navies they were designed like their predecessors laid down by the Continental Congress in the War of Independence to be larger and faster than comparable rates in Europe. The 44-gun frigates, *United States*, *Constitution* and *President*, were some 20 feet longer than the largest British 44s and two or three feet more in the beam;[4] they were also distinguished by a continuous deck above the main gun deck in place of the light gangways connecting foc's'le and quarterdeck in contemporary frigate classes. As commissioned they mounted thirty long 24-pounder guns in the main battery with twenty or twenty-two carronades – closely copied from the British model – throwing 32- to 42-pound balls on the spar deck above, and were undoubtedly the most formidable frigates of their day.

Construction was halted briefly in 1795 after Algiers had been appeased with cash supplemented by a present of four vessels built and armed in American yards, a conventional way of buying off the Barbary states. Subsequently work was resumed on the three most advanced vessels on the stocks, but the French privateer onslaught provoked accelerated construction of all six frigates, and many more warships were ordered. In addition merchant vessels were bought and fitted out as privateers. The crisis also led to the establishment of a Navy Department in Washington with its own state secretary; up to this point the navy had come under the Secretary of War.

The first Secretary of the Navy, Benjamin Stoddert, set about the creation of a disciplined and dedicated officer corps as one of his prime tasks; another was to build a battle squadron in addition to frigates to protect the substantial US investment on the high seas. Congress postponed the programme he proposed for twelve 74-gun ships of the line, and as the small US navy, assisted by swarms of private armed vessels, regained control of American and Caribbean trade routes the 74s were dropped altogether. Soon after the fall of the Directory late in 1799 negotiations with the new French Consulate led by Bonaparte re-established normal relations and in March 1801 Congress cut the navy to a peace establishment of just thirteen frigates, seven of which were to be laid up and only six kept in commission with reduced complements. It was to prove a false economy, particularly perhaps in the resulting loss of good officers; only thirteen captains were retained.[5]

Almost immediately trouble flared on the Barbary coast, from Tripoli this time, and when war between France and Great Britain was resumed after the short Peace of Amiens relations with Britain deteriorated rapidly. As before, the issues concerned the application of the prize laws as Britain responded to Bonaparte's continental system with a rigorous commercial blockade on France, Spain and their remaining colonies; more critical, perhaps, was the continued impressment of British sailors from American ships where they enjoyed higher pay and allegedly better conditions than in the Royal Navy, and fears on the part of British shipping interests that Americans were capturing key international carrying trades.

The alarm was raised in Parliament in 1804, after which the government made an Order in Council annulling the concession in the Jay Treaty allowing small American ships to enter British West Indian ports. Two years later HMS *Leander*, cruising off the approaches to New York, fired a shot across the bows of an inward-bound American schooner in order to stop and search her, then fired two more shots, one of which took off the head of the mate. Expression was given to the rage felt in New York by public exhibition of the mate's headless body at the corner of Wall and Water Streets.[6]

A more glaring example of British naval arrogance followed in June 1807: the US frigate *Chesapeake*, standing out to sea from Norfolk Roads, Virginia, was intercepted ten miles out by HMS *Leopard* and required on the authority of the admiral commanding the Halifax station to submit the men to inspection, since it was believed that some were British deserters. Her commander naturally refused, whereupon the *Leopard* fired a shot across her bows, and followed it with broadsides from point-blank range which killed three men, wounded another eighteen and seriously damaged the masts, shrouds and rigging. Caught entirely unprepared without locks on the guns and decks encumbered with baggage and furniture, the *Chesapeake*'s commander had no option but to submit. He returned to harbour afterwards in an agony of humiliation and rage. The feelings spread the length and breadth of the nation. Although the British government repudiated the *Leopard*'s action, a later British proclamation unequivocally restated the right of Royal Navy captains to reclaim British sailors serving in foreign vessels on the basis that British-born subjects retained their nationality unless formally freed from it by their own country.[7]

Collingwood, commanding the Mediterranean fleet as he had since the battle of Trafalgar, took a more reasoned view of the causes of the deterioration in relations with the United States, writing in a private letter:

> When Englishmen can be recovered in a quiet way, it is well; but when demanded as a National Right, which might be enforced, we should be prepared to do reciprocal justice. In the return I have from only a part of the ships, there are 217 Americans. Would it be judicious to expose ourselves to a call for them? . . . What should we say if the Russians were to man themselves out of English ships?[8]

The third American President, Thomas Jefferson, as concerned as Washington had been to avoid war, attempted to put pressure on Britain with an 'Embargo Act' prohibiting exports from the United States to belligerents – who by this date, December 1807, included practically the whole of Europe – and activated an earlier 'Non-Importation Act' prohibiting the import of specified British manufactures. The bans were denounced by the US financial and commercial community as infringements of individual freedom whose enforcement violated the Fourth Amendment to the Constitution securing the people against 'unreasonable searches and seizures'. In practice they hit American merchants harder than British, and by spring the following year, 1808, New York, which had moved far ahead of her erstwhile rivals, Philadelphia and Boston, to become undoubted commercial and shipping capital of the United States, was experiencing extraordinarily high rates of business failures, bankruptcies and mass unemployment, not least among sailors; some 500 ships lay idle in harbour.[9]

Trade stagnated throughout that year despite widespread evasion of the bans, but it was not until March 1809 when Jefferson stood down as President – electing to follow Washington's example of withdrawing at the end of his second term – that his successor, James Madison, formerly his Secretary of State, had the Embargo Act repealed and replaced with a Non-Intercourse Act prohibiting trade with Britain and France but allowing it with other states. The Non-Intercourse Act expired in 1810 but Madison offered an inducement to both main belligerents that if either agreed to recognize American neutral rights all trade with the other would be prohibited.[10] This was as unrealistic as the embargoes since Great Britain could do as she wished at sea. However, Napoleon promised to repeal his Berlin and Milan decrees and Madison, who had come to believe that British policy was designed to suppress American commerce, proclaimed non-intercourse with Britain unless she, too, repealed her Orders in Council by 2 February 1811; on the same day, 10 November 1810, he notified France that this would 'necessarily lead to war' with Britain unless she stopped molesting US ships.[11]

The British government could not comply without fatally undermining the commercial blockade of France; and since British merchants were unwilling to risk confiscation of their goods by trying to beat Madison's 2 February deadline, British-American trade collapsed. This coincided with the major disruption of Baltic trade caused by French occupation of the north German/Prussian ports, and led to industrial and social crisis in Britain. Opposition politicians called for the repeal of the offending Orders in Council. They were joined by industrialists, radical philosophers and a new school of scientific economists building on the foundations laid by Adam Smith. The arguments were finely balanced: on the one hand the nation could not sustain war against Napoleon and the consequent trade distortions, huge and growing debt, high taxes and social unrest indefinitely; on the other hand, lifting the blockade and concluding a compromise peace would result in exclusion from a continent dominated by Napoleon whose trade and industry would be revitalized by commerce with the United States; how long would this be sustainable?

In May 1812 the Prime Minister, Perceval, was assassinated and a new administration led by Lord Liverpool took the sensible decision to attempt a compromise with the United States. On 16 June the Foreign Secretary, Castlereagh, announced a temporary suspension of the Orders in Council for United States' shipping as a preliminary to negotiations. He had reason to believe that the major causes of dispute could be settled within an overall trade agreement as had been achieved soon after Madison came to power in 1809, only to be repudiated by Perceval's Foreign Secretary, Canning.

It was too late. Madison, ignorant of the change of government in London, had come under pressure from a war party led by politicians from western states who were eager to exploit Britain's isolation in Europe. They hoped to take Canada from her, so concluding the business begun in the War of Independence, and at the same time stop alleged British and Canadian incitement of native Indian tribes against US settlers. Madison had already recommended to Congress that war was the only way to resolve the maritime disputes with Britain, as indeed he had intimated to France earlier; and on 18 June the United States formally declared war against Great Britain.

The representatives of New England states whose merchants were bound up with British trade and capital and whose farms were supplying Lisbon and Cadiz with grain and other provisions for Wellington and the Portuguese and Spanish forces had generally voted against war. The belief that it would inflict serious damage on an economy already stunted by the Embargo and Non-Intercourse Acts was nowhere stronger than in the commercial quarter of New York, where the *Evening Post* carried a protest against Madison's war policy signed by fifty-six leading merchants.[12] Elsewhere in the city and the inland and southern regions of the United States resentment against the overbearing attitudes of the Royal Navy and shared sympathy with the ideals of the French Revolution ensured popular support for the war and for Madison, who was seeking re-election that year.

INSIDE A week of the outbreak of war with America Napoleon invaded Russia.[13] Both events were a consequence of Britain's control of sea routes. In the American case the link may have been opportunistic since war was against all that young republic's economic interests, but Napoleon's attack on Russia was a direct result of the leakage of British goods into the continent via the Baltic, and specifically of the tsar's failure to uphold the continental blockade. The attempt to impose a blockade was, in turn, the result of French naval failure, as exemplified at Boulogne, the Nile and Trafalgar.

However, the potentially grave effects for British commerce and industry of the American war superimposed on the continental blockade were immediately offset by Napoleon's Russian offensive. As early as July Saumarez was notified that peace had been signed by British, Russian and Swedish plenipotentiaries and the Admiralty instructed him that in view of the lack of enemies he might withdraw the greater number of his ships of the line from the Baltic 'and apply them to the blockade of Zealand [Denmark] where they will be of use to protect your convoys through the Belt'.[14] Meanwhile, trade was growing again after the crisis year, 1811: exports and re-exports through the Baltic increased from £2.3 million to a total for 1812 of £5.4 million – nowhere near the peak years of 1809 and 1810, yet showing a rising trend which would take British exports to northern Europe to a record value of £22.9 million in 1814.[15]

While Napoleon's strike east was achieving the reverse of its object of stopping up British trade, it had equally damaging effects on the French campaign at the other end of the empire in the Spanish peninsula, drawing off the better troops and leaving the marshals in command of separated armies without strategic drive or the unified direction of the Emperor. In addition large French forces were tied up guarding lines of communication against the Spanish guerrillas, and the mobility of each army was compromised by the French practice of living off the country. Wellington, who organized a network of supply depots stocked by sea and river transport, was able to outmanoeuvre his opponents, seize key fortresses on the Spanish-Portuguese border, Ciudad Rodrigo and Badajoz, and prevent the junction of the armies opposing him; thence he advanced into Spain and in July won a decisive victory at Salamanca over the Army of Portugal, now under Marshal Auguste Marmont. Afterwards he marched on Madrid, largely for moral and political effect. King Joseph retired from the capital with the Army of the Centre and on 12 August Wellington rode in, greeted for miles outside by crowds bringing laurel branches and flowers, wine, bread, grapes and other gifts, strewing the road before him with palm leaves and joining his men to march with them arm in arm. The scenes of adulation inside the city were even more tumultuous and extravagant.

It could only be a token conquest: with the more numerous French forces goaded at last into combining against him, he made a sally north-ward against their communications, then complying with his dictum that the real test of a general was 'to know when to retreat, and to dare to do it',[16] retired before superior numbers to Ciudad Rodrigo. Although back on the Portuguese border where he had started that year, the 1812 campaign decided the fate of the French in the peninsula: by concen-trating against him they had abandoned the greater part of Spain to the *guerrilleros*, and they were never to recover it.

At the same time the latest expression of the Grande Armée perished in the snows of Russia. Gathered by Napoleon from every part of Europe including Austria and Prussia, it had numbered over 450,000 at the start, the mightiest force ever assembled on the continent and endowed with the aura of the latest Caesar. The tsar's commander, Mikhail Kutuzov, had retired before it like Wellington in Portugal, leaving burnt fields and deserted villages. Napoleon had pursued with the image ever before him of the decisive battle that would enable him as so many times in the past to dictate terms to a broken enemy; but against the tsar's new strategy of withdrawal the very qualities that had given him his victories – the ability to make continuous forced marches and live off the enemy countryside – turned against him. He had inherited these methods and massed conscript armies from the Revolution and had made them his tool of conquest; now they proved his downfall. He was beaten in the advance. He lost 100,000 men to sickness and desertion before he reached Smolensk, rather over half the distance to Moscow.[17] The Russian army continued to retire eastward. When finally Kutuzov stood and faced him at Borodino Napoleon's effective strength had fallen to 130,000; by the end of that day he had less than 100,000 and the Russians had again withdrawn. Wellington, studying the campaign afterwards, found significance in the losses of men and some 10,000 horses sustained during the first marches into Russia in June and early July, and was sceptical of the story that they were caused by a storm of rain:

> those who know what an army is well know that a storm of rain in summer . . . does not destroy the horses of an army. That which does destroy them, that which renders those who survive nearly unfit for service throughout the campaign, and incapable of bearing the hardship of the winter, is hard work, forced marches, no corn or dry fodder at the period at which the green corn is on the ground, and is invariably eaten by the horses of the army. It is the period of the year at which of all others a commander who cares for his army will avoid enterprises the execution of which require forced marches or the hard work of the horses.
>
> In like manner, storms of rain do not destroy soldiers of the infantry . . . but forced marches on roads destroyed by storms of rain, through a country unprovided with shelter, and without provisions, do destroy soldiers, as every one left behind is without resource, is exposed, unsheltered and starving . . . and he must perish.[18]

Wellington observed that during the entire Russian campaign Napoleon's troops never received a ration that was not procured *à la maraude*, by forcing inhabitants to give up provisions without payment, and not only provisions; 'it is not astonishing', he concluded, 'that officers and soldiers so employed should become habitual plunderers.'

After Borodino Kutuzov left Moscow undefended. Napoleon rode in on 15 September to find the city practically deserted. Despite his profligate disregard of his men and horses on the march, he was now in a commanding situation. In the words of Leo Tolstoy only the simplest steps were necessary to retain it: 'not to allow the troops to loot; to prepare winter clothing – of which there was sufficient in Moscow for the whole army, and methodically to collect provisions, of which (according to the French historians) there were enough in Moscow to supply the whole army for six months'.[19]

Instead Napoleon decreed that detachments should enter Moscow in turn *à la maraude* for provisions. As they did so, discipline collapsed. And the soldiers, smoking their pipes or cooking within or outside the deserted timber houses of the enemy, caused fires in different quarters; fanned by strong winds these coalesced in a conflagration which gutted the city, sparing only the Kremlin. Napoleon's attempts to re-establish discipline were fruitless; even his own picked guards ran amok, pillaging and abusing or assaulting sentries placed over supplies gathered for the troops. As Tolstoy described it, the army, 'like a herd of cattle run wild and trampling underfoot the provender which might have saved it from starvation, disintegrated and perished with each additional day it remained in Moscow'.[20] The tsar, meanwhile, refused to treat with Napoleon. Finally in late October as the first snow fell, Napoleon could see nothing to do but order the retreat. As Tolstoy saw it: 'The members of what had once been an army – Napoleon himself and his soldiers – fled without knowing whither, each concerned only to escape from this position, of the hopelessness of which they were all more or less vaguely conscious.'[21]

Each took his plunder with him, not least Napoleon. Baggage trains clogged the road. Then partisan attacks began; detachments of Kutuzov's army, Cossack cavalry, peasants and landowners formed themselves into irregular bands which stalked the enemy column, laying ambush, attacking vulnerable units as they slept, cutting down stragglers, like the *guerrilleros* in Spain the expression of a nation rising to expel the alien invader. The Russian winter played its part, setting in early. Yet the prime cause of destruction of what had been the Grande Armée was internal: specifically its lack of an organized method of supply, a direct result of the French military practice of living off enemy land. Wellington was to sum it up: 'The system of the French army, then, was the cause of its irregularities, disorders and misfortunes; and of its loss.'[22]

Of over 450,000 men at the start, barely 25,000 returned from Russia; of these only some 10,000 were fit for service.

Napoleon left the pitiful survivors and rode in haste to Paris to quell another plot to oust him. But he could not disguise the catastrophe that had overtaken him. The spell of invincibility was broken. Throughout Europe the simmering spirit of revolt against his exactions in money and men and the restrictions placed on trade, nourished by British secret service funds, broke out in open demonstrations against his rule. Early in 1813 Prussia allied with Russia, and in March the two sovereigns jointly summoned all Germany to rise against him. Of the great powers, only Austria hesitated to commit. Talleyrand advised negotiation while there was still something to negotiate with. Instead, in the conviction that his authority rested on military might, Napoleon conscripted half a million more young men, withdrew troops from garrisons, recalled units of the Imperial Guard and veterans from regiments in Spain to create another Grande Armée in place of the one he had lost, and pushed forward into Germany. When Austria attempted to mediate a settlement in June, Napoleon told Prince Metternich, 'Your sovereigns get beaten twenty times, and yet return to their capitals. I cannot. For I rose to power through the camp.'[23] He was incapable of separating the interests and glory of France from those of his own person.

Lord Liverpool's government, meanwhile, seized the opportunity presented as if by miracle from the debacle in Russia, by subsidizing states which put troops into the field against France and promising Austria funds if she would join the alliance against Napoleon. Wellington was supplied with bullion for his army's expenses and reinforced with practically all the regular troops hitherto held at home against the threat of invasion – leaving only sufficient to quell civil disturbances. French forces in the peninsula had been thinned by Napoleon's levies for the Grande Armée and much reduced in age and quality; they were again dispersed over hundreds of miles and large numbers were engaged against the *guerrilleros* so that of a total of 200,000 in Spain the main force opposing Wellington under King Joseph and Marshal Jean Baptiste Jourdan mustered less than 60,000. Wellington's reinforcements brought his strength up to 52,000 British troops and 29,000 Portuguese trained by his own officers. He was supremely optimistic. During the winter he had prepared plans in the utmost secrecy to throw Joseph off balance by advancing north through Portugal into Spain, and his engineers and supply officers had reconnoitred routes through the mountainous country north of the Douro, supposedly impassable for an army. In February he had asked for a siege train to be sent to him at Corunna rather than Lisbon, from whence he could trans-ship the guns eastwards to ports on the Spanish Biscay coast.

He began his campaign in late May after rains had raised green forage for his horses, showing his confidence as he crossed the border into Spain with a rare flourish, sweeping off his hat and waving it behind him: 'Farewell Portugal! I shall never see you again!' He never did. His advance with guns and limbers manhandled over the rugged terrain of the northern border country turned Joseph's flank, forcing him to retire eastwards. Wellington followed him along the plain of the Douro and its tributary the Pisuerga before again striking north through mountainous country to outflank him – and by the same movement shortening the distance to a new supply depot he had had established at the port of Santander.

Joseph halted at the little town of Vitória at a junction of roads in the foothills of the Pyrenees, and there on 27 June Wellington fell on him, forcing him to retreat in confusion, leaving behind his guns, military stores, 2,000 prisoners and the royal baggage train filled with Joseph's Spanish booty and all the appurtenances of the court – pictures, books, state papers, boxes of Spanish dollars, silks, uniforms. Wellington was unable to pursue as his troops abandoned themselves to an orgy of looting – occasion of his notorious despatch describing them as 'the scum of the earth' and stating that it was 'impossible to command a British army'.[24]

Vitória was nonetheless decisive, and not simply in the peninsula. Joseph retreated with his army across the Pyrenees and shortly after news of his ejection from Spain reached the European capitals Austria agreed to join what is known as the Fourth Coalition against France. Napoleon had by this time fought two successful but not conclusive battles in Saxony with his new army against the Russians and the Prussians successively and had then refused terms proposed by Austria which would have removed his empire in central Europe – the occasion of his comments about his rise to power through the camp. Now, with Austria mobilizing against him and German detachments deserting the Grande Armée to join the Allies, he faced a potentially overwhelming concentration of forces under the Tsar, the Emperor of Austria, the King of Prussia and Crown Prince Bernadotte of Sweden, accompanied by volunteers of all nationalities including French royalists. They caught him outside Leipzig in October, squeezed his force into an ever tighter perimeter to the east of the town and on the 18th drove him into the outskirts. He escaped early the following morning from what is known as 'the Battle of the Nations' over the bridge across the river Elster, and retired westwards, losing men to disease, desertion and attrition as he had on the retreat from Moscow. When he crossed the Rhine into France similarly few were still with him.

He had lost two great armies in successive campaigns. Without conquests his whole system of paying for war had collapsed; operations in Spain, Russia and Germany had instead bled his treasury. His finances were again in ruins. The interest rates for French government borrowing had leaped to 10 per cent.[25] The French people had lost heart for war and the constant drain of young men for the armies, and were only held in submission by the police system he had established. He was, in Talleyrand's words, finished.[26] The only question was who and what kind of government should succeed him.

Napoleon consulted his own genius and did what he had always done: rejecting another generous peace proposal offering him the natural borders of France, the Rhine, the Alps, the Pyrenees, he raised more recruits, siphoned off more men from existing forces, including the former Army of Spain, now under Marshal Soult, and when the Allied armies invaded France in early 1814, marched against them. He had initial successes over separated columns in a campaign which has been judged the most technically brilliant of his career; yet in the wider strategic and political context it was the last throw of a gambler; he failed to prevent the Allies joining hands and occupying Paris, while in the south Wellington, having crossed the Pyrenees into Gascony, 'liberated' the merchant capital of Bordeaux, which immediately declared for a Bourbon restoration. Next, Wellington manoeuvred Soult's depleted army eastwards into Languedoc and finally on 10 and 11 April drove him from the fortress city of Toulouse. Entering the city next day, Wellington was greeted with as much fervour in the streets, where busts of Napoleon and imperial emblems were being destroyed, as if he had delivered it from foreign occupation.

At 5 that afternoon a British officer galloped in with despatches from Bordeaux: Napoleon had abdicated on the 6th. 'Ay,' Wellington replied, ''tis time indeed. You don't say so, upon my honour. Hurrah!' and the officer was treated to the sight of his unflappable chief spinning round on his heel, snapping his fingers.[27] Later that evening at a dinner attended by leading citizens of the city, and by Spanish, Portuguese,

French and British officers, Wellington proposed a toast to Louis XVIII. Directly afterwards General Miguel de Alava, who commanded Spanish troops attached to Wellington's army, stood and proposed his health, 'Lord Wellington, *Liberador d'Espana!*'

Immediately others were on their feet crying, '*Liberador de Portugal!*' '*Libérateur de la France!*' '*Libérateur de l'Europe!*' In the pandemonium of cheering that ensued for several minutes witnesses thought they detected Wellington's clear eyes cloud momentarily with emotion.[28]

Napoleon had not abdicated voluntarily. He had been manoeuvred off his throne in the end by Talleyrand, who had used his imperial position as Vice Grand Elector to preside over the minority of members of the Emperor's formerly subservient Senate still in Paris. They had elected him head of a provisional government, and decreed Napoleon deposed. There were numerous claimants for the vacant crown and there were proponents of a regency for Napoleon's infant son. Fearing a continuation of Bonapartism under another name, Talleyrand used the influence he had won with Tsar Alexander since his covert and treasonable meetings with him over five years before to block a regency and convince the tsar and the other Allied monarchs in Paris that the new order in Europe must be based on legitimacy – the restoration of the Bourbon line. He then had a Bill prepared for a constitutional monarchy almost identical to that of 1791 but with two elected chambers instead of one: this called in the name of the French people for the self-styled Louis XVIII, brother of the last King of France, to assume the throne 'and after him the other members of the House of Bourbon in the old order'.[29] It was formally enacted on 6 April.

Napoleon was at Fontainebleau then with the remnant of his army preparing to retire behind the Loire to rally troops from the south and continue the fight; his orders, made out with the usual detail, had been issued. His marshals were no longer prepared to follow him, though. They had no desire for civil war and, recognizing the hopeless situation, felt themselves released from their oath of allegiance by the Senate decree. Already in the early hours of that morning countermanding orders had gone out to the corps' commanders. Napoleon summoned them for a final appeal to their loyalty. It was met with silence. At last he, too, saw it was over and wrote a brief note renouncing for himself and his heirs the thrones of France and Italy, concluding that there was no sacrifice, 'not even that of his life, which he would not make in the interests of his country'.[30] The following day, it is believed, he took poison;

but the potion, apparently prepared during the retreat from Moscow for use in case he was captured by partisans, had lost its power. He was merely taken ill.[31]

The Allies were generous to a fault, granting him the island of Elba off Tuscany as a sovereign principality, an annual income of two million francs to be provided by France – which the French government proved unwilling to pay – and allowed him to retain the title Emperor.

He was, of course, to escape from exile the following spring for a final effort to impose his genius on Europe. The effort was doomed, for the decision of April 1814 was the product not of emperors and armies campaigning across the continent so much as innumerable sailors harnessing the winds of the world, and merchants, factory owners and workers, entrepreneurs, inventors, canal builders, engineers, financiers, stockjobbers and clerks, each following his own occupation but in sum drawing onwards the commercial-industrial juggernaut Britain had become. The trade figures reveal it. In 1793 imports had stood at an official value of £19.3 million, exports and re-exports at £20.4 million; by 1814 they had grown to £80.8 million and £70.3 million respectively, increases over the twenty years of almost unbroken war of 350 to 400 per cent.

The most spectacular advance had been in exports and re-exports to the continent through northern Europe, which had risen from £2.3 million in the slump year, 1811, to £22.9 million.[32]

Wellington was raised to a dukedom for his triumphant conclusion to the peninsular campaign inside southern France – no lesser honour would have been appropriate – but Admiral Sir James de Saumarez whose operational skill, resolution and extraordinary diplomatic tact had held the Baltic open for trade over most of the same period went unrewarded with a peerage until 1831 and is remembered now, if at all, chiefly as Nelson's second in command at the Nile. The campaigns of both commanders at either end of Napoleon's empire demonstrate the power of the naval ascendancy which underwrote Britain's commercial strength. From the beginning Wellington based his campaign in Portugal on seaborne supplies which were denied the enemy; when he took the offensive in Spain he had the egregious Commodore Sir Home Popham ranging the Spanish Biscay coast with a squadron headed by two of the line supplying the *guerrilleros* who were harassing the French, and establishing supply ports for his own army as he advanced north and eastwards. The money he needed to take his campaign over the Pyrenees into the south of France came by sea.

It was a remarkable operation, conducted by the brothers Rothschild. The family which was to have an incalculable influence on the course of nineteenth-century capitalism originated in Frankfurt, a commercial hub on the river Main close to its junction with the Rhine in the small German state of Hesse Kassel. Before the Revolutionary war the father of the dynasty, Mayer Amschel Rothschild, had been a dealer in coins and antiques, confined as a Jew to the segregated Jewish quarter of the city, yet with an entrée to the court through his coin business. With the outbreak of war he seized opportunities to provision Allied armies operating in the region and import the British textiles which were in great demand in Germany. The profits enabled him to extend his operations into banking. By the turn of the century he had become one of the richest Jews in Frankfurt.[33]

His wife had borne nineteen children; ten had survived; five were male, to whom alone, as they grew up, Mayer Amschel would entrust the family business operations. They were Amschel, born in 1773, Salomon, Nathan, Carl and Jakob or James, the youngest born in 1791. In 1799 he sent the twenty-two-year-old Nathan to Manchester to act as his agent for British textiles. Nathan had inherited his father's acute eye for profit margins, single-mindedness and bold, or with suppliers often harsh, self-assurance. Within seven years he had extended his client base through Germany and Switzerland and augmented his capital and his influence within the British Jewish community by marriage to the daughter of a leading London merchant, Levi Cohen. In 1811 he moved to London and set up on his own account as N. M. Rothschild at 2 New Court, St Swithin's Lane, in the City. His business in textile exports to the continent was by this time of necessity a smuggling operation using neutral-registered ships and false papers. He also smuggled gold to his younger brother James, in France, a breach of the continental system to which Napoleon turned a blind eye, believing his Treasury advisers who told him that England was economically weakened by the export of bullion.

The latest Rothschild biographer, Niall Ferguson, suggests that it was probably the scale of Nathan's bullion purchases in London that alerted the Commissary-in-Chief of the British army, Charles Herries, to his activities.[34] At all events, when in 1813 Wellington warned the government that his troops were unfed and unpaid and he would not take them, particularly his Spanish contingent, across the Pyrenees into France unless he received money – for 'without pay and food they must plunder; and if they plunder they will ruin us all' – Herries turned to Nathan, and in January

1814 gave him the task of financing the move into France. For this purpose Nathan called on his brothers on the continent to buy up bills of exchange on London, convert them into gold coins and deliver the gold to ships in the Dutch port of Helvoetsluys which were chartered by Herries to take them to the small Biscay harbour of Saint-Jean de Luz south of Biarritz, practically on the Franco-Spanish border. Nathan thus used continental bullion to finance the war against Napoleon.[35] Despite serious shortages of gold coins across the Channel, the task was accomplished efficiently. Impressed, Herries remarked to a colleague that although Rothschild was a Jew, 'we place a good deal of confidence in him'.[36]

The bullion shipments were a decisive factor in Wellington's invasion of France. They were equally decisive for the Rothschilds. They brought Nathan into personal relationships with Herries, British Treasury ministers and the Prime Minister, Lord Liverpool, and led to further commissions to transmit British subsidies to her continental allies. In 1815 Lord Liverpool told Castlereagh: 'I do not know what we should have done without him [Rothschild] last year.'[37]

While Wellington's spectacular campaigns in the peninsula leading to the invasion of France had weakened the French empire and exposed its vulnerability, it was Saumarez, prising open the northern end of the continental blockade, who had provoked Napoleon into occupying and intensifying repression on the north German and Prussian coast, raising the spirit of rebellion against him until finally Napoleon had been driven to his fatal adventure in Russia.

Yet in the end Britain had brought the war to a conclusion through the financial and diplomatic power riding on commercial strength. In the vital years of 1813 and 1814 she paid over £15 million in subsidies to keep the armies of the continental Allies in the field, and a further £5 million in subsidies was voted the following year when Napoleon escaped from exile in Elba.[38] Over the whole period of the war she paid some £60 million to subsidize her Allies. She was able to do this on a far smaller population base than France because of mounting customs revenues from increased trade and higher taxes on the wealthy and middling classes who benefited from commercial prosperity; not least of these was an effective version of Pitt's income tax, reintroduced on the resumption of war after the Peace of Amiens, which provided nearly a third of the additional tax revenue needed to defeat Napoleon.[39]

Customs and tax revenues were never entirely sufficient and it was ultimately the willingness of successive governments to add millions each year to the national debt, together with the credit won by First Lords of the Treasury over the previous century which kept the interest on this mounting borrowing under 6 per cent, only a point or so above peace rates,[40] that provided the margin for victory. Thus Pitt and his heirs offloaded a substantial proportion of the costs of preserving the British state on to future generations.

It was financial and naval strength founded on credit which allowed Britain to take the lead in successive coalitions against Revolutionary and Napoleonic France. Finally Pitt's disciple, Castlereagh, as Foreign Secretary in Lord Liverpool's government, left London for Allied head-quarters on the continent to hold the members of the fourth coalition together and insist there would be no peace in Europe until Napoleon was defeated. The hidden hand of the British government was equally persuasive: the lavish sums of secret service money dispensed by succes-sive Foreign Secretaries to fund anti-Republican resistance within France and raise insurrection throughout Napoleonic Europe contrib-uted greatly to the destabilization and final fragmentation of the French empire. Napoleon considered that it was not Castlereagh but one of the leading agents of the secret diplomatic network funded from London, the Corsican Carl André Pozzo di Borgo, who brought about his final downfall by persuading Tsar Alexander to march on Paris in 1814, and inducing Bernadotte to join him.[41]

Yet the downfall of Revolutionary and Napoleonic France cannot be considered in isolation as the result of particular characters and groups acting and reacting in the unusual circumstances of a revolutionary age, because it was in most respects a recapitulation in the most extravagant and costly form of all Anglo-French wars since the time of Louis XIV, France seeking military aggrandizement on the continent and an over-seas trading empire, Great Britain trumping her at sea and using the pro-ceeds of trade to subsidize continental armies against her. The rules were well established. The forces released by the Revolution were in a sense the herald of a darker age of whole nations making war rather than kings and armies, but in another sense they were the final violent expression of France's historic frustration in the face of British maritime supremacy, particularly under the elder Pitt in the mid-century Seven Years War which deprived France of her stake in north America and much of India.

Napoleon was not simply the military genius his admirers revere; he was heir both to the Revolutionary tradition of the nation in arms and to France's longer martial past; as such he personified a century of deliberation on ways of overcoming the maritime enemy. Genius or gambler, his defeat was conclusive proof that France had lost the century-long struggle; and that beneath the surface of contingent events, historic forces had favoured trade and sound finance over territorial conquest as a means of amassing wealth – as ever the sinews of war.

14

Lake Erie and Plattsburg Bay, 1813–1814

MEANWHILE THERE WAS the American war. For Great Britain it was a small matter compared with the life or death struggle against Napoleon; to Madison and the war party it had become a major predicament. The early attempts to invade Canada from the Great Lakes had ended in fiasco. The political calculation that Britain was isolated and vulnerable had been upset almost from the start; and with Napoleon's abdication the enormous strength of the Royal Navy had become available to throttle the young republic. A blockade stretching from New England to New Orleans had closed down even coastal trade; wharves and harbours the length of the land were occupied by idle ships. In the great port cities businesses had failed, stores closed, food prices escalated and unemployment and poverty were widespread.

In addition the Federal government had difficulty borrowing to pay for the war since the Bank of the United States, the central bank chartered by Congress in 1791 on the lines of the Bank of England to fund the debt from the War of Independence, issue notes and ensure a stable currency, had performed so successfully in the latter role it had attracted criticism from private state banks for restricting credit, and thus venture capital, in the rapidly expanding pre-war economy, also for encroaching on individual states' rights; when its charter expired in 1811 it was not renewed. The government had been obliged to borrow from private lenders, yet this was not easy since so many in the merchant and financial class were opposed to the war. Finally two immigrants, the German-born John Jacob Astor, who had amassed a fortune from the fur trade and New York property, and the French-born Philadelphian Stephen Girard, who had built a shipping empire, bought the US government bonds wholesale at a discounted price and sold them to colleagues at home and in Europe. By 1814 the government again desperately needed funds and the syndicate agreed to a further loan provided a new national bank were created to stabilize the economy. The government acquiesced. In 1816 the Bank of the United States would be reconstituted.

From the American perspective, practically the only good news to come from the war had been provided by the US Navy; and it had no connection with Congress or government, whose naval preparations had been perverse or absent. Since 1803 they had ordered well over 200 mostly very small gunboats for harbour and coast defence without, it appears, any strategic or tactical ideas for their employment.[1] Only six sea-going vessels – four gun brigs and two 14-gun schooners – had been built, or in one case bought; and after 1808 the striving for economy had been such that, despite increasing tension with Great Britain on the high seas, no vessels of any kind had been ordered and the existing sea-going navy had been allowed to fall into disrepair. By 1812, of the fine frigates laid down in response to the Barbary corsairs, two were so rotten they were beyond repair, three needed extensive repairs, one was refitting and only two were fully serviceable. The Navy Department was so pessimistic it was planned, in case of war, to strip down all frigates for use as floating harbour defence batteries and training depots for gunboat service, and rely largely on privateers to take the offensive by attacking British trade.[2]

The senior captains themselves made representations to Madison for an offensive strategy, and on news of the outbreak of war the only fully manned squadron of three frigates – one much in need of repair – and two 18-gun brigs put to sea on the initiative of Commodore John Rodgers commanding the 44-gun *President*. His aim was to hunt a British convoy reported to have sailed from Jamaica on 20 May. Two days out he came upon the lone British frigate, *Belvidera*. Her captain, Richard Byron, did not know of the American declaration but was aware of the delicacy of the situation, and when Rodgers failed to answer his signals, bore away. Rodgers followed, his large frigate drawing away from the rest of his squadron and gaining appreciably on Byron. By late afternoon he was within long gun range and opened with his bow chasers. The shots were extraordinarily accurate, two entering Byron's cabin in the stern and one the gunroom below. Byron returned fire equally accurately, but the turning point came when one of the American bow chasers exploded, killing or wounding its crew, injuring Rodgers who was cheering them on, and blowing away part of the foc's'le and the maindeck below. Rodgers ordered the helm over to bring the broadside to bear, then came round to open the other broadside, and continued the tactic so long that Byron, steering a straight course, was able to draw away from him and eventually escape.

The next round also went to the Royal Navy: on 16 July a British frigate squadron led by Captain Philip Broke (pronounced Brooke) in the *Shannon*, searching for Rodgers off New York, captured the US brig of war *Nautilus*. It was to be the last British success for some time. That evening Commodore Isaac Hull in the 44-gun *Constitution*, also looking for Rodgers after leaving the Chesapeake in haste on his own initiative to beat the anticipated blockade, sighted Broke's squadron off the New Jersey coast and closed, hoping it was Rodgers. At first light the following morning he realized his mistake, put about and ran. Broke chased, and as the wind died had all the squadron's boats lowered to tow the *Shannon*. Hull replied by joining all his available hawsers into two lines, each nearly a mile long, bending an anchor to each and rowing the anchors out ahead, dropping them alternately and heaving in to 'kedge' the ship along. It was gruelling and exacting work but executed so faultlessly that the big frigate drew away from the little flotilla of boats towing the *Shannon*, but not so far they lost her. Next morning a breeze got up and the chase continued under sail, both sides using all their art, heaving buckets of water aloft to wet the canvas to make it stretch and hold the wind better, balancing the sails to eliminate so far as possible rudder movements, trying different combinations of sails and different points of sailing. Still the *Constitution* with her longer waterline walked away, and next morning she was gone. It was a tribute as much to earlier American naval policy and design and to her Boston master builder as to Hull and his crew, superbly as they had sailed her.

Broke, who had been dismissive of the American service, had changed his view, writing to his wife on 21 July: 'I am sent in pursuit of an active and artful enemy, who will, if he can, do vast mischief to our trade, and perhaps (God forbid) evade after all the vengeance we intend to wreak on him.'[3] The Americans did do vast mischief in the early months as fishing schooners, pilot boats and all types of private vessels hastily armed and provisioned as privateers got to sea and played havoc with British trade, particularly in the West Indies. Larger craft mounting up to fourteen guns cruised further afield, even for a while disrupting

Wellington's supply shipping to the peninsula. But it was the US Navy which captured public imagination with a series of triumphs over Royal Navy ships in single combat.

First, on 19 August, was a meeting between the *Constitution* and the *Guerrier* of Broke's squadron. Isaac Hull had been attacking British trade off Newfoundland when he learned that Broke had appeared in the vicinity, and he made off southwards, by chance falling in with the lone *Guerrier* which Broke had detached to Halifax for repairs. Hull closed from to windward. Captain Dacres of the *Guerrier*, feeling fortune had chosen him as the first to thrash a Yankee in single combat, backed his main topsail to await him, issued the men a ration of grog and allowed eight Americans in the crew to go below out of the coming fight. His confidence was natural. Against French and Spanish ships British naval officers had come to anticipate victory as of right even if the odds were against them. As a result some had slipped from older standards of preparation for battle, or paid more attention to prettifying their ships than to gun drill; Dacres belonged to the former category. Besides the unavoidable repairs to be made in Halifax, the breeching ropes of several cannon were perished, their fittings rusty and the timber they passed through rotten; and it is probable the powder was damp.

If her batteries had been in immaculate condition and her guns' crews drilled to perfection, the *Guerrier* would still have been no match for Hull's ship. Both were rated frigates, yet the *Constitution* was in a superior class, 17 feet longer on the waterline, mounting fifteen 32-pounder long guns and twelve carronades 32-pounder on each broadside against the *Guerrier*'s fourteen 28-pounder long guns and eight carronades, an advantage in weight of shot of almost three to two. She had nearly double the men, 463 against 244 at quarters in the British ship, and all her masts and timbers were heavier; below her maindeck gun ports her sides were as thick as those of a British 74.[4]

After preliminary manoeuvring the *Constitution*'s weight of metal and the training of her guns' crews began to tell. The *Guerrier*'s mizzen mast fell over her starboard quarter, slewing her bows round, and Hull forged across ahead and raked from so close that the *Guerrier*'s bowsprit caught in his mizzen rigging, locking the two ships together. Boarders called away on both sides were unable to cross as a steep swell was lifting and dropping the vessels erratically. A musketry duel ensued until the American was swung clear by the wind, when the *Guerrier*'s remaining masts crashed over the side, leaving her unmanageable. She had 15 men killed, 63 wounded, many critically, and several of her guns were unshipped. Hull had only seven dead and seven seriously wounded, indicating deplorable British gunnery. He stood away to repair his rigging which had suffered from so many shot flying high, then headed back to take up a raking position across the *Guerrier*'s bows. Dacres called his officers for a brief council, at which it was decided to strike the colours. There was no alternative save useless slaughter.

The strategic and material results of the action were negligible. The *Guerrier* was so battered she was not worth repairing and commissioning in the US Navy, while the Royal Navy had 265 frigates, 168 of them in commission, and the loss of one was scarcely felt. Yet the moral effect was extraordinary. In America Hull and his ship's company became heroes, having accomplished what had eluded every European navy; they had lowered the arrogant Union flag in supposedly equal contest. British reaction was equally extreme and only explicable in the context of a general faith in the invincibility of the Royal Navy. The *Naval Chronicle* summed it up: 'An English frigate rated 38 guns should undoubtedly, barring extraordinary accidents, cope successfully with a 44-gun ship of any other nation.'[5]

Rodgers, meanwhile, in his pursuit of the West Indian convoy, picked up seven prizes, a meagre return for the force and effort deployed, and evading Broke, returned to Boston, there taking the advice of his junior captains to break the squadron into three detachments to hunt separately. In September Broke was superseded by Admiral Sir John Borlase Warren as commander-in-chief of a combined Halifax and West Indies station. Sir John had made his name and a huge fortune in command of a frigate squadron in the Revolutionary war, taking a record haul of 220 prizes during the single year 1795. He came with two 74s and plenipotentiary powers to make peace with Madison's government or with any willing state government. Amongst the New England merchant community the talk was of an armistice; one principal part of Warren's task was to conciliate and attempt to split the north-eastern states from Washington.

In October two more single-ship contests went to the Americans: on the 18th the sloop of war *Wasp* overpowered HMS *Frolic* of similar size and armament escorting a homeward-bound West Indian convoy. The *Wasp*'s superiority in gunnery was marked; she only lost 10 killed and wounded to the *Frolic*'s 58, over half her complement. Again the action had no strategic or material consequences since the *Frolic* saved her convoy and she and the *Wasp* were shortly retaken by a British 74.

A week later the American 44-gun frigate class again proved its supremacy. The *United States* under Captain Stephen Decatur chanced upon HMS *Macedonian* in the Atlantic after she had parted from an East India convoy. Against the American's broadside of fifteen long 24-pounders and eight carronades 42-pounder, the British frigate mounted fourteen 18-pounders and nine carronades 32-pounder, once again an inferiority in weight of shot of roughly two to three; there was a similar disparity in the complements – 290 to 478 men – and in the thickness of spars and timbers.[6]

Besides this Decatur's First Lieutenant, William H. Allen, had drilled the men at the great guns and small arms to high standards of speed and accuracy, whereas the British guns' crews had never been practised at a mark and there was no organization for battle. The captain, John Carden, was a disciplinarian and experienced fighting sailor, yet showed more concern for his band of French, German and Italian musicians and the smart turnout of his men, whom he paraded in different coloured costumes according to weather or whim, than for the fighting readiness of his ship, such was the effect of years of superiority on many Royal Navy officers. Unlike the unfortunate Dacres of the *Guerrier* Carden refused to excuse the Americans in his crew from fighting their fellow countrymen, threatening their spokesman with a pistol seized from the belt of a nearby boarder when ordering him to his action station on pain of death.[7]

News of the loss of the *Guerrier* and *Frolic* had not reached the *Macedonian*, and the men, contemptuous of the American service, were confident of victory. However, Carden was aware of the *United States'* powerful batteries since he had been aboard her as Decatur's guest the previous year in Norfolk, Virginia, and it was no doubt on account of this knowledge that he manoeuvred for position rather than sailing straight for the enemy in the manner of most British captains against European opponents. This played into Decatur's long suit as his heavier shot had a flatter trajectory and was consequently more effective at medium to long range. In this case it was not only more effective, but more rapid. Witnesses estimated that the American guns fired twice for every time the British fired. Realizing his mistake, Carden pointed his ship towards the *United States* in an attempt to close the range quickly, in so doing throwing his broadside guns out of bearing, while the American shot continued to pour in. A survivor from the British gun deck wrote:

It was like some awfully tremendous thunder storm whose deafening roar is attended by incessant streaks of lightning, carrying death in every flash and strewing the ground with the victims of its wrath . . . the scene was rendered more horrible by the presence of torrents of blood which dyed our decks.[8]

Still Carden closed. Coming within range of the American 42-pounder carronades the carnage and slaughter increased. Few of the *Macedonian*'s carronades were still on their mountings to reply, while the mizzen had fallen forward into the main top, the main yard and main topsail had been shot away and the rigging was cut to pieces. As a desperate resort, Carden had the foresail set to swing the bows towards the American to board her; even as the canvas filled a shot carried away the fore sheet and the frigate slowly turned back into the wind. The first lieutenant, a sadist who delighted in flogging, now showed his better side, rallying the surviving guns' crews amidst the barrage of round shot and grape. Finally the foremast and main topmast fell, and Decatur ceased firing and stood off to repair damage to his rigging. His frigate's hull was barely marked and casualties were only 12 killed and wounded against 36 killed and 68 wounded in the *Macedonian*. When he returned Carden had the colours struck against the pleas of the first lieutenant who was raving defiance to all Americans and calling for a renewal of the fight and sinking the ship alongside the enemy.

After news of this latest humiliation reached London, the Admiralty issued an order forbidding British 18-pounder frigates to engage US 24-pounder frigates in single combat. However, the *Naval Chronicle* printed a remarkable prophecy under the title 'The Retort Courteous':

> And as the War they did provoke,
> We'll pay them with our cannon.
> The first to do it will be Broke
> In his gallant ship, the *Shannon*.[9]

Broke was indeed burning for revenge: 'now the unlucky events of the *Guerrier*'s and *Frolic*'s actions bind us all to the service till we have restored the splendour of our flag,'[10] he had written to his wife before news of this latest defeat reached Halifax. More than that, he was not a commander who had fallen for the fetish of outward show. Everything in the *Shannon* was functional, especially the arrangements for fighting the batteries. He was a gunnery perfectionist. The powder in the magazines below the waterline was turned frequently and a machine pumped dry air in whenever the weather was fine. The timber quoins with which the cannon were elevated and the beds on which they ran were marked with deep scores so that gunlayers could feel the settings by touch at night or in thick smoke. The central score was for horizontal fire at point-blank range; on either side were scores for laying the gun horizontally when firing to windward or to leeward with the ship under a heavy press of sail as in chase. The gun barrels themselves were fitted with a foresight and a 'V' backsight which moved vertically up or down between uprights marked for different angles of elevation. A further check on elevation was provided by a plumb bob within a quadrant fixed to each breech. The carronades on the upper deck were similarly equipped.[11]

Broke had also devised what is probably the earliest system of 'director firing' designed to concentrate all guns of the battery on one point by night or in smoke when the target could not be seen by the gun captains. Lines of bearing cut into the deck radiated inboard from the gun ports, each filled with white putty and marked in degrees, each set of lines inclined marginally from the neighbouring set in order to focus all guns on a single point of convergence at point-blank range. On the upper deck before the mainmast a large compass was inscribed with angles of bearing corresponding to those at the gun ports. Broke could order all guns to a certain elevation and have them trained to the same point before, abaft or on the beam, then take his position at the upper deck compass and give the order to fire when he saw the enemy on the bearing to which the guns were trained.

It was a system of extraordinary refinement for the day, especially in view of the British attitude that it was only necessary to close the enemy to beat him. It is doubtful if there was another commander anywhere who had taken such meticulous steps to calibrate and sight his guns. He held frequent great gun drills, exercised the gun captains firing at a barrel in the sea and rewarded those hitting with half a pound of tobacco.[12] He also held 'blindfold' firing exercises using his director system to convince sceptics that it worked and that the balls hit the sea almost as closely bunched as when the guns were laid by eye. To prevent exercises lapsing into formalism he tested his officers with hypothetical emergencies to which they had to react. Regular small arms drill for the marines and boarders and in fine weather cutlass drill and single-stick exercise for the men had welded his ship's company into a singularly effective and adaptable fighting unit. Rumours of his methods must surely have reached the *Naval Chronicle*.

Before he had a chance to realize them in action, the Royal Navy suffered another loss to the Americans. On 29 December USS *Constitution*, now under Commodore William Bainbridge, came upon HMS *Java* with an American prize off the coast of Brazil. Captain Lambert of the *Java* had not received the Admiralty order forbidding frigates of his 18-pounder class from engaging the large Americans, and directly he recognized her as an enemy he ordered his prize crew to steer for San Salvador while he headed straight for her. This time it was the American who initiated a manoeuvring contest during which her heavier broadsides made a shambles of the *Java*'s decks. Lambert, like Carden, made a desperate attempt to board, but his foremast fell, his ship lost way and Bainbridge was able to wear and rake from across his bows, then take up a position off his quarter and complete the ship's destruction. Finally an unmanageable wreck with 24 killed and 100 wounded, the *Java* struck her colours. Bainbridge took the survivors off, then burned the shattered hulk.[13]

'The public will learn with sentiments which we shall not presume to anticipate', *The Times* commented when the news reached London, 'that a *third* British frigate has struck to an American.' Five hundred merchantmen were reported captured by American privateers; three frigates had submitted in single combat. 'Can these statements be true,' the paper asked, 'and can the British people hear them unmoved?'[14]

In February 1813 Broke, cruising in the hope of meeting Rodgers, made an entry in the on-going letter he was writing to his wife:

> you can't imagine the pains I have bestowed on this *graceless wooden wife* of mine, particularly since she ran away with me here . . . I think she will do me credit if she finds an opportunity, and I am sure the other wife will make me happy if I quit this *game of honor*.[15]

That same day, his eventual opponent, Captain James Lawrence of the US sloop of war *Hornet*, gained the easiest of the American successes to date against HMS *Peacock*, a brig of war whose brilliant paintwork did justice to her name; so artistically was she maintained she was known on the West Indies station as 'the yacht', but her crew were unpractised in gunnery. Lawrence, who like all American commanders constantly exercised his men at the guns, overcame her in under fifteen minutes; after which she sank so quickly she carried down nine of her wounded and three of Lawrence's men attempting to rescue them.

As James Lawrence joined the list of American naval heroes, Broke became increasingly anxious in case 74s arriving from England to reinforce the blockade would lock the American navy in port and prevent him taking on one of their frigates to restore the honour of the flag; and that spring 1813, hearing that Rodgers in Boston with the *President* and *Congress* was nearly ready for sea, he flaunted the *Shannon* close off the harbour with another frigate in company to lure him out, sending in messages via fishing boats detailing the armament and complements of his two ships, challenging him to come out and fight and promising to send away any other British warships which might attempt to interfere. 'Equal combat is my one wish,' he assured him, 'that we may try whether your papers are correct in saying that the English have forgotten how to fight!'[16]

Rodgers did not oblige him. It is not clear why: probably he was wary of two British 74s he knew were in the offing although out of sight, and in any case considered the war against British trade of more importance; possibly he needed time to work up his ships' companies. He slipped out when a change of wind and squalls forced Broke to beat out seawards from what had become a lee shore. However, a third US frigate, the *Chesapeake*, was still in Boston preparing for sea. The following month Lawrence was appointed to command her. Broke saw another opportunity. Lawrence was young, likely to be confident after his late easy victory and was rumoured to be hot-headed. He was also well known for having challenged another British sloop to single combat before he met the *Peacock*. Broke sent his companion frigate away, stood in close off Boston alone and on 31 May sent in a very carefully worded challenge to Lawrence:

> Sir, as the *Chesapeake* appears now ready for sea, I request that you will do me the favour to meet the *Shannon* with her, ship to ship, to try the fortune of our respective flags. To an officer of your character, it requires some apology to proceed to further particulars.[17]

He did so nevertheless, pledging his honour that the *Shannon* would not receive support, detailing her exact armament and the number of her complement and suggesting a rendezvous 'from six to ten leagues East of Cape Cod Lighthouse; from eight to ten leagues East of Cape Anne's light; on Cashe's ledge in latitude 43 North'. Finally, he urged him not to imagine he was impelled by personal vanity or depending upon Lawrence's ambition; both had nobler motives:

the result of our meeting may be the most grateful service I can render my country; and . . . you, equally confident of success, will feel that it is only by repeated triumphs, in *even combats*, that your little navy can hope to console your country for the loss of that trade you can no longer protect.

The celebrated US naval historian, A. T. Mahan, has likened this famous challenge to that of a French duellist 'nervously anxious lest he should misplace an accent in the name of a man whom he intended to force into a fight and kill. It was provocative to the last degree.'[18]

Lawrence's orders were to proceed to the mouth of the St Lawrence and attack British troop and supply convoys. While stating that it was impossible to conceive a more important naval service 'in a national point of view than the destruction of the enemy's vessels with supplies for his army in Canada and his fleets on this station', they did leave him freedom to exercise his own judgement.[19] It was evident, however, that unless the weather changed he could not get out of Boston without meeting the *Shannon*. If he waited she might be rejoined by her former consort or even by a 74, since the blockade was tightening by the month. Lawrence probably reasoned it was better to meet her at once, bring her in, make rapid repairs and sail again before a replacement should arrive. At all events, as 1 June dawned fair and bright and the *Shannon* slid down before a light northerly breeze past the spur of Nahant close in to the cluster of islands fringing the approaches to Boston harbour and fired a single, teasing gun, he had already made his decision. He had a gun fired in reply and the fore topsail loosed; and a white flag was hoisted bearing the slogan 'FREE TRADE AND SAILORS' RIGHTS'. Women were sent ashore, the anchor cable hove short and the ship prepared for sea. By noon Lawrence was under way.

He was surrounded by fishing craft crowded with Bostonians eager to experience the anticipated triumph at close quarters, while ashore people thronged the waterfront and roofs of buildings; others began preparations for a grand celebration supper to which surviving British officers would be invited alongside Lawrence and his officers and men, and at the Navy Yard a wharf was cleared to accommodate the shattered hull of the *Shannon* when she was brought in. Seldom can confidence have run so high.

Yet the two ships could not have been more evenly matched. The *Chesapeake* was not one of the 44-gun super-frigates; like the *Shannon*, she mounted fourteen long 18-pounders each side of her gun deck. Above she had ten carronades 32-pounder; the *Shannon* had eight carronades 32-pounder and two long 9-pounders on specially devised high-angle swivel mountings for use against an enemy's fighting tops or her wheel. Lawrence had an edge in numbers of men, 440 – 279 of whom had served on her previous cruise – against 330 men and boys in the *Shannon*;[20] he had exercised them at the great guns twice in his first four days in command and found them expert. He could not have known of the supremely trained crews of his opponent and their unique system for horizontal fire.

Directly Broke saw that Lawrence had accepted the challenge, he stood out to sea in case he should suffer mast or rigging damage which would leave him crippled and prey to boarding parties from the shore, and cleared ship for action. Lawrence followed, setting studding sails alow and aloft. The breeze had been backing into the south-west. Bright sunlight burnished canvas tapering in tiers against the blue of the sky.

By about 4 p.m. Broke had run some 15 miles from the land which had fallen out of sight below the horizon; he shortened sail to allow Lawrence to catch him, and at 5.10, as the *Chesapeake* came within two miles, had the drum beat to quarters. Putting on a top hat as better protection for his head than a uniform cocked hat, he went to the break of the quarterdeck and summoning the men told them they had acquired such skill with the great guns he believed no frigate afloat could stand beside them.

'Throw no shot away. Aim every one. Keep cool. Work steadily. Fire into her quarters – don't try to dismast her. Kill the men and the ship is yours!'

He reminded them of the date: the Glorious First of June, and told them he had great hopes of adding another shining laurel to it, for he had no doubt they would triumph. Finally he charged them to remember their comrades from the *Guerrier*, *Macedonian* and *Java*. 'You have the blood of hundreds to avenge today. The eyes of all Europe are upon you!' Several of the listening men wept openly with emotion.[21]

After they had dispersed to their action stations Broke went to each of the 9-pounder swivel guns' crews in turn and instructed them to concentrate on the American's wheel, telling them, 'She must not get away.'

Lawrence, approaching in his wake, had made a similarly stirring appeal to his own men, reciting the unbroken list of American frigate successes and concluding with a reminder of his own swift victory in the *Hornet*: '*Peacock* her, my lads! *Peacock* her!'[22]

Both had shortened to fighting sail by now. By current doctrine Broke should have worn to bring his broadside to bear, but this would have initiated a manoeuvring contest at comparatively long range; he wanted to draw Lawrence alongside at close range where his superior gun discipline would tell, and he kept the wheel amidships and his jib and mainsail shivering, challenging the American to come up whichever side he chose. Lawrence accepted the bait, bringing his ship up in style on Broke's starboard quarter as close as prudent seamanship allowed, his bowsprit almost over Broke's taffrail before he luffed to parallel the *Shannon*'s course with only some 40 yards between them. The officers of the *Shannon*'s starboard batteries had the quoins under the breeches of their guns adjusted for horizontal fire to windward under the present easy press of canvas. The men were silent. When Lawrence's men roared three cheers across the diminishing stretch of water they did not respond. Broke insisted on silence at drill and in action in case orders were misheard.

As Lawrence ranged up with about a knot more in speed, the *Shannon* held a steady course. The captain of her fourteenth, aftermost 18-pounder waited as he had been instructed until the American's foremost gun protruding from the second gun port from her bow came in line with his sights, then jerked his firing lanyard. The flintlock snapped shut; sparks flew from the priming powder and the piece erupted, jumping towards him; gunsmoke blowing back through the port clouded all view. The aftermost carronade roared from the deck above; to his left the thirteenth gun went off and leaped inboard. Broke, standing in the starboard gangway port above, watched the first shots striking through the side timbers of the American gun deck. Satisfied that the pieces were laid well, he started walking back towards the quarterdeck.

Forward in the *Chesapeake* the execution was dreadful. Practically all the foremost gun's crew were dead or wounded, and as their ship continued overtaking, death and destruction spread aft. Her guns in bearing were replying, but firing from the windward position without Broke's meticulous arrangements for horizontal fire, much of the shot struck on or near the waterline; few found the British gun decks.[23]

Lawrence, already wounded in the leg by a marksman in the *Shannon*'s top, realized that he had too much speed, particularly as his canvas was now blanketing the *Shannon*'s sails, and ordered the helm down for a brief luff to spill the wind from his canvas. His jib sheet had been cut by the *Shannon*'s fire, and two helmsmen had been felled by Broke's 9-pounder swivel shot; the wheel was smashed and the tiller ropes cut. As the jib blew free the mizzen canvas escaped from its brails and stretched flat against the rigging, pulling the stern round, and with the steering out of action what had begun as a temporary deviation to check the ship's progress became an uncontrollable swing into the wind. The remaining sails were caught aback and she lost way, then began drifting astern towards the *Shannon*'s bow. Broke ordered his helm up and mizzen topsail shivered in an attempt to turn the bow away, but the jib stay had been cut by shot, the sails were still blanketed and she fell off the wind only slowly. Meanwhile shot from his 18-pounders beat in through Lawrence's stern windows, striking clouds of splinters from timbers, cutting down the so far unscathed men of the *Chesapeake*'s after quarters.

On the quarterdeck Lawrence realized that his ship was about to drift into the *Shannon* and called for the boarders. But below all was confusion. No body of men could have withstood the raking hail of shot, grape and splinters scouring the deck. Many were taking refuge on the starboard side by the galley, others lying on deck, while a steady stream of wounded were being helped or carried down to the cockpit. A few men from the centre division followed their lieutenant, Cox, with drawn sword up the main hatchway. Gaining the quarterdeck, Cox found that Lawrence had been hit by a second musket ball just above the groin and was clinging painfully to the binnacle. Cox sheathed his sword and, ordering the men to 'Rush on!' took hold of his captain and with two sailors assisting helped him to the ladder and down to the cockpit, where Lawrence insisted the men be told to fire faster and exhorted them not to give up the ship.

The pace of the *Chesapeake*'s sternway had increased; six minutes after the first shot from the *Shannon*, her wrecked port quarter gallery ground against the *Shannon*'s starboard side by the fifth maindeck gun from forward, while above her spanker boom swung against the fore shrouds. Broke's bo'sun lashed it there to hold the ships together. Broke had already ordered the marines to the foc's'le. He himself was standing on a foc's'le carronade mounting, gazing through the gunsmoke at the American's quarterdeck. He had no intention of going across himself, but he suddenly realized there was no one opposing him. Lawrence's marines and after carronade crews had been in an intolerable position, exposed to concentrated fire from the *Shannon*'s forward carronades, the musketry of the marines and marksmen in the tops. Dropping the speaking trumpet he was carrying, he drew his sword and shouting, 'Follow me who can!' jumped on to the shaft of the working anchor, thence over the hammocks in their nettings and down to the protruding muzzle of the American's aftermost carronade, using it as a step up to the hammocks atop her bulwarks, from which he dropped down to the enemy quarterdeck.

He was accompanied by the marine sergeant, his coxswain and others armed with cutlasses, while several men were swarming along the American's spanker boom just above. Broke led his party forward on the bloodied deck past dead and wounded and on to the port gangway towards a group gathering for defence of the foc's'le. Behind him a party of Americans emerged from the main hatch and forced some of his fol-lowers to retreat, before a second wave of yelling, oathing Shannons came over the bulwarks with pikes and cutlasses and drove them back. The officer leading the Americans was felled by a cutlass blow to the head, after which the new boarders stormed along the gangways to relieve Broke and his close supporters on the foc's'le. Their arrival broke the resistance. Some of the defenders climbed out through carronade ports and lowered themselves down to enter the main gundeck ports, others stampeded for the main hatch. Below, Lieutenant Cox and a mid-shipman had laid and fired the two aftermost 18-pounders on the port side whose muzzles were practically against the *Shannon*'s side. As the men came tumbling down the ladder Cox ran towards them with drawn sword to halt the panic, but immediately realized it was of no use.

Virtually the only resistance now came from marksmen in the *Chesapeake*'s tops firing down on the Shannons below; several were picked off by a midshipman sitting astride the *Shannon*'s main yard and their companions fled down the shrouds. Another midshipman in the *Shannon*'s fore top, seeing a fleeting opportunity as the wind pushed the *Chesapeake*'s head round and her fore yard briefly touched the *Shannon*'s, rushed out along the yard and on to the American yard brandishing a French cavalry sabre he had acquired from a prize. The American fore topmen made off down the weather shrouds. Broke was trying to restrain his men in a blood-frenzy from slaughtering the outnumbered Americans remaining on the upper deck when he was attacked from behind by three of those chased down. A shouted warning allowed him to turn in time to parry a thrust from a pike seized by one assailant from the deck and he put his sword through the man, but the second knocked off his top hat with a clubbed musket and the third brought a sabre down on his bare head, parting his skull to the brain cavity. As he fell, stunned, the enraged Shannons near by chased and cut down all three.

The wind had torn the two ships apart by this time and a small blue ensign had been raised by the Shannons above the Stars and Stripes at the *Chesapeake*'s mizzen peak, a signal to the senior officer aboard the *Shannon* to order the ceasefire. From the first gun it had taken eleven minutes to overpower the American frigate as timed by the *Shannon*'s gunner in the magazine below the waterline. Broke was attended by a midshipman and the captain of the fourteenth maindeck gun, who bound the neckerchief he had been wearing about his head over the deep gash in his captain's skull, then pointed to the blue ensign flying over the Yankee colours before lifting him to his feet and helping him to sit on a carronade slide.

Miraculously, Broke would survive and eventually recover. Lawrence, lying in the cockpit below and calling for the ship to be blown up rather than surrender, did not. As the *Chesapeake* was towed to Halifax he lapsed into a delirious coma, gesturing for his officers to hurry up the boarders and crying out constantly, 'Don't give up the ship!' He died on 4 June and was buried with full honours in Halifax; later his coffin was taken under a flag of truce for reburial in Salem, and from thence to a ceremonial funeral in New York, and a final resting place in Trinity Churchyard, Broadway.

News of the victory was received ecstatically in Britain. The Secretary to the Admiralty referred to it as unexampled in the naval annals of Great Britain. The *Naval Chronicle* wrote of 'the most brilliant act of heroism ever performed'.[24] Poets drew the conclusion, 'Britannia rules the wat'ry world, / Sole empress of the Main', and in London salons the toast was to 'An Irish river and an English Broke'.[25]

An analysis of the damage recorded for both ships provides conclusive proof that Broke's victory was the result of his arrangements for horizontal fire, assisted a little by Lawrence's overconfidence in approach: of some 54 round shot which struck the *Chesapeake*, between 35 and 44 pierced her main gun deck, nine her upper deck bulwarks; thus between 80 and 99 per cent of her shot was effective against American men at quarters. The *Shannon* was hit by fewer than half the number of round shot, only 25; and of these less than half hit the battery decks, the rest were on or about the waterline copper. The *Chesapeake* was also struck by some 306 grapeshot against 119 hits on the *Shannon*.[26] Much of the disparity was the result of the *Chesapeake*'s guns being thrown out of bearing when she became unmanageable. Yet this was no accident: it was the work of Broke's superbly trained 9-pounder swivel guns' crews who deliberately destroyed the wheel.

Casualties reflected the difference in horizontally effective fire. The American figures are not known with any precision, but between 70 and 108 were killed or mortally wounded, a sufficiently high proportion to ensure the defeat of any warship of the day, especially since it occurred in such a short period. The *Shannon* lost 23 killed, probably no more than 15 in the gunnery exchanges before the boarders went across. Adding the wounded to the totals on both sides it appears that during those fearsome eleven minutes well over 20 men per minute were killed or incapacitated – a far higher casualty rate than had occurred over the course of any naval engagement before.[27]

The lessons of the action were not lost on the British service; a number of officers, enthused by what they heard of Broke's gunnery innovations, wrote to ask for details, and two subsequently wrote books on naval gunnery which spread the essence of his teaching. In *Observations upon the Defective Equipment of Ships' Guns* Captain John Pechell observed that it was necessary 'to have the means of directing a broadside to be fired in a horizontal line when the ship heels under a press of sail, the enemy enveloped in smoke, or engaged in a dark night',[28] and he went on to describe Broke's methods of concentration fire and the training drills which he himself had copied in his ship after witnessing them aboard the *Shannon*. An even more influential *Treatise on Naval Gunnery* written by Sir Howard Douglas,[29] son of Rodney's flag captain at the battle of the Saints, also a noted gunnery innovator, leant quite as heavily on Broke's ideas and contributed much to the eventual foundation of the Royal Naval gunnery training establishment, HMS *Excellent*, which was later to become a seedbed of gunnery progress.

THE CAPTURE of the *Chesapeake* did not mark the end of British humiliation at the hands of the US Navy. The most significant occurred on Lake Erie that autumn. The conquest of Canada was one of the prime aims of the war party supporting Madison, and since the failure of their initial plans to invade from both western and eastern ends of Lake Erie and from the north end of Lake Champlain they had been engaged in a naval building race with the British on the shores of the lakes to gain command of these vital waters through which the US-Canadian border ran.

The British took over armed vessels of the Canadian Provincial Marine, bought and armed lakes' trading vessels and established building yards at Kingston and York, now Toronto, on Lake Ontario and Detroit on Lake Erie to construct new warships. The US Navy Department similarly authorized their naval commanders on the lakes to purchase trading vessels and sent shipbuilders from New York to establish yards at Presque Isle, now Erie, on the southern and eastern shore of Lake Erie and Sacket's Harbor at the eastern end of Lake Ontario. These master craftsmen performed miracles of rapid improvisation in daunting conditions. At Sacket's Harbor Henry Eckford, a Scot who had emigrated to Canada at the age of sixteen, learned his trade in Quebec, then moved to New York, where he opened his own yard in 1800 near the present Brooklyn Navy Yard, rapidly completed a 20-gun ship-rigged sloop and a 24-gun corvette and several smaller craft including a 16-gun schooner which he launched in twenty-three working days.[30] At Presque Isle, Lake Erie, Noah Brown built two 20-gun brigs, a schooner and several gunboats from locally cut timber, much of the ironwork and cables and rigging salvaged from a derelict schooner he found frozen in the lake ice.

In late August 1813 this motley flotilla sailed under the command of the senior naval officer, Lieutenant Oliver Hazard Perry, for the western end of the lake and anchored in Put-in-Bay in the Bass Island group opposite the mouth of the Detroit river, challenging the British to come out and fight. The senior British officer, Commander Robert Barclay, obliged on 9 September. Against Perry's two new 20-gun brigs, named *Lawrence* and *Niagara*, and seven smaller craft mounting from one to four guns, Barclay had two 19-gun ship sloops, *Detroit* and *Queen Charlotte*, taken over from the Canadian Provincial Marine and approximately the same size as the US brigs, together with four smaller craft. Since the issue would be decided between the two larger, square-rigged craft on each side the forces appeared evenly matched. However, there was a crucial difference. Whereas Perry's two brigs each mounted eighteen carronades 32-pounder and two long 12-pounders, Barclay's sloops were armed with a miscellaneous selection of long guns, chiefly 9-pounders and 12-pounders with two 24-pounders and only two carronades.[31] This gave Barclay an advantage in a medium- to long-range action outside the effective range of carronades, but if Perry could close, each of his two

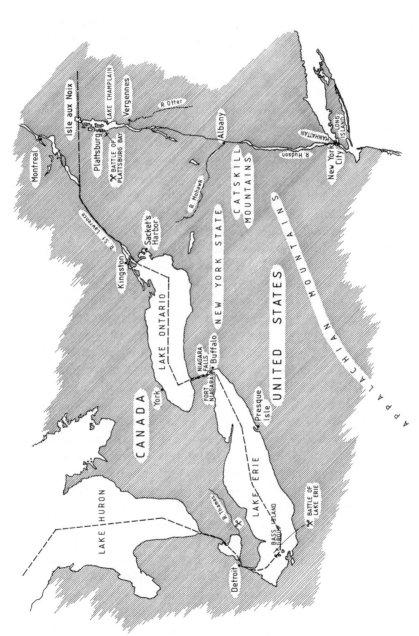

Map 3   The Great Lakes' Campaign, 1813–1814

square-riggers would have an advantage in weight of broadside of 300 against under 150 lbs. Given the British predilection for close action this meant the odds were on Perry, especially as the assorted calibres of the British long guns would make cartridge preparation, shot distribution and accurate elevation of the different pieces for long-range fire confusing in the extreme.

The British flotilla was sighted in the north-west by Perry's lookouts at dawn on 10 September, and he weighed and steered towards them, forming line of battle. The wind was light from the south-east, giving him the weather gage, thus the choice of distance at which the action would be fought. However, as he pressed on in his flagship, *Lawrence*, to close the range, holding his fire for nearly half an hour after Barclay opened, his consort *Niagara* held back out of range of the British guns. Consequently Barclay's two square-riggers, *Detroit* and *Queen Charlotte*, and an armed schooner were able to concentrate their fire on the *Lawrence*, which they gradually reduced. By 2.30 in the afternoon, more than two hours after the first shots, Perry's ship was a wreck, unmanageable and all her guns silenced. He took boat to the so far undamaged *Niagara* and, favoured by a freshening wind, sailed straight for Barclay. The British vessels had been severely mauled in action with his former flagship, and this new onslaught with the *Niagara*'s heavy carronades served by fresh crews completed their destruction. By 4 o'clock Barclay had struck his colours and surrendered the entire squadron.

After repairing damages, Perry moved an American force 4,500 strong, under the western army commander, General William H. Harrison, across the lake. The British and their native Indian allies under the Shawnee chief Tecumseh retreated; Harrison followed and routed them on the Thames river on 5 October, thus securing the north-west for the United States. The battle had another important result for American western settlers: Tecumseh, who had organized and led an intertribal Indian alliance to resist white expansion, was killed; with his death Indian resistance in the Ohio valley and southwards virtually collapsed.

Perry, promoted to captain, joined the roll-call of American naval heroes, and justly so. Next year, 1814, with the abdication of Napoleon, the British were able to concentrate fully on the American war. The naval blockade was drawn so tight that scarcely anything could move in or out of US ports, and raids were mounted on coastal cities while large invasion forces massed in Canada. US Navy gunboats proved of no use in protecting the coast. Baltimore was bombarded and a marine force took Washington DC and burned many of the public buildings; the Americans themselves burned the Navy Yard and destroyed a frigate and a sloop under construction and two older frigates to prevent them falling into enemy hands.

On the lakes meanwhile the British and their native Indian allies held US forces to a stalemate in operations on Lake Huron,[32] while gathering an army for the invasion of New York state via Lake Champlain. Anticipating this, in March the US government despatched Adam and Noah Brown, the New York shipbuilder who had performed wonders on Lake Erie, to Vergennes on the Otter river leading from the southern end of the lake. The British had a new 16-gun brig, a flotilla of gunboats and were constructing a frigate at Isle aux Noix at the head of the lake. The Browns were instructed to build a ship and six gunboats. Having completed the task and returned to New York, they received orders in late June to go back to Vergennes and build a 24-gun brig as rapidly as possible. Adam Brown departed at once with 200 tradesmen and workers and on 6 September his new brig, *Eagle*, joined the Lake Champlain flotilla.[33]

She was just in time. A British army of 14,000 veterans under Sir George Prevost, Governor-General of Canada, supported by the British lake flotilla under Commodore George Downey, was advancing south along the western side of the lake with the object of continuing the invasion of New York state down the Hudson river valley. The officer commanding the US flotilla, Lieutenant Thomas Macdonough, decided to bar their passage and fight at anchor. He selected a defensive position in Plattsburg Bay, disposing his ships carefully with springs to their cables so that they could be swung to face any direction of attack. As on Lake Erie the battle would be decided by the larger vessels on each side, the British 36-gun frigate *Confiance* and 16-gun brig *Linnet*, the American 26-gun corvette *Saratoga* and 24-gun brig *Eagle*, supported by a 7-gun schooner *Ticonderoga*. Yet again the Americans had the advantage in weight of shot at close range: Macdonough's flagship *Saratoga* mounted a total of eighteen carronades 42-pounder and 32-pounder, the *Eagle* twelve carronades 32-pounder and the *Ticonderoga* five carronades 32-pounder, whereas Downey's flagship *Confiance* had only six carronades 24-pounder, her main battery consisting of long 24-pounder cannon.

Downey attacked on 11 September. After fierce exchanges lasting one and a half hours both sides had suffered heavy damage and losses, but Macdonough was able to haul the *Saratoga* round with his springs to bring his hitherto disengaged broadside to bear on the *Confiance* which was now too crippled to match the manoeuvre. Downey was forced to surrender with his whole squadron. Plattsburg Bay was as decisive a victory as Lake Erie since Sir George Prevost, deprived of naval support to protect his supplies, turned back and retired to Canada. As American troops and militia had repulsed another British incursion at Fort Niagara, the serious threat of invasion from Canada had been averted. Moreover, news of this second major reverse disposed the British government towards peace.

Madison certainly needed peace. Besides the disastrous effects of the British blockade on commerce and employment and the chaotic state of public finances, influential opinion in New York and New England had hardened against a war which was destroying their prosperity, and there was open discussion on leaving the Union. British and American negotiators had been talking for some months at Ghent, and on 24 December 1814 peace was agreed on the pre-war status quo. It allowed Madison the illusion of victory before the full power of the Royal Navy destroyed American overseas commerce and shipping as it had destroyed French commerce. And it allowed the British government and people a much needed respite from the heavy costs of war.

Before peace was ratified in Washington in February 1815, Stephen Decatur made a final bid to get to sea with one of the super-frigates. His *United States* had been blockaded in New London since May 1813; now he and his crew transferred to the *President* in New York, and in January 1815 he took advantage of a north-easterly gale to slip out, but the frigate grounded on a shoal and was pounded by heavy seas for two hours before he could work free. The following morning he was sighted by a British squadron and ran, outpacing all but one frigate, the *Endymion*. He rounded on her and in the ensuing duel both ships suffered such damage that when the rest of the squadron came up he had little option but to surrender. The big American frigates had been much admired and the *President* was commissioned in the British service. She soon proved to have been so strained by her grounding outside New York she was condemned and broken up, but a new ship was built on her lines and named HMS *President*. It was a fitting end to a naval war that had seen the young American service achieve something no European navy had been able to do: in diverse ways it had taught British naval officers a lesson.

15

Napoleon's Nemesis

THE WAR AGAINST Napoleonic France had been concluded formally by the Treaty of Paris on 30 May 1814. The terms were indulgent since the Allies had restored a Bourbon to the throne as Louis XVIII and wanted to give the French people no excuse to topple him. No indemnity was demanded for the ravages and extortions visited on the continent over the past quarter-century; nor was there any requirement to return the multitude of works of art Napoleon had looted. France was reduced to her historic frontiers, yet these were drawn marginally wider than they had been in 1789, and Britain handed back the overseas colonies she had taken, with the exception of Mauritius in the Indian Ocean and the West Indian islands of Tobago and St Lucia which had become British by the Peace of Amiens.

The more complex task of reconstituting the map of Europe and fashioning an enduring peace had been postponed to a congress to be held in Vienna in November. Here, amidst unending celebration of the pleasures of the old aristocracies the Revolutionaries had aimed to displace, the Allies sought to capitalize on their triumph: Russia laid claim to Poland, Prussia to Saxony. Castlereagh for Great Britain advanced the goals of a balance of continental power, England's strategy from at least the sixteenth century, the creation of barrier states to contain French expansionism, and a system of collective security. Pitt had outlined such a peace in 1805, laying particular stress on the great powers engaging by treaty to support one another against any attempt to 'infringe' their respective rights or possessions and so establishing a 'public law' in Europe.[1]

In pursuit of these goals, Castlereagh found it necessary to bring France into the scales to curb Russian and Prussian ambitions. By a secret treaty signed between Britain, Austria and France on 3 January 1815, these three undertook to act together and if necessary put troops in the field to defend whoever might be attacked as a result of claims made at the peace conference. Talleyrand, French Foreign Minister again under Louis XVIII, savoured his triumph, reporting to Louis, 'The [Allied] Coalition is dissolved . . . France is no longer isolated in Europe . . . Your Majesty possesses a federal system which fifty years of negotiation might not have constructed.'[2] In truth, like Vergennes before him, he had always believed in partnership between Great Britain, France and Austria to guarantee the stability of Europe. The terms of the secret treaty were leaked to Russia and Prussia, who then realized the necessity for compromise.

Alongside *Realpolitik* Castlereagh attempted to persuade the other powers to join the crusade against the slave trade. It had become a ruling passion in Britain. Earlier that year some three-quarters of a million people from all parts of the kingdom had signed 800 petitions urging the government to persuade the restored Bourbon monarchy to end the French trade.[3] As before, this was regarded in France as the purest *hypo-crisie anglaise* designed to allow the Royal Navy to search and seize French ships. It was particularly resented in the former French slaving ports – Nantes, Bordeaux, Le Havre – where peace brought the promise of a resumption of the trade ruined by the British naval blockade, and the authorities hoped to persuade the new government to reintroduce a bounty on slaves landed in the West Indian islands now restored to France. Nonetheless, to conclude the Treaty of Paris, Talleyrand had been forced into a general statement that France would do everything possible to suppress the traffic, and Louis XVIII had had to promise to abolish the French trade within five years.

This was not sufficient for British abolitionists. When Wellington returned to London in the summer of 1814 he was struck by 'the degree of frenzy existing here about the slave trade'. He had not been aware of it while campaigning; now, he found, 'People in general appear to think that it would suit the policy of the nation to go to war to put an end to that *abominable* traffic.'[4]

In December 1814 Great Britain and the United States pledged in the Treaty of Ghent which ended the war between them to 'use their best endeavours' to end the slave trade. At Vienna in February 1815

Castlereagh succeeded in having a similar declaration signed by the sceptical diplomats of France, Russia, Prussia, Austria, Spain, Portugal and Sweden denouncing the African slave trade as 'repugnant to the principles of humanity and universal morality'[5] and enjoining those powers with colonies to end it as soon as possible. Castlereagh was to attempt to bring the powers together to implement this pious resolution with a permanent international conference on the trade in London the following year, but the institution achieved little beyond the collection of information. The struggle would continue for decades. The irony was that both 'Anglo-Saxon' powers leading the crusade were directly or indirectly dependent on the institution of slavery: cotton produced by slave labour in the southern United States had become that country's chief export and over half went to British factories whose ever-rising output of finished textiles provided the impetus for industrial growth and accounted for up to 50 per cent of the declared value of British exports.[6]

Meanwhile Napoleon escaped from Elba. Aware of the tensions between the powers at Vienna, informed of dissatisfaction with Louis' regime in France, he determined to lead a patriotic uprising to overthrow the puppet monarch imposed on the French people and once again lead them to glory over their enemies. He had lost more armies than any warlord in history, in Egypt, in Russia and in Germany, yet he retained the rhetorical skills that had originally inspired them. Landing on the south coast of France on 1 March 1815, between Antibes and Cannes, he issued a series of proclamations informing the French people they had not been beaten, only betrayed by generals within, and he invited them to rally round him, tear down the white cockade and raise the tricolour once more to redeem Paris from the shame: 'How long will you serve a prince who was the enemy of France for twenty years and boasts that he owes his seat upon the throne to a Prince Regent of England?'[7]

Avoiding the main road to Paris, he took his followers northwards through the foothills of the Maritime Alps, and the miracle he willed unfolded. Villagers attached themselves; Louis' troops sent to apprehend him were overcome by his aura as their former Emperor and joined him instead. By the time he reached Lyons he commanded an imperial progress. Perhaps it is not surprising: he had controlled the press of France over the decade of his stunning conquests and he was offering glory again after humiliation. Thus, in the imagery evoked in his proclamations 'the Eagle with the tricolour' flew from steeple to steeple until it reached the pinnacles of Notre Dame in Paris,[8] and Louis XVIII fled.

News of Napoleon's escape and progress towards Paris concentrated minds at Vienna. Talleyrand drafted a declaration skilfully indicting Napoleon Bonaparte, not France, for harbouring revolutionary designs against the peace of Europe, whereby he had placed himself outside civil and social relations and delivered himself up to public justice.[9] It was signed by the delegates of all powers present on 13 March, and twelve days later Russia, Prussia, Austria and Great Britain each pledged themselves to place 150,000 troops in the field against him and, in a repeat of the Chaumont Treaty which had held them together the previous March, agreed not to make a separate peace. Wellington, who had relieved Castlereagh as head of the British delegation at the Congress, was appointed to command the Allied armies in the Low Countries. As before, Britain was to be paymaster; in May the House of Commons voted by 160 to only 17 to provide subsidies of over £5 million.[10] Anticipating a government order to transmit subsidies to the coalition, Nathan Rothschild had been buying gold since March.[11]

Napoleon first attempted to split Austria and Britain from the other powers – bidding for British approval with an imperial edict abolishing the French slave trade. His messages went unanswered, and the coalition armies gathered. His options were to await the inevitable invasion of France and conduct a defensive campaign in the north to defend Paris against one enemy at a time as he had done the previous year, or launch an offensive. Inevitably he chose to advance and strike; it was the pattern of his career. Wellington was to comment later, 'he never in his life had patience for a defensive war.'[12] Belgium had been much on his mind in exile. He had told British visitors that the French would never give up hope of recovering the lost Belgian provinces. It was, besides, an obvious target; Brussels lay under 40 miles from the French frontier defended by a mixed force of some 90,000 British, Hanoverians and other Germans and Dutch-Belgians under Wellington, and somewhat to the east of them 120,000 Prussians under Marshal Prince von Blücher. If he could insert himself between them, overcome each in turn with the 125,000-strong army he had gathered in the north, and take Brussels, it would boost his authority in France, shake the coalition, perhaps even topple the British government, and the way would be clear for further advance into Holland.

There was fanatical *esprit* among his troops. It was not simply his own person the Allies had to contend with, as Talleyrand had implied, but a substantial portion of disillisioned, humiliated Republicans and army veterans. Only seven of his marshals had rallied to him but his Army of the North was compared for fervour to the first Revolutionary armies; there were no foreign units; all were French; one officer reported 'an absolute frenzy for the Emperor, and against his enemies'.[13] His other advantage was that no war had yet been declared; thus Wellington and Blücher could not send patrols across the French border to report his movements. This enabled him to concentrate while they were still dispersed along the frontier not knowing when or where the attack might come. Moving with a speed reminiscent of his youthful campaigns, early on 15 June he crossed the border into Belgium and seized Charleroi.

Wellington in Brussels learned of it that afternoon, but confirmation that it was the main thrust, not a feint, did not arrive until late that night. He issued orders for his forces to concentrate at Quatre Bras, the crossroads on the Brussels road 10 miles north of Charleroi. The dancing and gaiety at the Duchess of Richmond's ball which he attended that night with his staff and officers, so many of whom were to fall in the coming days, has entered legend. He retired early. Next day he was at Quatre Bras by 10 o'clock; from there he rode a few miles south-easterly to Saint-Amand and Ligny where Blücher was concentrating his army. Surprised to find the Prussians deploying on the forward slopes fully visible to the French gunners, he commented that if he put his own men in full view like that he would expect to see them 'damnably mauled'. Gneisenau, Blücher's chief of staff, rejoined stiffly that Prussians liked to see their enemy. Promising to bring his men to Blücher's aid so long as he was not attacked too heavily himself, he rode back to Quatre Bras.

The French artillery mauled the Prussians dreadfully that day and finally their infantry broke Blücher's centre; Wellington was unable to come to his support as Napoleon sent his left wing under Marshal Ney to oust him from Quatre Bras. Ney and his leading corps commander, General Honoré Reille, had fought in the peninsula and knew Wellington's talent for conjuring troops from concealed positions at critical moments. Their lengthy reconnaissance and preparation against such surprises gave time for more units of Wellington's force to reach the lines, and when the assaults came they were held off. It was a crucial check on Napoleon's route to Brussels. Equally crucial was Gneisenau's decision that night to retreat northwards rather than eastwards. It meant he would remain in touch with Wellington. Learning this next morning, the 17th, Wellington retired northwards in parallel and established new defensive lines on the reverse slopes of Mont Saint-Jean before the village of Waterloo some 10 miles south of Brussels. It was a position he had reconnoitred earlier in the year and was ideally suited to his tactics of concealment. On the gentle forward slopes up which the enemy must advance were three clusters of substantial farm buildings; he garrisoned these as pockets of resistance to disrupt and break the momentum of the assault.

He made his decision to stand and fight conditional on receiving one Prussian corps. He was promised two; and in the early hours of the next morning, the 18th, he received word from Blücher that the two corps would march at dawn to join him, and should Napoleon attack, Blücher himself would follow with his entire army.[14] Napoleon believed he had dealt with the Prussians at Ligny, and discounted them. He also discounted warnings from his chief of staff, Soult, together with Ney and Reille, about Wellington's use of ground and the firepower and tenacity of the British infantry – with the implication that flanking manoeuvres would be more effective than a frontal assault.

Brushing aside this counsel, he ordered an artillery bombardment, to be followed by a direct attack in mass to overawe and break the Anglo-Allied centre as he had broken the Prussians at Ligny. It took time to move the guns into position through ground soaked by torrential rains during the night, and it was about 11.30 before they opened fire. At about the same time assaults were launched against Wellington's advanced positions in the farm complexes. The attacks were repulsed, and since Wellington had hidden his units on Mont Saint-Jean beyond the crest of the slope the gunners had few targets on which to aim the bombardment. More disturbing for the French staff, before one o'clock substantial bodies of troops were sighted some six miles off on their right wing; the suspicion formed and was shortly confirmed by a prisoner that these were Prussians – General von Bülow's corps, 30,000 strong, with the rest of Blücher's army not far behind.

Napoleon was not diverted. At about 1.30 he had Ney launch the frontal attack on the ridge of Mont Saint-Jean. Four vast columns mustering in all some 16,000 men started forward to the beat of drums, preceded by skirmishers darting through the high green corn of summer. Wellington had seen it many times since his initial encounter with Junot at Vimeiro, but not with so many columns, each formed on a wide front to increase their firepower. His field artillery came up to the crest of the slope and opened, cutting cruel swathes through the ranks. The human tide pressed on, clamorous with imprecations, defiance and cries of loyalty to the Emperor, gaps closing while others were opened by shot.

As they neared the top Wellington's officers called their units up and extended them in line, two deep, across the advancing hordes. Each Allied detachment had been stiffened by British redcoats. It was on these Wellington placed his reliance. Asked a few days before how he considered his chances, he had pointed to a British private soldier who happened to be near by: 'It all depends upon that article whether we do the business or not. Give me enough of it, and I'm sure.'[15] Whether he had enough at Mont Saint-Jean must have been his chief concern. Much of the regular British army including his peninsula veterans had been sent to Canada for the American war and was still on the way back. Of his force of over 67,000, just under 24,000 were British; about half of these had seen service in the peninsula.[16]

In the event it proved just sufficient. The advancing columns were broken by disciplined volleys of musketry and thrown back in disorder down the slopes with bayonets, or in one sector which gave way, by cavalry charge. The French artillery resumed pounding the ridge, finding such an accurate range Wellington withdrew his line 100 yards or so, whereupon Ney, mistaking the movement for retreat, launched his cavalry up the slope. The Anglo-Allied infantry formed in squares and received them with close-range volleys and barriers of bayonets from which mounts swerved; as the cuirassiers and lancers raged impotently around and between the squares Wellington called up reserve cavalry which drove them off. Ney responded by sending up more cavalry in wave after wave; they too were driven back in the most sustained mounted actions of the Napoleonic wars.

Von Bülow, meanwhile, deploying cautiously on the French right, drew off Napoleon's reserves, and when in the early evening the farm immediately below Wellington's centre on the Brussels road at last fell, Napoleon refused Ney troops to exploit the potentially crucial gain. Finally, in a last desperate throw to break Wellington's centre, Napoleon ordered his elite Imperial Guard up the trampled and bloodied slope of Mont Saint-Jean. Unsupported by cavalry, they were met by infantry redeployed in line to meet them, and like the first massed columns of the day, their leaders were cut down by close-range musketry and driven back with bayonets. As the third wave broke Wellington raised his plumed cocked hat bearing the cockades of all the Allies and, waving it in the direction of the French, galloped along the whole line shouting to his commanders to charge.

Napoleon, deathly pale, recognized defeat. His staff hurried him into a carriage but the French rout was such he soon had to take to horse to escape capture. In contrast to Wellington, who had ridden everywhere about his lines, rallying the men, calling up reserves, seizing opportunities for his cavalry, Napoleon had shown none of the activity or flare of his youth and had left Ney to conduct the main assault. Above all, it seems, he had been unable or unwilling to recognize the tactical lessons of the peninsula. 'Damn the fellow, he is a mere pounder after all!' Wellington had exclaimed of him at one point in the action;[17] asked later if the French had fought better than usual, he replied, 'No, they have always fought the same since I first met them at Vimeiro.'[18]

It had been a critical day, nonetheless. The unreliability of several of the Allied units together with Bülow's tardiness in deployment had resulted in a number of perilous situations. 'It was the most desperate business I was ever in,' Wellington confided to his brother, 'and never was so near being beat';[19] and to a civilian enquiring the following day, he described it as 'a damned serious business . . . the nearest run thing you ever saw in your life', adding, 'By God, I don't think it would have been done if I had not been there.'[20] The list of dead or wounded officers was extraordinarily long; tears ran down his face as it was read out to him. He believed he had been shielded by the hand of God, for every member of his staff had been cut down at his side. 'Next to a battle lost', he was to tell Lady Shelley, 'the greatest misery is a battle gained.'[21]

For Napoleon and the fervently loyal army he had led, it was the end. Over 30,000 had been killed or wounded, almost 7,000 taken prisoner – against just over 16,000 Anglo-Allied and some 7,000 Prussian casualties.[22] Two battalions of Guards escorted Napoleon, falling asleep on his horse,[23] to Paris; the rest of the surviving troops melted into the countryside and made their way home. Napoleon's chief reaction to defeat appears to have been to blame Ney for wasting his cavalry. As ever, he wanted to raise another army which he would lead in the defence of Paris. But the politicians of the parliament he had established to give his new reign liberal credentials knew that France was beaten, bankrupt and needed peace. He was the obstacle. On 22 June, the fourth day after the battle Wellington chose to call after his headquarters village, Waterloo, rather than Mont Saint-Jean where the broken remains of men and horses lay in sickening furrows of churned mud and crops, Napoleon was forced to sign a second abdication. Three days later Louis XVIII proclaimed a second Bourbon restoration, and in early July the Allied armies under Wellington made a second triumphal entry to Paris.

The Congress of Vienna had already completed its work. The Final Act incorporating a multitude of separate agreements to reshape the map of Europe had been signed on 9 June, before Waterloo. It has been criticized for reinstating the old order, ignoring ideas of democracy and nationalism unleashed by the French Revolution, but it was designed deliberately to contain France by statesmen whose experience was imprinted with the destructiveness of the French drive for territorial aggrandizement and tribute under the Revolution and Empire. A buffer state was created on France's north-eastern border by joining Holland, Belgium and the bishopric of Liège in a new kingdom of the Netherlands under the House of Orange. In this context, the Dutch stranglehold on Antwerp was finally ended by a treaty opening the river Schelde to international commerce. A similar code was applied to the Rhine.

As with French overseas colonies, in order to ensure the viability of the new state Great Britain handed back most of the Dutch colonies she had seized during the wars, with the notable exceptions of the Cape of Good Hope and Ceylon. Territorially the Netherlands was to be buttressed by Prussia which, at Castlereagh's insistence, gained territories along the left bank of the Rhine to protect that great trading river, as well as part of Saxony and part of Poland. Austria gained compensation particularly in northern Italy, and Russia gained Finland and dominion over a new kingdom of Poland. In Germany the hundreds of individual principalities were consolidated into just thirty-nine states joined in a loose German confederation to be presided over by Austria.

Thus the British goal of balance between the great continental powers was roughly achieved at the expense of liberal and national aspirations. As for Pitt's goal of establishing a public or international law in Europe, this was addressed in November that year when the Quadruple Alliance of 1813 between Britain, Austria, Russia and Prussia was renewed and the powers agreed in addition to meet from time to time to confer on European problems and uphold the Vienna settlement. At the resulting Congress of Aix-la-Chapelle in 1818 France, by then no longer deemed the public enemy, was admitted to the great power fold.

In the meantime Talleyrand – whose life's work may be said to have been directed to such a goal – and Wellington engineered Louis XVIII's second coming. The regicide Fouché and all who had participated in Louis XVI's execution were granted amnesty, and Fouché was appointed Minister of Police; he had played much the same role in Napoleon's second abdication as Talleyrand in his first. Talleyrand himself headed the government as President of the Council and retained his post as Foreign Minister. As an admirer of the British constitution he persuaded Louis to institute a hereditary upper chamber to balance an elected lower chamber; and true to all past French statesmen who had attempted to imitate by decree institutions which had evolved naturally in the supreme maritime power of the day, he set about choosing the hereditary peers himself, in the words of one witness 'as if it had been a question of invitations to a dinner or ball'.[24] As ministers dropped in to see him they were asked to suggest names. At the same time he attempted to ensure that elections to the lower chamber also resulted in a majority favourable to his government. Instead, the voting produced a preponderance of extreme royalists who wanted to turn the clock back, and his government of moderates was soon brought down.

France at last had the British style of constitutional monarchy Necker and the practical men of 1789 had wanted, yet French politicians had not been raised in the pragmatic spirit of its operation; moreover, the wounds of the Revolution were still bleeding, the divisions between reactionary royalists and radical Jacobins too bitter for the moderation that oiled the British and American systems. Above all, perhaps, French political culture was still steeped in abstract ideas and the spirit of central regulation that flowed from them. As the philosopher, John Stuart Mill, was to tell Alexis de Tocqueville, 'We [British] have never considered government from such a lofty point of view . . . We have not done this deliberately, but from our sheer inability to comprehend general ideas on the subject of government or anything else.'[25]

Not surprisingly the constitution would not take deep root. Yet it held sufficiently long for France to redevelop economically and rejoin the comity of powers. Much credit belongs to Louis XVIII, a Bourbon who may not have forgotten much, but was willing to learn; and not least to Castlereagh, Wellington and Tsar Alexander for aiding his rule by insisting on moderation rather than vengeance for Napoleon's hundred-day adventure. In the second peace treaty of Paris finally concluding the Napoleonic wars an indemnity of 700 million gold francs was demanded from France over a five-year period together with the costs of an occupation army to enforce payment;[26] this was hardly commensurate with the costs of French pillage and destruction over the period of the wars, and Wellington, who painstakingly allotted the sums to be paid to individual states, had consulted bankers to ensure that France could pay without undue strain.[27] Appropriately, this time the art works Napoleon had looted were reclaimed, a small matter but highly emotive for Parisians, and Wellington was bitterly attacked when he sent officers to the Louvre to collect the treasures and ensure despatch to their former owners. Those who impugned him may not have known that he had played a central role in curbing a Prussian appetite for a Carthaginian peace, and saved Napoleon from execution.

THE LONELY Atlantic island of St Helena was chosen for Napoleon's second exile. Taken aboard a British warship in July 1815, he was described by her commander as remarkably strong and well-built, but corpulent, as a result of which 'he had lost much of his personal activity, and, if we are to give credit to those who attended him, a very considerable portion of his mental activity was also gone. It is certain his habits were very lethargic while he was on board the *Bellerophon*.'[28] The lethargy may perhaps have stemmed from defeat; it may also have contributed to defeat, for his whole conduct of the campaign after his initial breakout to Charleroi had been distinguished by uncharacteristic sluggishness. What can scarcely be in doubt is that, even if he had prevailed at Mont Saint-Jean, he would still have been doomed; for behind Wellington and Blücher were the armies of Russia, Austria, and in the south Spain, and British veterans were returning from America; above all the British government had been voted the funds to keep the alliance together, and the French treasury was empty.

Napoleon died on St Helena in 1821. He remains a potent symbol of glory to admirers, by no means all French. By any objective assessment he was the ultimate French disaster. He cannot, of course, bear the whole historic weight: he was merely the charismatic representative of France's warrior and agricultural past, supported by and supporting all those groups and systems of belief carried forward through or benefiting from the revolutionary changes. Ultimately, it was France's industrial and financial failure in face of the British financial and technological revolution that proved decisive. The failure was apparent even before 1789, becoming more marked during the Revolutionary war when French overseas trade was crippled by the British naval blockade.

With the decline of French Atlantic and Mediterranean ports and manufacturing hinterland French industry had refocused in the northern and eastern regions, and Paris itself, both to supply the armies and to export goods to the European markets brought under French control by conquest. As noted, Napoleon's continental blockade was an attempt on the one hand to ruin British trade but on the other to provide French manufacturers with a huge protected market; by 1810 it had reached over 40 million consumers.[29]

Woollen and particularly cotton manufacturing had been hugely stimulated. Machines such as spinning jennies had been imported from England before the Revolution and enterprising merchants had employed Englishmen to construct and run factories powered by running water.[30] During the Empire weaving had been revolutionized with a punched-card apparatus invented by a native of Lyons, Joseph-Marie Jacquard. His remarkable invention, adapted later for analytical and statistical machines, automatically reproduced patterns in the weave by selecting and controlling the coloured warp threads on the loom – releasing children who had hitherto been employed for this task. The silk weavers of Lyons reacted like 'Luddites' in Britain by wrecking 'Jacquard' looms, but the advantages of the system were so evident that by 1812 some 11,000 were in use across France.[31] And in a rare reversal of the general direction of technological exchange, within a few years of the end of the war they had been adopted in British textile mills.

Another result of blockade and the reorientation of French industry towards the European market was the improvement and extension of inland waterways. One notable example was the Saint-Quentin canal in north-east France. Constructed between 1802 and 1809 by Barnabé Brisson, a civil engineer who had trained at the École Polytechnique in Paris, one of the outstanding educational institutions founded in the Revolution, it linked the textile industry of the Saint-Quentin region with the Belgian waterway network and the North Sea via the rivers Escaut and Lys; the English Channel via the Somme; and Paris and Le Havre via the rivers Oise and Seine.

The French iron and armaments industries had naturally been stimulated by war, but results had been uneven. The first large ironworks outside Great Britain using coke derived from coal rather than timber charcoal as fuel had been founded at Le Creusot in east central France before the Revolution with the technical aid of the celebrated British iron-master John Wilkinson and his brother.[32] Wilkinson was the inventor of a precision cylinder-boring machine vital to the success of James Watt's steam engines; he had also taught the French how to bore cannon from solid castings – rather than casting the barrel around a central core which was afterwards withdrawn – hugely improving the accuracy. In the command economy of 1793 when ironworks were taken under the control of the French Republic attempts were made to introduce coke firing and improve production by disseminating scientific information; and new steelworks were set up, the workers similarly provided with instructive literature on the latest British methods. Outcomes were disappointing. As soon as conquest brought French armies to the Rhine French steel was abandoned in favour of the German product.[33] As for Le Creusot, the naval cannon it cast proved so brittle orders were discontinued and the works confined to producing cannon balls and ballast. As with steel, heavy armaments production became focused on the conquered regions of Belgium, Luxembourg and the west bank of the Rhine. However, real expansion in iron manufacture, like that in the textile industry, came from serving the huge domestic market protected from British imports.[34]

In the long term the chief beneficiaries of the protected market were the middlemen, the export-import merchants, army contractors, agents and bankers of the cities on the eastern borders of France and the annexed territories, particularly Strasbourg. These amassed fortunes from legal and contraband trade across the tariff barrier erected to favour French industry at the expense of the satellites. But in overall national terms, despite the increasing value of such exports into Europe, these never made up for the loss of the maritime trades of the west and south-west. And from 1813 as the Empire and the protective barrier collapsed, British goods of generally higher quality and lower cost flooded into the continent once more and much of the expanded French textile and iron industries was wiped out. Neither the demands of war nor the protected market, nor even tutelage from central government functionaries, had provided the conditions necessary for technological advance sufficient to catch up with, let alone overtake, British industry. Except in certain specialized fashion lines, French goods could no more compete with the mass-produced articles from British factories than they had before the wars; indeed the relative position had altered in Great Britain's favour.[35] Napoleon's continental system had not only failed in both principal aims, it had set French industry back by decades. The statistics are inadequate, but it has been estimated that it took some thirteen years from Napoleon's final defeat for French foreign trade to regain the level it had reached in the final year of the *ancien régime*.[36] Moreover, there were few, if any, improvements in French agriculture during the period, and it is believed that Napoleon's wars alone cost the lives of over a million young Frenchmen.[37]

The catalogue of disaster prompts the question, central to the whole period of Anglo-French conflict, of why France failed. She appeared to have all the advantages over her island rival: she was larger and more populous and spread across more diverse climatic regions of forest and fertile land served by navigable rivers, and faced three trading axes, the Mediterranean, Atlantic and English Channel leading to the Baltic. Recent estimates suggest that her population at the time of the Revolution was almost three times and her gross national product perhaps double that of Britain.[38]

Moreover, French scientists, intellectuals and inventors were at least the equal of their British counterparts: the Parisian Antoine-Laurent Lavoisier was the founder of modern chemistry; Gaspard Monge, prominent both in the establishment of the metric system and the École Polytechnique during the Revolution, was a pioneer in analytical geometry; the *Encyclopédie* was a showcase of progress in the natural sciences; Jacquard's punched-card system was a more complex apparatus than anything devised in Britain. Marc Brunel, father of the more famous Isambard Kingdom Brunel, was a French engineer who came to England as an émigré and mechanized the making of timber blocks for warship rigging in Portsmouth dockyard in 1799; his other inventions included the ground-breaking antecedent of the tunnel-boring shields in use today. The list is long, for France was ahead of England in formal education and technical training.[39] This was evident even in the navy: French warships were generally of better design and when captured, as so many were, their lines were often taken and copied for subsequent British classes. Yet she was unable to capitalize on her strengths.

The evidence is unequivocal; she had fallen technologically and materially well behind Britain before the Revolution. The journals of two remarkably observant and intelligent young French noblemen, François and Alexandre de la Rochefoucauld, make this crystal clear. They toured England and Scotland in 1784 and 1785, surely engaged in industrial espionage, so detailed are their descriptions of English factories, canals, mines, machines and working conditions and pay scales. They found the contrast even in the standard of hostelries 'too much to our [French] disadvantage . . . The differences between us and the English, which I am constantly made aware of, sometimes grieves me: we are inferior to them in a great many ways.'[40] They were shown over the great ironmaster, John Wilkinson's works and noted that 'several thousand pieces of mechanism we [French] cannot cast' were sent daily to France, an exaggeration perhaps, but this was the information they were given.[41] At Matthew Boulton's factory in Birmingham they saw the steam pumps for which he was famous and also 'a machine with two cylinders which makes an instant copy of a letter' whose secrets they could not fathom. The impression left from reading their journals is that even if the industrial revolution in Britain was not in full flood before the French Revolution, everything was in place, the canals, mines, ironworks, steam engines, powered textile machinery, driven entrepreneurs and local finance. As for the prime factor, François commented at Derby, 'their superiority over us in the great numbers of their machines must be acknowledged.'[42]

The conclusion from the material disparity can only be that the French political system and culture formed of and dominated by land-holding values could not adjust or compete with a very different merchant culture protected by and in command of the sea. The struggle lasted so long and the final rounds were fought so fiercely and run so close, each side reverting to its naked character – the warrior horde against the ruthless merchant trader – that the result has, to borrow Tocqueville's phrase, the validity of a scientific experiment. France's 'greatest frustration' was her martial-bureaucratic ethos.

16

The Sceptre of the World

GREAT BRITAIN EMERGED from the Napoleonic war as the supreme world power. Her network of bases extended along all trade routes: in the Mediterranean Gibraltar, Malta and the Ionian Islands; on the routes to the east the Cape of Good Hope, Mauritius and Ceylon with its magnificent harbour of Trincomalee. There was a gap on the final leg to China since the Dutch East Indies possessions had been handed back, but this was made good within four years by the occupation of a small island called Singhapura at the tip of the Malay peninsula. Singapore was acquired through local individual initiative, not government action. Its prime strategic location at the entrance to the South China Sea had been noted previously by officers of the Honourable East India Company, and it was a particularly energetic and ambitious Company servant, Sir Stamford Raffles, who seized it in January 1819 to provide a base from which to protect far eastern trade and a commercial entrepôt to break the hold which the Dutch were re-establishing in the region. 'Our object is not territory but trade,' he wrote. 'One free port in these seas must eventually destroy the spell of Dutch monopoly.'[1]

In the west Britain had added Trinidad, St Lucia and Tobago to her string of West Indian islands, and on the mainland of central America the former Dutch possessions of Demerara and Essequibo – later to form British Guiana. She retained bases on the slaving coast of Africa from which to prosecute her crusade against the slave trade. This was to carry a high cost in lives and permanent ill-health. Average mortality rates on the west African coast would soon amount to 70 per thousand men, against under 10 per thousand in home and Mediterranean squadrons, while annual sickness rates would reach 1,500 per 1,000 men. In the five years from 1839 to 1844, 385 officers and men died from fevers contracted in the coastal swamps or from the slaves they were freeing or were killed in action with slavers; nearly 500 more were invalided out of the service.[2]

Britain also retained Heligoland, her trading entrepôt in the German Bight. In the Pacific, she had planted a colony on the eastern shore of Australia, which had been charted and claimed for the British Crown and named New South Wales by Captain James Cook on the first of his epic voyages of Pacific exploration in 1770. The British government's prime motive for sending Cook and two previous expeditions to the South Seas had been commercial: to find the supposed great southern continent, *terra australis incognita*, in order to extend British trade and manufacture into a new hemisphere.[3] This was glossed with all the Enlightenment apparatus of scientific investigation. The motive for establishing a colony in New South Wales was surely the same, although no documentary proof has been discovered. This time it was glossed with the need to ease overcrowding in Britain's gaols. The first fleet of eleven ships carrying almost 1,000 settlers, the majority of them convicts, 570 of whom were male, 160 female, had sailed in spring 1787 under Captain Arthur Phillip, whose instructions were to take possession of the entire territory from the eastern coast and islands westward to the 135th meridian – roughly halfway across the continent. Arriving in January 1788, Phillip had established a base settlement inside the splendid natural harbour of Port Jackson at a bay on the southern shore named Sydney Cove – between the sites of today's defining images of the city of Sydney, the harbour bridge and the opera house. Surviving extreme hardship in the early years, by 1815 the settlement had established outposts along the coast and on Norfolk Island and Tasmania; during the next decade settlers would emigrate to southern and western Australia and the British Crown would claim the whole continent.

The other large British territorial holdings overseas were in Canada and India. Canada, where British colonists who had remained loyal to the Crown during the American revolution coexisted with descendants of the original French settlers and indigenous peoples, was governed much as the now independent American colonies had been through provincial governors presiding over an executive council and a legislature made up of an elected lower chamber balanced by an aristocratic upper chamber whose members were appointed by and loyal to the governor.

The British Parliament controlled external relations, trade and navigation and retained the ultimate sanction over legislation.

India was very different. During incessant warfare between rival
European East India companies, particularly the British and French,
each side allying with local rulers eager for advantage over their own
rivals, the British company had gained great tracts of territory and
become a power in its own right. However, the costs of administration
and defence overwhelmed its trading finances and forced it to seek
government aid, in return for which it had progressively ceded control
over Indian affairs. In 1784 Pitt's administration had established a Board
of Control in London with members appointed by the government to
oversee the company's directors, while in India a Governor-General
appointed by the Crown was given greater powers over his own governing council in Calcutta and the subsidiary administrations in Madras
and Bombay. The Honourable Company retained control over its commercial activities and its ancient monopolies of trade with India and
China, but as a power in India it had been reduced, in the words of one
scholar, to a 'quasi-state department'.[4]

Pitt had sweetened the pill by drastically reducing the duties paid on
tea, the major commodity imported from China in the company's ships,
clawing the revenue back by imposing a tax on windows. Hitherto about
half the tea entering Britain had been smuggled in. The reduction of
duties to some 10 per cent of the wholesale price[5] made smuggling
redundant, and by reducing the retail price led to increased consumption, to the huge benefit of the company.

The growth in quantity of tea imports to Britain was matched by
increasing exports of Indian opium to China; indeed the two trades were
complementary as the silver the company was required to pay for tea at
Canton was obtained from the sale of opium to other Chinese, also at
Canton. It was not a direct transfer since opium was banned by the
Chinese government for reasons of health and public morale; the
company had to distance itself from the illegal supply or forfeit its rights
in legal trades. So, while the cultivation of the opium poppies, particularly in Bengal, and the factories established to process the poppyheads'
narcotic juice were East India Company monopolies, the finished
product, the dried and pressed brown cakes of opium, were auctioned
in Calcutta to independent merchants who despatched them in non-
company ships to Canton Bay, there to be bought at high price by
Chinese smugglers who bribed the Chinese officials supposed to prevent

them bringing the drug ashore. Thus the Honourable Company, while promoting the contraband trade, washed its hands of formal complicity,[6] an artifice which must have left even French connoisseurs of *la perfidie anglaise* wide-eyed in admiration.

The company controlled supply carefully to ensure that it did not outpace growth in the number of Chinese users, thereby, as it has been put, effectively 'growing silver',[7] and far more cheaply than it could be mined. Moreover, since this kind of 'silver' did not continue to circulate but was consumed by its addicts it was a perfect system for growing money in infinite quantities. With the three-way exchange, opium–silver–tea, the company entered what was to prove its final phase on a surge of exceptional profits.

Meanwhile British territory in the subcontinent had been extended. The cause or pretext had been Bonaparte's 1798 expedition to Egypt and fear of French designs on India. These had coincided with the appointment of a new Governor-General of India, Lord Mornington, otherwise Richard, later Marquess Wellesley, elder brother of Arthur, the future Duke of Wellington, who was already in Madras in command of a British infantry regiment. Mornington combined deep hostility to the French Revolutionaries with determination to pursue an active, forward policy in securing the company's Indian territory. It might be said he was an imperialist, or that he was responding to perceived threats to the British position in India. Mogul rule had collapsed leaving a residue of rival princes and alliances, and if the French were to succeed in getting a force into India they would certainly find allies to join them in a campaign against the British.

Colonel Arthur Wellesley was not convinced of the danger, believing with his invariable good sense that it was unlikely the French could insert more than 3,000 troops, and he advised waiting at least until their own forces were better prepared.[8] Mornington charged him with this task and, when he had completed it, lost no time in striking at the most hostile of French clients, Tippoo Sahib, Sultan of Mysore, the state adjoining Madras in southern India. In March 1799 an army of over 20,000, including 5,000 British regulars, organized, drilled and supplied under Wellesley's exacting gaze, together with 16,000 troops sent by the Nizam of Hyderabad, a British ally, moved from Madras into Mysore and, joined by a small force from Bombay, stormed and took Tippoo's fortress capital, Seringapatam, in May. Tippoo himself was killed in the assault.

A part of his territory was annexed by the company, another part went to the Nizam for his aid. Wellesley himself stayed on in Seringa-patam as commander-in-chief and civil governor of the region until in 1803 – following the resumption of war with France after the Peace of Amiens – he was called upon by Mornington to lead one arm of a two-pronged assault on the next perceived threat. This was the Mahratta confederacy, a leaderless and chaotic mix of states stretching across central India from the west coast to Bengal. The campaign succeeded on both fronts; the divided Mahrattas were forced into treaties giving the company more territory, more leverage, more client princes. Above all, the British had established an aura of victory. If they had not entirely filled the power vacuum left by the Moguls, they had advanced to a position from which, in the unstable state of the subcontinent, they could only be drawn forward.

Alarmed both by the annexations and the costs of the campaign which had been met by a hastily arranged loan of £6.5 million on the London market, the government recalled Mornington. But on the ground in India there could be no turning back. One eminent historian of British India, the late Sir Penderel Moon, who had first-hand experience as an administrator in the later days of the Raj, asserted that it was 'the French example and French rivalry that drew [the British] unwittingly along the road to conquest'.[9] In a sense this must be true. It is also true that the advance was not directed either by the British government or the court of the Honourable East India Company in London, but, in Lawrence James's words, 'by a handful of individuals most of whom, if pressed on the matter, would have argued that British supremacy in India was the only practical solution to the problems they faced as commanders and administrators'.[10] Mornington was one. As a historically significant by-product of his rule his younger brother, Arthur, taught himself his trade and discovered his true genius as a soldier.

In 1813 the British government had ended the fiction of the Honourable Company's territorial holdings in India by claiming sovereignty for the Crown. At the same time it ended the company's trade monopoly with India. This was a demonstration of the power of the new industrial pressure groupings, particularly perhaps the Manchester Chamber of Commerce. Confident in the ability of British factory-made goods to penetrate this hitherto closed market of millions, they had demanded free trade. Their success over the following decades at the expense of thousands of Indian handloom weavers and other craft workers would make it more than ever vital for the British to hold

India.[11] The company was permitted to retain its China trade and tea monopolies, but in the event these had a mere twenty years more to run: when the charter again came up for renewal in 1833 both were annulled. Thus free trade triumphed throughout the eastern seas, at least for British merchants and shipowners; Japan remained closed to all intercourse and China restricted overseas trade to the Canton river.

Such was the shape of Great Britain's second empire after the loss of her American colonies; it was built by and for traders. The framework of strategic islands or non-territorial bases along the trade routes together with large territorial holdings in three oceans was rendered invulnerable by her navy – although governments were always sensitive to the potential overland threat to India. The lifeblood pulsed through the maritime arteries in ever greater volumes from the cotton mills of Lancashire, Yorkshire, the midlands and lowland Scotland, driven at first by water, increasingly by steam engines, and from her iron and steel works and brass foundries and machine shops. These manufactures dominated markets in Europe, the United States, the countries of south America as they emerged from colonial rule and in the peace after the great wars flooded Africa and Asia, reversing the balance of trade with the east which had hitherto exported much to the west but desired little in return except silver bullion in payment.[12]

The force of British industry blowing around the world was exceeded only by the power of the London capital market. The leading bankers in the market, particularly the third-generation immigrant from Protestant Germany, Alexander Baring, and the recent Jewish immigrant, Nathan Rothschild, mediated post-war history by stabilizing the European nations impoverished by Napoleon – not least France herself – so guaranteeing the Vienna settlement. In the process they changed the political culture of western Europe for ever by imposing the British way in finance: a funded state debt guaranteed by a national assembly, not a monarch, a transparent budget and a central tax-collecting bureaucracy.[13] At the same time they financed the emerging south American countries and helped fund the states of the United States as they expanded westward.

Baring stole the initial advantage over his main rival by taking control of French finances. France, of course, already had a British-style constitution imposed by Wellington and Talleyrand; she also had the advantage of a very small public debt – since, as noted, *assignat* inflation had wiped out the accumulated Bourbon and Revolutionary debt and Napoleon had shunned state borrowing. It stood at scarcely over £50 million (1,200 million francs) compared with the British national debt after the wars of almost £900 million.[14] Nevertheless, France lacked a revenue surplus sufficient to pay the war indemnity imposed by the second peace treaty, and the Paris capital market was too weak to raise the necessary sum: the 5 per cent state bonds named *rentes* had fallen to 50 per cent of their face value. Baring stepped in, supplying the French government with almost 300 million francs (*c.* £13 million) in exchange for *rentes*. His intervention shored up Louis XVIII's administration and enabled it to raise two further substantial sums the following year by issuing *rentes* directly to the public. Baring underwrote one of these issues which proved popular with British investors as the interest was twice that on British government 3 per cent Consols.[15] Wellington, still in Paris attempting to settle the portions of the French war indemnity due to different European states for the losses inflicted on their private citizens, wrote to the Prime Minister, Lord Liverpool: 'Baring, having the French finances in his hands . . . has to a degree the command of the money market of the world. He feels his power, and it is not a very easy task to counteract him.'[16]

Baring made a huge profit on the rising value of his *rentes*. At much the same time Nathan Rothschild pulled off a similar master-stroke in London. He had been buying 3 per cent Consols steadily on a rising market; by July 1817 his holding was £1.6 million at face value, and he started selling. This was several months before the price peaked and began to fall, and he eventually realized a profit of over a quarter of a million pounds. Niall Ferguson suggests that he had inside information from the Chancellor of the Exchequer, who was planning a large issue of 3.5 or 3.25 per cent government stock which was bound to depress the 3 per cents, as it did.[17] It was Nathan's extensive funding operations for the War Office which had brought him close to British ministers, and on this interpretation persuaded the Chancellor he owed him something in return. Nathan's late father, Mayer Amschel Rothschild, had taught the brothers about 'sticking to a man in government' and had told them that if a highly placed person entered into a financial partnership with a Jew, 'he belongs to the Jew'.[18] He had been a master of cementing such partnerships with loans and other financial favours. At all events, the coup added to Nathan's celebrity and laid a substantial foundation for his further operations.

First and most significant of these was a loan to the Prussian government, which had ended the war with a debt smaller than France's,[19] but with far smaller resources to meet it. Nathan made it clear that he needed security beyond the good faith of Prussia's monarchical government, pointing out that the British had invested in French loans believing the representative system of government there afforded a guarantee 'which could not be found in a Contract with any Sovereign uncontrolled in the exercise of executive powers'.[20] The final contract designated revenues from the Prussian royal estates to service the loan, imposed a British-style sinking fund for repayment and led to a 'Decree for the future Management of the State Debt' which declared that no new loan could be raised without first summoning the Imperial Estates assembly, essentially linking future state borrowing to constitutional reform.[21] King Frederick William III was afraid of reform, equating it with Jacobinism; he therefore borrowed no more, to his and Prussia's loss.

The Prussian loan was important more for innovations offering advantages to British investors: the loan was in pounds sterling and the interest was paid half-yearly in sterling in London, not Berlin, making it both as convenient to hold and as immune from exchange-rate fluctuations as any British stock. The system was generally copied and marked the start of large-scale British investment in foreign stocks, since they paid more than British government stock. The Prussian loan also represented a large step towards a truly international bond market, since the bonds were issued simultaneously in London, Berlin, Frankfurt, Hamburg, Amsterdam and Vienna. The Rothschilds were uniquely qualified to initiate this step since the five brothers now operated from five capitals – Nathan in London, James in Paris, Salomon in Vienna, Amschel in Frankfurt and Carl in Naples – cooperating in the exchange of intelligence, advice and decisions so closely they were, in Niall Ferguson's words, 'to all intents and purposes component parts of a multinational bank'.[22]

As such they soon overtook Baring in combined capital resources and became the acknowledged captains of world finance; in particular, Nathan in London was credited with the capacity to make or break the ambitions of the greatest powers. Metternich's secretary coined for him the epithet '*Finanzbonaparte*';[23] Niall Ferguson has called him 'the prototype financial master of the universe'.[24]

James Rothschild won a commanding position in Paris after Baring's initial post-war coup, and over the next forty years foreign loans raised in Paris practically equalled the value of those raised in London, a measure of the change wrought in France by constitutional government. It was also an indication that financiers, merchants, government contractors and army generals who had profited from the Napoleonic wars and those who had gained by purchase of the confiscated church and émigré estates after the Revolution were investing in foreign stocks at the expense of domestic industry, which languished by comparison even with that of the Belgian provinces of the new Dutch state on its north-eastern border, let alone with Great Britain[25] and the United States of America.

The impressions of foreign visitors to Britain in this period of con-summation after the great French wars are strikingly similar to those of visitors to the United Provinces during its golden age of maritime supre-macy in the seventeenth century: opulence, freedom of expression, the unusual liberties enjoyed by women, and in the industrial quarters intense activity, were especially noted. Some of the most vivid vignettes come from the Prussian Prince Pückler-Muskau, who toured Britain between 1826 and 1828 in search of a wealthy bride to pay off debts inherited with his estate. In this he failed. One of his best prospects, the only daughter of a rich jeweller, had already turned down two peers of the realm because she intended marrying for love; she turned Pückler down because it had become known in English society that he had divorced his first wife in order to marry an heiress. He had been warned early in his tour that he would not find a wife in England since divorce was only recognized on grounds of infidelity and an English girl in his sort of second marriage would regard herself more as a mistress. At the time he had thought this 'entirely too absurd'; but after the jeweller's daughter proved 'by her stupidity to be such an incurable English woman and prudish',[26] he virtually gave up hope of success.

More usually he found English women, young and not so young, lively, pretty and companionable. He extolled the attractions of one married woman, Lady Garvagh, with 'her slender form . . . and the most beautiful English complexion', to an extent that suggests he was much smitten.[27] After a long walk in Brighton alone with another young woman who had just been 'finished' in Paris, he remarked, 'they give unmarried girls in England uncommon freedom, once they are "out"',[28] paralleling foreigners' comments on young Dutch women in the seven-teenth century.[29]

Pückler had come to England in some awe of the English: 'among us the very name Englishman serves instead of the highest title'.[30] His experiences served if anything to enhance the preconception. Two days spent at the Houses of Parliament during a period of political crisis, during which he heard speeches of 'blinding splendour' by Brougham and Canning in the Commons and in the Lords the great Duke of Wellington, 'the hero of the century', struggling over his words and admitting his deficiency as an orator, moved him deeply:

> There is something great about this gathering of the country's representatives. The simplicity in appearance, the dignity and experience, this gigantic power in the outside world and unassuming family relationship on the inside ... In contemplating this twofold senate of the people of England one begins to understand why the English nation is, as yet, the first on the face of the earth.[31]

He confessed he had felt both elevated and depressed, 'the former when I fancied myself an Englishman, the latter when I remembered that I was German'.

Travelling to the source of the Thames outside Cheltenham, he was seized with poetic fancy, musing on the ships and treasure this stream carried on its lower reaches with 'the capital of the world' lying on its banks, from which 'its all-powerful trade rules the four corners of the world!' Then he thought of Rothschild 'without whom no power in Europe today seems able to make war'.[32] He had introduced himself to Nathan earlier in his tour after a visit to the London Stock Exchange, whose jobbers and dealers he characterized as a 'restless, comfortless throng of damned souls ... self-interest and greed gleamed in every eye.'[33] His access to Rothschild's counting house had been impeded by a van loaded with silver ingots; inside, he found the Russian ambassador paying court, Nathan responding without ceremony in a peculiar mode of speech, half German, half English with a German accent 'declaimed with an imposing self-possession'.[34] From another visitor we have a description of Nathan's appearance as 'very common ... with heavy features, flabby pendant lips and a projected fish eye'.[35] All, however, attested to his instant ability to fix a rate and his phenomenal memory for the details of any deal.[36] Such was the 'lion' of the City.

Pückler saw the main faults of the English arising from the very businesslike habits of time, order and despatch to which they owed their success carried over into social life, producing a dullness, narrow views, routine habits of thought, prejudices and 'unbounded desire for, and deference to, wealth'.[37]

Although Pückler was moving in elevated social circles, all this chimes with seventeenth-century descriptions of Dutch bourgeois society, as does the overwhelming impression he gives of the wealth, order and prosperity everywhere: 'these thousands of snug, charming farmhouses . . . this continual throng of elegant carriages, riders and well-dressed pedestrians, are peculiar only to England.' And riding out one spring morning, he was captivated by a vision of countryside we can only dream of today, meadows which 'shimmered blue, yellow, red and lilac. Cows waded belly-deep among these bright flowers . . .'[38]

He was struck by the elegance and unostentatious comfort of the London clubs which surpassed anything conceived of in Germany, and by 'the outstanding cleanliness in all the houses', and was almost overwhelmed by the luxurious standards and abundant breakfasts in the inns. In his first his room had a gargantuan bed with three mattresses; on the washstand, not the single water bottle, jug and basin provided in German and French hotels, 'but instead real tubs of Chinese porcelain in which one can plunge half one's body without trouble; taps which in an instant provide just the flow of water one desires', together with half a dozen large towels, footbaths and a host of other comforts.[39]

Of course Britain had hideous areas in and around the centres of manufacturing industry, where wan-faced workers, including high proportions of children, served endlessly turning machines like machines themselves. Pückler was fascinated and appalled by 'the smoking, swarming, teeming factory town of Birmingham'. He visited a plant there equipped with an 80-horsepower steam engine, spending some hours in 'horrid, dirty, stinking holes which serve as the various workshops', and was allowed to manufacture a button.[40] Yet he found that in general the English of all strata enjoyed greater material well-being than their counterparts on the continent, commenting: 'What with us is called prosperity is here looked upon as mere sufficiency, and this extends through all classes.'[41] The observation was reinforced on his return home – still single – through France where he found, even in Paris, 'something dead . . . miserable and dirty' when compared with the 'bustle, splendour and neatness of England'.[42]

This was January 1829, well over a decade since Napoleon's final defeat and about the time French foreign trade at last regained the level it had reached in 1789. Pückler had sensitive antennae: the following year Parisians would rise in another street revolution to bring down a Bourbon king.

*

JUST AS art had flourished and taken new directions in the merchant societies of Renaissance Italy and the seventeenth-century United Provinces, so British commercial society was complemented by an efflorescence of original genius, particularly in painting, poetry and the novel. Seventeenth-century Dutch art had replaced images of the divine with human, sometimes gross reality, domesticity and living, wind-driven ships and seas. In Britain the focus shifted to the divine in nature, and in the hands of J. M. W. Turner to light itself, source of all visual impressions.

Reverence for the natural world and its moods had been foreshadowed in the work of earlier eighteenth-century British poets. The Scot, James Thomson, working in London in the third decade of the century, was first to take the astonishing step of making nature subject and plot of an extended poem. 'When nursed by careless Solitude I lived, / And sung of nature with unceasing joy'[43] – two lines from Thomson's *The Seasons* introduced another motif of what came to be known as the 'Romantic' movement in British poetry, cultivation of the imagination in isolation from the materialist or mercenary world. It was hardly surprising that the note should have been sounded first in London. 'Hail, ever-pleasing Solitude!' Thomson opened another short piece, 'Companion of the wise and good!'[44] The refrain was taken up by other poets, notably Thomas Gray, whose *Elegy written in a Country Church-yard* extolling the virtues of humble lives far from the reach of ambition touched deep chords in the public. A huge success when published in 1751, it remains an imperishable monument to English landscape and unpolished virtue. Its theme and mood had been prefigured in an earlier piece by Gray, 'Ode on the Spring':

> With me the Muse shall sit and think
> (At ease reclined in rustic state)
> How vain the ardour of the crowd,
> How low, how little are the proud,
> How indigent the great![45]

At the same time in mid-century feelings for the natural as opposed to the formal or classical had begun to manifest themselves in country estates. The most celebrated agent of change, Lancelot 'Capability' Brown, began his career as a gardener's boy and would have remained one of those unknown toilers eulogized by Gray had the English imagination not already been seized by 'nature'. Establishing himself as a landscape gardener to the gentry, Brown made his reputation creating the apparently natural lakes and vistas in the grounds of Blenheim Palace, seat of the Dukes of Marlborough. His sobriquet 'Capability' came from his habit of assuring clients that their grounds were 'capable of improvement'. The 'natural' effects he created with weaving paths and grassy banks reflected in sheets of smooth water, set off by single trees or clumps or winding belts of woodland, were the antithesis of the geometrical arrangements on the continent exemplified by the formal gardens of Versailles. Besides 'improving' more British landed property than any other landscape architect and defining an English rural idyll, Brown's influence spread across Europe; the 'English garden' remains a feature of several continental cities and private estates. Voltaire created one at his chateau on the Swiss border which is still tended today; Jean-Jacques Rousseau was affected by the same emanations.

The British Romantic movement achieved most complete expression in the period of the French Revolutionary and Napoleonic wars just as landscape and working lives in parts of the country were being blighted by industry. In 1789 the engraver, painter, poet and printer-publisher William Blake brought out his first major illustrated and exquisitely hand-coloured volume of verses, *Songs of Innocence*. Their deceptive simplicity could hardly have been further from the certainties of the Revolutionaries in Paris. 'Little lamb, who made thee? / Dost thou know who made thee?'[46] His answer in the final lines: 'Little lamb, God bless thee, / Little lamb, God bless thee' is surely as profound an insight as any achieved by Enlightenment science or philosophy. Blake was a mystic who had 'seen' angels and the soul ascending from his younger brother when he died. His vision pierced rationality. Pückler in the City of London had noted self-interest and greed in every eye. Blake, in *Songs of Experience* (1794), recorded in every face in London 'Marks of weakness, marks of woe'.[47]

Blake's multi-layered genius as artist and poet defies categorization. His contemporaries, the Scot Robert Burns and the giants of English Romantic poetry, Lord Byron, Samuel Taylor Coleridge and William Wordsworth, consummated the shift towards reverence for and through nature and the elevation of emotion over reason. Ironically the Scots philosopher, David Hume, had used reason to prove the invalidity of reason fifty years before, concluding that it was the simple 'slave of the passions'.[48] The theme now permeated British literature. In the greatest examples it was accompanied by a sense of the oneness of nature, in which, contrary to established religion, man was merely a part of the whole. In 'To a Mouse' (1785) Robert Burns saw himself as 'earth-born companion, / An' fellow mortal' of the 'Wee . . . tim'rous beastie', and regretted that man's dominion had 'broken Nature's social union'.[49] Coleridge, in his surpassing epic *The Rime of the Ancient Mariner* (1798), used the allegory of a sailor killing an albatross to suggest the evils that follow when mankind breaks the unity of nature:

> 'He loved the bird that loved the man
> Who shot him with his bow.'
>
> The other was a softer voice,
> As soft as honey-dew:
> Quoth he, 'The man hath penance done,
> And penance more will do.'[50]

The message was more than a century and a half ahead of its time. Burns and Coleridge and his intellectual foil, Wordsworth, and the meteors in their train at the opening of the industrial age, Keats and Shelley, raised an unmatched paean to nature, truth and beauty; but on the ground the reality was to be a ruthless subjugation of nature by means of the products of the new industries. In a wider sense, the gulf between ideals and the darkness at the heart of human desire was expressed most vividly among British Romantic poets by Byron both in his life and writing.

Meanwhile the search for truth through nature was pursued on canvas most brilliantly by J. M. W. Turner and John Constable, the former a youthful prodigy, the latter a craftsman who achieved genius through painstaking observation and effort. In Constable's portraits of everyday activity on and about the river Stour near his home in Suffolk the land-scape is as meticulously honest as the human figures; the trees have weight and shade; their bark is rough; their upper branches sway; clouds pile against the broad East Anglian sky; the river moves and ripples with the current. To the French master, Théodore Géricault, painting in the grand style of Rubens who followed the Italian Renaissance masters, the simplicity and extreme naturalism achieved by Constable came as a revelation. His disciple Eugène Delacroix was equally struck. *The Hay-wain* and *View on the River Stour near Dedham* exhibited at the Paris Salon in 1824 affected him to such an extent he is said to have repainted parts of his own exhibit, *Scènes des massacres de Scio*. Afterwards he left for England where in association with Constable and Turner he developed a freer, more English style. Through these two French artists who influenced French painting through to the Impressionists, Constable in particular seems to have mediated the direction taken by modern art.[51]

Turner took a more direct route. The journey may be said to have started in the summer of 1802. He was twenty-seven and had established himself as the most outstanding British landscape artist of his generation. The Peace of Amiens allowed him to travel to the continent for the first time, and it was in the mountains of Switzerland that he developed that inner eye for the drama of nature that came to dominate his work. His sketchbooks reveal him casting off strictly pictorial representations as inadequate to convey his innermost response to what he was experiencing; or in the words of David Blayney Brown, curator of the Tate Gallery's Turner collection, 'it was that year [1802] on the Montenvers, perhaps, or the Mer de Glace, that Turner began the process of becoming a modern artist – the *first* modern artist.'[52]

He worked up his sketches in London over the following years of war. His increasingly free, impressionistic style was at the opposite pole to the mannered heroics of contemporary French painting. The contrast between his *Snowstorm: Hannibal and his Army crossing the Alps* (1812) and Jacques-Louis David's *Napoleon on the St Bernard Pass* (*c.* 1800) could not be more palpable. Turner's canvas is filled with the fury of the storm over a pitiless landscape, Hannibal and his troops reduced to tormented victims. In David's picture, which Turner had seen in Paris during his travels, the mountain pass is a mere backdrop to an idealized portrait of the Emperor on a rearing grey steed, a stilted fiction anticipating those which would be used to promote the twentieth-century dictators. It is only necessary to place these two canvases side by side to gauge the gulf between mercantile and territorial societies.

Fittingly, Turner was much drawn to maritime subjects, and he brought to them a power and intensity not attained even by the Dutch seventeenth-century masters, capturing the raw moods of the moving sea or the solidity and extraordinary menace of a first rate ship of the line or the chaos at the heart of a storm. In his later canvases he seems to have attempted to see through the material world to the spirit of creation; objects melt into barely visible shapes in swirling vortices of fantastical light.

At the time Romanticism took hold of British artistic and intellectual life a completely antithetical movement was developing, termed

'Utilitarianism'. It originated with a jurist named Jeremy Bentham, who laid the basis in 1789 with his *Introduction to the Principles of Morals and Legislation*. There were many sources for his inspiration, including the British philosophers John Locke and David Hume, although he evidently did not accept Hume's scepticism about the authority of reason since his system is reasonable to the ultimate degree; it is also pragmatic, might indeed be described as common sense on stilts. Although very British in this respect, an important spur to Bentham's thinking had been the French *philosophe* Claude-Adrien Helvétius, whose *De l'esprit* he had read in 1769.[53]

Helvétius had attacked all forms of morality based on religion – for which *De l'esprit* had been publicly burned – and like many British philosophers from Locke onwards defined 'the good' as pleasure or happiness. He believed character to be effectively the sum of education an individual had received, and that his or her education was dependent on the institutions and laws established by government for the instruction and education of the good or virtuous society. The concept inspired Bentham whose particular interest was law reform; his *Principles of Morals and Legislation* sought to provide a scientific footing for such legal, social and moral reforms. The basis was to be a calculation of the consequences of every act in terms of the balance of pleasure over pain. He considered the pursuit of pleasure – in all sensual and intellectual forms – and avoidance of pain as the two primary motivators of human conduct, and since he followed the philosophical school holding pleasure to be 'the good', pleasure was for him both the motive or explanation for action and its virtuous result. He termed this 'the greatest happiness principle' or, borrowing from Hume, 'the principle of utility'. 'The greatest happiness for the greatest number' was to be the scientific and moral basis for legislation.[54]

The basic unit of the 'principle of utility' was the individual. Bentham was a disciple of Adam Smith and the idea that the individual's drive for pleasure had a beneficial moral effect on society can be likened to Adam Smith's proposal in *The Wealth of Nations* that the individual's economic self-interest advanced the prosperity of society. In Bentham's calculus of benefit each individual was 'to count for one, and none more than one', an argument assuming social equality. The political implications included votes for all, including women; and Bentham and his influential followers, James Mill and his son John Stuart Mill and the economist David Ricardo, played an important role in the debates leading to the great Reform Act of 1832 which rationalized the electoral system and extended the vote to the middle classes. They continued to influence much subsequent legislation, while John Stuart Mill and his wife, Harriet, were to become the most potent publicists for women's suffrage.

As a system Utilitarianism was worked out in detail by Jeremy Bentham, but just as Locke's philosophy in the late seventeenth century seemed to reflect the imperatives of the moneyed interest then rising to dominance in Britain, so Bentham's system was finely attuned to the demands of the rising British middle classes. He was not contemptuous of continental metaphysical philosophers, as Locke had been; he simply ignored them, as he ignored motives for actions, whether derived from religious, aristocratic, cultural, internal or even philosophical values such as his German contemporary, Immanuel Kant, proposed. The sole considerations, as summarized by John Stuart Mill in his *Utilitarianism* (1863), were that actions were right 'in proportion as they tend to promote happiness; wrong as they tend to promote the reverse of happiness'.[55] It was a philosophy for logicians or accountants – and of course 'Socialists', a term which first appeared in Britain in 1827 – but as its name implies it proved useful, and in amended and refined forms it has survived as a useful tool.

Bentham had one point of affinity with the Romantic poets: he explicitly extended considerations of happiness to non-human animals.[56] This has hardly penetrated human consciousness outside Anglo-Saxon cultures today; for the late eighteenth century it was a breathtaking intuitive leap. However, if one accepts Wordsworth's evaluation of poetry as 'the most philosophic of all writing' whose object is 'truth . . . carried into the heart by passion', the classical Utilitarians must be found wanting.[57]

Poetry and the novel were, in any case, more effective disseminators of British middle-class values abroad.[58] Napoleon, who had a fierce appetite for books and eclectic tastes, chose several English novels – in French translation since he did not read English – for the library he took with him into exile in Elba. Three were by women. *Julia* by Ann Radcliffe was a 'Gothic' tale, an extremely popular genre, from which he would have learned of the British only that they enjoyed stories of suspense set in impossibly romantic locations. The other two would have been illuminating. They were novels of manners combining social observation and characterization with authentic dialogue, *Camilla, or a Picture of Youth* by Fanny Burney, a pioneer in the form, and *The Absentee* by

Maria Edgeworth, which dealt with the current scandal of absentee English landlords in Ireland.[59]

Both women were precursors of Jane Austen, who gave the form its highest artistic expression. At the time Napoleon chose his books for exile *Sense and Sensibility*, *Pride and Prejudice* and *Mansfield Park* had come out anonymously under the authorship of 'a Lady' so he would not have known her name. She was to produce three more polished gems and be taken up by one of the lions of literary publishing, John Murray, before she died in 1817. Her social range was confined practically to the country gentry and upper middle-class circles of London and Bath in which she moved. Within this compass her piercing eye for the foibles of character, her intelligence, wit and mischief and her delineation of the inner moral life of her heroines illumined universal truths. In the context of social history, her novels mirror the emotional individualism that had spread through the upper and middling echelons of British society, enhancing the role of women. The basis of the phenomenon, described in the social sciences as the rise of 'the individualistic nuclear child-oriented family which is the sole outlet of both sexual and affective and erotic bonding',[60] has so permeated western culture it is hard to appreciate how unusual it has been historically and geographically. It had made an appearance in Dutch bourgeois society in the seventeenth century and was undoubtedly connected with merchant values, which explains its rarity hitherto when the extended family in varied forms with wider kinship organization had been the norm. Lawrence Stone considers the advance of the nuclear family, as opposed to kinship groupings, as 'certainly one of the most significant transformations that has ever taken place, not only in the most intimate aspects of human life, but also in the nature of social organization'.[61] Jane Austen must be counted one of its most effective and entertaining publicists.

SUCH IN outline were the artistic and intellectual achievements Great Britain carried from the wars which had brought her world power. They were as much a product of her wealth and free entrepreneurial society as her manufacturing inventions. They did not include great music, whose home was Vienna. Nor did they embrace the construction of theoretical systems with which to comprehend the moral universe; that was left to continental 'idealist' philosophers whose home was Germany. And it was from Copenhagen, not London, that the great German system-builders, Kant and Georg Wilhelm Friedrich Hegel, would be laid low: the Dane Søren Kierkegaard punctured the conceit that earthlings embedded in existence could conceive the nature of that existence from the outside, as it were through the eyes of God; truth was subjectivity. Not many heeded or even understood him at the time.

It was in the material sphere that British industrial genius and capital now transformed the world. The specifics are well known; they derived from the harnessing of coal-fired steam power to manufacture and to transport by land and sea, and associated advances in iron-founding and engineering. Progress was achieved not by government direction, but as in Adam Smith's model, through the drive and ingenuity of self-interested individuals, many of them uneducated. George Stephenson, father of the railway, taught himself to read and write as an adult at night school and learned mathematics by studying with his son when he brought back homework from school. The passenger train drawn on iron rails by a steam-powered locomotive with which he inaugurated the railway age in 1825 evolved from a mine-owner's project to transport coal to the nearest river communications centre at Darlington in north-east England. Within a decade of its success 1,000 miles of railways radiated from London in every direction, linked Edinburgh and Glasgow and the industrial midlands with Manchester and Liverpool. All lines had been built by private companies financed from the London capital market or more usually by provincial joint stock banks. By this time, 1836, Britain was producing 10 million tons of iron annually, her nearest competitor, Belgium – which had broken away from the United Netherlands in 1830, financed by the Rothschilds – was producing under three million tons, France just a million tons.[62]

The railways, bridges, tunnels and ships built by the engineering Napoleon of the age, the French émigré's son, Isambard Kingdom Brunel, were also financed by private enterprise. Brunel had the grand concept of linking London and New York by railway and steamship, and achieved it briefly in 1841 with the completion of the Great Western Railway line from London to Bristol; he had inaugurated a transatlantic steam passenger and cargo service from the port three years previously with his paddle-wheeler *Great Western*; his *Great Britain*, the first large ship to be built of iron and propelled by screw instead of paddle wheels, entered service in 1845, although her transatlantic career was cut short after her maiden voyage to New York by grounding. She can be seen today in Bristol gloriously restored to her original condition, living proof of the robustness of her design and construction.

On the continent railway construction, which began in Belgium in the early 1830s, was generally planned and subsidized by governments since capital was in short supply and central regulation was the norm.[63] Neither of these considerations applied in Britain, yet the British government did give a decisive fillip to steam shipping with mail subsidies. The first was awarded to the Peninsular Steam Navigation Company in 1837, the year the young Queen Victoria ascended the throne. In return for an annual payment of £29,600, the company undertook to carry the mails on a regular weekly basis to ports on the Iberian peninsula between Vigo and Gibraltar.[64] This was a commercial, not a strategic decision; the government's aim was economy. When the company showed it could deliver the mails more rapidly and cheaply than the Admiralty sailing packets used hitherto, the system of contracting out to private enterprise was applied to all mail routes. On the important transatlantic run the contract was gained by Samuel Cunard (1840) with ships running from Liverpool, dooming Brunel's attempts from Bristol. The significance of mail subsidies can be gauged from the fact that in those early years when marine engines were huge and low-powered and devoured coal ravenously, only those steamship lines awarded mail contracts survived on long sea routes.

The Peninsular Company itself won further mail contracts to Malta, Alexandria and the east, augmenting its name to the Peninsular & Oriental Steam Navigation Company – P & O to generations of imperial administrators, army officers and merchants. Mails and passengers were carried overland from Alexandria across the isthmus to Suez, where the P & O's eastern ships took them via Aden and Galle in Ceylon to Madras and Calcutta. By 1851 the company had won further mail contracts to Australia, Singapore and China and had sewn up the Indian subcontinent with a service to Bombay. Mails and passengers now reached the seat of imperial administration in Calcutta in little over six weeks when under sail around the Cape of Good Hope they had taken from five to six months.[65]

The novelist William Makepeace Thackeray has left a vignette of the mail officer aboard the P & O *Lady Mary Wood* in 1844:

> now our attention was drawn from the land to a sight of great splendour on board. This was Lieutenant Bundy, the guardian of Her Majesty's mails, who issued from his cabin in his long, swallow-tailed coat with anchor buttons; his sabre clattering between his legs, a magnificent shirt collar of several inches

in height rising around his good-humoured, sallow face; and above it a cocked hat that shone so I thought it was made of polished tin ... The authority of Her Majesty's Lieutenant on the steamer is stated to be so tremendous that he may order it to stop, to move to go to larboard, starboard or what you will; and the Captain dare only disobey him *suo periculo*.[66]

Mail subsidies gave British steam shipping a head start over all rivals and in turn stimulated the ancillary industries, marine engine-building, iron ship construction and coal mining; while the necessary establishment of coaling depots on the steamer routes expanded the network of British overseas bases. The majority of naval officers brought up in the high art of seamanship and shiphandling under sail naturally viewed steam engines with their coal and filthy smoke and dust and the grimed engineers and firemen who attended them much as Romantic poets viewed the industrial blight spreading from the manufacturing cities. Nevertheless the Admiralty, contrary to legend, made full use of the skills of the private marine engineering firms. This was the real and no doubt unintended benefit the government gained from the mail subsidies. Paddle-wheel gunboats were built for coast defence at home and river and coastal operations overseas, particularly in the campaign against the African slave trade; and when the screw propeller proved superior to paddle wheels, the Admiralty began fitting auxiliary steam engines turning screws to ships of the home battle fleet, still the foundation of overseas dominion and maintained at a strength equal to the combined fleets of the only likely opponents, France and Russia.[67]

The East India Company also ordered large numbers of steam gunboats to maintain British influence in Egypt and Mesopotamia and on the Indus river in north-west India for fear of French and Russian designs on the overland routes to the subcontinent. Others were ordered to China where trade relations were breaking down. Since the Honourable Company's last legal monopolies had ended in 1834 increasing quantities of opium had been smuggled into China by British traders supplied by the company, which retained control of Indian production, and by Americans buying the drug from ports in the Ottoman Turkish empire; the Chinese reacted to the drain of silver and importation of drug dependence with harsh measures, burning stocks and the offshore receiving ships or hulks, torturing Chinese merchants, seizing British hostages.[68] This was to provide a pretext in 1839 for the first 'Opium War'.

The underlying cause was more fundamental: the irresistible dynamic of British/western trade meeting the incomprehension of the Confucian bureaucracy in Peking. The Chinese Celestial Empire was self-sufficient; trade was a despised occupation; and contact with foreign traders was strictly controlled. Only limited numbers of Chinese merchants were licensed for commerce with the barbarians in restricted locations. Naturally these formed a cartel which kept prices artificially high, while local officials levied arbitrary duties. All attempts by the East India Company to normalize trade and open more Chinese ports had been resisted. A major effort had been made as early as 1793 when the British government in concert with the East India Company had despatched an extravagant diplomatic mission to Peking under Lord Macartney, a former governor of Madras. The court he paid had been regarded by the Chinese as submission, his gifts as tribute; his mission had ended in failure.

From 1834 independent China traders headed by William Jardine of Jardine Matheson joined the Honourable Company in calls to the British government to send out warships to force China open.[69] And in response to increasing anarchy as Chinese attempts to apprehend smugglers extended to all western merchant vessels, the Foreign Secretary, Lord Palmerston, convinced himself that there were only two possible courses of action: to withdraw completely from China or 'to bring the Chinese government to reason with vigorous measures'.[70] He had the First Lord of the Admiralty prepare for the second solution. A strong naval force was gathered but before it could sail open war had broken out, precipitated by a British sailor committing murder and the Chinese authorities, according to custom, demanding hostages.

The Chinese retreat into isolation for over two centuries had left them entirely vulnerable to the instruments of warfare developed in the west. Some of the cannon in their forts had been cast three centuries earlier. Their foot soldiers were armed with bows and crossbows, swords, spears or stones and shields; their few muskets took three men to serve, aim and fire.[71] In the first naval action fought in November 1839 two British warships of the East Indies squadron, a 26-gun frigate and an 18-gun sloop, routed twenty-nine Chinese war junks in under half an hour, sinking five, causing one to explode and crippling many others.[72] The following year the particular service squadron from England arrived in the Canton river headed by three ships of the line and carrying 20,000 British and Indian troops. A blockade of the coast was established, offlying islands seized and the merchants of Canton and Macao forced to resume trading on British terms. Afterwards the squadron headed northwards, dealing in similar fashion with other ports up the coast on the way to the Yangtse river.

At home a young William Gladstone, from the opposition benches in the Commons, denounced as aggression this exhibition of naked power on behalf of the manufacturers of opium grown in India: 'We, the enlightened and civilized Christians, are pursuing objects at variance both with justice and religion.'[73] Palmerston asked why, if the motives of the Chinese government were to promote moral habits, they did not prohibit opium-growing in their own country; the fact was 'this was an exportation of bullion question, an agricultural interest-protection question. It was the poppy interest in China.'[74] Outrageous as the reply appears, Palmerston did not lack moral bearings: he was as personally committed to the abolition of the slave trade as he was to the promotion of British commerce, and wielded British power in that cause quite as vigorously. In this he represented the majority of his countrymen.

The key to British success in China proved to be the steam gunboats, chiefly those of the Honourable Company. Their ability to manoeuvre independently of the wind, tow sailing warships into action, transport troops and stores, support troops ashore and finally to lead and tow the sailing warships up the Yangtse river to strike at China's transport jugular, the Grand Canal linking the northern to the southern provinces, proved decisive. The *Nemesis*, an iron vessel 184 feet in length, built by John Laird of Birkenhead and armed with a 32-pounder cannon at bow and stern, each able to swing to either broadside, together with fifteen smaller cannon and several rocket launchers, was reported by her captain to have instilled terror in the Chinese: 'they call her the devil ship and say that our shells and rockets could only be invented by the latter. They are more afraid of her than all the line of battle ships put together.'[75]

In August 1842, with many sea ports and the vital internal north–south waterway under British control, the Chinese government acknowledged its impotence and bowed to British demands. By the Treaty of Nanking and a supplementary treaty the following year, the ports of Amoy, Foochow, Ningpo, Shanghai and Canton were opened to trade and residence with rights for British people to be tried by British courts; the island of Hong Kong at the mouth of the Canton river was ceded to Britain and a war indemnity of £5.8 million was conceded. Subsequently the United States and other western powers were able to negotiate similar rights for their citizens.

The first 'Opium War' might be better named the first China Trade War: the East India Company, Jardine Matheson and other agency houses and independent merchants who summoned up British government forces were, of course, driven by the unique profits made from the manufacture and smuggling of opium, but the greater aim had always been to open the vast country to regular and orderly trade. The war was as significant for the role played by steam gunboats. It was not the first campaign in which they took an important part; they had done so in operations in the Levant in 1840. But by bringing British power to the very heart of the Celestial Empire they had been instrumental in securing complete capitulation. The lessons were clear.

Hong Kong was to prove an inspired choice for a trading entrepôt. Its splendid harbour was protected by the mainland hills from the northeast monsoon and summer typhoons. Like Singapore, it was declared a duty-free port from the beginning and grew at a prodigious rate as the emporium of trade with China, serving also as coaling station and main naval base for the British East Indies squadron.

Free trade and relaxation of the Navigation Laws whereby colonial trades and all imports to Britain had been reserved to British ships or ships of the country producing the goods were the pacific and beneficial arms of the British drive for world markets. William Pitt, a disciple of Adam Smith, had first attempted to liberalize trade after the American war in the 1780s, but his project had been shattered by the outbreak of the Revolutionary war. The baton was picked up by a liberal Tory government in the 1820s: customs duties imposed during the war to raise revenue were reduced and a Reciprocity Act was passed in 1823 which permitted treaties with other countries to allow their ships to bring goods to Britain and pay reduced duties provided they reciprocated. The aim was to increase the volume of trade by lowering barriers. The process was continued throughout the 1840s; by 1846 all raw materials except timber and tallow and many semi-finished goods could be imported duty-free, while the duty on manufactured goods was reduced from 30 to 10 per cent.[76]

This was, of course, exactly what British industry needed: cheaper raw materials allowed lower finished prices; and since few foreign manufactures could compete with the British factory-made article, protective tariffs were unnecessary. Economists of the 'Manchester School' centred on that hub of manufacturing dominated political debate, raising the cause of free trade into a moral crusade with predictions that the international prosperity which resulted would lead eventually to the 'harmonization of mankind's general desires and ideals'.[77] One of the leading polemicists, a calico-printing industrialist turned politician named Richard Cobden, argued during the 1830s and 1840s for a new direction for foreign policy based on promoting international economic expansion through the free movement of men and materials. His ideal was succinctly conveyed by the title of a pamphlet he put out in 1842: *Free Trade as the Best Human Means for Securing Universal and Permanent Peace.* An immensely comforting doctrine for British industrialists and politicians alike, it would endure repeated disappointments in practice. The record reveals that it never penetrated meetings of the Board of Admiralty.

However, other nations did initially follow the path of free trade, to Britain's great advantage: between 1840 and 1847 alone her imports rose by 44 per cent, exports by 34 per cent.[78] The other chief beneficiary was the United States of America. Her shipping industry had benefited hugely from her neutral status during the greater part of the French wars. Now it was able to profit from the easing of the British Navigation Laws, which were finally abolished in 1849. The Americans had a tradition of building fast ships; this was joined to what that shrewd observer of American life, Alexis de Tocqueville, described as 'a sort of heroism in their manner of trading',[79] by which he suggested that they showed none of the prudence of European sailors: they seldom waited for favourable weather to leave port, seldom shortened sail at night and did not seek harbour to repair damages. Americans were often shipwrecked, he observed, but no traders completed their voyages so rapidly, hence charged such low freight rates. British shipping, which had been sheltered by the Navigation Laws, found it difficult to compete or adjust. By the 1830s American ships were carrying over 75 per cent by value of US exports and 90 per cent of imports.[80] By 1840 they had 2.14 million tons of merchant shipping against a British total of 2.72 million tons,[81] and seemed on course to overtake the mistress of the seas. No doubt they would have done so had Britain not taken such a decisive lead in marine engine design and the construction and employment of iron steam ships, soon to supersede sail.

Merchant traders of the US port cities, New York, Philadelphia, Boston, Baltimore, besides breaking into the European and far eastern trades and carrying the produce of the southern states of the Union, had penetrated the formerly protected markets of the Caribbean and central and south America. They could not compete with British manufactures or finance, but had helped to establish for the United States a moral sway, in Tocqueville's words, 'as the most enlightened, the most powerful, and the most wealthy members of the great American family'.[82] The fifth US President gave expression to the idea in an address in December 1823 which was recognized from mid-century as the 'Monroe Doctrine'. He warned Europeans that any attempt to oppress or control any nation in the Americas would be viewed as a hostile act against the United States. The declaration had been inspired by a British invitation to issue a joint statement forbidding future colonization in south America. James Monroe made it unilaterally. In view of Britain's overwhelming naval and financial power it had little practical application and was not invoked when Britain repossessed the Falkland Islands off Argentina in 1833; for all that, it accurately reflected the perception of the United States' pre-eminence in the western hemisphere. From 1845, when the United States annexed the former territory of Texas from Mexico, once a Spanish colony, now independent, the idea had been encapsulated in the doctrine of the United States' 'manifest destiny to overspread the continent allotted by Providence'.[83]

'Manifest Destiny' served, like the Spanish and Portuguese missions to spread Christianity, as a cover for naked conquest: with victory over Mexico in 1848 the United States acquired the huge territories now forming California, Arizona, New Mexico, western Colorado, Utah and much of Wyoming.[84] And 'Manifest Destiny' rendered subjugation of native inhabitants of the continent by a materially more powerful, land-hungry people an acceptable, even admirable goal. It was simply inevitable. As white settlers trekked westwards creating new states from wilderness, the dispossessed of the wilderness became aliens in their own land, reinforcing the settlers' sense of the superiority of their own culture. And we have it from the observations of an English gentlewoman, Fanny Trollope, who travelled the United States in 1829 and 1830, that the Americans, no doubt because of the freedoms and equality of opportunity enjoyed in their pioneer society – so unlike the old stratified societies of Europe – considered themselves 'the most moral people on earth'. She read and heard it asserted time and again in conversation and from the pulpit.[85]

At the same period in Australasia British free immigrants opening southern and western Australia were disinheriting the aboriginal natives; and from 1840 – the year convict transportation was ended – Britain claimed sovereignty over the nearby islands of New Zealand and settlers began establishing a white ascendancy over the Maoris who had arrived over a thousand years before. As in the American mid-west, the taming of native inhabitants with treaties, unequal purchase, the interpretation of Anglo-American law, theft, firearms and not least the spread of diseases hitherto unknown in the wilderness went hand in hand with belief in moral and racial superiority. History had always been driven thus. It was simply the turn of the Anglo-Americans; their claims seemed justified to them by their extraordinary scientific and material progress; certainly the power this gave them was irresistible.

The dynamo of United States expansion was New York City. Philadelphia, once financial capital of the nation, where the Bank of the United States had been resurrected in 1816, had been comprehensively eclipsed by the 1830s. New York owed its dominance to unparalleled sea and inland communications. Whereas Philadelphia could only be reached by large ocean-going ships at high tide, the quays encircling the south end of Manhattan Island on which New York stood could be approached by the largest vessels. Frances Trollope, who arrived there by river boat from the interior, referred to its unparalleled advantages of position and unimaginable beauty: 'Situated on an island . . . it rises like Venice from the sea, and like that fairest of cities in the days of her glory, receives into its lap tribute of all the riches of the earth.'[86]

The description was precise. The master stroke by which the city had reinforced its ascendancy was the construction of a canal from Albany on the upper reaches of the river Hudson, which was navigable from New York, via the Mohawk river valley to Buffalo on the eastern shore of Lake Erie. It was a gigantic enterprise involving 360 miles of excavation, chiefly by Irish immigrant labourers, and the creation of eighty-two locks to raise the level 500 feet. Although a public venture run by the state of New York, it was in effect the work of the Manhattan mercantile elite who held political power.[87] It was financed by bonds issued by a New York investment bank whose grandest client, Baring Brothers, found no difficulty in selling them to British investors; the majority of the funding came from Britain and Europe.[88]

On the completion of the Erie Canal in 1825 New York achieved the prime middleman position between on the one hand the new agricultural states of the mid-west, Ohio (1803), Indiana (1816), Illinois (1818) and the territories that would form Michigan and Wisconsin, and on the other hand ocean-borne manufactures from Britain and the produce of Asia and the east. Manhattan merchants already brokered and shipped the bulk of the produce of the southern plantation states. With growth in trade with the mid-west stimulated by a 90 per cent reduction in freight rates from Buffalo to New York City – from $100 a ton by land to $10 by canal – and the completion over the next few years of more canal projects which sucked in the commodities of other regions, New York became the supreme national emporium.

As in Venice, Amsterdam and London before it, all professional and information services associated with commerce were concentrated in a small area, in this case around the Bank of New York on Wall Street near the southern tip of Manhattan. Opposite the bank in the recently built Merchants' Exchange, the New York Stock and Exchange Board dealt in a greater volume of stocks than any American exchange, and set prices for the continent. The several banks in the city disposed of more capital than Philadelphian banks – and in the early 1830s played a key role in bringing down the second Bank of the United States. New York's banks asserted financial dominance, but the Federal government was left without a central issuing house or lender of last resort. The assets of New York insurance companies also exceeded those of the insurance industries of Philadelphia, Boston and Baltimore combined.[89]

The commercial heart of Manhattan was surrounded by offices and warehouses of shipping agents, commodity merchants and hundreds of wholesale companies which bought imported goods at auction and shipped them on commission via coasting vessels and canal boats to country stores in the interior. Horse-drawn goods wagons, carts and carriages jammed the streets; those leading east and west were closed with views of the bowsprits and high masts and yards of ships alongside the Hudson and East river quays; across the water shipbuilding yards lined the Brooklyn and Hoboken shores.

The 'Battery' fortifications guarding the southern tip of the island had been converted into a green and tree-lined promenade which Frances Trollope supposed more beautiful than any other city could boast;[90] from there the magnificent avenue, Broadway, ran north, lined with attractive shop fronts with neat awnings past another green park surrounding the City Hall, and a long way beyond past slum tenement blocks crowded with the teeming labour force of immigrant Irish, Germans and free blacks. The offices of many of the forty-seven newspapers, eleven of them daily papers, published in the city by the early 1830s, were congregated in the streets leading off City Hall Park. As focus of internal and external communications Manhattan had become the national clearing house for news; nearly a million copies of New York papers were shipped out upstate and interstate each month.[91] The city had also taken the lead in book and periodical publishing.

North of City Hall Park and west of Broadway lay the fashionable residential areas where the merchant patriciate lived in grand style, their wives, as in seventeenth-century Amsterdam, raising 'republican children' while creating an environment in which their husbands could escape the pressures of the office. This was the role for which women of the middling and upper social classes were groomed. Frances Trollope was struck by the separation of the genders in most social activities in the United States and the little influence women had in public life or even in society compared with their counterparts in England.[92] This would be partially redressed within the next two decades as women authors, journalists and editors came to prominence and women asserted themselves in campaigns for women's rights and the abolition of slavery in the southern states. Yet up to mid-century feminist agitation achieved little more than legislation giving women the right to control their own bank deposit accounts. One individual achievement stands out: the British-born immigrant to New York, Elizabeth Blackwell, succeeded in gaining admittance to the Geneva Medical College in upstate New York and in 1849 graduated at the top of her class to become the first female doctor of medicine in any modern country. It was a foretaste of what might be, although on her return to New York City she was refused employment as a physician. Forced to set up independently, she founded the New York Infirmary for Women and Children.

Soon after the boom in canal building 'railway mania' was sparked by Stephenson's success in England. New York again took the lead. The Mohawk and Hudson Railroad Company, formed in 1831 with major funding by John Jacob Astor, was the first of many lines built to improve the city's communications with the interior – and within Manhattan itself – culminating in 1851 with the New York and Erie railroad. The growth of internal trade, western settlement – and speculation in land values – and the volume and value of dealings as railroad company stock came on the New York stock market exceeded that generated by canals; and as in the British model, railroads stimulated iron founding, engineering, mining and multiple industrial innovations. Steam engines were employed in shipbuilding yards and rope walks, and in 1846 the first steam grain elevator was installed in New York harbour. By mid-century the aggregate horsepower of steam engines employed in the United

States as a whole amounted to nearly 1.7 million against 1.3 million for Great Britain; the figure for France was under 0.4 million.[93]

Americans had always defined themselves in relation to the elemental regions of the interior beyond the bounds of cultivation; and given the continued cultural sway of Great Britain – despite bitter feelings towards her as a nation – and the influence of the Romantic poets and painters, it is not surprising that the erosion of the American wilderness, first by agriculture, then by canals and railroads and the great conurbations that sprang up almost overnight in their track, should have become a theme of American literature and art. The New Yorker, Washington Irving, known as the first American man of letters, conveyed the tension with his Catskill hills tales in *The Sketchbook of Geoffrey Crayon, Gent* (1819–20), while in the first truly American novel, *The Pioneers* (1823) by James Fenimore Cooper, also a New Yorker, the conflict was personalized: the chief character, the scout known as Leatherstocking, seemed to be the spirit of the wilderness struggling vainly against the advance of civilization: he continued to do so in four subsequent 'Leatherstocking' novels.

The collision of the pastoral with the primeval was conveyed on many canvases, the most poignant perhaps *View from Mount Holyoke, Northampton, Massachusetts, after a Thunderstorm* (1836) by Thomas Cole, a pioneer of American landscape painting. Cole painted himself into the picture, a tiny figure with an easel on the wild side as if confronting the groomed farmland he portrayed beyond the bends of the Connecticut river. Cole had emigrated from England at the age of seventeen, studied at the Pennsylvania Academy of Fine Arts in Philadelphia and made his name with canvases of the Hudson river valley and Massachusetts landscapes worked up in the English mode from pencil sketches made on his expeditions. During a sketching trip in the Catskills, New York state, in 1835 Cole confided in his journal how the painter of American scenery had 'privileges superior to any other; all nature here is new to Art.'[94] The same year he wrote an 'Essay on American Scenery' in which he condemned the democratic, expansionist and 'meagerly' utilitarian direction in which the nation was being taken by its seventh President, Andrew Jackson.[95] He was already engaged in a series of paintings depicting a civilization rising from primitive beginnings, through maturity to decline and desolation. The centrepiece on which he worked that year represented *The Consummation of Empire* in vainglory, luxury and excess. There are grounds for believing this to be an allegory of 1830s New York; it is even suggested that a central figure robed in red and receiving the acclamation of crowds is Jackson, the 'American Caesar'.[96]

A year after Cole's death in 1848 his one-time unofficial pupil, Asher Brown Durand, painted a moving tribute, *Kindred Spirits*, depicting Cole with brush and palette and their mutual friend William Cullen Bryant, a prolific nature poet, standing together on a rocky ledge overlooking a gorge in the wilderness. Cole was forerunner of a school of landscape artists influenced by Turner and Constable yet distinctly American, who recognized that the threatened wilderness was both unique and sublime and that they only need reproduce it to evoke its grandeur, as they did. In doing so they played a significant part in defining American identity.[97]

As in Turner's *Snowstorm: Hannibal crossing the Alps*, human figures in their canvases were dwarfed by luminous skies, mountains, lakes and forests. Yet increasingly settlement was taming the wilds. The population of the Union had increased at a phenomenal rate, chiefly from immigration as the poor of particularly Ireland and Germany sought escape from destitution, starvation or repression; these immigrants were, of course, a necessary element in the dynamic of the nation. By mid-century the population had swollen from four millions in 1790 to over 23 million, fast approaching Great Britain with 27 million and France with 34 million.[98] France, formerly by far the most populous nation in western Europe, had fallen well behind both her rivals in rate of increase of numbers, as in industrialization.

THAT PENETRATING observer, Alexis de Tocqueville, who toured the United States in 1831 and 1832 with an equally enquiring companion, Gustave de Beaumont, discovered the answer to France's comparative stagnation in lower Canada. As noted in the Introduction, he found that the descendants of the original French settlers here were in thrall to bureaucratic regimentation from the centre, as a result of which they lacked the political confidence to manage their own affairs or the commercial enterprise or prosperity of the New England communities he and Beaumont had studied. In contrast to the vigour of American society, theirs was static.[99]

American commercial drive was portrayed by Frances Trollope in terms Tocqueville might have used: 'Nothing can exceed their [Americans'] activity and perseverance in all kinds of speculation, handicraft and enterprise, which promises a pecuniary result.' She quoted an

Englishman long resident in the country remarking that he had never heard a conversation between Americans in the street, in the coffee house, the theatre or at home without the word 'dollar' coming up.[100] She declared she had no wish to do business with them 'lest, to use their own phrase, "they should be too smart for me"',[101] but had nothing but praise for the boldness and energy with which they undertook and completed public works. 'Nothing stops them if a profitable result can be fairly hoped for. It is this which has made cities spring up amidst the forests with such inconceivable rapidity.'[102]

Tocqueville and Beaumont attempted to discover how public works were launched and carried through and were astonished to find that there was no single agency or method: large public enterprises were usually undertaken by the state, but there was no rule and counties, towns or private companies were constantly in competition with the state, as when private or municipal turnpikes or toll roads ran parallel to state highways. They were particularly struck by the 'private associations' – by which they meant the corporations that flourished in Andrew Jackson's America – responsible for so many ambitious projects, and noted that they had accomplished works 'which the most absolute kings and the most opulent aristocracies would certainly not have been able to undertake and finish in the same time'.[103]

Synthesizing his first impressions, Tocqueville concluded that the dominating passion of Americans was commercial gain. They assessed the value of everything from the answer to a single question: 'how much money will it bring in?' To all appearances they seemed to be 'a company of merchants gathered together for trade'.[104] Later, he and Beaumont visited England, in Birmingham discovering parallels to the behaviour they had imagined unique to Americans: 'They work as if they must get rich by the evening and die the next day,' Tocqueville noted. 'They are generally very intelligent people, but intelligent in the American way.'[105] Beaumont described a manufacturer they met: 'No elegance; good nature; polite; sometimes indiscreet; embarrassingly obliging; it's *absolutely America*.'[106]

Like Pückler before them, the two were overwhelmed by the city, which Tocqueville described as an immense workshop in which they heard only the sound of hammers and the whistle of steam escaping from boilers, saw only busy people with faces grimed with smoke. 'Everything is black, dirty and obscure, although every instant it is winning silver and gold.'[107] Other impressions of England echoed

Pückler's: '*Quel luxe!*' he wrote at the end of accounts of visits to Chelsea and Greenwich;[108] and of the English countryside: 'the Eden of modern civilization. Magnificently kept roads, new and clean houses, fat herds . . . more dazzling riches than anywhere else in the world.'[109] And he and Beaumont left the country after their tour, like Pückler, with the feeling they had passed through 'the most powerful, the most active, the most successful social entity on earth'.[110]

Their fascination with British and American attitudes provides the clearest evidence of the profound cultural and material gulf between France and the two Anglo-Saxon empires. The essence of the difference, they concluded – as of the differences they had observed between New England and former French lower Canada – was the degree of administrative control exercised by central government. In Britain and the United States it was minimal. Parishes, towns and counties were managed by locally elected councils in America or local justices of the peace in England.[111] Disputes were taken to the courts. Central government did not intervene. In France, by contrast, central government bureaucracy penetrated every *département, arrondissement* and *commune* with a web of complex rules to guide local functionaries and ensure uniformity throughout the country, so emptying the localities of political freedom or initiative.[112] The system carried over into commercial relations. Railway construction was delayed until central government could take it in hand. This was not due to lack of capital; as noted, France invested almost as much abroad in this period as Great Britain. All industry was subject to government influence and interference. Trained scientists, engineers, architects and technicians turned out by the excellent higher education system were sucked into government service rather than private associations or corporations as in Britain and America, further strengthening the hold of the centre.[113]

The imbalance rendered the centre itself vulnerable. Local and legal restraints inherent in the British and American systems had not been grafted on to the constitutional monarchy otherwise copied so faithfully from the British model. When feeling in the country diverged from the direction the government was taking the administration lacked the political antennae to detect the coming storm or the popular institutions to deflect it. In July 1830 the last of the French Bourbon kings, Charles X, formerly the Comte d'Artois, who had succeeded on the death of his elder brother, Louis XVIII, in 1824, was forced from the throne by a popular and parliamentary uprising provoked by a desperate attempt to close newspapers opposing the government. Violence reminiscent of 1789 erupted on the streets of Paris. Mobs sporting tricolour cockades manned barricades formed across the streets with felled trees backed by paving stones and doors wrenched from houses.

Charles was succeeded by the liberal Louis-Philippe, formerly Duc d'Orléans. The upper bourgeoisie and intelligentsia, including Tocqueville and Beaumont, rejoiced, believing this was France's 1689 – England's 'Glorious Revolution' remained a potent political image. James Rothschild moved his support deftly from the old to the new regime.[114] But the doctrines of administrative centralization and what Tocqueville called the 'system of uniformity that delights the superficial and metaphysical minds of our age'[115] continued; and in 1848 a third popular insurrection removed Louis-Philippe.

Tocqueville, who had warned of the impending revolution weeks before, diagnosed its causes as retention of all political power and influence by a single class – the upper bourgeoisie – denying most people any part in public affairs, together with fantastical socialist theories on the role government could play in relations between workers and employers, and ultra-centralizing policies 'which had come to persuade the multitude that it depended on the state not only to save them from misery, but to afford them comfort and well-being'.[116] He and Beaumont identified socialism as heir to the bureaucratic spirit of pre-Revolutionary France, categorizing its doctrines as denial of liberty, contempt for the individual, 'a new form of servitude'.[117] This was particularly prescient that year, 1848, when two German disciples of Hegel, Karl Marx and Friedrich Engels, brought out the *Manifest der Kommunistischen Partei* (*The Communist Manifesto*). The fruit of Tocqueville's American tour, *De la démocratie*, in English translation *Democracy in America*, had established his reputation on both sides of the Atlantic among the leading political savants of the day, but he was as little heeded on the dangers of socialism as Kierkegaard on Hegel's fundamental misconceptions.

Louis-Philippe abdicated and a Second Republic was proclaimed. It was not sufficient for radicalized workers who took to the streets of Paris again in June. They were bloodily suppressed, after which Tocqueville and Beaumont were coopted on to a commission to draw up a new constitution. But the tensions between the opposing extremes of socialism and reaction could not be contained within a liberal programme, while the elected President of the new Republic, Charles-Louis-Napoleon-Bonaparte, son of Napoleon's brother Louis, preferred to surmount the conflict by promoting himself to the people as the strong man they needed, reminding them of the nation's former imperial grandeur. In December 1851 he staged a coup and dissolved the Assembly. The unresolved conflicts of 1789 were to be reconciled once again by a Bonaparte; weary or incapable of a politics of compromise, France turned back to *la gloire*. Next year Bonaparte would take the title of Emperor Napoleon III – since Napoleon's son who had died earlier had been styled by his adherents Napoleon II.

The revolutions that toppled French regimes in 1830 and 1848 had counterparts in most western states, with varying results. The two Anglo-Saxon nations were exceptions. In Great Britain radicals and middle classes alike were appeased by the Great Reform Act of 1832; in the United States by the extension of suffrage – in five new states to all males – and appeals made by Andrew Jackson in the 1828 Presidential election over the heads of the political parties to the mass of the people. 'Jacksonian democracy' is seen as a turning point in the political development of the United States. However, for both nations a speech by the younger Pitt in 1792 linking the unprecedented prosperity of the country with the constitution bequeathed it in 1689 would have seemed appropriate: 'It is this union of liberty with law which . . . affords to property its just security, produces the exertion of genius and labour, the extent and solidity of credit, the circulation and increase of capital.'[118]

Tocqueville and Beaumont would most certainly have agreed. Tocqueville noted, however, that England, having garnered the trade of the whole world, had to maintain this 'extraordinary and abnormal state'.[119] The implication was that she – and the United States – were, in effect, balanced on a wheel of perpetually increasing trade and prosperity and could not afford to slow or stop or they would fall, an insight with perilous present-day resonances.

The United States faced more immediate perils than revolution: dissolution or civil war. There was a seemingly unbridgeable moral and ideological divide between the southern states where slavery was practised and the northern states in which Black African-Americans were free. This was nothing new: the constitution had been forged in a compromise over slavery. Yet by mid-century the situation had been exacerbated by the westward spread of the nation and the formation of new 'slave' states in the south and 'free' states in the north. By 1848, when gold was discovered in the recently annexed territory of California slave and free states were precisely balanced at fifteen each. The following year the Californians requested admission to the Union as a free state, thereby provoking political crisis, for if the slave states lost parity in the Senate they were powerless to block legislation harmful to their interests. The dilemma was resolved after months of bitter negotiation with a series of measures known collectively as 'the compromise of 1850'; California was admitted as a free state, but the south was compensated in other ways. It was a triumph of the politics of accommodation as practised in Britain and America, but the crippling schism remained.

Elsewhere among western nations slavery was becoming an anomaly. It had been abolished throughout the British empire in 1834, in the French and Danish colonies in 1848, and owing largely to the power diplomacy of Canning, Palmerston and other British Foreign Secretaries and the activities of Royal Naval slave patrols, slave trading was banned by most western European nations and the newly independent states of south America. Its survival was practically confined in the west to Brazil, Cuba and the southern United States.[120] The evil effects on both slaves and slave-owning societies were detailed graphically by Tocqueville and other European visitors to America; Frances Trollope was particularly eloquent about the moral degradation resulting from ownership of slaves, especially among poorer whites, 'often as profoundly ignorant as the negroes they own'.[121] In the Preface to the fifth edition of her *Domestic Manners of the Americans* published in 1839, she insisted that until the Union abolished slavery it must be a negative Union:

> It is life and death bound up together; and if the courage, enterprise and indus-
> try of the Eastern and free Western States would escape the rottenness that
> must inevitably spread if they continue thus linked together, they must submit
> to the mortifying necessity of lessening the map of their Federal territory.[122]

She was right on wider grounds than the pure moral principle behind the British and American abolitionists. The move to free trade animating the dominant commercial-industrial and middle classes in Britain and their Utilitarian publicists embraced every political and commercial freedom from the unrestricted movement of labour, capital and goods to individual political and moral autonomy. Slavery had no place in the new order; and British trading interests had come to realize its negative impact on normal trade and investment.[123] This is not to suggest that the abolitionist movement was in any way hypocritical, simply that the new trading and political imperatives had reached congruence with its moral drive. As John Stuart Mill put it: 'The spirit of commerce and industry is one of the greatest instruments not only of civilization in the narrowest, but of improvements and culture in the widest sense.'[124]

The institution of slavery in the southern states debarred the United States from leading the advance of freedom and progress. France had ruled herself out by retreating into her martial and bureaucratic past under Napoleon III. The other populous continental power, Russia, had not emerged from feudalism. It remained for Great Britain to show the way, for good or ill, to the modern world. Like the United Provinces before her, she had survived the most terrific onslaught of the most powerful territorial hosts, and had done so for much of the time completely on her own. By adding industrial to naval and merchant strength she had emerged as a new kind of world power without a peer. No continental despot could bring her down; she had ended history's greatest frustration: her people would enjoy ever-rising material prosperity.

The Great Exhibition of 1851 in Hyde Park, London, provided a fitting demonstration. Appropriately the initiative came from an outsider, the German Prince Albert, consort to Queen Victoria. The Crystal Palace in which it was housed was a triumph of prefabricated engineering, design and innovation. Walls and arches of clear glass panes were supported by an intricate framework of slender iron rods and enclosed 23 acres of floor space. Some 14,000 exhibits were displayed, nearly half British, the rest from around the world. The American stands which included false teeth, Colt's pistol and McCormick's mechanical reaper excited particular interest.

The Prince Consort had explained his idea in a speech the year before:

Nobody, who has paid any attention to the peculiar features of our present era, will doubt for a moment that we are living at a period of most wonderful transition, which tends rapidly to accomplish that great end, to which, indeed, all history points – the realization of the unity of mankind . . .

The distances which separated the different nations and parts of the globe are rapidly vanishing before the achievements of modern invention . . . On the other hand, the great principle of division of labour, which may be called the moving power of civilization, is being extended to all branches of science, industry and art.[125]

The exhibition proved a huge success, drawing thousands of visitors from around the world. And if Queen Victoria's description of the opening on 1 May as 'the greatest day in our history' was influenced a little by pride in her beloved Albert, whose 'dearest name is immortalized with this great conception',[126] when viewed objectively, the Great Exhibition can be seen as a demonstration of political freedom and the achievements of peace; hitherto Great Britain's historic triumphs had been on the seas and fields of war.

Glossary of Nautical Terms

abaft   Towards the *stern*.

abeam   At right angles to a vessel's *fore-and-aft* line.

admiral of the red/white/blue   The three squadrons into which a British fleet was divided historically were distinguished by colour; the admirals commanding the squadrons (each subdivided into three divisions) flew corresponding ensigns, red ensigns for the senior squadron, generally placed in the centre of the line of battle, and always led by the commander-in-chief, ranked admiral of the fleet. His *van* division was led by the vice admiral of the red, his rear division by the rear admiral of the red. The white squadron, ranked second and generally placed in the *van*, would be commanded by the admiral of the white and its subdivisions would be led by a vice admiral of the white (*van*) and a rear admiral of the white (rear); the junior squadron, the blue, was similarly commanded with an admiral, vice admiral and rear admiral of the blue, each flying a blue ensign. On first achieving flag rank, an officer became a rear admiral of the blue; his next step up was to rear admiral of the white, then rear admiral of the red, after which he became a vice admiral of the blue, and so on up the colour divisions. Promotion was automatic as vacancies occurred. After the battle of Trafalgar, a new rank of admiral of the red, who was formerly admiral of the fleet, was created as a reward for senior admirals and a tribute to the navy's successes.

aft   The *stern* part of a vessel.

after/aftermost   Adjectival forms of *aft*.

a-lee (*helm*)   To put the *tiller* down – i.e. to *leeward*.

astern   In a vessel's wake.

back (wind)   To change direction anticlockwise.

(sails)   To *brace* the *yards* so that the wind catches their *sails* from ahead, checking the vessel's progress.

beam   The extreme width of a vessel.

'on the beam': the direction at right angles to a vessel's *fore-and-aft* line.

bear (verb)   To lie in a certain direction from the observer, usually expressed in *points* from compass north or from the *fore-and-aft* line of the vessel.

bear away   To put the *helm* (*tiller*) towards the wind, so steering further off (or away from) the wind.

bear down   To put the *helm* (*tiller*) away from the wind, so steering up (or closer) into the wind.

'bear down on': to sail towards.

bear up   As *bear away*: to steer further off (or away from) the wind.

bearing   The horizontal angle to an object from a reference point, usually compass north or the *fore-and-aft* line of the vessel.

beat   To work a vessel to *windward* by sailing *close-hauled* on alternate *tacks*.

bend   To make fast to: as to *bend* a sail to a *yard*, *bend* a *cable* to an anchor.

bilge   The lowest part of the ship inside the *hull* either side of the *keel*; also applied to the lowest side timbers of the *hull*.

binnacle   The wooden housing of the compass.

bitts   Stout oak uprights on the *forecastle* and upper deck around the masts on which anchor *cables*, *sheets*, *halyards* and other ropes used to work the vessel are secured (belayed).

blanket (verb)   *Sails* are said to be *blanketed* when their wind is masked, for instance by the *sails* of another vessel close to *windward*.

block   A timber casing through which rope is *rove* around a lignum-vitae pulley wheel (sheave) to lead the rope in a desired direction, or with two or more blocks each with one or more sheaves, to create a purchase (*tackle*) with which to work *yards* and *sails*.

boarding   Laying a vessel alongside another (when fighting) in order to *enter* men in her.

bore (verb)   The past tense of *bear*; (of guns) pointed towards.

bouse (bowse)   To *haul* hard, to set taut.

bow   The *foremost* part of a vessel.

bowsprit   A spar projecting out from the *bow*, to which *forward stays* are led.

brace (verb)   To *haul* a *yard* around horizontally to trim its *sail* to the wind.

braces   Ropes from the *yardarms* for *hauling* the *yards* round horizontally when trimming *sail*.

brail (verb)   To gather a *sail* up to its *yard* so that it loses wind.

brails (noun)   The ropes used to *brail* up the *sails*.

breech   The end of the gun housing the *charge*.

breeching   A stout rope made fast to the vessel's side and around the *breech* of a gun to secure the piece and in action restrain its recoil.

bring to   To stop the forward movement of a vessel under *sail* by *bracing* the fore *yards* until the wind catches their *sails* from *ahead* (*backing* their *sails*), thus counteracting the impulse given by other *sails*.

broadside   The main armament guns on one side of a vessel; it was usual to fire them by *quarters*, sections (or platoons) or as they bore on target rather than all together.

bulwarks   The raised sides of a vessel above the upper deck to prevent seas washing aboard or men falling overboard.

cable   (1) A large-diameter rope, especially for use with an anchor. (2) A distance of a tenth of a nautical mile, thus 200 yards or 100 *fathoms*.

canister   Anti-personnel shot consisting of small iron balls packed inside a cylindrical case fired from *cannon* or *carronades*.

cannon   A cast-iron or -bronze gun with a length-to-diameter-of-bore ratio of 18–22 to 1.

capstan   A drum set vertically on a spindle in the deck and turned manually with capstan bars to heave in *cables* and *warps*.

carriage (gun-)   A box-like timber structure to support a *cannon*. The sides reduced in height in steps towards the rear (*inboard*) end to allow the *breech* to be levered up or down when *laying* the gun for *elevation*; the whole was mounted on small timber wheels (*trucks*) to allow recoil when the piece was fired.

carronade   A short, large-bored cast-iron gun manufactured by the Carron Iron Foundry Co. of Falkirk, Scotland, from 1779. Accurate casting allowed the shot to fit more snugly in the bore than was the case with conventional *cannon*, thus less of the propellant gases escaped around the ball and a smaller *charge* could be used; consequently less metal was needed to contain the explosion and the gun was much lighter than a *cannon* firing the same weight of shot. Uniquely, the guns were cast with a raised sight at mid-length for aiming, and were fitted with a screw-thread *elevation* mechanism which worked through a projection of the *breech* termed the 'elevating screw box'. Carronades were served by far fewer men than required to serve *cannon* and although less effective at medium to long *range* they were devastating at close *range*, and were subsequently copied for both the French and United States navies.

cartridge A canvas, cloth, paper or flannel bag containing the propellant *charge* for *cannon* and *carronades*.

charge The gunpowder whose rapid combustion produced gases which expanded to propel the shot from guns.

chase-guns Long guns mounted either side of the *stem* or *sternpost* to fire ahead or *astern*.

claw off To *beat* off a *lee shore*.

close-hauled Sailing with the *yards braced* forward to the maximum extent in order to steer as close as possible (between six and seven *points*, or 67–79 degrees) towards the direction from which the wind is blowing.

come to the wind To point a vessel closer towards the direction from which the wind is blowing.

convoy A number of ships under escort by warships or armed merchantmen.

course (1) The direction along which a vessel is steering. (2) The lower sail on fore- and main-*masts*.

de'd (deduced) reckoning Calculation of navigational position worked entirely from courses steered and speeds measured since the last known position, with allowance for tides or currents.

downwind To *leeward*, away from the direction from which the wind is blowing.

ebb A falling tide.

elevation (of gun) The angle the bore is inclined above the horizontal – achieved by levering the *breech* end with *handspikes* against the stepped sides of the *carriage* and placing timber wedges (*quoins*) to hold the *breech* at the required height above the bottom timber (bed) of the *carriage*, or with *carronades*, turning the elevating screw.

enter to clamber aboard an enemy vessel after *boarding* her.

fall off When a vessel turns from the wind or the set *course* due to damage aloft or inattention on the part of the crew.

fathom A nautical measure of six feet, used for *sounding* depths and measuring *cables*.

fend off Ward off; prevent from *boarding*.

fetch When sailing, to reach a point of land or another vessel, or bring it *abeam*.

first rate See *rate*.

flagship A vessel carrying (and flying the flag of) the admiral (or commodore) commanding a fleet, squadron, division or detachment.

flood A rising tide.

fluky (wind) Inconstant.

fore-and-aft Direction aligned with the vessel's *keel*.

forecastle (fo'c'sle) The *forward* end of the upper deck, or a deck raised above the upper deck at the *forward* end, in warships mounting light guns.

foremast See *masts*.

foremost Furthest *forward*.

foresail See *sails*.

forward Towards the *bow*.

frigate A *ship*-rigged, single main gundeck warship built for speed and employed as a scout for a fleet or squadron, despatch vessel, commerce raider or *convoy* escort.

gaff The angled spar at the mizzen lower *mast* to which the head of the *fore-and-aft sail* called the spanker is *bent*.

go about To turn a vessel to the opposite *tack*, either by *tacking* or *wearing*.

grape (shot) Small iron shot arranged in tiers around an iron pin attached to a circular bottom plate of a size to fit the bore of a great gun and contained in a canvas bag. In the nineteenth century the balls were contained between four circular iron plates connected by a central iron bolt and screwed tight with a nut. This shot was particularly effective when fired from *carronades* at close *range* to batter an opponent's *bulwarks*, cut his rigging and kill or disable men on his upper decks.

guerre de course Originally in international maritime law the right of a merchant vessel licensed as a *privateer* by *letter of marque* or *reprisal* to capture enemy merchantmen, the term has broadened to include any belligerent action against an enemy's trade.

gunwale (pronounced *gunn'l*) The uppermost timber of a vessel's side.

halyard A rope to hoist (or lower) a *yard* or *fore-and-aft sail*.

handspike A timber lever for moving, *laying* and *training* great guns.

hard up to Close by.

hatch An opening in a deck to permit access for persons, stores, cargo or guns.

haul To pull on a rope.

haul round To turn a vessel.

haul the wind (or haul to the wind) To point a vessel closer to the direction from which the wind is blowing.

hawser A large-diameter rope (5 inches or more in circumference) used for securing a vessel alongside a quay or towing, *warping* or *kedging* her against wind or tide.

heave to To stop the forward motion of a sailing vessel by shortening and/or *backing* some *sail*, followed by lashing the *helm* down (to *leeward*) so that she alternately comes up into and falls off the wind, thereby making no progress.

heel (noun) The angle a vessel is leaning to one side.

(verb) To cause a vessel to lean over to one side, usually for repairs or cleaning or painting.

helm The *tiller*; but since the adoption of the steering wheel the term had come to embrace the position at the wheel.

hull The main body of a vessel.

hulling shot Shot striking the hull of an opponent as opposed to his *masts*, *sails* or rigging.

impress See *'press*.

inboard Towards the centre line of a vessel.

inshore Towards the land.

jib   The *fore-and-aft* sail set on the *stay* leading from the fore top*mast*-head to the *jib-boom* end.

jib-boom   The spar secured to and extending ahead from the *bowsprit*.

jury rig   Makeshift *mast* or *masts* and spars rigged in order to sail a vessel to a safe haven after she has lost her *masts*.

kedge (verb)   To *warp* a vessel off a shoal or in shallow water against a contrary wind or tide by means of an anchor taken away from the ship by boat and dropped in the desired direction.

kedge anchor   A small anchor for use in *kedging*.

keel   The principal centre-line timber running from *stem* to *sternpost* at the bottom of a vessel on which the *hull* structure is raised.

keel-hauling   Lowering a man over one side of a vessel from a rope from the *yardarm* and *hauling* him under the vessel and up the other side with a rope from the opposite *yardarm*, a punishment employed, comparatively rarely, in the Dutch and British navies.

langridge (or langrage or langrel)   An assortment of nails, bolts or jagged pieces of metal in a container to fit the bore of a *cannon* or *carronade*, employed chiefly by *privateers* firing from close *range* to cut rigging and sails and disable men.

larboard   That side of a vessel to the left when looking *forward*, later termed *port*.

lask   To sail with the wind on the *quarter*, i.e. well *abaft* the *beam*.

lay   To give a gun its proper *elevation* for the *range* to the target.

lead   A lead weight on a line marked in *fathoms* used for *sounding* the depth of water beneath a vessel.

lead down (verb)   Sail towards.

lee   The side opposite that from which the wind is blowing.

lee shore   Land towards which the wind is blowing.

leeward (pronounced *lieuw'd*)   The direction away from the wind, or *downwind*.

leeway   A vessel's drift *downwind* from the *course* she is steering.

letter of marque/reprisal   The commission for a *privateer* to attack enemy trade.

lie to   To stop in the open sea to keep a fleet together at night or in poor visibility, or to repair damage, or in heavy weather to prevent storm damage.

line ahead   Each vessel following in the wake of her next ahead.

liner   A *ship of the line*.

luff   The leading edge of a *sail*.

luff up   To turn the *bow* towards the direction from which the wind is blowing.

make post   See *post captain*.

masts   The three masts of a *ship* were named, from *forward*, foremast, mainmast, mizzenmast; each was formed of three separate timbers, a lower mast, topmast and topgallant (t'gallant) mast; the uppermost section of the latter was termed the royal mast. Each took its name from the mast of which it formed a part, thus 'fore topmast', 'main royal' etc.

match   A small-diameter line (rope) impregnated with incendiary composition, kept alight in action and used to fire the great guns. By the time of the French Revolutionary war flintlocks had superseded matches in the British navy, although not it seems in the French and Spanish navies.

mizzen   See *masts* and *sails*.

Navigation Laws   Acts passed in all leading trading nations restricting the carriage of merchandise to or from the nation's ports to the nation's own ships (or ships of the country of origin of the goods in the case of imports) in order to encourage the shipping industry and enlarge the stock of sailors, who would be needed in war; they also tied colonies to the mother country by stipulating that imports to the colonies had to come from or via the mother country and the staples of colonial produce had to be shipped to the mother country. The laws were a part of the 'mercantilist' system described and deplored by Adam Smith, which sought to protect national trading and colonial interests against foreign rivals.

offing   The direction away from land towards the open sea.

pay off (verb)   (1) For a sailing vessel's *bow* to fall off the wind, i.e. to *leeward*. (2) To settle the accounts of wages owing at the end of a warship's commission.

point   (1) One of thirty-two divisions of the compass card, each point representing 11¼ degrees. (2) An angular measurement of direction with reference to the ship's *fore-and-aft* line, e.g. four points on the *starboard bow*, 45 degrees to starboard from right ahead.

point blank   The *range* at which a gun is *laid* horizontally.

poop   The short, uppermost deck at the *stern* of a vessel.

port   (1) An opening in the ship's side – e.g. gun port. (2) See *larboard*.

post captain   In the Royal Navy, the commander of a *rated* warship. Once an officer was 'posted' or 'made post' he would ascend the 'captains' list' automatically year by year as vacancies occurred at the top, thence on to and up the 'flag list', starting as a rear *admiral* of the blue. It was the decisive step for an officer.

'press (impress)   To require the service of men for the defence of the country, advancing them a sum of money (prest). Naval service being unpopular, force was often needed to recruit men from merchant vessels, seaports and sometimes even inland towns.

privateer   A privately owned and armed vessel commissioned by *letter of marque* to operate against enemy merchant ships.

prize   (1) An enemy vessel captured by a warship or *privateer.* (2) Cargo taken from a merchant ship and condemned as contraband by an admiralty court.

prize crew   The party sent aboard a captured *prize* to sail her into port.

prize money   The proceeds from the sale of captured ships or cargoes condemned in an admiralty court and distributed in settled proportions among the commanding admiral, the capturing ship's captain, officers and crew.

put about   To change *tack.*

quarter   That part of a vessel between about mid-length and the *stern.*

'on the quarter': the direction from a vessel midway between *abeam* and *astern.*

quarterdeck   The length of the upper deck *abaft* the main*mast.*

quarters   The stations allotted to the men in action and for different evolutions.

quoin   Triangular timber wedge employed to support the *breech* of a *cannon* at the desired height.

raise   To sight an object or feature as it first appears above the horizon.

rake (verb)   To fire from a position across an enemy's *bow* or *stern* so that the shot sweeps the length of his decks; thus 'raking' fire.

range (gunnery)   The distance to the target.

rate   Warships were 'rated' according to the number of guns in their batteries; first rates mounted 100 guns or over on three gun decks; second rates from 84 to 100; third rates 70 to 84 on two gun decks, the most numerous type in both British and French navies being '74's; fourth rates 50 to 70; fifth rates were by this date largely frigates mounting 32 to 36 guns on a single main gun deck; and sixth rates were smaller frigates mounting up to 32 guns. After 1810 in the Royal Navy as ships had become larger the number of guns for each rate was increased.

reach   To sail with the *sails* more or less square to the wind, thus with the wind on or *abaft* the *beam*.

reef   To shorten sail by gathering a horizontal section up to the *yard* and securing it with short lengths of rope sewn into the sail known as reef points.

reeve (past tense **rove**)   To thread a rope through a *block* or eye.

royal   See *masts* and *sails*.

rudder   A vertical timber piece hinged on the *sternpost* and angled by the *tiller* to steer the vessel.

sails   Square sails were spread from *yards* secured to *masts* at right angles to a vessel's *fore-and-aft* line but with freedom to swing laterally. Sails took their name from their mast, the lowest, largest square sails being the foresail and mainsail, or fore*course* and main*course* on the fore and main *masts* respectively; above them were the topsails, above them the topgallant, or t'gallant sails and highest of all the royals, thus the main royal, the mizzen topsail etc. Triangular *fore-and-aft* sails were set from *stays* or in the case of the mizzen mast from a *gaff*; see also *studding sail, jib*.

schooner   A vessel with two or more masts, each rigged with *fore-and-aft sails*; originally with square topsails on the fore*mast*.

set (noun)   (1) The angle at which a *sail* is set. (2) The direction in which a tidal stream or current is running.

(verb)   (1) To rig a *sail* for sailing. (2) To trim a *sail* to the proper angle to the wind.

sheets   Ropes from the bottom corners (clews) of square *sails* used to trim the *sail* to the wind; *fore-and-aft sails* have only one sheet from the *after* clew.

ship   A generic term for sea-going vessels, but strictly a three-*masted* vessel with a *bowsprit* and square *sails* on all *masts*.

ship of the line   A warship powerful enough to fight in the line of battle; by this era a ship with two or more gun decks.

shiver (verb)   Describes the shaking motion of especially the leading edges (*luffs*) of sails when a vessel was pointed too far into the wind (too close to the wind) or when the wind shifted to cause the same effect.

shrouds   Standing (fixed) ropes from the *mast* heads down to the vessel's sides (or, in the case of topmasts and t'gallants, to the sides of the *tops* of the *masts* below) *abaft* the *mast* to give it support from lateral and astern wind pressure.

sounding   Measuring the depth of sea below a vessel by 'heaving' the *lead* over the side.

spanker boom   The spar holding the foot of the spanker (*fore-and-aft*) *sail* set from the lower mizzen *mast*.

spring   *Hawser* led *aft* from the *bow* or *forward* from the *stern* of a vessel to a buoy, *cable* or to a mooring bollard ashore if making fast alongside.

stand after/away/in/on   Respectively, to pursue/retreat from/proceed in (to harbour/shore/danger)/proceed.

stay   A standing (fixed) rope running from a *mast* head and secured on deck to support the *mast* from pressure from *forward* or in the case of a backstay from *aft*.

steerage way   Sufficient forward motion for the *rudder* to take effect.

stern   The end of a vessel furthest from the *bow*.

sternpost   The *aftermost* central timber rising from the *after* end of the *keel*.

sternway   proceeding *stern* first.

studding sail   A small *sail* spread from a spar extending a *yard* outwards (outboard), so increasing the normal (plain) *sail* area to gain extra speed in light winds.

stunsail   Colloquial term for a *studding* (or steering) *sail*.

sway aloft   *Haul* an object up from the deck.

swivel   A light gun mounted on a vertical pin on the *bulwarks* and thus free to point in any direction.

tack (noun)   The direction a sailing vessel is moving relative to the wind; thus on the starboard tack means 'with the wind on the vessel's *starboard* side'.

(verb)   To turn a sailing vessel through the wind to the other *tack* (noun) – i.e. to *put her about* by first turning the *bow* towards the wind.

tackle (pronounced taikle)   A rope rove through two or more *blocks* in order to gain a mechanical advantage when *hauling*.

taffrail   The curved timber top of the *stern* of a warship.

take off way   Reduce speed through the water.

t'gallants   Topgallant *sails*; see *masts* and *sails*.

tiller   A timber attached to the *rudder* head through which leverage is exerted to angle the *rudder* and so steer the vessel. The turning force was applied by ropes wound around the drum of the wheel and led through *blocks* at the ship's sides, thence *inboard* to the *forward* end of the tiller.

top   A platform constructed just below each *mast* head to spread the *shrouds* of the *mast* above; used by sharpshooters to fire down or lob grenades on the enemy decks when *boarding* or in close action.

train (verb)   To aim a gun for direction.

trucks   Small timber wheels for gun *carriages* to allow recoil after firing.

van   The leading squadron or division of ships.

vangs   Ropes leading from the outer end of the *gaff* to the ship's sides at the *stern* to control the spar and prevent the *sail* (spanker) sagging to *leeward*.

veer (wind)   To change direction clockwise.

warp (noun)   A light *cable* used in moving a vessel by *hauling* her along.

(verb)   To heave a vessel along by means of *cables* or *warps* led to the *capstan*.

wear (past tense **wore**)   To put a sailing vessel on the opposite *tack* by first turning her *bow* away from the wind.

weather   The side or direction from which the wind is blowing.

weather gage   The position to *windward* of the enemy.

weigh   To raise the anchor from the seabed.

wind direction   The *point* from which the wind is blowing.

windward   That side or direction from which the wind is blowing.

yard   Spar to which a square *sail* is *bent*.

yardarms   The ends of a *yard*.

References and Notes

Abbreviations used:

Enc. Br.	*Encyclopaedia Britannica*
MM	*Mariner's Mirror*
MOD	Ministry of Defence
NMM	National Maritime Museum, Greenwich, London
NRS	The Navy Records Society
SCRO	Suffolk County Record Office, Ipswich, Suffolk

Introduction

1. Ericus Walten, cited Israel, p. 856.
2. See Pieter de Groot, cited Bromley & Kossman, p. 23.
3. The second of *Two Treatises of Government*, 1690, cited Charles Ess, Drury University, Internet.
4. Laslett (ed.), pp. 368–9.
5. Cited Buruma, p. 38.
6. Cited Fisher, p. 697.
7. A. de Tocqueville, *Oeuvres complètes*, Paris, 1951, v, pp. 377–8, cited Drescher, p. 29.
8. Pocket notebook, 4 Jan. 1832, cited Schleifer, p. 128.
9. To father, 3 June 1831, Tocqueville's Letters Yale Bla 1 Paquet 15, pp. 2–3, cited ibid., p. 122.
10. Alphabetic notebook 'C' *Centralization*, 24 Aug. 1833, Tocqueville, *Journeys*, pp. 61–2.
11. Ibid., 'U' *Uniformity*, ibid., p. 66.

12. Tocqueville, *Democracy*, i, p. 91.

13. Pocket notebook, 3 Oct. 1831, cited Schleifer, p. 127.

14. A. O. Hirschman, 'Rival Interpretations of Market Society . . .', *Journal of Economic Literature*, 20 (1982), p. 1465, cited Fukuyama, p. 254.

15. 'Introduction' to Tocqueville, *Democracy*, ii, p. xviii.

16. Smith, i, p. 398.

17. Ibid.

18. Vergennes to Montmorin (French ambassador to Spain), 1 Nov. 1782, cited J. Dull, *The French Navy and American Independence*, Princeton Univ. Press, 1975, p. 316.

19. *Enc. Br.*, vi, p. 283.

20. Amendment VI, ibid., iii, p. 573.

21. See Padfield, *Maritime Supremacy*, pp. 225–6.

22. E. L. Jones, p. 1.

23. Ibid., pp. 75–6.

24. Francesca Bray in J. Needham, *Science and Civilisation in China*, vol. vi, *Biology and Biological Technology*, Part II, 'Agriculture', CUP, 1984, p. 612, cited ibid., p. 82.

25. See J. Needham, ibid., iv, pp. 495–7, 487–90, 516 note.

26. E. L. Jones, p. 153.

27. Needham, op. cit. (ref. 25 above), p. 683.

28. Reischauer, p. 84.

29. See Milton, pp. 101–4, 129–30, 139, 144, 294–5, 360.

30. For the horrific mass executions of Christians, see ibid., pp. 351ff.

31. See E. L. Jones, pp. 140–1; Landes, pp. 157–8.

32. John Locke, *Two Treatises of Government*, pp. 401, 368, cited Pipes, p. 35.

33. Padfield, *Maritime Supremacy*, p. 82.

34. Ibid., p. 184.

35. Cormack, p. 27.

36. Rodger, p. 345.

37. J. von Archenholz, *A Picture of England, 1789–91*, quoted Roy Porter, *English Society in the Eighteenth Century*, 1982, p. 273, cited Christie, p. 58.

38. 7 Sept. 1833, 'Last Impressions of England', Tocqueville, *Journeys*, p. 67.

39. The Rev. Edmund Paley, *The Works of William Paley, DD . . .*, 4 vols, 1838, iii, p. 258, cited Christie, p. 54.

40. Eric Robinson, 'An English Jacobin: James Watt Junior, 1769–1848', *Cambridge Historical Journal* II (1953–5), p. 350, cited Christie, p. 59.

41. William Paley, *The Principles of Moral and Political Philosophy*, from Edmund Paley, op. cit. (ref. 39 above), cited Christie, p. 163.

42. Burke, p. 276; the editor's footnote states: 'Burke's interpretation of the social significance of the French Enlightenment, once dismissed as an emo-

tionally exaggerated conspiracy theory, has been confirmed by recent scholarship.'

43. See Burke, p. 277 footnote.
44. Ibid., p. 277.

Chapter 1: The French Revolution, 1789

1. Germaine de Staël, *Considérations sur la révolution française*, ed. J. Godechot, Paris, 1983, p. 226, cited Yalom, p. 148.
2. Marquise de Villeneuve-Arifat, *née* Mlle de Nicolay, cited ibid., p. 17.
3. Tocqueville, *L'Ancien Régime*, pp. 149, 148.
4. Ibid., p. 169.
5. See ibid., p. 173.
6. On 'the General Will', see B. Russell, pp. 724ff.
7. Ibid., p. 727.
8. Palmer, *Democratic Revolution*, p. 471.
9. *Boswell on the Grand Tour* . . . (1764), NY, 1953, pp. 223–4, cited Pipes, p. 39.
10. See Schama, pp. 141–6.
11. Ibid., p. 306; Wright, p. 7.
12. See Glete, i, p. 292; P. Kennedy, *Great Powers*, pp. 105ff.
13. See Schama, p. 231.
14. See Glete, i, pp. 278–9, 282.
15. See ibid., p. 371 footnote.
16. See Cormack, p. 23; see Scarfe, *Innocent Espionage, Highlands, passim.*
17. See Glete, i, p. 276, ii, pp. 553, 580–1: 1790, 145 British ships of the line, total 334,000 tons displacement; 73 French ships of the line, total 231,000 tons displacement.
18. See Palmer, *Democratic Revolution*, p. 454; Schama, p. 237; but Soboul, p. 98 has deficit of *c.* 126 million livres (*c.* 20 per cent of expenditure).
19. Schama, pp. 116–17: Schama goes so far as to state that the stereotypes of a British aristocracy open to new blood and a French aristocracy closed to new entrants should be completely reversed.
20. Ibid., pp. 326–8.
21. See Palmer, *Democratic Revolution*, p. 478; Wright, p. 23.
22. *Enc. Br.*, x, p. 71.
23. See Wright, pp. 33–4, and p. 32 above.
24. Soboul, p. 168.
25. Wright, p. 35; Schama, pp. 448, 576, and p. 581 states that only 10 per cent of eligible voters voted.
26. Soboul, p. 236; Schama, p. 595.
27. Cited Soboul, p. 236.
28. Germaine de Staël, *Considérations*, op. cit. (ref. 1 above), cited Yalom, p. 158.

29. See Wright, p. 62; Schama, pp. 646–7; Schama, p. 646 states it as 'unlikely that more than 6 per cent of the seven million entitled to vote did so'; which would mean that less than half a million voted!
30. Cited Soboul, p. 286.
31. See Israel, pp. 1098ff., especially p. 1103.
32. Soboul, pp. 283–4.
33. Sparrow, p. 6.
34. See Soboul, p. 292; Schama, p. 709.

Chapter 2: The Terror, 1793

1. Green, p. 765.
2. Ibid., p. 763.
3. Burke, pp. 183–4.
4. Ibid., pp. 170, 174.
5. Tocqueville, *L'Ancien Régime*, p. 15.
6. J. R. Jones, p. 252.
7. 'The Middlesex and Surrey Justices Act', June 1792; see Sparrow, p. 7; see J. R. Jones, pp. 257–8.
8. See P. Pringle's 'Introduction', in Goddard, pp. x–xi.
9. Trevelyan, p. 55.
10. P. Pringle in Goddard, p. 55, although Maximilien de Lazowski in Scarfe, *Innocent Espionage*, pp. 200–1, thought London no more lawless than Paris, and headed his paragraph on the subject, 'Pleasing absence of police'.
11. See Sparrow, pp. 7, 14–15.
12. See ibid., pp. 19–24.
13. Ibid., pp. 23–4.
14. See Yalom, p. 191.
15. Cited Soboul, p. 303.
16. Cited ibid., p. 305.
17. Diary, 31 May–2 June, cited ibid., p. 325.
18. Ibid.
19. Convention decree, 23 Aug. 1793, cited Schama, p. 762.
20. See, for instance, Talleyrand: 'If historians strive to discover the men to whom they can give honour or attribute the blame [for] . . . the French Revolution, they will be wasting their time. It had no authors, nor leaders, nor guides. The seed was sown by writers who . . . wishing to attack prejudice, overthrew the principles of religion and social life, and by incompetent ministers, who increased the embarrassment of the Treasury, and the discontent of the people.' Treatise on the Duke of Orleans, prob. 1793, cited Duff Cooper, p. 70.
21. See Palmer, *Twelve Who Ruled*, pp. 227–32.

22. Talleyrand memo, dated 25 Nov. 1792, found in Danton's papers, cited Duff Cooper, p. 67.
23. Ibid., p. 66.
24. See Fouché's speeches at Nevers, 22 Sept., 22 Oct. 1793, cited Cole, pp. 41–2; and see Soboul, p. 348.
25. Germaine de Staël, *Considérations*, op. cit. (ch. 1, ref. 1), cited Yalom, pp. 149–50.
26. See, for instance, Soboul, p. 325.
27. See, for instance, Wright, p. 97.
28. Schama, p. 787.
29. Robespierre's speech 5 Feb. 1794, cited Wright, p. 130.
30. Cited C. W. Cole, *Colbert and a Century of French Mercantilism*, Cass, 2 vols, 1964, i, p. 334.
31. Robespierre's speech 5 Feb. 1794, cited Wright, p. 129; and see Palmer, *Twelve Who Ruled*, p. 264.
32. *Boswell on Tour*, op. cit. (ch. 1, ref. 9), pp. 223–4, cited Pipes, p. 39.
33. See Yalom, pp. 21, 146, 242.
34. See Padfield, *Himmler*, p. 42.
35. *Émile*, see Yalom, p. 32.
36. See Wright, p. 95; Yalom, p. 238.

Chapter 3: The Glorious First of June, 1794

1. Lewis, *Social History*, p. 318.
2. R. Hill, pp. 8–9, 201–5.
3. Ibid., p. 22.
4. Ibid.
5. See Rodger, p. 256.
6. Lewis, *Social History*, pp. 31–4, 288ff.; Rodger, p. 254.
7. Austen, *Persuasion*, p. 36.
8. Ibid., p. 72.
9. Ibid., p. 71.
10. Southey, p. 7.
11. Ibid.; and see Oman, p. 10.
12. Nelson to Wm. Locker, Feb. 1799, cited V. Sharman, author *Nelson's Locker*, The Nelson Society, in letter to *The Times* (London), 2 Jan. 2001, 'Letters'.
13. Oman, p. 30.
14. Rodger, p. 274.
15. Cited Southey (unsourced), p. 27.
16. Description from midshipman of *Barfleur*, cited Oman, p. 47.
17. Southey, p. 31; Oman, p. 70.
18. Cited Mahan, *Nelson*, p. 52.

19. Cited Oman, p. 99.
20. Cited Mahan, *Nelson*, p. 86; Southey, p. 43.
21. Cited Schama, p. 727.
22. See Cormack, pp. 191–5.
23. 14 Sept. 1793, cited Oman, p. 121.
24. Cited ibid. (unsourced), p. 130.
25. See Cormack, pp. 109–17.
26. Jeanbon, *Rapport des représentans*, pp. 21–3, cited Cormack, p. 259.
27. Law of 19 *Vendémiaire*, see Cole, p. 43.
28. Cole, p. 56.
29. Cited ibid., p. 51.
30. C. Josselyn, *The True Napoleon*, New York, 1902, said by Napoleon of his time at the Military Academy at Brienne, cited Wheeler, p. 9.
31. Gen. Westermann to Committee of Public Safety, cited Schama, p. 787.
32. Charles Philippe Henri Ronsin, cited Schama, p. 789.
33. See Wright, p. 92; Schama, p. 789.
34. Tunstall, p. 205.
35. Cited Cormack, p. 276.
36. Cited Padfield, *Nelson's War*, p. 19.
37. Kemp, p. 403.
38. J. D. Spinney, 'Rodney and the Saintes . . .', *MM*, vol. 68, no. 4 (Nov. 1982), pp. 379–80.
39. Rodney to Lord Sandwich, 27 Jan. 1780, Barnes & Owen, iii, p. 211.
40. Issued in New York, 15 Oct. 1781; see Tunstall, p. 177.
41. See ibid., pp. 151, 154.
42. Mahé de la Bourdonnais, 1746.
43. See Tunstall, pp. 194–5, 199.
44. '*très-exercée et leste dans ses mouvements*', Tunstall, pp. 201–2.
45. Corbett, *Fighting Instructions*, p. 258; Jackson, i, p. 12.
46. *Queen Charlotte*'s signal log, Jackson, i, p. 47; this source is used for times of signals and manoeuvres hereafter unless otherwise stated.
47. Dr Thomas Trotter, cited Lloyd, *Health of Seamen*, p. 265.
48. See, for instance, Robert Wilson's account of action in Thursfield, p. 155.
49. Dr Thomas Trotter, cited Lloyd, *Health of Seamen*, p. 265.
50. Corbett, *Fighting Instructions*, p. 258.
51. See, for instance, log of *Ramillies*, Jackson, i, p. 96: 'ships to act as circumstances will admit to engage them either to windward or leeward'; ditto log of *Tremendous*, ibid., p. 87.
52. A lieutenant, cited Barrow, p. 253.
53. 5 June 1793, Newnham Collingwood, p. 21.
54. Lt. Edward Codrington's account, cited Warner, *First of June*, p. 53.
55. Signal lieutenant's log entries, *Queen Charlotte*, Jackson, i, p. 47.

56. Barrow, pp. 267–8, and for remainder of these exchanges.
57. Jeanbon, *Journal sommaire*, pp. 26–7, cited Cormack, p. 280.
58. Cormack, p. 280.
59. M. Lewis (ed.), *Narrative of Sir William Dillon*, 2 vols, NRS, 1953, cited Warner, *First of June*, pp. 79–80.
60. Barrow, p. 288.
61. Cited Warner, *First of June*, p. 92.
62. 13 July 1799, cited Barrow, p. 379.

Chapter 4: St Vincent, 1797

1. Cited Mahan, *Nelson*, p. 114.
2. Cited Oman, p. 148.
3. Ibid., p. 159.
4. Cited Mahan, *Nelson*, p. 144.
5. Cited Oman, p. 163.
6. Cited Mahan, *Nelson*, p. 154.
7. Ibid., p. 162.
8. Fleurus on the river Meuse.
9. Cormack, pp. 286–7.
10. Israel, p. 1122; see Ferguson, *Banker*, p. 1037 for gulden exchange rate of 11.25 to the pound in 1798.
11. Treaty of Basel.
12. Memo, Chairs of East India Company to Lord Hillsborough, 7 Nov. 1781; India Office, Home Misc., S, vol. 155, p. 80, cited Harlow, i, p. 108.
13. See Israel, p. 1127.
14. Sparrow, pp. 26–8.
15. See Corbett, *Spencer Papers*, i, p. 66.
16. See Sparrow, pp. 56–7; Corbett, *Spencer Papers*, i, pp. 66–7.
17. Corbett, *Spencer Papers*, i, p. 67.
18. See Sir J. Borlase Warren to Spencer, Quiberon Bay, 3 July 1795, ibid., p. 81.
19. Sparrow, p. 59.
20. See ibid., p. 61.
21. Sir J. Borlase Warren to Spencer, Quiberon Bay, 28 Aug. 1795, Corbett, *Spencer Papers*, i, p. 105.
22. By July 1795 *assignats* had lost 97 per cent of their face value: Godechot, p. 178.
23. See Sparrow, p. 67.
24. Duff Cooper, p. 83.
25. See Belloc, p. 50.
26. Leoben, 18 Apr. 1797.

27. See Godechot, p. 192.

28. This was the Comte d'Antraigues: Sparrow, p. 123.

29. See Harbron, pp. 117–18.

30. See Glete, ii, pp. 376, 552ff., 631.

31. See Ehrman, iii, p. 100.

32. See Richard Saxby, 'The Blockade of Brest in the French Revolutionary War', *MM*, vol. 78, no. 1 (Feb. 1992), p. 29.

33. Ehrman, iii, p. 5.

34. Ibid., p. 6.

35. Capt. Duckworth's copy in NMM DUC/1/18, cited Tunstall, pp. 213ff.

36. Jervis to the respective captains, HMS *Victory*, at sea, 28 Aug. 1796, cited Tucker, i, p. 206.

37. Cited Berckman, p. 146; Tucker, i, p. 225.

38. Earl Spencer, Admiralty, to J. Jervis, 1 Feb. 1797, cited Tucker, i, p. 225.

39. Cited Oman, p. 119.

40. Position from *Victory*'s log, noon 14 Feb. 1797: 'Cape St Vincent N 49 E 11 leagues'; Jervis's later despatch gave a position eight leagues from Cape St Vincent.

41. Tucker, i, p. 254.

42. Ibid., pp. 255–6.

43. Jervis to First Lord, cited Lloyd, *St Vincent*, p. 40: 'set t'gallants', Jackson, i, p. 241; Jackson is followed hereafter unless otherwise noted.

44. Parsons, p. 258.

45. See p. 87; Corbett, *Fighting Instructions*, p. 258 (ch. 3, ref. 45).

46. Cited Tucker, i, p. 257.

47. Parsons, p. 259.

48. Tucker, i, p. 258.

49. Tunstall, p. 218.

50. Jackson, i, p. 222.

51. Drinkwater Bethune, p. 79.

52. Ibid., p. 38.

53. Collingwood to his wife, *Excellent*, off Lagos, 17 Feb. 1797, Warner, *Life and Letters*, p. 68.

54. Ibid.

55. 'Account of the Proceedings of the *Captain*', Nicolas, iii, p. 343.

56. Padfield, *Nelson's War*, p. 69.

57. 'Account of the Proceedings', op. cit. (ref. 55 above), p. 343.

58. Nelson to Suckling, off Lagos, 23 Feb. 1797, Nicolas, iii, p. 356.

59. 15 Feb. 1797, ibid., p. 349.

60. Drinkwater Bethune, pp. 87–9.

Chapter 5: Camperdown, 1797

1. Petition from *Queen Charlotte* to Earl Howe, 7 March 1797, cited Lewis, *Spithead*, p. 135.
2. For Dr Trotter's analysis of festering resentments, see Lloyd, *Health of Seamen*, p. 239.
3. Ehrman, iii, p. 22.
4. See Barrow, p. 388.
5. Archives *Ministère des Affaires Étrangères: Mémoires et Documents*, France, 590/198, cited Sparrow, p. 118.
6. Gill, p. 299, claims that the phrase in the Spithead petition 'in the respect due to us' points to the 'Rights of Man'.
7. See Camperdown, pp. 14ff.
8. Barrow, p. 354.
9. *Queen Charlotte* petition to Lord Howe, op. cit. (ref. 1 above), p. 135.
10. Peter Cullen's Journal, 12 May 1797, aboard frigate *Espion* at the Nore, Thursfield, p. 84.
11. Howe to Sir Evan Nepean, Barrow, p. 337.
12. Cormack, p. 299.
13. Cited Oman, p. 224.
14. Mahan, *Nelson*, p. 257.
15. *Theseus*, off Santa Cruz, 24 July [1797], 8 p.m., cited Oman, p. 237.
16. Lloyd & Coulter, p. 141; see also P. D. Gordon Pugh, *Nelson and his Surgeons*, E. & S. Livingstone, Edinburgh and London, 1975.
17. Cited Oman, p. 247; and see Joseph F. Callo, 'Nelson at Santa Cruz', *Naval Review*, vol. 85, no. 2 (April 1997), p. 135.
18. Cited Oman, p. 248.
19. Tunstall, p. 219.
20. Ibid., p. 220.
21. Wolfe Tone's diary, 19 July 1797 aboard *Vrijheid*: 'Our ships exercise at the great guns and small arms every day; they fire incomparably well', cited Lloyd, *St Vincent*, p. 130.
22. Camperdown, p. 215.
23. Cited ibid., p. 259.
24. Journal of Robert Young, surgeon of *Ardent*, cited Lloyd, *St Vincent*, p. 147.
25. Ehrman, iii, pp. 66–8, 100.
26. Speeches 24 Nov., 4 Dec. 1797 respectively, cited ibid., p. 104.

Chapter 6: The Nile, 1798

1. George Ellis to George Canning, 11 Sept. 1797, Harewood Collection, Geo. Canning Mss GC/63, Leeds District Archive, cited Sparrow, p. 138.

2. James Talbot to Lord Grenville, Nov. 1797, cited Sparrow, p. 148.

3. Bankers: Walter Boyd, William Herries; see Sparrow, pp. 130, 141–3, 160.

4. Cited Bryant, *Endurance*, p. 219.

5. See Duff Cooper, p. 102.

6. Bonaparte to Talleyrand, 13 Sept. 1797 from Passariano, cited Lloyd, *The Nile*, p. 10.

7. Duff Cooper, p. 102; Lavery, p. 15.

8. See Harlow, i, pp. 317–19.

9. Bonaparte's orders from Paris, 22 April 1798, see Lloyd, *The Nile*, p. 132; Lavery, p. 23.

10. Fisher, p. 826.

11. St Vincent to Nelson, 2 May 1798, cited Warner, *The Nile*, p. 12; and see Michael Duffy, 'British Naval Intelligence and Bonaparte's Egyptian Expedition of 1798', *MM*, vol. 84, no. 3 (Aug. 1998), pp. 281ff.

12. St Vincent to Lord Spencer, 1 May 1798, Nicolas, iii, p. 11.

13. Nicolas, iii, pp. 17–18.

14. Wm. Hardman, *A History of Malta during the Period of the British and French Occupations, 1798–1815*, London, 1909, reprinted Valetta, 1994, p. 74, cited Lavery, p. 90.

15. Corbett, *Spencer Papers*, ii, p. 438.

16. Nicolas, iii, p. 24.

17. General Order, *Vanguard* at sea, 8 June 1798, cited Tunstall, p. 225.

18. Ibid.

19. Nelson to Lord Spencer, *Vanguard* off islands of Ponza, 15 June 1798, Nicolas, iii, p. 31.

20. Nelson to Sir Wm. Hamilton, *Vanguard* off Naples, 17 June 1798, Nicolas, iii, p. 32.

21. Nelson to Sir Wm. Hamilton, *Vanguard* off Naples, 18 June 1798, ibid.

22. Nelson to British consul, Alexandria, *Vanguard* at sea, noon, Alexandria bearing S 68 E 233 miles, 26 June 1798, ibid., p. 37.

23. Brueys to Bonaparte, 13 July 1798, cited Lloyd, *The Nile*, p. 36.

24. See Nelson to his captains, 20 July 1798, Nicolas, iii, p. 46.

25. Rose, i, p. 215 note.

26. Edward Berry, *An Authentic Narrative of the Proceedings of His Majesty's Squadron . . .*, London, 1798, cited Nicolas, iii, p. 50.

27. See Tunstall, p. 226; in Jackson, ii, p. 51, this signal is given as 'Haul to the wind on the larboard tack'.

28. *Vanguard*'s signal log, Jackson, ii, p. 51, followed hereafter unless otherwise stated; and see Tunstall, p. 226.

29. See Rear Admiral Villeneuve to Blanquet, Paris, 12 Nov. 1800, cited Jackson, ii, p. 75.

30. See John Crossland 'Secrets of the Burning Deck Revealed', *The Times*,

London, 11 Dec. 1984; and Richard Beeston, 'Divers Reveal Nelson's Blast from the Past', ibid., 28 June 1999, citing Frank Goddie: the French were 'too far out from the shore, too far apart from each other and failed to secure the head of their line'.

31. Memo of Capt. Webley of *Zealous*, Jackson, ii, pp. 26–7.

32. See Berry, *Authentic Narrative*, op. cit. (ref. 26 above), p. 50.

33. John Nicol, *The Life and Adventures of John Nicol, Mariner*, ed. G. Grant, Edinburgh, 1822, reprinted London, 1937, cited Lloyd, *The Nile*, p. 51.

34. Capt. R. W. Miller to his wife, Jackson, ii, p. 42.

35. John Nicol, op. cit. (ref. 33 above), cited Lavery, p. 216.

36. *Vanguard*'s surgeon wrote, 'the cranium was bare for more than one inch; the wound was three inches long': cited Warner, *The Nile*, p. 104.

37. Cited Tours, p. 145; see also the diary of 'a young Irish widow' [Mrs St George], 9 Oct. 1800, in ibid., p. 157.

38. Sparrow, pp. 87–95.

39. Parsons, p. 217.

40. See p. 148; Sparrow, pp. 130, 141–3, 160.

41. See Sparrow, pp. 22, 103–4, 134–5, 142.

42. H. M. C. Dropmore, v (1799), pp. 42–4, cited Sparrow, pp. 188–9.

43. See Sparrow, pp. 189–90.

44. Ibid., pp. 190–1.

45. Comte de las Casas, *Le Mémorial de Sainte-Hélène . . .*, Édition Gérard Walter, 1956, cited Sparrow, p. 191.

46. Sir Sidney Smith to General Kléber, commanding the army Bonaparte had left in Egypt: 'I engaged General Bonaparte, in leaving him a free passage, to return to take command of the Army of Italy, which no longer exists', cited Sparrow, p. 192; and see Warner, *The Nile*, pp. 158, 293.

47. Coup of 18–19 *Brumaire*, Year VIII: 9–10 Nov. 1799.

48. See Sparrow, p. 203.

Chapter 7: Copenhagen, 1801

1. Belloc, pp. 201ff.; and see Sparrow, pp. 215, 217 for Fouché's and Talleyrand's plot to oust Bonaparte if he failed; and Duff Cooper, p. 125.

2. Treaty of El Arish, 22 Jan. 1800.

3. Treaty of St Petersburg, 16 Dec. 1800.

4. The 'young Irish widow', Mrs St George's diary entry, 3 Oct. 1800, cited Tours, pp. 155–6.

5. 'Admiral Nelson is little, and not remarkable in his person . . . but he has great animation of countenance, and activity in his appearance; his manners are unaffectedly simple and modest', Mrs Cornelia Knight, Journal, 22 Sept. 1798, cited Tours, p. 122.

6. Mrs St George's diary entry, 9 Oct. 1800, cited ibid., pp. 155–6.

7. See Lesley Edwards, 'Horatia Nelson and Lady Hamilton's Twins', *MM*, vol. 8, no. 3 (Aug. 2000), pp. 313–15; and see correspondence in *The Times*, London, 19–20 Aug. 1999, especially Cdr J. G. B. Swinley's letter, 19 Aug. 1999, stating that Horatia's twin was *not* deposited in the Foundling Hospital; and see Pocock, p. 13.

8. Act of Union, 1 Jan. 1801.

9. Treaty of Florence, March 1801.

10. Fisher, p. 833.

11. See Sparrow, pp. 224–32.

12. Ibid., p. 236.

13. Nelson to Troubridge, cited Pope, pp. 219–20.

14. *Polyphemus* signal log, Jackson, ii, p. 95, which will be followed hereafter unless otherwise stated.

15. Rear Admiral Thomas Graves to his brother, *Defiance*, off Copenhagen, 3 April 1801, Jackson, ii, p. 102.

16. Lt.-Col. W. Stewart's account, Nicolas, iv, p. 308.

17. Capt. Robert Otway's biography, cited Mahan, *Nelson*, p. 483; however, Mahan also cites the biography of Parker's secretary: 'it was arranged between the admirals that, should it appear the ships which were engaged were suffering too severely, the signal for retreat would be made to give Lord Nelson the option for retiring, if he thought fit', Mrs and Dr Gatty, *Recollections of the Life of the Rev. Dr A. J. Scott*, p. 70.

18. Lt.-Col. W. Stewart's account, Nicolas, iv, p. 309.

19. Mahan, *Nelson*, p. 484.

20. Lt.-Col. W. Stewart to Sir Wm. Clinton, 6 April 1801, NMM AGC/14, cited Ole Feldbaek, 'Humanity or Ruse de Guerre? Nelson's Letter to the Danes', *MM*, vol. 73, no. 4 (Nov. 1987), p. 343.

21. L. V. Harcourt, *The Diaries and Correspondence of the Rt. Hon. George Rose*, London, 1860, i, pp. 347–8, cited ibid.; and see Mahan, *Nelson*, p. 489.

22. Pope, p. 414.

23. Cited Mahan, *Nelson*, p. 486.

24. See Pope, Appendix III, p. 530: Danes, 370 killed, 106 died of wounds, 559 wounded; British, 256 killed, 688 wounded; and Oman, p. 703.

25. Vice Admiral Cronstedt to King Gustavus IV Adolphus, Riksarkivet, Stockholm, cited Feldbaek, 'Humanity', op. cit. (ref. 20 above), p. 346.

26. Lt.-Col. W. Stewart to Sir Wm. Clinton, 6 April 1801, NMM AGC/14, cited Feldbaek, ibid., p. 347.

27. A. M. Broadley and R. G. Bartelot, *Nelson's Hardy; His Life, Letters and Friends*, London, 1909, pp. 63–5, cited Feldbaek, ibid., p. 348.

28. Feldbaek, ibid., p. 349.

29. Baron Stedingk to Gustav III, 29 March 1801, cited Sparrow, pp. 239–40.

30. Sparrow, p. 240.
31. Cited Mahan, *Nelson*, p. 494.
32. Ibid., pp. 506–7.

Chapter 8: Warriors and Merchants

1. Bergeron, p. 65.
2. See Tocqueville, *L'Ancien Régime*, especially p. 66.
3. François Crouzet, 'Politics and Banking in Revolutionary and Napoleonic France', in R. Sylla, R. Tilly, G. Tortella (eds.), *The States, the Financial System and Economic Modernization*, Cambridge, p. 45, cited Ferguson, *Cash Nexus*, p. 114.
4. See Bergeron, pp. 39–40; Geoffrey Ellis, 'War and the French Economy (1792–1815)', in Aerts & Crouzet, p. 7.
5. See Ferguson, *Cash Nexus*, p. 179.
6. See Bergeron, p. 34; Fisher, p. 840.
7. See Hufton, pp. 432–3 on Diderot and Rousseau.
8. Ibid., p. 486.
9. Bergeron, p. 25.
10. See Cole, p. 116; Sparrow, pp. 287–91; Fisher, pp. 840–1.
11. Thomas, pp. 495, 520.
12. See H. J. K. Jenkins, 'The Heyday of French Privateering from Guadeloupe, 1796–98', *MM*, vol. 64, no. 3 (Aug. 1978), pp. 245–50; H. J. K. Jenkins, 'Guadeloupe's Commerce Raiding, 1796–98; Perspectives and Contexts', *MM*, vol. 83, no. 3 (Aug. 1997), pp. 303–9.
13. Duff Cooper, p. 146.
14. Burke, p. 279.
15. Ibid., p. 278.
16. See Ferguson, *Cash Nexus*, p. 152.
17. Ibid., p. 394.
18. Ehrman, iii, pp. 265–72.
19. Mitchell & Deane, p. 281; and see George Rose, *A Brief Examination into the Increase of the Revenue, Commerce and Manufacture of Great Britain from 1792 to 1795*, London, 1799, cited G. J. Marcus, *A Naval History of England*, ii, Allen & Unwin, 1971, p. 209.
20. P. Kennedy, *Naval Mastery*, p. 166.
21. Cited Bryant, *Endurance*, p. 308.
22. 'Alphabetic notebook', 24 Aug. 1833, Tocqueville, *Journeys*, pp. 61–2, cited in fuller form in Introduction above, p. 7.
23. See Stone, *Family*, p. 167.
24. See Stone, *Broken Lives*, p. 19.
25. See Oman, p. 512.

26. See Stone, *Broken Lives*, p. 24.

27. Vickery, p. 9.

28. See Amanda Vickery, 'A Nation of Material Girls', *BBC History Magazine*, vol. 2, no. 9 (Sept. 2001), p. 30; and Scarfe, *Innocent Espionage*, p. 216.

29. Vickery, 'Material Girls', op. cit. (ref. 28 above), p. 31.

30. See Stone, *Family*, p. 239.

31. See ibid., p. 286.

32. Austen, *Emma*, p. 1.

33. See Padfield, *Maritime Supremacy*, pp. 69–81; Stone, *Family*, p. 420.

34. Cited Stone, *Family*, p. 214.

35. Ibid., p. 220.

36. Austen, *Persuasion*, p. 224.

37. See Hufton, pp. 453–4, 505–6.

38. Yalom, p. 234.

39. M. G. Jones, *Hannah More*, Cambridge, 1952, cited Talbott, p. 131.

40. See Sir James Watt, 'James Ramsay, 1733–1789; Naval Surgeon, Naval Chaplain and Morning Star of the Anti-Slavery Movement', *MM*, vol. 81, no. 2 (May 1995), p. 166; and see Talbott, pp. 129–31; Thomas, pp. 491–4.

41. Thomas, p. 496.

42. Ibid., p. 508.

43. Cited ibid., p. 514.

44. Cited ibid., pp. 545–6.

45. *Parliamentary History*, vol. 29, cols 1055–7, cited ibid., p. 528.

46. See Thomas, p. 540.

47. In 1792 the Danish government prohibited the slave trade to their islands because they thought it certain that Britain would abolish the trade shortly, and too many sailors on slave ships died: ibid., pp. 525–6.

48. Cited Robertson, p. 422.

49. See Thomas, p. 494: 'Moral conviction was in truth the determining element in the unusual chapter of British parliamentary history about to begin.'

Chapter 9: Bonaparte's Army of England, 1803

1. Glete, ii, p. 386.

2. See Sparrow, p. 267.

3. At Orbe, see ibid., p. 262.

4. See J. R. Jones, p. 271.

5. See Sparrow, pp. 272ff.

6. See J. R. Jones, p. 279: 'From the evidence of the instructions he sent to colonial governors, he anticipated a resumption of war with Great Britain at some time in the second half of 1804.'

7. See Schom, pp. 122, 72–4.

8. See ibid., pp. 72, 74–7; Pocock, pp. 95–6.

9. See Glete, ii, pp. 375–82: 1805, British battle fleet 357; French battle fleet 129, Spanish battle fleet 104; the British battle fleet was thus 153 per cent of the French and Spanish fleets combined.

10. See Julian de Zulueta, 'Trafalgar – the Spanish View'; *MM*, vol. 66, no. 4 (Nov. 1980), p. 297: the Spanish fleet needed 89,350 men; there were only 53,147 registered sailors in the country, and only some 5,800 of these were used to the high seas.

11. Cited Mahan, *Nelson*, pp. 88–9.

12. Report of Rear Admiral Gravina and Capt. Valdés, Museo Naval, Madrid, Misc. Ms 1927, cited Zulueta, op. cit. (ref. 10 above), p. 293.

13. Cited Zulueta, op. cit. (ref. 10 above), p. 298.

14. Dr Thomas Trotter, *Observations on Scurvy*, cited C. Lloyd, 'Cook and Scurvy', *MM*, vol. 65, no. 1 (Feb. 1979), p. 27.

15. See Zulueta, op. cit. (ref. 10 above), p. 298.

16. See Introduction, p. 22.

17. NMM SIG/B/82; and see Lewis, *Navy of Britain*, p. 541; Tunstall, pp. 242–4.

18. See Ehrman, iii, p. 705: 'If Pitt and his colleagues had risked forcing the pace they had done so deliberately, and did not seem unduly cast down by the result.'

19. Archivo 'Don Alvaro de Bazán' at El Viso del Marqués, Legajos Expediciones a Europa (1804), cited Zulueta, op. cit. (ref. 10 above), p. 301.

20. See Padfield, *Maritime Supremacy*, pp. 204–5.

21. See Michael Steer, 'The Blockade of Brest and the Victualling of the Western Squadron, 1793–1805', *MM*, vol. 76, no. 4 (Nov. 1990), pp. 312–14; also Richard Saxby, 'The Blockade of Brest in the French Revolutionary War', *MM*, vol. 78, no. 1 (Feb. 1992), pp. 31–5.

22. Cited Schom, p. 203.

23. Mahan, *Nelson*, p. 578, makes the further point that Napoleon's efforts in the Mediterranean were confined to feints and demonstrations; he did not contest Nelson's use of Sardinia as a fleet base.

24. 17 Jan. 1805, cited Schom, p. 182; and see Fuller, ii, pp. 374–5.

25. Robertson, p. 416; for Pitt's ideas, later adopted at the Congress of Vienna, see Ehrman, iii, pp. 731–4.

26. Dacres Adams Papers, 6/100 Paris 10 July, cited Sparrow, p. 306.

27. See Desbrière, i, pp. 117–18.

28. Ibid., p. 119; and see David Howarth, 'The Man who Lost Trafalgar', *MM*, vol. 57, no. 4 (Nov. 1971), p. 366.

29. Schom, p. 241; Belloc, p. 253; Sparrow, p. 305; Duff Cooper, p. 153, states that Napoleon wrote to Talleyrand on 13 August saying that he would be

in Vienna by November to deal with the Russians if they showed themselves.
30. Belloc, p. 253.
31. Napoleon to Duroc, 31 Aug. 1805: 'The army is in full movement . . .', cited Fuller, ii, p. 387.

Chapter 10: Trafalgar, 1805

1. Mahan, *Nelson*, p. 577.
2. Ibid., p. 571.
3. Cited Corbett, *Fighting Instructions*, p. 310.
4. To Dr Mosely, cited Mahan, *Nelson*, p. 581 without date.
5. Dr Gillespie, cited ibid., p. 595.
6. Dr Beatty, cited ibid.
7. Dr Gillespie, cited ibid.
8. Cited ibid., p. 582.
9. Cited Schom, p. 198.
10. See Lewis, *Social History*, pp. 348–50, 361ff.
11. To Decrès, 22 Jan. 1805, cited Howarth, 'Man who Lost Trafalgar', op. cit. (ch. 9, ref. 28), p. 363.
12. ibid.
13. See Zulueta, 'Spanish View', op. cit. (ch. 9, ref. 10), p. 303.
14. 10 May 1805, cited Mahan, *Nelson*, p. 656.
15. The French had landed 1,000 sick on arrival and had buried that number during their stay: Oman, p. 574; as for the Spanish, Gravina wrote to Decrès, 16 Sept. 1805: 'If we had remained for another month we would have lost half our men, rendering perhaps impossible our return to Europe', cited Zulueta, 'Spanish View', op. cit. (ch. 9, ref. 10), p. 305.
16. Cited Oman, p. 575.
17. Cited Mahan, *Nelson*, p. 671.
18. See pp. 215–16 above, cited Howarth, 'Man who Lost Trafalgar', op. cit. (ch. 9, ref. 28), p. 366.
19. See Desbrière, i, pp. 132–3.
20. Gravina to Decrès, 8 Aug. 1805, cited Zulueta, 'Spanish View', op. cit. (ch. 9, ref. 10), p. 305.
21. See p. 85.
22. See pp. 87–91, 95–8.
23. See pp. 141–4.
24. See Tunstall, p. 247.
25. See Mahan, *Nelson*, p. 688.
26. Cited Ehrman, iii, p. 790.
27. Cited Oman, pp. 588–9.

28. Cited ibid., p. 594.
29. Mahan, *Nelson*, p. 683.
30. Cited ibid., p. 690.
31. Cited L. Kennedy, p. 309.
32. Respectively Captains George Duff and Edward Codrington, cited ibid., p. 310.
33. To an officer, anonymous, who copied it to the *Naval Chronicle*, cited Mahan, *Nelson*, p. 693.
34. Cited ibid., p. 609.
35. Cited ibid., pp. 611–12.
36. Cited ibid., pp. 696–7.
37. Tunstall, p. 249.
38. Cited Mahan, *Nelson*, p. 698.
39. For discussion of progress in tactics, see Mahan, *Nelson*, pp. 694ff.; Tunstall, pp. 248ff.
40. Fuller, ii, p. 390.
41. Cited Howarth, 'Man who Lost Trafalgar', op. cit. (ch. 9, ref. 28), p. 368.
42. Gravina to Godoy, 28 Sept. 1805, cited Zulueta, 'Spanish View', op. cit. (ch. 9, ref. 10), p. 309.
43. See minutes of Council of War, 8 Oct. 1805, cited Desbrière, ii, pp. 105–6; and letter of Don Antonio de Escaño, a representative at the Council, to Don Enrico Macdonell, cited ibid., ii, pp. 107–9.
44. Villeneuve to his captains, *Bucentaure*, Toulon Roads, 21 Dec. 1804, cited Desbrière, ii, p. 130.
45. Gen. Lauriston to Napoleon, 21 Aug. 1805, cited ibid., ii, p. 113; and see Howarth, 'Man who Lost Trafalgar', op. cit. (ch. 9, ref. 28), p. 308.
46. Gravina to Spanish government, 18 Oct. 1805, cited Zulueta, 'Spanish View', op. cit. (ch. 9, ref. 10), p. 310.
47. Ibid.
48. Escaño's Report on the Battle of Trafalgar, 17 Dec. 1805, cited ibid., pp. 307–11.
49. Desbrière, i, p. 211.
50. Zulueta, 'Spanish View', op. cit. (ch. 9, ref. 10), p. 311.
51. *Victory*'s log, 6.0 a.m., Jackson, ii, p. 183. The *Victory*'s and *Euryalus*'s signal logs are used hereafter unless otherwise stated.
52. Cited Oman, p. 620.
53. John Brown to Thos. Windever, *Victory*, Chatham, 28 Dec. 1805, cited Thursfield, p. 364.
54. Newnham Collingwood, pp. 127–8.
55. Cited Mahan, *Nelson*, p. 726.
56. Cited Oman, p. 621.
57. See Mahan, *Nelson*, pp. 729–30; Oman, pp. 622–3.

58. Admiral Hercules Robinson, cited W. C. Russell, p. 136.

59. A single yellow flag with a blue fly added to the appendix of the printed signal book, to which Nelson appended the explanation: 'The Admiral will probably advance his Fleet to the van of theirs before he makes the Signal in order to deceive the Enemy by inducing them to suppose it is his intention to attack their van', NMM Tunstall Collection TUN/61; and see Tunstall, pp. 250–1, 258.

60. See Maj.-Gen. Contamine of Villeneuve's expeditionary force: 'The swell took our ships abeam, made them roll heavily and our aim uncertain', cited Desbrière, ii, p. 144.

61. Newnham Collingwood, p. 124.

62. Mahan, *Nelson*, p. 731.

63. Desbrière, i, p. 280; Mahan, *Nelson*, p. 732.

64. See W. James, iv, p. 57.

65. Desbrière, i, p. 284.

66. Surgeon's post-mortem examination report, cited Nicolas, vii, pp. 258–61.

67. Capt. Lucas' Report, cited Desbrière, ii, p. 217.

68. Desbrière, i, p. 285.

69. Capt. James Atcherley, RM, of *Conqueror*, cited Warner, *Trafalgar*, p. 120.

70. Cited Howarth, p. 185.

71. Midshipman Babcock of *Neptune*, cited Fraser, p. 281.

72. Capt. Lucas' Report, cited Desbrière, ii, pp. 217–18.

73. Cdr Bazin, 2nd in cd. *Fougueux*, Report, cited ibid., pp. 230–2.

74. Dr Beatty's narrative, Nicolas, vii, pp. 244ff.

75. Rev. A. J. Scott (Nelson's secretary) to Mr Rose, 22 Dec. 1805, cited Nicolas, vii, pp. 245ff.

76. Ibid.; Lt. George Browne of *Victory* to his parents, 4 Dec. 1805, gave the time of Nelson's death as 4.49; time of death in *Victory*'s log 4.30.

77. Capt. Blackwood to Hon. Mrs Blackwood, 22 Oct. 1805, 1 o'clock at night, cited Nicolas, vii, p. 224.

78. To Blackett, *Queen*, 2 Nov. 1805, cited Newnham Collingwood, p. 136.

79. Cited Oman, p. 635.

80. Lord Fitz Harris's 'Note Book', Malmesbury IV, p. 341n., cited Ehrman, iii, p. 790.

81. Zulueta, 'Spanish View', op. cit. (ch. 9, ref. 10), p. 313.

82. Collingwood to Mrs Moutray, *Queen*, off Carthagena, 9 Dec. 1805, cited Nicolas, vii, p. 238.

83. Escaño's Report on the Battle of Trafalgar, 17 Dec. 1805, cited Zulueta, 'Spanish View', op. cit. (ch. 9, ref. 10), p. 313.

84. See Howarth, p. 239; Pocock, pp. 217–18.

85. See Glete, ii, p. 386.

86. See Ehrman, iii, p. 707.

87. Glete, ii, p. 390.
88. Paul Fontin, *Les Sous-marins et l'Angleterre*, Paris, 1902, p. 78, cited Naval Intelligence Department Report No. 676, Ministry of Defence Library, London.
89. Capt. Blackwood to Hon. Mrs Blackwood, 23 Nov. 1805, cited Nicolas, vii, p. 227.

Chapter 11: The Empire of the Oceans

1. Duff Cooper, pp. 149–52.
2. Treaty of Pressburg, 26 Dec. 1805.
3. Gabriel Ouvrard, see Sparrow, p. 315.
4. Treaty of Schönbrunn, 15 Dec. 1805.
5. Ehrman, iii, pp. 823, 829.
6. George Rose, cited ibid., p. 829.
7. Cited ibid., p. 830.
8. See Duff Cooper, p. 155.
9. See R. Hill, pp. 45–6.
10. See Padfield, *Maritime Supremacy*, p. 120.
11. See Duff Cooper, p. 158; Sparrow, pp. 338–40.
12. Cited R. Hill, p. 46.
13. See Fisher, p. 848.
14. See Duff Cooper, pp. 158, 162.
15. Sir Robert Wilson to Canning, 26 June 1807, cited Sparrow, p. 343.
16. To Brooke Taylor, PRO FO 95/84, Most Secret No. 2, 16 July 1807, cited Sparrow, p. 344.
17. PRO FO 353/56, cited Sparrow, p. 343.
18. PRO FO 95/84, No. 3, 22 July 1807, cited Sparrow, p. 344.
19. Ibid.
20. Duff Cooper, p. 161.
21. See Sparrow, p. 346.
22. See ibid., p. 344.
23. *Hansard*, 1808, p. 66, cited Robertson, p. 509.
24. See Glete, ii, p. 393.
25. Cited Bryant, *Victory*, p. 215.
26. See Duff Cooper, p. 164; Fisher, p. 852.
27. In which context, a previous French Foreign Minister, the Comte de Vergennes, had viewed Great Britain as a 'restless and greedy nation . . . powerfully armed and ready to strike': see Padfield, *Maritime Supremacy*, p. 239.
28. See Thomas, pp. 525–6, 548.
29. June 1806, cited Thomas, p. 552.
30. Thomas, p. 530.

31. See Woodman, p. 13; P. Kennedy, *Naval Mastery*, p. 155.
32. See Crowhurst, p. 95; A. N. Ryan, 'The Defence of British Trade with the Baltic', *English Historical Review*, vol. xxiv, no. ccxcii (July 1959), pp. 461–2; and see Ryan, pp. 187ff.
33. Cited R. Hill, p. 47.
34. Admiralty circular, 3 Feb. 1808, cited ibid., p. 49.
35. See A. N. Ryan, 'Defence of British Trade', op. cit. (ref. 32 above), p. 463; R. Hill, p. 51.
36. See Sparrow, p. 337.
37. See John D. Grainger, *The Navy in the River Plate, 1806–1807*, NRS, 1996, p. 36, cited Woodman, p. 69; and see R. Hill, p. 40.
38. *US Rolla* judgement, cited R. Hill, p. 40.
39. To Lady Collingwood, *Ocean*, off Toulon, 15 May 1808, Newnham Collingwood, p. 355.
40. Gen. Trochu, cited Aldington, p. 115.
41. Cited Aldington, pp. 115–16.
42. Ibid., p. 131.
43. Schönbrunn, 14 Oct. 1809.
44. Wellington to Lord Liverpool, 31 Jan. 1810, cited Aldington, p. 146.
45. Lord Liverpool to Wellington, 27 Feb. 1810, cited Parkinson, p. 108.
46. Parkinson, p. 126.
47. Ibid., p. 132.
48. Wellington: 'if anyone wishes to know the history of this war . . . it is our maritime superiority gives me the power of maintaining my army while the enemy are unable to do so', cited Woodman, p. 10.
49. J. R. Jones, p. 295, states that the opening of Spanish markets in 1808 resulted in the tripling of British exports 1808–9. Mitchell & Deane, p. 311, suggests a quadrupling, thus exports to foreign West Indies and South America, 1807, £1.3 million; 1808, £4.8 million; 1809, £6.4 million; total trade in same direction, exports and imports, 1807, £2.6 million; 1808, £7.7 million; 1809, £11.5 million.
50. See Padfield, *Maritime Supremacy*, p. 2.
51. Glete, ii, p. 376.
52. Paul Webb, 'The Frigate Situation of the Royal Navy, 1793–1815', *MM*, vol. 82, no. 1 (Feb. 1996), table 5, p. 38; Glete, ii, p. 382.
53. Glete, ii, p. 383.

Chapter 12: The Continental Blockade

1. Lord Mulgrave, 1st Lord of the Admiralty, to Saumarez, 20 Feb. 1808, and Admiralty instructions to Saumarez, 21 March, 16 April 1808, cited Ryan, pp. 7, 12–13.

2. Saumarez draft letter, *Victory*, off Port Baltic, 30 Aug. 1808, Ryan, p. 42.

3. Duke (surgeon) to Saumarez, *Victory*, off Port Baltic, 12 Sept. 1808, Ryan, pp. 46–7.

4. Saumarez to Pole, Sec. to Admiralty, 2 Sept. 1808, Ryan, p. 44.

5. Saumarez to Rajalin, off Carlskrona, 6 Aug. 1808, ibid., p. 26.

6. Saumarez to Pole, 21 Nov. 1808, ibid., p. 57.

7. Dixon to Admiralty, 9 Nov. 1809, cited Ryan, 'Defence of British Trade', op. cit. (ch. 11, ref. 32), p. 457.

8. Ryan, ibid., pp. 444–5, citing J. J. Oddy, *European Commerce: Shewing New and Secure Channels of Trade with the Continent of Europe*, 1804. Neither Mitchell & Deane nor François Crouzet in *L'Économie britannique et le blocus continental*, Presses Universitaires de France, 1958, analyse the figures for the Baltic separately, but the extraordinary rising trend of trade in northern Europe is clear: thus Mitchell & Deane, p. 311, has the official value of exports and imports to northern Europe in 1793 as £10.7 million; 1801, £21.7 million; 1809, £19.3 million.

9. Boris V. Anan'ich, Sergei K. Lebedev, 'Russian Finance during the French Revolution and the Napoleonic Wars', in Aerts & Crouzet, pp. 41–2.

10. Saumarez to Pole, London, 21 Nov. 1808, Ryan, pp. 52–3.

11. Saumarez's 'Explanation', 21 Nov. 1808, ibid., p. 56.

12. See P. Kennedy, *Naval Mastery*, p. 171; Mitchell & Deane, p. 311.

13. 'Instructions to a Commander of a Danish Privateer', in Saumarez to Croker, Sec. of Admiralty, 6 June 1810, Ryan, pp. 126–7.

14. Saumarez to Yorke, 1st Lord of the Admiralty, *Victory*, Hanö Bay, 25 July 1810, ibid., p. 139.

15. Mitchell & Deane, p. 289.

16. Saumarez to Yorke, *Victory*, Hanö Bay, 20 Sept. 1810, Ryan, p. 152.

17. C. Wright & E. Fayle, *A History of Lloyds*, London, 1928, pp. 187ff., cited Ryan, p. 150; and see Crowhurst, p. 94; and Ryan, 'Defence of British Trade', op. cit. (ch. 11, ref. 32), pp. 461–2.

18. Wilkinson to Saumarez, 20 June 1811, Ryan, p. 184; and see Ferguson, *Banker*, p. 62, describing Mayer Amschel Rothschild of Frankfurt caught with smuggled goods worth around 100,000 gulden (c. £90,000), which were publicly burned; in addition, he was fined some 20,000 francs (c. £870). Another Frankfurt firm was fined over 360,000 francs (over £15,000). An observer wrote, 'The extent of general confusion which this has caused beggars description.'

19. Napoleon to Metternich, Sept. 1810: 'I shall have war with Russia on grounds that lie beyond human possibilities, because they are rooted in the cause itself', cited Bryant, *Victory*, p. 390.

20. Gneisenau to Saumarez, 8 Sept. 1811, Ryan, p. 189.

21. Saumarez to Gneisenau, Wingo Sound, 28 Sept. 1811, ibid., p. 193.

22. Johnson to Culling Smith, 13, 15 March 1811, PRO FO 7/111, cited Sparrow, p. 374.
23. Duff Cooper, p. 176.
24. Fouché dismissed 2 June 1810, see Sparrow, pp. 386ff.
25. See Ellis, 'French Economy', op. cit. (ch. 8, ref. 4), p. 9.
26. See Padfield, *Maritime Supremacy*, p. 77.
27. Eric Buyst & Joël Mokyr, 'Dutch Manufacturing and Trade during the French Period (1795–1814) in a Long Term Perspective', in Aerts & Crouzet, p. 70.
28. See L. Neal, 'A Tale of Two Revolutions: International Flows, 1789–1810', ESCR Quantitative History Conference, Hull, 1989, cited ibid., p. 67.
29. See Ellis, 'French Economy', op. cit. (ch. 8, ref. 4), p. 10.
30. See Bergeron, pp. 39–42.
31. Glete, ii, p. 387.
32. See Florin Aftalion, 'The Financing of the Wars of the Revolution and the Empire', in Aerts & Crouzet, p. 23.
33. Count Montholon, *History of the Captivity of Napoleon*, London, 1846–7, ii, p. 309, cited Wheeler, p. 74.
34. Ibid., p. 79.
35. See Ferguson, *Cash Nexus*, p. 181.
36. Aftalion, 'Financing the Wars', op. cit. (ref. 32 above), p. 28.
37. Mitchell & Deane, p. 311.
38. See J. R. Jones, pp. 302, 307; Mitchell & Deane, p. 311, records a fall from £7.8 million in 1810 to £1.4 million in 1811.
39. See J. R. Jones, p. 308.

Chapter 13: The American War, 1812

1. See Burrows & Wallace, p. 32.
2. Jenkins, 'Guadeloupe's Commerce Raiding', op. cit. (ch. 8, ref. 12), pp. 305–7.
3. Ibid., p. 307.
4. Chapelle, p. 127.
5. Ibid., pp. 175–6.
6. Burrows & Wallace, p. 410.
7. See J. R. Jones, p. 305; Robertson, p. 455.
8. To Vice Admiral Thornborough, 18 Oct. 1807, Newnham Collingwood, p. 330.
9. Burrows & Wallace, pp. 411–12.
10. Macon's No. 2 Act, May 1810, see J. R. Jones, p. 306.
11. See ibid.

12. Burrows & Wallace, pp. 423–4.
13. 28 June 1812.
14. Melville, 1st Lord of the Admiralty, to Saumarez, July 1812, Ryan, p. 185.
15. 'Official values of imports and exports and re-exports according to regional direction', Mitchell & Deane, p. 311.
16. B. H. Liddell Hart, 'Wellington', in Parker, p. 75.
17. Aldington, p. 174.
18. Wellington's memorandum on the war in Russia, 1812, cited Aldington, p. 355.
19. Tolstoy, p. 1104.
20. Ibid., p. 1110.
21. Ibid., p. 1132.
22. Wellington's memorandum, op. cit. (ref. 18 above), p. 357.
23. Cited Fisher, p. 865.
24. Guedalla, *The Duke*, p. 238.
25. Ferguson, *Cash Nexus*, p. 181.
26. Duff Cooper, p. 215.
27. Guedalla, *The Duke*, p. 248.
28. See Aldington, p. 199.
29. Cited Duff Cooper, p. 231.
30. Belloc, p. 416.
31. Roberts, p. 117.
32. Mitchell & Deane, pp. 281–2; 1793 figures 'official values'; 1814 figures 'computed or declared values'.
33. See Ferguson, *Banker*, p. 48.
34. Ibid., p. 94.
35. Larry Neal, *The Rise of Financial Capitalism*, Cambridge, 1990, pp. 180–90, cited ibid., p. 95.
36. Herries to Sir George Burgman, cited Ferguson, *Banker*, p. 95.
37. Ibid., p. 96.
38. See Ferguson, *Cash Nexus*, p. 286; Ferguson, *Banker*, p. 90; Robertson, p. 453.
39. See Ferguson, *Cash Nexus*, p. 70.
40. Ibid., p. 184.
41. See Sparrow, p. 394.

Chapter 14: Lake Erie and Plattsburg Bay, 1813–1814

1. See Chapelle, p. 208.
2. Ibid., p. 244.
3. Broke to Louisa Broke, 21 July 1812, Saumarez Papers SCRO HA 93 877/13.

4. See Padfield, *Broke*, p. 98.

5. Ibid., p. 101.

6. See ibid., p. 106.

7. Ibid., p. 109.

8. Leech, cited ibid., p. 110.

9. *Naval Chronicle*, vol. xxviii, 1812, p. 422.

10. To Louisa, 26 Nov. 1812, Saumarez Papers SCRO HA 93 877/13.

11. See Padfield, *Broke*, pp. 27ff., for Broke's gunnery arrangements.

12. Ibid., p. 38.

13. The *Constitution* probably lost 10 killed and had 44 wounded, although the official report stated 34 killed and wounded: see ibid., p. 117.

14. *The Times*, London, 20 March 1813.

15. To Louisa, 14 Feb. 1813, Saumarez Papers SCRO HA 93 877/14.

16. Padfield, *Broke*, p. 134.

17. A copy of Broke's famous challenge is in the Saumarez Papers SCRO HA 93.

18. Mahan, *War of 1812*, p. 134.

19. Cited Padfield, *Broke*, p. 150.

20. Ibid., p. 231.

21. Ibid., p. 161.

22. Ibid., p. 162.

23. See 'Analysis of the Battle', Appendix A, ibid., pp. 240ff. This analysis is followed hereafter.

24. *Naval Chronicle*, vol. xxx, 1813, p. 41.

25. See Padfield, *Broke*, pp. 194–5.

26. 'Summary of Shot', Appendix B, ibid., p. 245.

27. See computation of casualties, ibid., pp. 231ff.

28. Capt. S. J. Pechell, *Observations on the Defective Equipment of Ships' Guns*, 1825, MOD Library, Naval section.

29. Sir H. Douglas, *A Treatise on Naval Gunnery*, John Murray, 1829.

30. Chapelle, p. 273.

31. Ibid., pp. 169–70.

32. See B. Gough, *Fighting Sail on Lake Huron*, US Naval Institute Press, Annapolis, 2002, for the critical importance of these operations in preserving the Canadian border at the subsequent peace negotiations.

33. Chapelle, p. 298.

Chapter 15: Napoleon's Nemesis

1. Ehrman, iii, pp. 730–4.

2. Cited Duff Cooper, p. 257.

3. Thomas, p. 583.

4. To Sir H. Wellesley, London, 29 July 1814, cited Aldington, pp. 206–7.

5. See Thomas, p. 584.

6. See Hobsbawm, *Revolution*, p. 38.

7. Cited Guedalla, *Hundred Days*, p. 26.

8. Ibid., p. 25.

9. '*la vindicte publique*', see ibid., pp. 53–4.

10. Robertson, p. 467.

11. Ferguson, *Banker*, p. 104.

12. Guedalla, *Hundred Days*, p. 99.

13. Unnamed French brigadier, cited ibid., p. 110.

14. Ibid., p. 132; Roberts, p. xxxi.

15. Aldington, p. 212.

16. See ibid., p. 220.

17. Alice, Countess of Strafford, *Personal Reminiscences of the Duke of Wellington* . . ., 1904, p. 179, cited Roberts, p. 172.

18. To Mr Creevey, cited Guedalla, *Hundred Days*, p. 143. For the most succinct and cogent analysis of the tactics and fighting at Waterloo, see Keegan, pp. 134ff.

19. To his brother, William, 18 June 1815, cited Roberts, p. 184.

20. To Mr Creevey, cited Aldington, pp. 142–3.

21. Cited ibid., p. 229.

22. Casualty figures from Aldington, p. 227.

23. Count Flahaut to Prince Pückler-Muskau, 11 Feb. 1827, cited Pückler-Muskau, p. 93; for the profound implications of the French rout on the idea of the Revolution, see Keegan, pp. 178ff.; and for Wellington's comment that Waterloo was won on the playing fields of Eton, see Keegan, p. 194: Wellington was suggesting that 'the French had been beaten not by wiser generalship or better tactics or superior patriotism but by coolness and endurance, the pursuit of excellence and intangible objectives for their own sake which are learnt in game playing'.

24. Eugène Vitrolles, cited Duff Cooper, p. 275.

25. Tocqueville, *Journeys*, p. 81.

26. See Ferguson, *Banker*, p. 121.

27. See Aldington, pp. 245–8, 235–6.

28. Capt. F. Maitland, *Narrative of the Surrender of Bonaparte* . . ., 1826, p. 208, cited Roberts, pp. 195–6.

29. See Ellis, 'French Economy', op. cit. (ch. 8, ref. 4), p. 11.

30. See Louis Bergeron, 'Les Milieux d'affaires, la Guerre et la Paix (1792–1815)', in Aerts & Crouzet, pp. 17–18.

31. *Enc. Br.*, vi, p. 467.

32. Bernal, ii, p. 530.

33. See Denis Woronoff, 'Production d'Armaments, Progrès Technique et

Croissance Économique pendant la Révolution et l'Empire', in Aerts & Crouzet, p. 90.

34. See ibid., pp. 93–4.
35. See Ellis, 'French Economy', op. cit. (ch. 8, ref. 4), p. 11.
36. i.e. 1826, see ibid.
37. See Bergeron, p. 113.
38. See Ferguson, *Cash Nexus*, p. 398.
39. See Hobsbawm, *Revolution*, pp. 29–30.
40. Scarfe, *Innocent Espionage*, p. 23.
41. Ibid., p. 101.
42. 28 Feb. 1785, ibid., p. 51.

Chapter 16: The Sceptre of the World

1. Cited Keay, p. 449.
2. See Sir James Watt, 'The Health of Seamen in Anti-Slavery Squadrons', *MM*, vol. 88, no. 1 (Feb. 2002), p. 70; and Padfield, *Rule Britannia*, pp. 113–14.
3. See Padfield, *Maritime Supremacy*, p. 233.
4. The late Prof. Roberts, cited Keay, p. 391.
5. See Hobhouse, p. 143; Keay, p. 391.
6. See Hobhouse, pp. 145–6; Keay, pp. 454–5.
7. Hobhouse, p. 148.
8. Aldington, p. 58.
9. Cited Godfrey Hodgson, reviewing Penderel Moon, *The British Conquest and Dominion of India*, Duckworth, 1989, *Independent*, 19 May 1989.
10. L. James, p. 63.
11. See Hobsbawm, *Revolution*, pp. 34–5.
12. Ibid.
13. Ferguson, *Cash Nexus*, pp. 287ff.
14. Ferguson, *Banker*, p. 90.
15. Ibid., pp. 122–3.
16. Cited ibid., p. 123.
17. See ibid., pp. 126–7.
18. Salomon Rothschild to Nathan Rothschild, Oct. 1815, cited ibid., p. 82.
19. 188 million thaler (*c.* £32 million), see ibid., p. 131.
20. Nathan to Amschel Rothschild, *c.* Dec. 1817, cited ibid., p. 132; Ferguson, *Cash Nexus*, p. 288.
21. See Ferguson, *Banker*, p. 132.
22. Ibid., p. 283.
23. Cited Ferguson, *Cash Nexus*, p. 290.
24. Ibid., p. 289.

25. See Hobsbawm, *Revolution*, pp. 106, 316; Hobsbawm, *Capital*, pp. 40, 309.
26. Pückler-Muskau, pp. 154–5.
27. Ibid., p. 143.
28. Ibid., pp. 95–6.
29. See Padfield, *Maritime Supremacy*, pp. 69ff.
30. Pückler-Muskau, p. 46.
31. Ibid., pp. 113–15.
32. Ibid., p. 194.
33. Ibid., p. 26.
34. Ibid., p. 29.
35. Cited Ferguson, *Banker*, p. 275.
36. Nathan Rothschild's obituary, *The Times*, London, cited ibid., p. 281.
37. Pückler-Muskau, p. 46.
38. Ibid., p. 105.
39. Ibid., p. 23, and see p. 64.
40. Ibid., pp. 71–2.
41. Ibid., p. 193.
42. Ibid., p. 242.
43. 1726–30, in Lonsdale, p. 180.
44. 'Hymn to Solitude' (1729), in ibid., p. 191.
45. Written 1742, published 1748, in ibid., p. 349.
46. 'The Lamb', in ibid., pp. 690–1.
47. 'London', in ibid., p. 694.
48. E. C. Mossner's Introduction, in Hume, p. 22.
49. Lonsdale, p. 706.
50. Samuel Taylor Coleridge, *The Rime of the Ancient Mariner*, Arno Press/ Mayflower Books, NY, 1979, p. 10.
51. See Waldemar Januszczak reviewing Lucien Freud/Constable exhibition, Grand Palais, Paris, *Sunday Times*, 13 Oct. 2002.
52. Blayney Brown, p. 26.
53. B. Russell, p. 748.
54. *Enc. Br.*, xviii, p. 505, and see Singer, p. 15.
55. John S. Mill, 'Utilitarianism', *Internet Encyclopedia of Philosophy*.
56. *Enc. Br.*, xviii, p. 505, and see Singer, pp. 15ff.
57. Preface to W. Wordsworth, Samuel T. Coleridge, *Lyrical Ballads*, 2nd edn, London, 1801.
58. See pp. 27–8 above.
59. See Ben Macintyre, 'Bookworm Boney loved English Tales', *Sunday Times*, 31 Jan. 1998.
60. Stone, *Family*, p. 427.
61. Ibid., p. 428.

62. Hobsbawm, *Revolution*, p. 316.
63. Ibid., pp. 175–6.
64. Padfield, *P & O*, p. 15.
65. Ibid., p. 23.
66. Cited ibid., pp. 21–2.
67. See Padfield, *Rule Britannia*, p. 17; Glete, ii, Appendix 2 gives for 1850 aggregate British fleet 550,000 tons deadweight; French fleet 316,000 tons deadweight; Russian fleet 231,000 tons deadweight.
68. See Hobhouse, p. 149.
69. Headrick, pp. 44ff.
70. Padfield, *Rule Britannia*, p. 95.
71. See Headrick, p. 90; Padfield, *Rule Britannia*, p. 96.
72. Padfield, *Rule Britannia*, p. 95.
73. Magnus, p. 52.
74. Guedalla, *Palmerston*, p. 189.
75. Capt. Hall of *Nemesis* to John Laird, May 1841, India Office Records L/MAR/C 593, pp. 543–4, cited Headrick, p. 50.
76. C. P. Hill, p. 151.
77. Padfield, *Rule Britannia*, p. 86.
78. C. P. Hill, pp. 153–4; and see Ferguson, *Cash Nexus*, p. 61.
79. Tocqueville, *Democracy*, i, p. 509.
80. *Williams's Register*, 1833, cited ibid., p. 398.
81. Headrick, p. 146.
82. Tocqueville, *Democracy*, i, p. 513.
83. *Enc. Br.*, vii, p. 777.
84. See Batty & Parish, p. 13.
85. Trollope, p. 259.
86. Ibid., p. 297.
87. See Burrows & Wallace, p. 451.
88. Ibid., p. 445.
89. See ibid., p. 431.
90. Trollope, p. 298.
91. Burrows & Wallace, pp. 440–1.
92. See Trollope, pp. 299ff., 239, 244.
93. Hobsbawm, *Capital*, p. 309.
94. Marshall Tymn (ed.), *Thomas Cole: The Collected Essays and Prose Sketches*, St Pauls, Minnesota, 1980, p. 131, cited Tim Barringer, in Wilton & Barringer, p. 49.
95. Ibid., p. 51.
96. See ibid., pp. 51–2, 102–3.
97. Ibid., p. 39.
98. See Hobsbawm, *Capital*, p. 309; Hobsbawm, *Revolution*, p. 169; and see

G. R. Taylor, 'American Economic Growth before 1840', *Journal of Economic History*, Dec. 1964, pp. 427ff.

99. A. de Tocqueville, *Oeuvres complètes*, Paris, 1951, v, pp. 377–8, cited Drescher, pp. 25–30.

100. Trollope, pp. 258–9.

101. Ibid., pp. 327–8.

102. Ibid., p. 308.

103. See Schleifer, p. 75.

104. Tocqueville's preliminary synthesis, in Schleifer, p. 42.

105. Tocqueville, *Journeys*, p. 94.

106. Yale MSS (B) C.X.3, *L'Irlande* notes, 'Hallem Manufacturier', cited Drescher, pp. 63–4.

107. Tocqueville, *Journeys*, p. 94.

108. Cited Drescher, p. 57.

109. '*Mémoire sur paupérisme*', p. 294, cited Drescher, p. 134.

110. Cited Drescher, p. 104.

111. Alphabetic Notebook: 'C' *Centralization*, 24 Aug. 1833, Tocqueville, *Journeys*, pp. 61–2.

112. See Drescher, pp. 85–6.

113. See ibid., p. 132.

114. Ferguson, *Banker*, p. 232.

115. See Schleifer, p. 77.

116. Tocqueville to Senior, 10 April 1848, *Oeuvres: Correspondance d'Alexis de Tocqueville*, (2nd edn) 1867, cited Drescher, p. 144.

117. Tocqueville speaking in Constitutional Assembly, 12 Sept. 1848, cited Drescher, pp. 151, 144–7.

118. Pitt's Budget speech, 17 Feb. 1792, cited Ehrman, iii, p. 419.

119. In *Moniteur*, 20 Jan. 1845, p. 125, cited Drescher, p. 164.

120. See Thomas, pp. 673–6.

121. Trollope, p. 209.

122. Ibid., 1839 edn, p. xiv.

123. See James Walvin, 'British Abolitionism, 1787–1838', in Tibbles, pp. 92ff.

124. J. S. Mill, Introduction to Tocqueville, *Democracy*, ii, p. xlviii.

125. Speech by Prince Albert at a Banquet at the Mansion House, City of London, 1850, in Golby, p. 1.

126. Queen Victoria to the King of the Belgians, 3 May 1851, in ibid., p. 4.

Select Bibliography

Abbreviations used:

NRS   The Navy Records Society
PRO   Public Record Office, Kew Gardens, London
SCRO   Suffolk County Record Office, Ipswich, Suffolk
OUP   Oxford University Press, Oxford
CUP   Cambridge University Press, Cambridge

The place of publication is London unless otherwise shown.

Aerts, E., & Crouzet, F., *Economic Effects of the French Revolutionary and Napoleonic Wars*, Leuven Univ. Press, Leuven, Belgium, 1990
Aldington, R., *Wellington*, Heinemann, 1946
Anderson, R. C., *Naval Wars in the Baltic*, Francis Edwards, 1969
Austen, J., *Pride and Prejudice*, 1795, Macmillan edn, 1942
—— *Emma*, 1796, Macmillan edn, 1942
—— *Persuasion*, 1818, Pan edn, 1969
Barnes, G. R., & Owen, J. H. (eds.), *The Private Papers of John, Earl of Sandwich . . . 1771–1782*, NRS, 4 vols, 1932–8
Barrow, J., *Richard Earl Howe*, John Murray, 1838
Batty, P., & Parish, P. J., *The Divided Union; a Concise History of the Civil War*, Tempus, Stroud, Gloucestershire, 1999
Belloc, H., *Napoleon*, Cassell, 1932
Beloff, M., *The Age of Absolutism, 1660–1815*, Hutchinson, 1954
Bennett, G., *Nelson the Commander*, Batsford, 1972
Berckman, E., *Nelson's Dear Lord*, Macmillan, 1962

Bergeron, L., *France under Napoleon*, trans. R. R. Palmer, Princeton Univ. Press, Princeton, 1981

Bernal, J. D., *Science in History*, vol. 2, *The Scientific and Industrial Revolutions*, C. A. Watts, 1954

Blayney Brown, D., *Turner in the Alps, 1802*, Tate Gallery Publications, 1998

Bromley, J. S., & Kossman, E. H., *Britain and the Netherlands in Europe and Asia*, Macmillan, 1968

Bryant A., *The Years of Endurance, 1793–1802*, Collins, 1942

—— *Years of Victory, 1802–1812*, Collins, 1944

—— *The Age of Elegance, 1812–1822*, Collins, 1950

Burke, E., *Reflections on the Revolution in France*, ed. J. C. D. Clark, Stanford Univ. Press, Stanford, 2001

Burrows, E. G., & Wallace, M., *Gotham: A History of New York City to 1898*, OUP, NY, 1999

Buruma, I., *Voltaire's Coconuts; or Anglomania in Europe*, Weidenfeld & Nicolson, 1999

Camperdown, Earl of, *Admiral Duncan*, Longmans Green, 1898

Chapelle, H. I., *The History of the American Sailing Navy; The Ships and their Development*, Bonanza Books, NY, 1949

Christie, I. R., *Stress and Stability in Late Eighteenth Century Britain: Reflections on the British Avoidance of Revolution*, OUP, 1984

Clark, K., *Civilisation: A Personal View*, John Murray, 1969

Clerk, J., *An Essay in Naval Tactics*, Edinburgh, 1804

Cole, H., *Fouché: The Unprincipled Patriot*, Eyre & Spottiswoode, 1971

Corbett, J. S., *Fighting Instructions, 1530–1816*, NRS, 1904

—— *Signals and Instructions, 1776–1794*, NRS, 1908

—— (ed.), *The Private Papers of George, second Earl Spencer . . . 1794–1801*, vols I & II, NRS, 1913–14 (*see* Richmond for vols III & IV)

Cormack, W. S., *Revolution and Political Conflict in the French Navy, 1789–1794*, CUP, 1995

Crawford, A., *Reminiscences of a Naval Officer; A Quarter-Deck View of the War against Napoleon*, London, 1851, reprinted Chatham Publishing, 1999

Crowhurst, P., *The Defence of British Trade, 1689–1815*, Dawson, Folkestone, 1977

Desbrière, E., *The Naval Campaigns of 1805: Trafalgar*, trans. C. Eastwick, 2 vols, OUP, 1933

Drescher, S., *Tocqueville and England*, Harvard Univ. Press, Cambridge, Mass., 1964

Drinkwater Bethune, Col., *A Narrative of the Battle of St Vincent with Anecdotes of Nelson*, 1840, reprinted Blackmore, 1969

Duff Cooper, *Talleyrand*, Jonathan Cape, 1932

Ehrman, J., *The Younger Pitt*, vol. 3, *The Consuming Struggle*, Constable, 1996

Ekins, C., *Naval Battles, 1744 to the Peace in 1814*, London, 1824

Ferguson, N., *The Cash Nexus: Money and Power in the Modern World, 1700–2000*, Allen Lane, 2001

——— *The World's Banker; The History of the House of Rothschild*, Weidenfeld & Nicolson, 1998

Fisher, H. A. L., *A History of Europe*, Edward Arnold, 1936

Fraser, E., *The Enemy at Trafalgar*, Hodder & Stoughton, 1906

Fukuyama, F., *The Great Disruption: Human Nature and the Reconstitution of Social Order*, Profile Books, 1999

Fuller, J. F. C., *The Decisive Battles of the Western World*, vol. 2, *From the Defeat of the Spanish Armada to the Battle of Waterloo*, Eyre & Spottiswoode, 1955

Fuller, M., *Women in the Nineteenth Century and Other Writings*, ed. D. Dickenson, OUP, 1994

Gardner, J. A., *Above and Under Hatches; The Recollections of James Anthony Gardner*, NRS, 1906, reprinted Chatham Publishing, 2000

Gill, C., *The Naval Mutinies of 1797*, Manchester Univ. Press, Manchester, 1913

Glete, J., *Navies and Nations: Warships, Navies and State Building in Europe and America, 1500–1860*, Almquist & Winsell, Stockholm, 2 vols, 1993

Goddard, H., *Memoirs of a Bow Street Runner*, Museum Press, 1956

Godechot, J., *France and the Atlantic Revolution of the Eighteenth Century, 1770–1799*, trans. H. H. Rown, The Free Press, NY, 1965

Golby, J. M., *Culture and Society in Britain 1850–1890*, OUP, 1986

Gordon, J. S., *The Great Game: A History of Wall Street*, Orion Business Books, 1999

Green, J. R., *A Short History of the English People*, Harper & Brothers, NY, 1886

Guedalla, P., *The Duke*, Hodder & Stoughton, 1931

——— *Palmerston*, Hodder & Stoughton, 1937 edn

——— *The Hundred Days*, Hodder & Stoughton, 1939 edn

Harbron, J. D., *Trafalgar and the Spanish Navy*, Conway Maritime Press, 1988

Harlow, V. T., *The Founding of the Second British Empire*, vol. 1, *Discovery and Revolution*, Longmans Green, 1952

Headrick, D. R., *The Tools of Empire*, OUP, 1981

Hill, C. P., *British Economic History, 1700–1939*, Edward Arnold, 1961

Hill, R., *The Prizes of War: The Naval Prize System in the Napoleonic Wars, 1793–1815*, Sutton Publishing, 1998

Hobhouse, H., *Seeds of Change; Six Plants That Transformed Mankind*, Sidgwick & Jackson, 1985 (rev. edn Papermac, 1999)

Hobsbawm, E., *The Age of Revolution; Europe 1789–1848*, Weidenfeld & Nicolson, 1962

——— *The Age of Capital, 1848–1875*, Weidenfeld & Nicolson, 1975

Howarth, D., *Trafalgar: The Nelson Touch*, Collins, 1969

Hufton, O., *The Prospect Before Her: A History of Women in Western Europe*, vol. 1, *1500–1800*, Fontana, 1997

Hume, D. A., *A Treatise of Human Nature*, ed. E. C. Mossner, Penguin, 1969

Israel, J., *The Dutch Republic: Its Rise, Greatness and Fall, 1477–1806*, OUP, 1995

Jackson, T. S. (ed.), *Logs of the Great Sea Fights*, 2 vols, NRS, 1899

James, L., *Raj: The Making and Unmaking of British India*, Little, Brown, 1997

James, W., *Naval History of Great Britain . . .*, 6 vols, London, 1826

Jones, E. L., *Growth Recurring: Economic Change in World History*, OUP, 1988

Jones, J. R., *Britain and the World, 1649–1815*, Fontana, 1980

Keay, J., *The Honourable Company: A History of the English East India Company*, HarperCollins, 1991

Keegan, J., *The Face of Battle*, Jonathan Cape, 1976, Penguin edn, 1978

Kemp, P. (ed.), *The Oxford Companion to Ships and the Sea*, OUP, 1976

Kennedy, L., *Nelson and his Captains*, Collins, 1951, reprinted Penguin, 2001

Kennedy, P., *The Rise and Fall of British Naval Mastery*, Allen Lane, 1976

—— *The Rise and Fall of the Great Powers: Economic Change and Military Conflict from 1500 to 2000*, Unwin Hyman, 1988

King, P., *Fear of Power: An Analysis of Anti-statism in Three French Writers*, Frank Cass, 1967

Landes, D. S., *The Wealth and Poverty of Nations: Why Some are So Rich and Some So Poor*, Little, Brown, 1998

Lane, F. C., *Venice, A Maritime Republic*, Johns Hopkins Univ. Press, Baltimore, 1973

Laslett, P. (ed.), *John Locke, Two Treatises of Government*, CUP, 1960

Lavery, B., *Nelson and the Nile: The Naval War against Bonaparte, 1798*, Chatham Publishing, 1998

Leech, S., *A Voice from the Main Deck – the Experiences of Samuel Leech*, London, 1844

Lewis, M., *The Navy of Britain: A Historical Portrait*, Allen & Unwin, 1948

—— *A Social History of the Navy, 1793–1815*, Allen & Unwin, 1960

—— *The Navy in Transition, 1814–1864: A Social History*, Hodder & Stoughton, 1965

—— *Spithead, an Informal History*, Allen & Unwin, 1972

Lloyd, C., *St Vincent and Camperdown*, Batsford, 1963

—— *The Nile Campaign*, David & Charles, Newton Abbot, 1973

—— (ed.), *The Health of Seamen*, NRS, 1966

Lloyd, C., & Coulter, J. L. S., *Medicine and the Navy, 1714–1815*, Livingstone, Edinburgh, 1961

Locke, J., *see* Laslett, P.

Lonsdale, R. (ed.), *The New Oxford Book of Eighteenth-Century Verse*, OUP, 1984

Magnus, P., *Gladstone: A Biography*, John Murray, 1954

Mahan, A. T., *The Life of Nelson; the Embodiment of the Sea Power of Great Britain*, Sampson, Low, Marston, 1899

—— *Sea Power in its Relation to the War of 1812*, 2 vols, Sampson, Low, Marston, 1905

Milton, G., *Samurai William; The Adventurer Who Unlocked Japan*, Hodder & Stoughton, 2002

Mitchell, B. R., and Deane, P., *Abstract of British Historical Statistics*, CUP, 1962
Morogues, Vicomte de, *Tactique navale*, trans. 'A Sea Officer', 1767
Newnham Collingwood, G., *Correspondence of Vice Admiral Lord Collingwood*, 1828
Nicolas, N. H., *The Despatches and Letters of Lord Nelson*, 7 vols, John Murray, 1844–6
Oman, C., *Nelson*, 1946, reprinted Greenhill Books, 1996
Padfield, P., *Broke and the Shannon; a Biography of Admiral Sir Philip Broke*, Hodder & Stoughton, 1968
—— *Guns at Sea; a History of Naval Gunnery*, Hugh Evelyn, 1973
—— *Nelson's War*, Hart Davis, 1976
—— *Rule Britannia; the Victorian and Edwardian Navy*, Routledge & Kegan Paul, 1981
—— *Beneath the Houseflag of the P & O*, Hutchinson, 1981
—— *Himmler; Reichsführer-SS*, Macmillan, 1990
—— *Maritime Supremacy and the Opening of the Western Mind; Naval Campaigns that Shaped the Modern World, 1588–1782*, John Murray, 1999
Palmer, R. R., *The Age of Democratic Revolution*, Princeton Univ. Press, Princeton, 1959
—— *Twelve Who Ruled: The Year of Terror in the French Revolution*, Princeton Univ. Press, Princeton, 1969
Parker, B. (ed.), *Famous British Generals*, Nicholson & Watson, 1951
Parkinson, R., *The Peninsular War*, Hart-Davis MacGibbon, 1973
Parsons, G. S., *Nelsonian Reminiscences; Leaves from Memory's Log*, 1905
Pipes, R., *Property and Freedom*, Harvill Press, 1999
Pocock, T., *The Terror before Trafalgar; Nelson, Napoleon and the Secret War*, John Murray, 2002
Pole, J. R., *The Foundations of American Independence 1763–1815*, Collins, 1973
—— (ed.), *The Revolution in America 1754–1788*, Macmillan, 1970
Pope, D., *The Great Gamble: Nelson at Copenhagen*, Weidenfeld & Nicolson, 1972
Pückler-Muskau, Prince, *Pückler's Progress: The Adventures of Prince Pückler-Muskau in England, Wales and Ireland . . .*, trans. F. Brennan, Collins, 1987
Reischauer, E. O., *Japan Past and Present*, Charles Tuttle, Tokyo, 1946
Richmond, H. W. (ed.), *The Private Papers of George, second Earl Spencer . . . 1794–1801*, vols III & IV, 1923–4 (*see* Corbett for vols I & II)
Roberts, A., *Napoleon and Wellington*, Weidenfeld & Nicolson, 2001
Robertson, C. G., *England under the Hanoverians*, Methuen (rev. edn), 1930
Rodger, N. A. M., *The Wooden World; An Anatomy of the Georgian Navy*, Collins, 1986
Rose, J., *Memoirs and Correspondence of Admiral Lord Saumarez*, 2 vols, 1838
Rowland, K. T., *Steam at Sea*, David & Charles, Newton Abbot, 1970
Rudé, G., *Europe in the Eighteenth Century; Aristocracy and the Bourgeois Challenge*, Sphere Books, 1974

Russell, B., *History of Western Philosophy*, Allen & Unwin, 1946
Russell, W. C., *Admiral Lord Collingwood*, Methuen, 1891
Ryan, A. N., *The Saumarez Papers*, NRS, 1969
Scarfe, N., *Innocent Espionage: The La Rochefoucauld Brothers' Tour of England in 1785*, The Boydell Press, Woodbridge, Suffolk, 1995
——— *To the Highlands in 1786: The Inquisitive Journey of a Young French Aristocrat*, The Boydell Press, Woodbridge, Suffolk, 2001
Schama, S., *Citizens: A Chronicle of the French Revolution*, Knopf, NY, 1989
Schleifer, J. T., *The Making of Tocqueville's Democracy in America*, Univ. of North Carolina Press, Chapel Hill, 1980
Schom, A., *Trafalgar: Countdown to Battle, 1803–1805*, Michael Joseph, 1990
Singer, P., *Writings on an Ethical Life*, Fourth Estate, 2001
Smith, A., *The Wealth of Nations*, 2 vols, 1776–8, reprinted J. M. Dent & Sons, 1910
Soboul, A., *The French Revolution, 1787–1799*, trans. A. Forrest & C. Jones, New Left Books, 1974
Southey, R., *The Life of Nelson*, Blackie, 1813
Sparrow, E., *Secret Service; British Agents in France, 1792–1815*, The Boydell Press, Woodbridge, Suffolk, 1999
Stone, L., *The Family, Sex and Marriage in England, 1500–1800*, Penguin (abridged edn), 1984
——— *Broken Lives: Separation and Divorce in England, 1660–1857*, OUP, 1993
Talbott, J. E., *The Pen and Ink Sailor: Charles Middleton and the King's Navy, 1778–1813*, Frank Cass, 1998
Thomas, H., *The Slave Trade; The History of the Atlantic Slave Trade 1440–1870*, Picador, 1997
Thursfield, H. G. (ed.), *Five Naval Journals, 1789–1817*, NRS, 1951
Tibbles, A. (ed.), *Transatlantic Slavery; Against Human Dignity*, HMSO, London, 1994
Tocqueville, A. de, *Democracy in America*, trans. H. Reeve, 2 vols, Schocken Books, NY, 1961
——— *Journeys to England and Ireland*, trans. G. Lawrence & K. P. Mayer, Faber & Faber, 1958
——— *L'Ancien Régime* (originally *L'Ancien Régime et la Révolution*, 1856), trans M. W. Patterson, Blackwell, Oxford, 1947
——— *The Old Regime and the French Revolution*, trans. S. Gilbert, Doubleday, NY, 1955
——— *see also* Drescher, S., and Schleifer, J. T.
Tolstoy, L., *War and Peace*, Macmillan & OUP, 1942
Tours, H., *Life and Letters of Emma Hamilton*, Gollancz, 1963
Trafalgar, Committee appointed by the Admiralty, to enquire into the tactics of, Cd. 7120, HMSO, 1913

Trevelyan, G. M., *Illustrated English Social History*, vol. III, *The Eighteenth Century*, Longmans Green, 1942

Trollope, F., *Domestic Manners of the Americans*, 1839, reprinted Century, 1984

Tucker, J., *Memoirs of Admiral Earl St Vincent*, 2 vols, 1844

Tunstall, B., *Naval Warfare in the Age of Sail: The Evolution of Fighting Tactics, 1650–1815*, ed. N. Tracy, Conway Maritime Press, 1990

Vickery, A., *Women's Lives in Georgian England*, Yale Univ. Press, New Haven, 1998

Warner, O., *Trafalgar*, Batsford, 1959

—— *The Battle of the Nile*, Batsford, 1960

—— *The Glorious First of June*, Batsford, 1961

—— *The Life and Letters of Admiral Lord Collingwood*, OUP, 1968

Wheeler, H. F. B., *Maxims of Napoleon*, London, *c.* 1905

Wilton, A., & Barringer, T., *American Sublime; Landscape Painting in the United States 1820–1880*, Tate Publishing, 2002

Woodman, R., *The Victory of Seapower: Winning the Napoleonic War 1806–1814*, Chatham Publishing, 1998

Wright, D. G., *Revolution and Terror in France, 1789–1795*, Longmans, London & NY, 1990

Yalom, M., *Blood Sisters: The French Revolution in Women's Memory*, Basic Books, NY, 1993

Index